BLACK ICE

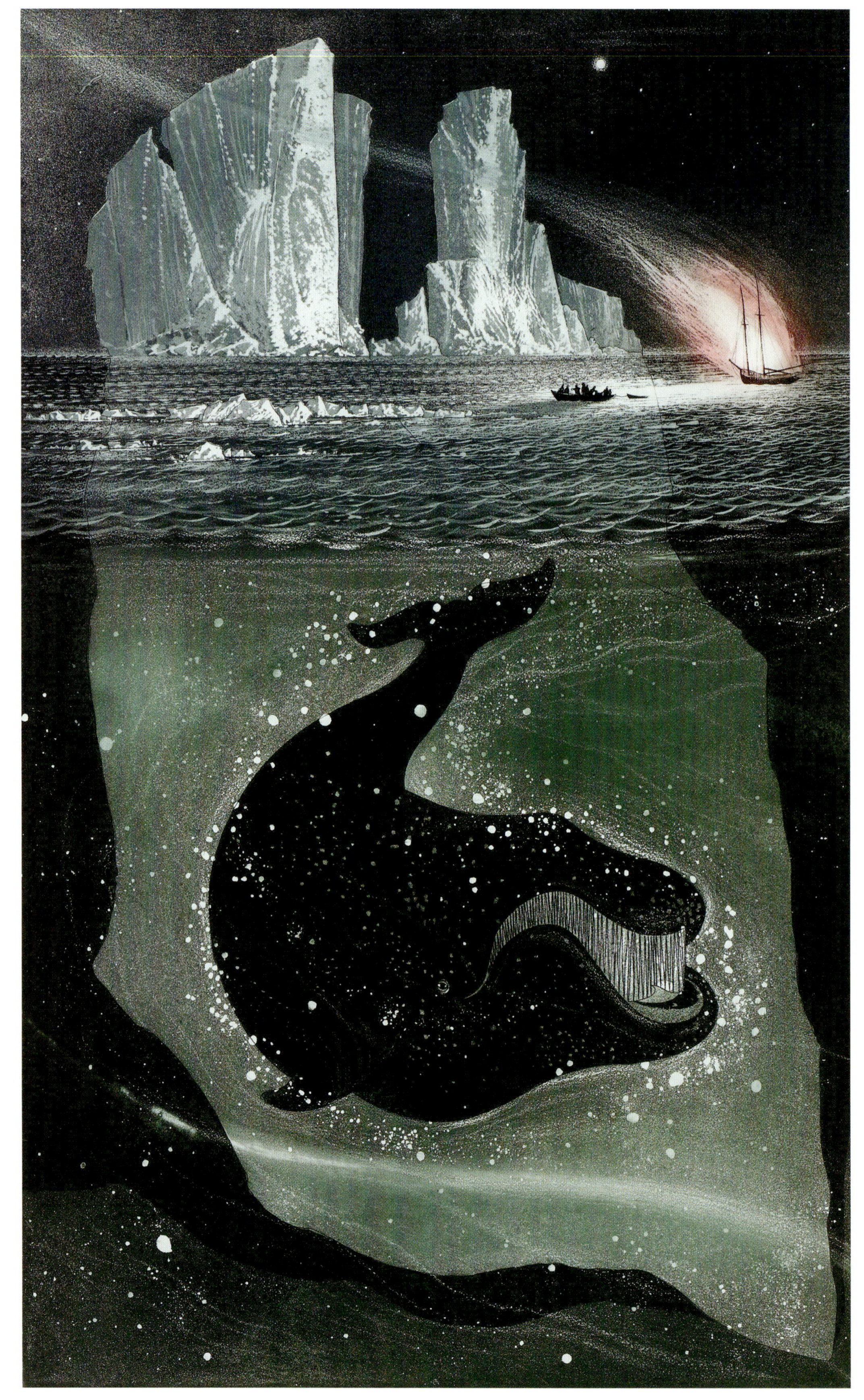

BLACK ICE

David Blackwood Prints of Newfoundland

Katharine Lochnan

WITH *Gary Michael Dault, Derek H.C. Wilton and Martin Feely, Sean T. Cadigan, Caoimhe Ní Shúilleabháin and Michael Crummey*

Douglas & McIntyre

Art Gallery of Ontario

14 15 16 17 18 5 4 3 2 1

Douglas and McIntyre (2013) Ltd.
P.O. Box 219
Madeira Park BC Canada V0N 2H0
www.douglas-mcintyre.com

Art Gallery of Ontario
317 Dundas Street West
Toronto ON Canada M5T 1G4
www.ago.net

Cataloguing data available from
Library and Archives Canada
ISBN 978-1-77162-057-4 (pbk.)

Editing by Trena White
Cover and interior design by Peter Cocking
Front cover image: David Blackwood,
Fire Down on the Labrador, 1980 (detail)
Back cover image: David Blackwood,
Outward Bound for the Labrador, 1980
Frontispiece: David Blackwood,
Fire Down on the Labrador, 1980
Printed and bound in Canada by Friesens
Text printed on acid-free paper
Distributed in the U.S. by Publishers Group West

We gratefully acknowledge the financial support of the Canada Council for the Arts, the British Columbia Arts Council, the Province of British Columbia through the Book Publishing Tax Credit and the Government of Canada through the Canada Book Fund for our publishing activities.

The exhibition *Black Ice: David Blackwood Prints of Newfoundland* was organized by the Art Gallery of Ontario and ran from February 5 to June 12, 2011. The exhibition subsequently travelled to The Rooms (St. John's, NL), and the Art Gallery of Greater Victoria (Victoria, BC).

Supported by

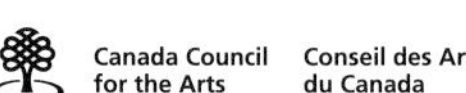

Contents

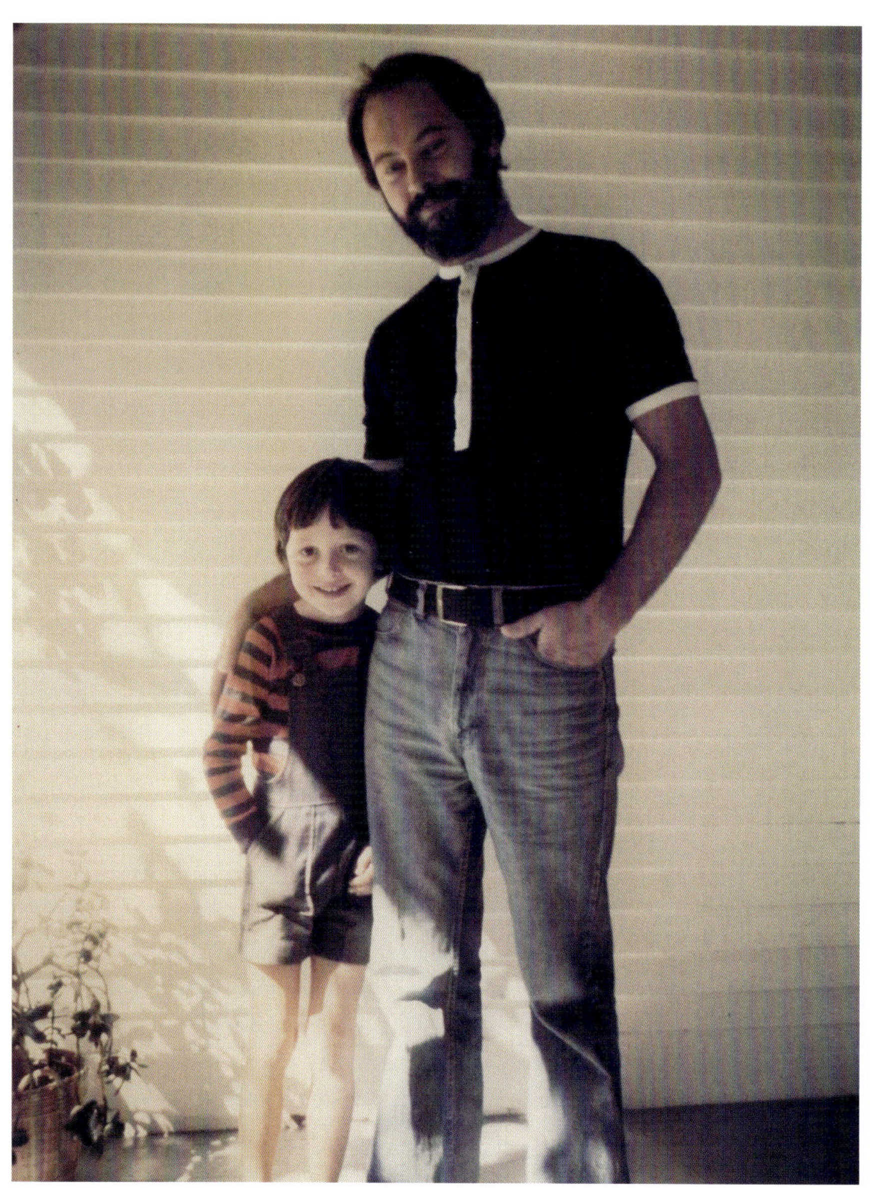

David Blackwood with David Blackwood Jr. (1971–2005)

Dedicated to the memory of

DAVID BONAR BLACKWOOD

(DAVID JUDAH)

July 12, 1971–March 10, 2005

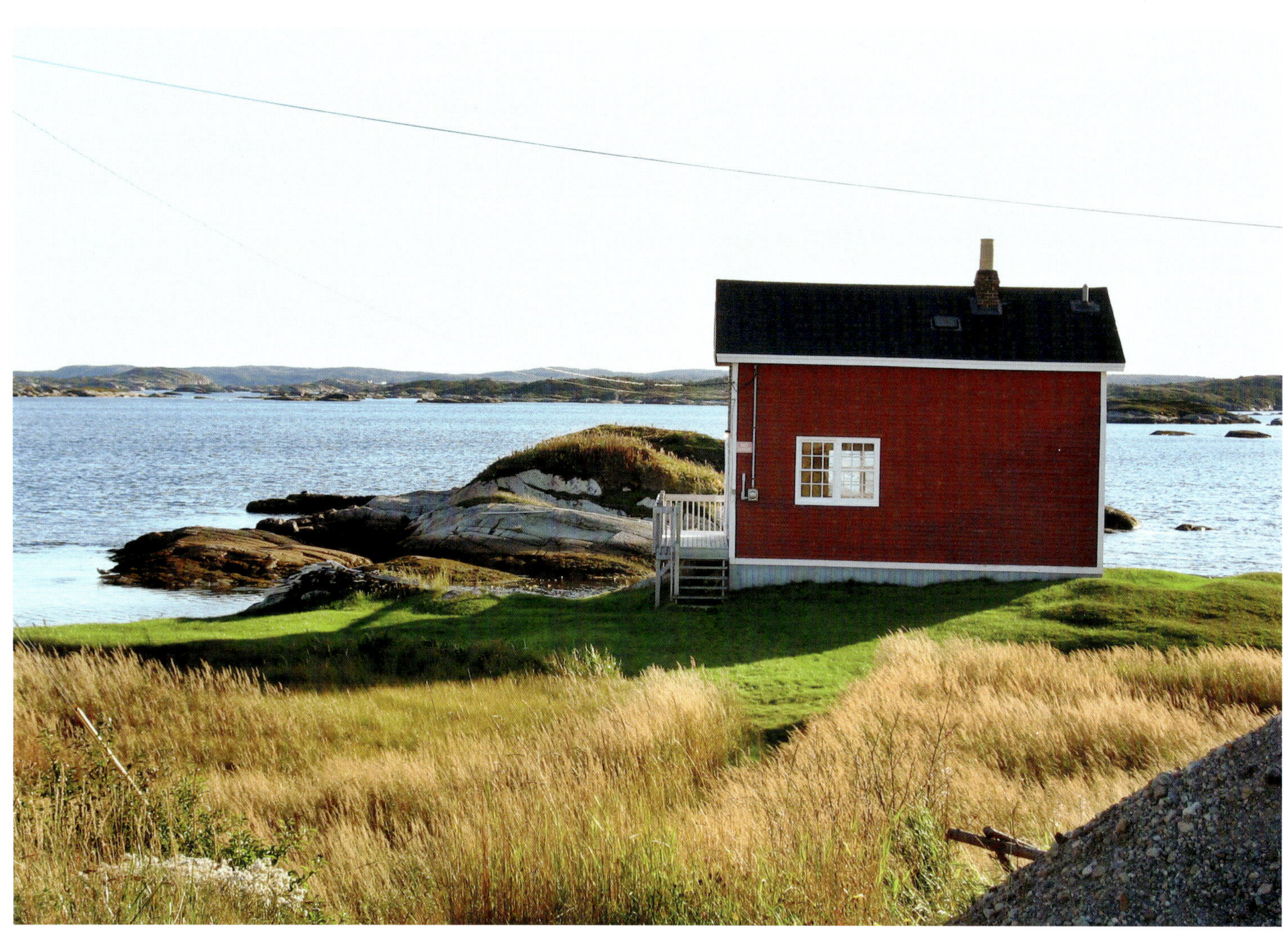

David Blackwood's studio, Wesleyville, Newfoundland, September 2009

Director's Foreword

THERE IS in the work of David Blackwood a deep impulse to keep memory alive. In a world that pursues the constantly new, Blackwood devotes himself to telling the story of his family, his history and his remembered community with a sentiment of resonance and wonder. He grasps his past of remote fishing villages in Newfoundland and holds tight, pulling his experience into the present in the belief that the stories of ethics, commitment and community all express timeless value in the face of adversity. And they do.

Blackwood came of age as an artist at the moment in the early 1960s when abstract expressionism gave way to pop art as a dominant movement, and he matured as colour field painting and minimal art challenged the very tenets of narrative storytelling that he had embraced. He did so with conviction and sustained commitment to his craft—he became a master printmaker by being open to the experiences of others and through his rigorous exploration of method and technique. And he did so largely from outside the art world, working in his studio in Port Hope, Ontario, teaching at the Trinity College School and meeting his audiences through commercial rather than museum exhibitions.

In the mid-1990s, the Art Gallery of Ontario gratefully received from David Blackwood the first gift of his works, enabling it to become the institution of record for his work. The gift of prints and related drawings and watercolours continues to grow over time, and Blackwood has pledged to add his own personal archives in due course. The AGO recognizes the importance of Blackwood's contribution to Canada and the art of this place, and in committing resources to care for the works and to make them available to a broad public the AGO underlines Blackwood's enduring achievement.

Edited and assembled by Dr. Katharine Lochnan, Senior Curator and the R. Fraser Elliott Curator of Prints and Drawings at the AGO, *Black Ice* explores Blackwood's work through the lenses of geology, history, folklore and the literature of Newfoundland. I would like to acknowledge all those who have helped bring Dr. Lochnan's vision and this publication into fruition, including Jill Cuthbertson, Iain Hoadley, Daniel Naccarato, Jim Shedden and Sandy Sparks in Exhibitions; Syvalya Elchen, Ian Lefebvre, Jane Rhodes and Sean Weaver in Photographic Resources; Debbie Johnsen, Milijana Mladjan and Brenda Rix in Curatorial; Marilyn Bouma-Pyper in Design; and Lee Rickwood in Media. My heartfelt thanks goes to the community of supporters who made a significant contribution towards the realization of this project: Salah Bachir and Jacob Yerex, John and Joyce Pollock, Samuel and Esther Sarick and an anonymous donor. Their generous commitment to David Blackwood and his work, and to the AGO, is exceptional and deeply appreciated.

We have created this publication to honour Blackwood's art and to deepen the public understanding of his contribution. In this exploration of Blackwood's work, the context of his creation and his commitment to the great storytelling traditions of community are analyzed and celebrated and placed in an enduring context.

MATTHEW TEITELBAUM
Michael and Sonja Koerner Director, CEO
Art Gallery of Ontario

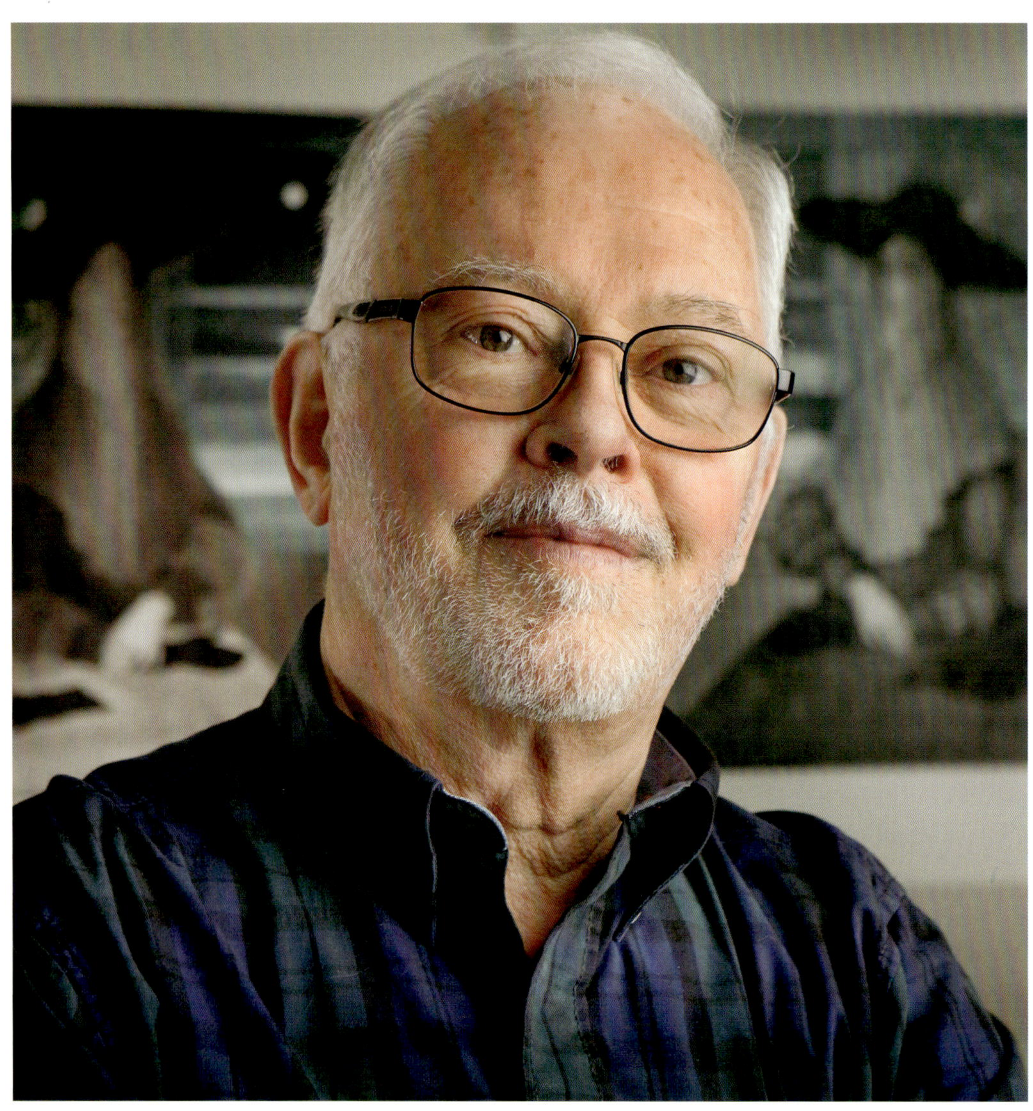

David Blackwood, 2010

Acknowledgments

IT HAS BEEN a great pleasure working with David Blackwood on this project. I would like to thank David and his wife, Anita, for opening up their house and studio repeatedly to facilitate work on it. I would also like to thank David for introducing me to Wesleyville and Bonavista North.

Our perspective has been inspired in part by the Limestone Barrens Project led by curators Charlotte Jones, Sean McCrum and Stuart Reid in 2004–2006. Sponsored by the Ireland Newfoundland Partnership (INP), this venture explored artistic responses to three analogous limestone landscapes: the Burren in County Clare, Ireland; the Northern Peninsula of Newfoundland; and the Bruce Peninsula in Ontario.

Since its inception in 1996, the INP has funded collaborative research projects, several of which facilitate a contextual reading of David Blackwood's work. I would like to thank Agnes Aylward, former president of the INP, for her interest in this project, and her assistant, Kristy Clarke, for putting me in touch with grant recipients and organizing my Irish research trip. Among those who greeted me warmly and shared their research on Newfoundland are John Ennis, head of humanities at Waterford Institute of Technology; Ruan O'Donnell, head of the Department of History at the University of Limerick; and catalogue contributors Martin Feely of National University of Ireland, Galway, and Caoimhe Ní Shúilleabháin of Dublin and Brussels. I am grateful to Edward O'Loghlen, Medical Section, James Hardiman Library, National University of Ireland, Galway, for assisting in many ways with on this project.

I would like to thank Ron Rompkey, professor of English at Memorial University, for helping me to plan a research trip to Newfoundland, and Noreen Golfman, dean of graduate studies at Memorial University, for introducing me to the novelist Michael Crummey, who has made a valuable contribution to this book. I am obliged to Sheila Perry, director, and Caroline Stone, curator, at the Rooms in St. John's for arranging my visit to the archives and museum at the gallery, and for introducing me to Sean Cadigan. I would like to thank Sharon Driscoll for showing me Blackwood sites in the St. John's area.

I am grateful to Paul Gilbert for arranging with Noel O'Dea of Target Marketing and Communications in St. John's to assign Patrick Dunn to take documentary film footage of David Blackwood, Derek and Susan Wilton and myself in Wesleyville in September 2009.

My sincere thanks to all the authors who enthusiastically embraced this project and whose cutting-edge perspectives on Newfoundland have greatly enriched our understanding of the prints and their context. Furthermore, I would like to extend my gratitude to the skilled and professional staff at Douglas & McIntyre who were integral in publishing this book, in particular Peter Cocking, Scott McIntyre, Caroline Skelton and Trena White.

I would also like to thank my director, Matthew Teitelbaum, whose support for the acquisition of David Blackwood's work and for this project made the whole thing possible.

DR. KATHARINE LOCHNAN
Senior Curator and the R. Fraser Elliott
Curator of Prints and Drawings
Art Gallery of Ontario

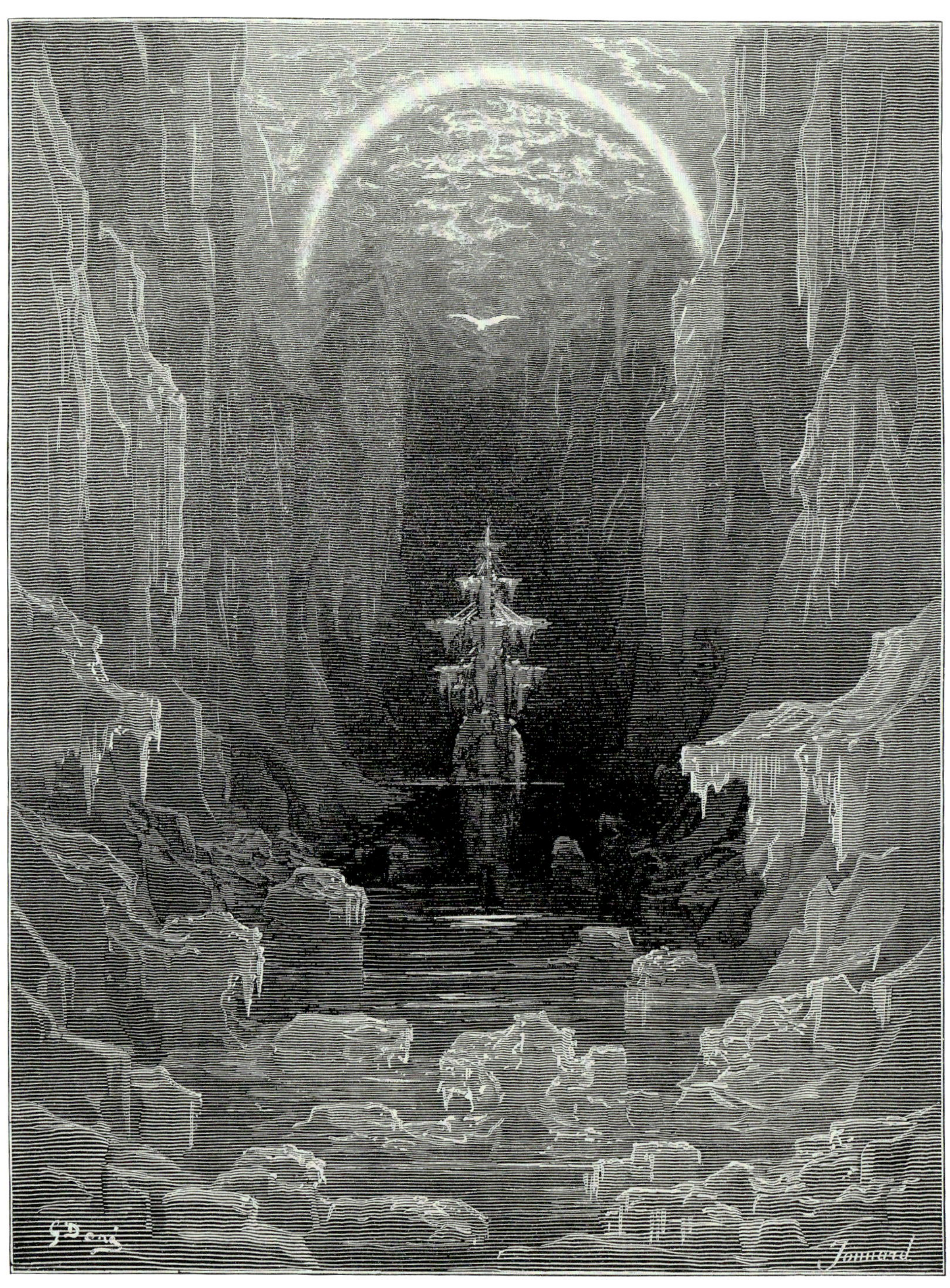

Gustave Doré, *Ship Encountering Icebergs*. Plate from "The Rime of the Ancient Mariner" by Samuel Taylor Coleridge (edition published in Milan, 1966). Wood engraving

SAMUEL TAYLOR COLERIDGE

BRITISH · 1772–1834

The Rime of the Ancient Mariner · 1797

. . .

And now there came both mist and snow,
And it grew wondrous cold:
And ice, mast-high, came floating by,
As green as emerald.

And through the drifts the snowy clifts
Did send a dismal sheen:
Nor shapes of men nor beasts we ken—
The ice was all between.

The ice was here, the ice was there,
The ice was all around:
It cracked and growled, and roared and howled,
Like noises in a swound!

LINES 51–62

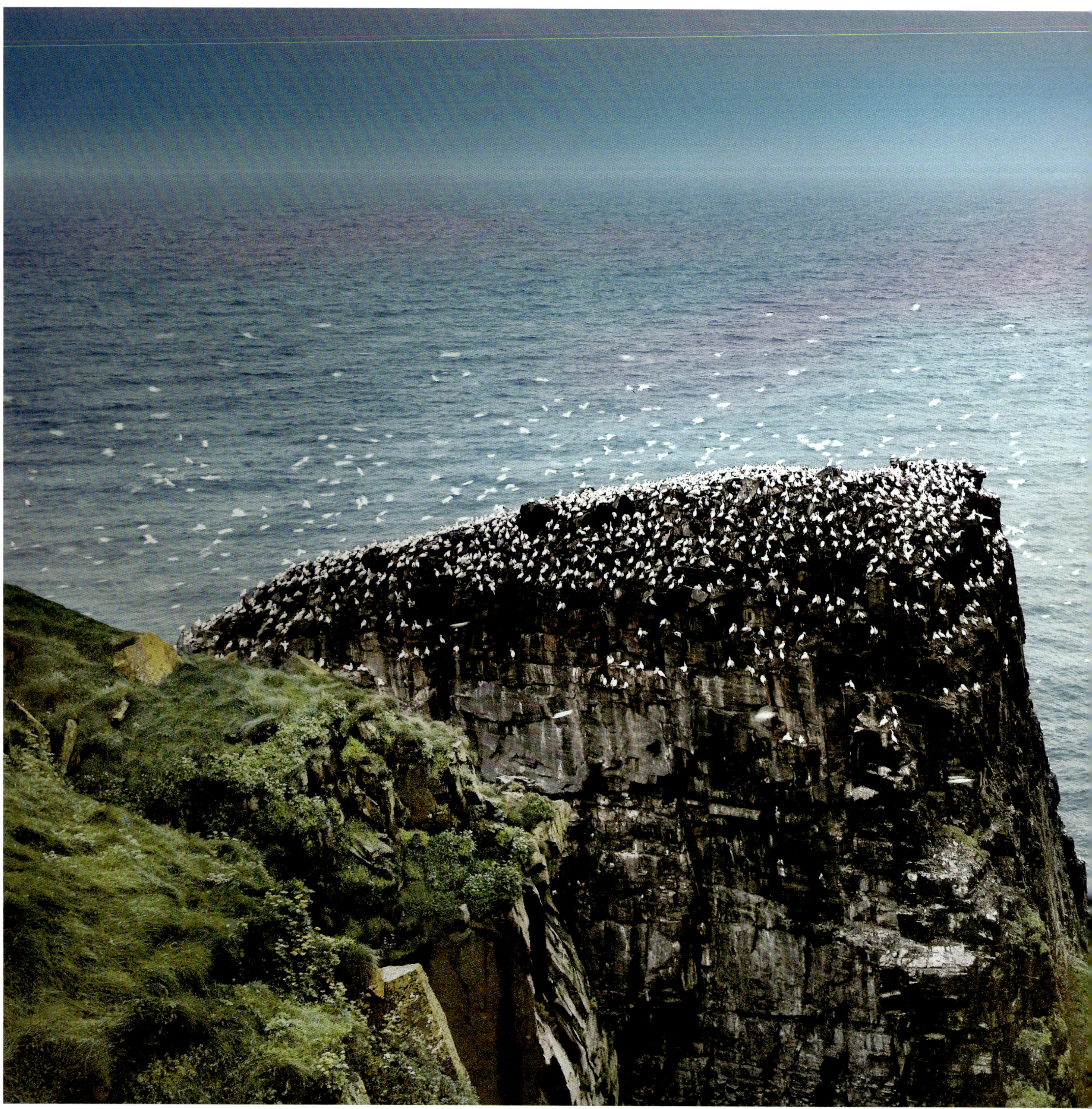

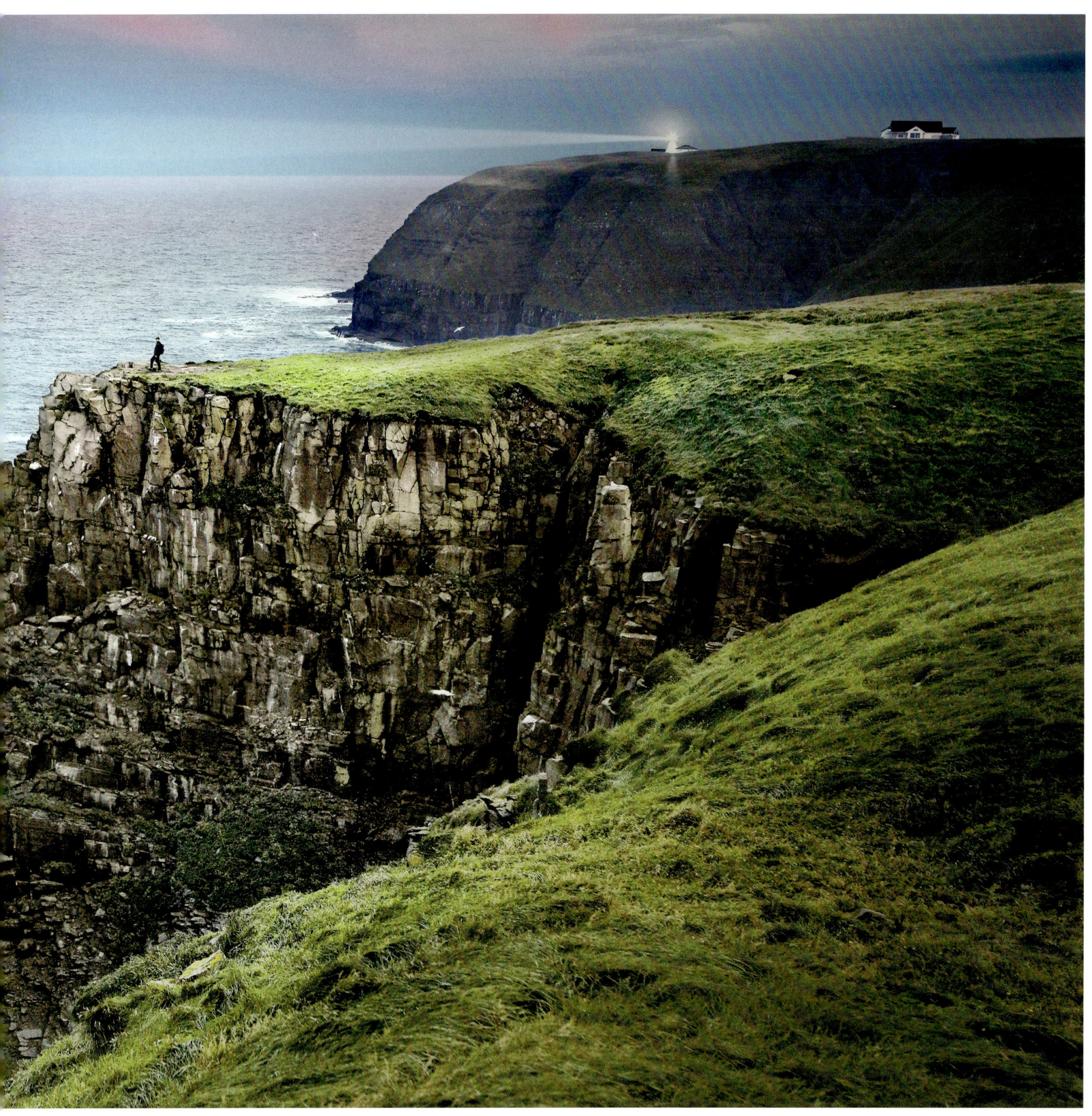

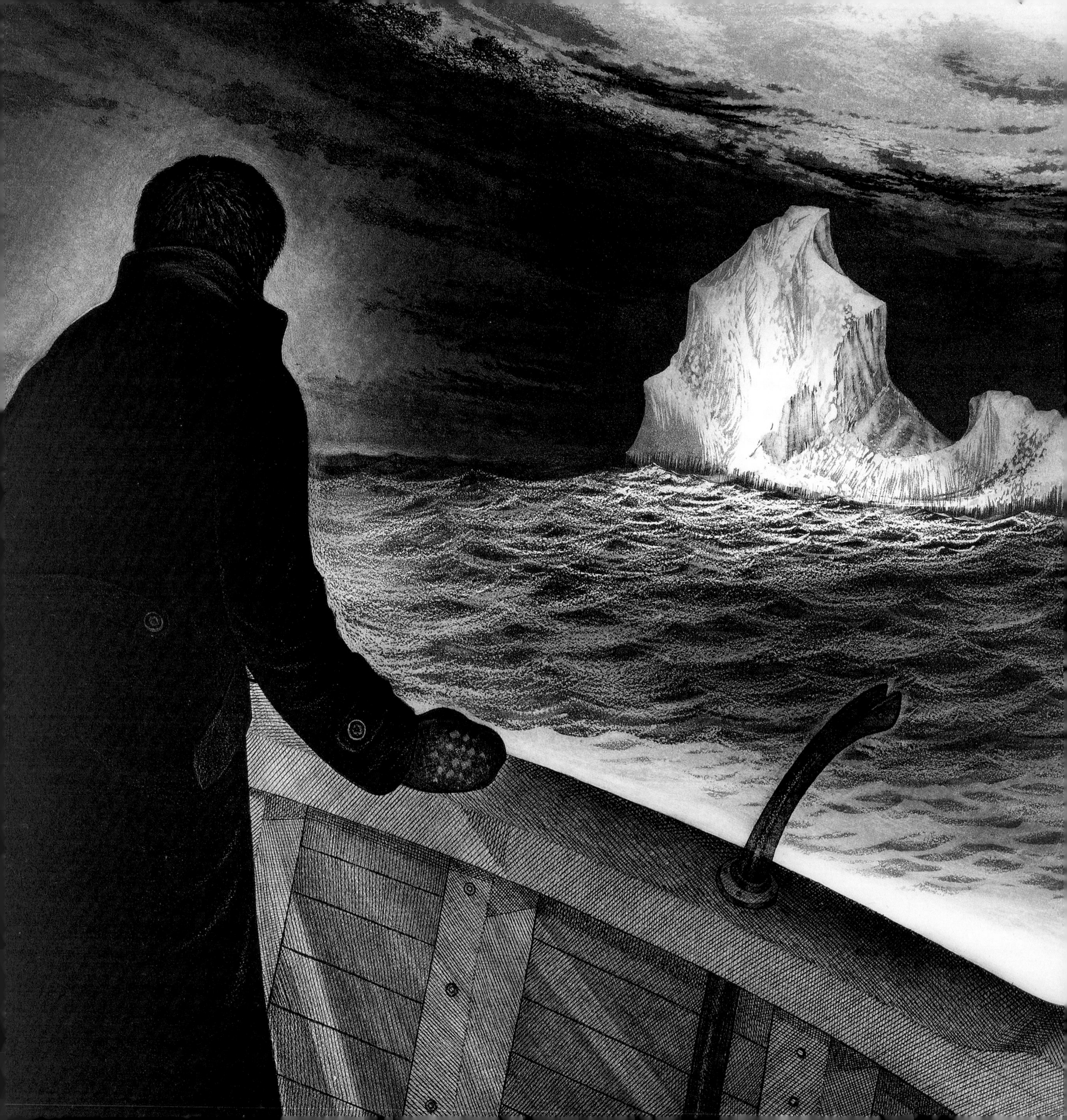

Black Ice

DAVID BLACKWOOD'S PRINTS OF NEWFOUNDLAND

Katharine Lochnan

I WILL NEVER FORGET my first encounter, in May 1961, with the landscape of David Blackwood: the eerie nocturnal experience of standing alone on the deck of an ocean liner listening to the orchestra playing in the salon below, and watching the northern lights glowing pink, yellow, green and white—opening and closing like fans and rustling like silk—as the ship moved slowly past towering icebergs, towards the mouth of the St. Lawrence River, displacing the heaving, groaning pack ice that blocked the Labrador Sea. Perhaps that is one reason why I was riveted by my first sight of David Blackwood's etchings of Newfoundland in the late 1970s.[1] No one has captured that spectacular landscape more brilliantly: the starkness, monumentality and breadth of vision of the etchings continue to resonate with me just as strongly three and a half decades later.

facing: Detail from **Captain Lew Kean Passing**, 1979 (plate 37)

facing: Reconstruction of Viking houses, L'Anse aux Meadows, Newfoundland

Newfoundland was formed of land masses torn from the west coasts of Ireland and Africa by continental drift, borne northwest by the opening up of the Atlantic Ocean and coalescing off the east coast of Labrador.[2] Long before its Northern Peninsula was briefly settled by Vikings in the eleventh century, it was home to the indigenous Beothuk. The rich fishing grounds off the Grand Banks attracted seasonal transatlantic expeditions during the seventeenth century and permanent British settlements in the eighteenth century. In 1763, following the Seven Years War, Newfoundland came under British rule.

From the seventeenth century on, West of England sea captains sailed from Bristol across St. George's Channel to southeast Ireland, where they picked up provisions and labour from the Waterford area before sailing to Newfoundland.[3] Newfoundland became such an important destination for Irish emigrants that it was given its own name in the Irish language: Talamh an Éisc, meaning "land of the fish." Under the British, its political, religious, social and economic structure reflected that of Ireland: English Protestants ruled the colony and ran the fishing industry, whereas Irish Catholics provided much of the workforce on land and on sea. This ethnic divide is still reflected in the distribution of distinct Protestant and Catholic communities as well as those of English and Irish descent. Their rich cultural legacy is embedded in the surnames, language, customs, accents and music of Newfoundland. Belittled in Blackwood's youth, Newfoundland is seen today by historians, linguists, musicians and folklorists on both sides of the Atlantic as a precious time capsule of English and Irish culture and a great creative force in its own right.[4]

Wesleyville

The small Protestant outport of Wesleyville in Bonavista Bay on the Cape Freels Peninsula, where David Blackwood was born in 1941, was founded by men from the West of England. Despite its size and its marine focus, it contained almost all the resources needed for his artistic formation. Its history, religion, economy, education, folklore and people fed the tapestry of his imagination and his appetite for the romantic sublime.

As Derek Wilton observed while standing on the outcropping behind Blackwood's former school in Wesleyville, Blackwood's etchings are "rooted in granite." If his deeply bitten copper plates resemble the fissures in the rock, the powerful underlying rhythms of their compositions capture those of the maritime environment. Like the place that inspired them, their dramatic narratives are riven with seismic shifts. This inhospitable, glacier-scoured landscape is in a state of constant transformation. Situated on the western edge of the Atlantic Ocean, covered for six months of the year by snow and ice, it gave rise to, as Blackwood said, "a constant preoccupation with the weather... You are constantly aware of the gales and winds, and the

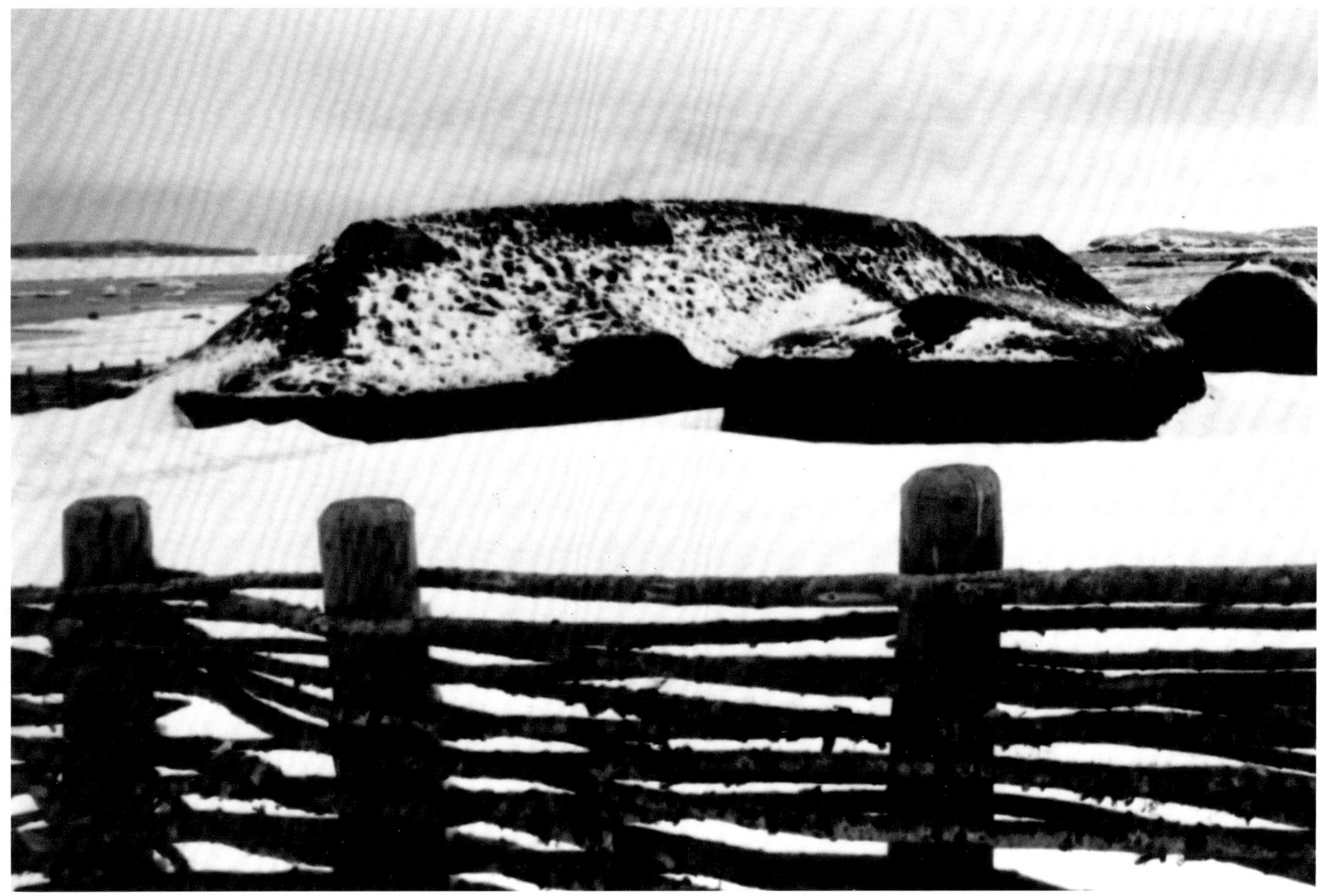

sea roaring, and wetness coming in... You hear it at night whirling around the buildings. You tie things down, tie things on to one another."[5] It is also incredibly beautiful, reminiscent of Connemara on the west coast of Ireland, where virtually identical landscapes bear witness to their joint geological birth.[6]

David Blackwood's grandfather, Captain Albert Blackwood, and his father, Captain Edward Blackwood, were sea captains who expected him to follow in their footsteps. His father began to take him cod fishing up the Labrador coast when he was still an infant. Like his father before him, Captain Edward Blackwood took his son to work beside him from the age of ten. They would anchor the family schooner, the *Flora S. Nickerson*, in a good harbour, put out the cod traps, then later retrieve them and salt the fish below deck.

Blackwood's ambitions did not coincide with those of his father, and, as he recalls, when his father presented him with a fishing boat at the age of fourteen, he was "really put out... What *was* I supposed to do with this thing? Here I was hating school, and wanting to draw and paint all the

below: David Blackwood as an infant on the Labrador coast

facing: Wesleyville school

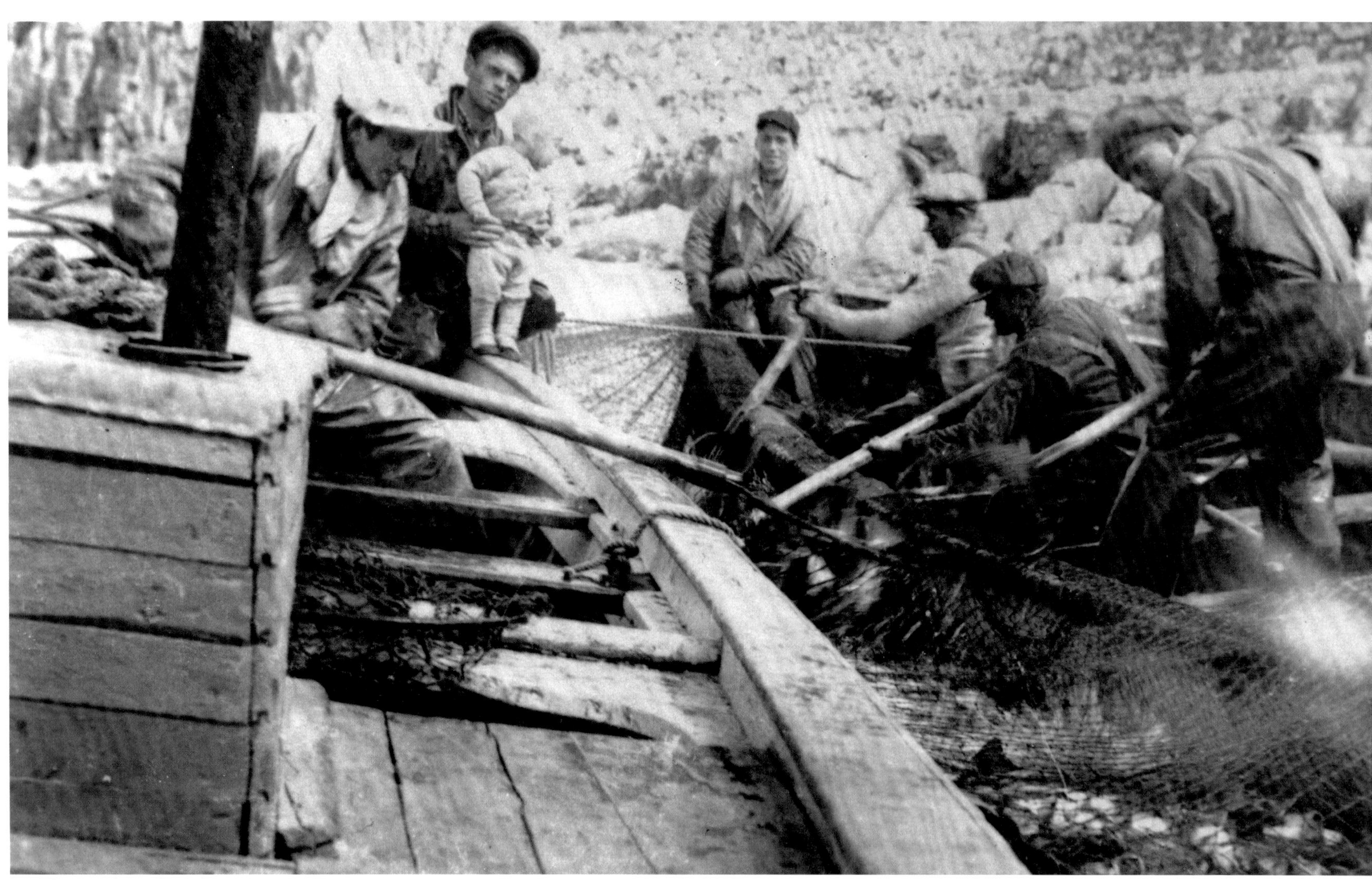

time."[7] His father bought from an uncle sixty lobster traps, which Blackwood and a friend rebuilt. The following year they became lobster fishermen, getting out of bed at five on April mornings, when there was still Arctic ice out on the waters, and hauling up their traps before heading off to school.

Following Newfoundland's entry into Confederation with Canada in 1949, and the implementation of Premier Joey Smallwood's resettlement program, which was designed to close down the outports, fishing and sealing ceased to be major economic drivers in Wesleyville. Captain Edward Blackwood spent increasing amounts of time on land, engaged in road construction. David Blackwood's time at sea was not wasted, however: it is thanks to this first-hand experience that his subjects possess such intensity and authenticity.

Methodism was the philosophical bedrock of Wesleyville. Amid the deep uncertainties of life, the Methodist church, built on the highest point of the rock, was the focal point of the community, and its highly visible steeple a symbol of its aspirations. Preachers constantly reminded their congregations that "we could be here today, gone tomorrow," because of the asymmetrical relationship between the power of man and that of nature. As a child Blackwood was spellbound by preachers who could turn the darkest and most colourful Old Testament stories into gripping serials at Sunday school. The dramatic starkness and simplicity of his epic narratives pitting man against nature can be traced to his Methodist youth.

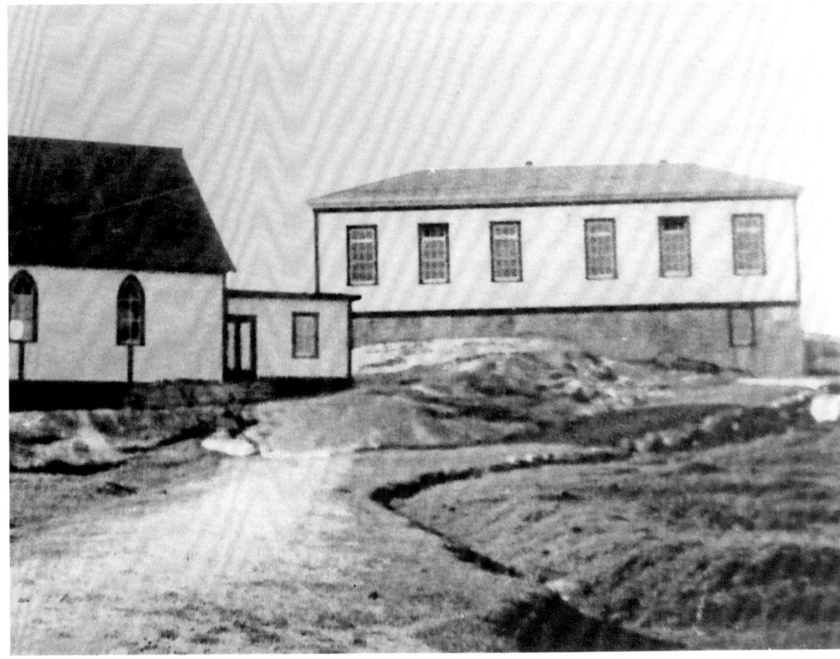

Given the remoteness of Bonavista North, Blackwood considers it "a miracle" that he received the support of the community to follow his artistic ambitions. The Methodists viewed reading, writing and education as being of primary importance. Earnest, hard-working and frowning on joviality, the Methodists nonetheless admired those who could tell stories, sing or play a musical instrument. They valued technological progress and the development of a strong work ethic. These attributes are reflected in Blackwood's command of etching and printing techniques and the disciplined structuring of his workday.

Music also played an important role in Blackwood's formation. He was introduced to it at church, where he listened to the organ and sang in the choir. Methodist hymns with stirring words were a source of inspiration for him,

facing: Jubilee Methodist Church, Wesleyville, 1930s

especially Blessed John Henry Newman's "Lead, Kindly Light" and William Whiting's "Eternal Father, Strong to Save." Although aware of the Newfoundland folk tradition, he was drawn to classical music, particularly the works of Beethoven, Rachmaninov and Mendelssohn. He loved the Sunday-night concerts that were broadcast on CBC Radio from Massey Hall in Toronto. After moving to Toronto, he was able to attend the concerts in person and was thrilled to meet Stravinsky in 1961. Among his many pleasures was hearing the Mendelssohn Choir sing Handel's *Messiah* at Christmas.

History and English were Blackwood's favourite subjects at school. His history teacher, who had been in Europe during the Second World War and had visited Versailles and Rome (including the Sistine Chapel), was able to bring the places he had seen, and the activities that had taken place in them, vividly to life. Blackwood was drawn to the more colourful historical personalities, and in third grade he painted a portrait of King Louis XIV based on one by the French artist Hyacinthe Rigaud. His English teacher made texts exciting by reciting and performing them and relating them to the world of his students. Blackwood became a devotee of Shakespearean tragedy, especially *Macbeth* and *Julius Caesar*, as well as the great British Romantic poets Shelley and Keats, and the Victorians Tennyson and Coleridge. His favourite poem was Samuel Taylor Coleridge's "The Rime of the Ancient Mariner."

As Newfoundland was still under British rule until 1949, Canadian history was only of marginal interest and was taught in a very dry manner. Not so Newfoundland history. Blackwood feels that his work actually "goes back 150 years because my grandfathers' and great-grandfathers' experiences have reached me through my father. The verbal tradition was still alive in my time, story-telling was a very important activity in every outport home. These stories were strongly visual and have influenced my work more than anything else."[8] He grew up listening to the dramatic tales of seamen who gathered in kitchens to share stories and sing songs about their adventures at sea. Strong personalities in their own right, they painted fantastic images using colourful narratives.

No one has described these men more vividly than the great Canadian writer Farley Mowat, Blackwood's next-door neighbour and one-time collaborator:

> *They were the outport men and women of Newfoundland whose minute villages clung precariously to the rocks and bones of a bleak island wracked by the impassioned fury of the North Atlantic. Between wind and weather they clung to life and living with a tenacity that is beyond the capacity of modern man to comprehend, let alone emulate.*
>
> *But they did more—much more—than just endure. In summer and winter, in autumn and in spring they sallied out from their embattled roosting places to fling the primordial challenge back to*

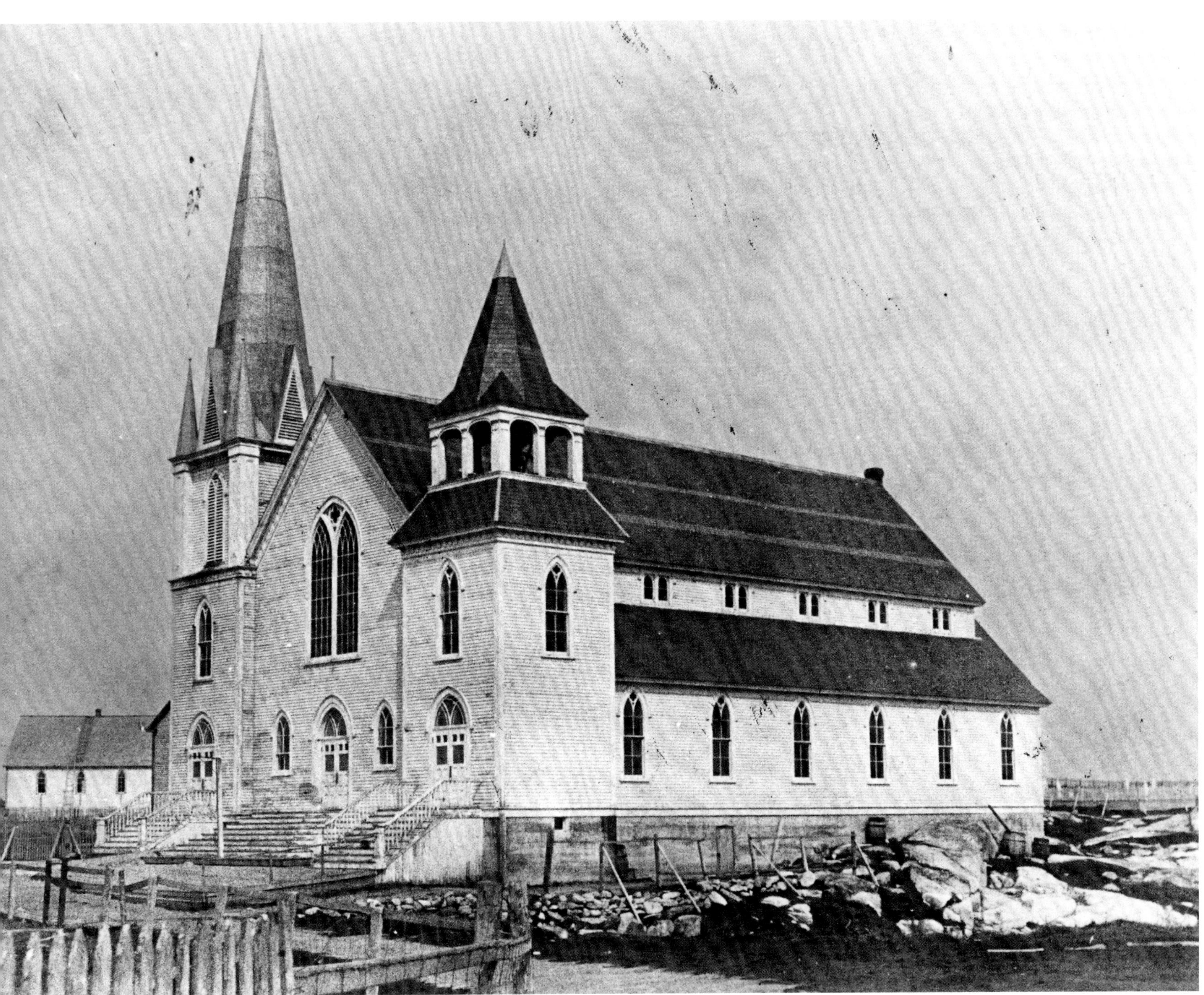

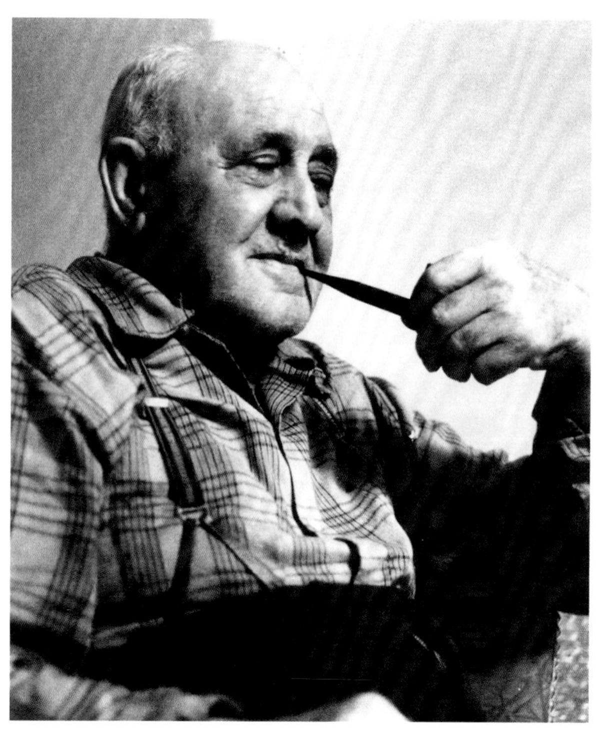

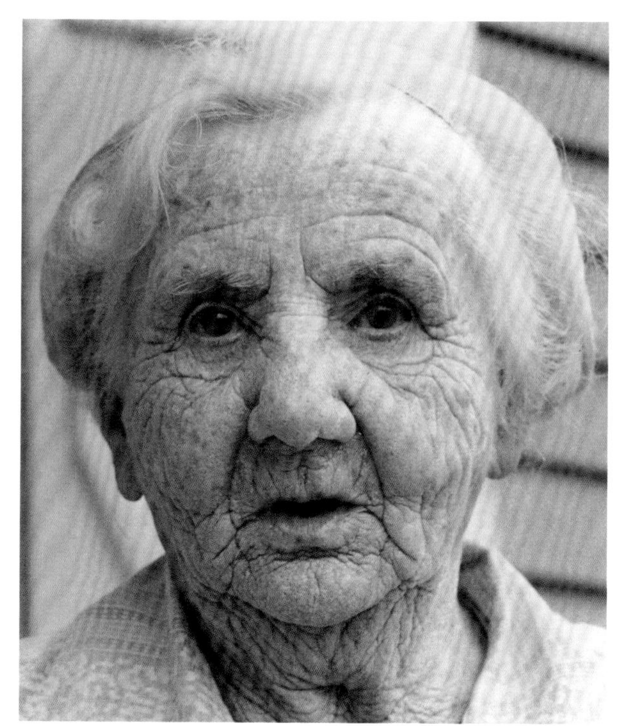

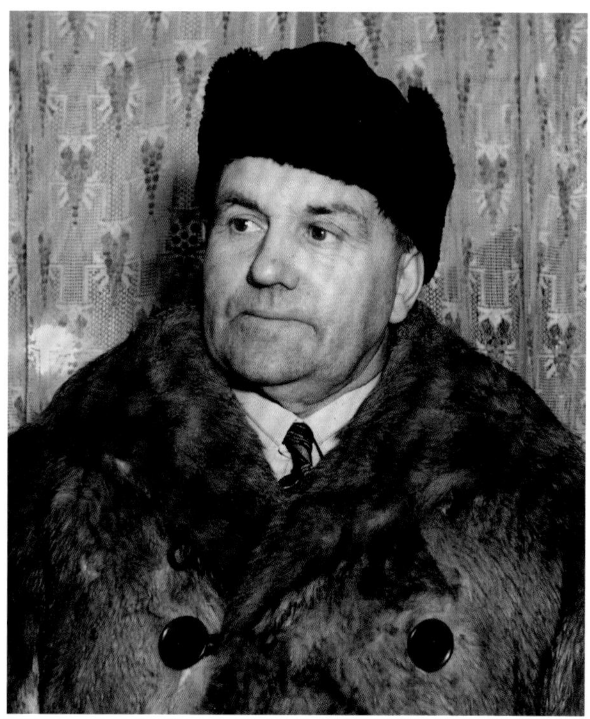

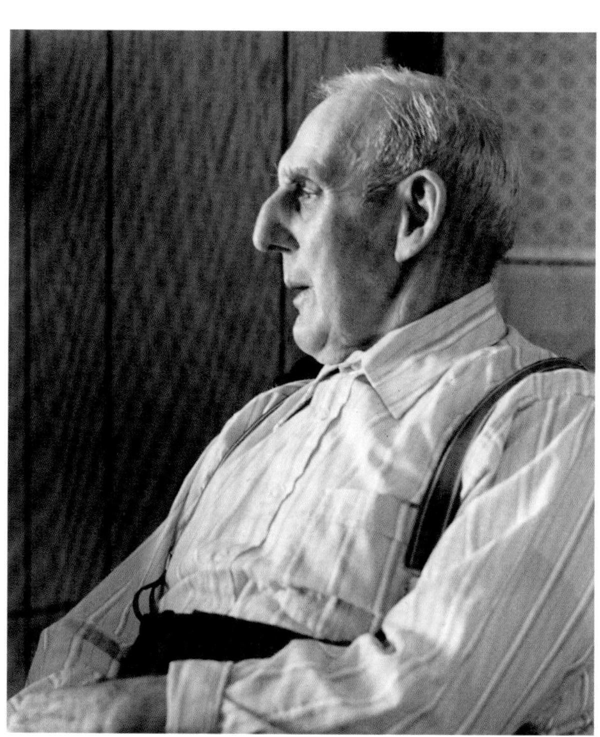

facing, clockwise from top left: Captain Llewellyn Kean smoking his pipe, 1969; Aunt Mary Fifield, Wesleyville; Captain Sid Hill, Wesleyville, 1952; Captain Bax Ford, Wesleyville, 1968

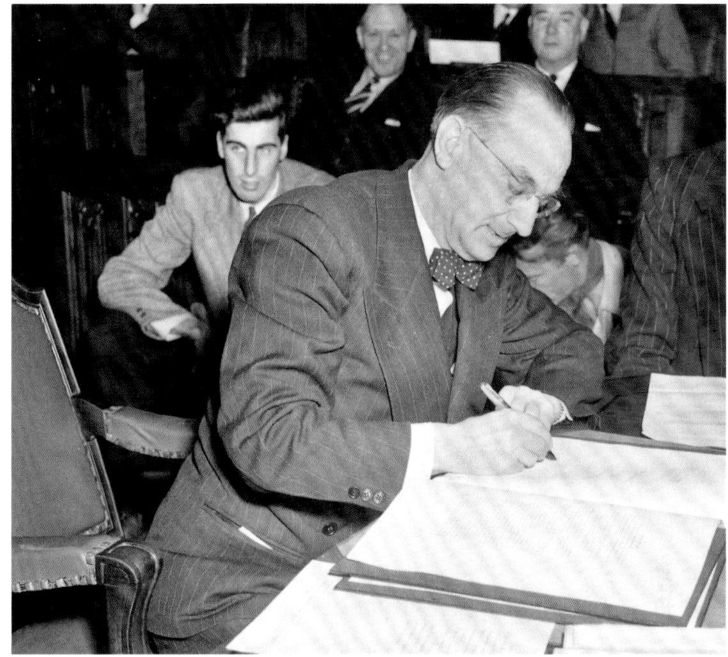

right: Joseph Smallwood signing the agreement that admitted Newfoundland into Confederation, Ottawa, Ontario, December 11, 1948. The Honourable A.J. Walsh, Chairman of the Newfoundland delegation, is on the right.

those unyielding elementals—the roaring sea; the mad and bitter gales; the entombing fog, the green, destroying ice. They were winnowed and culled by a merciless environment so that their strength grew greater with each succeeding generation. They were evolving in the manner that has been decreed for all living things; they were becoming—had already become—magnificent, functional human entities, secure within themselves.[9]

Blackwood vividly recalls the controversy over whether to join Canada or the United States of America that split Newfoundland down the middle, and the opposition to Premier Joey Smallwood's resettlement strategy. He recalls the trauma of family members forcibly uprooted from their homes on Bragg's Island, and the response of his grandfather, who locked himself up and refused to leave. Witnessing the disintegration of first the way of life, then the communities and finally the buildings themselves was the equivalent to "the shot fired across the bow" to Blackwood. As a young adult he decided to devote his professional and personal life to recording his early memories of these communities and assisting in the preservation and restoration of Wesleyville to ensure that the way of life, the stories, the people, their values, their cultural heritage and the knowledge of the built environment would be passed down.

Blackwood made good use of the two local libraries. He learned about the artistic profession at the age of ten from a book in the school library entitled *A Life of Millet*. Published at the turn of the twentieth century, it was richly illustrated with black and white reproductions of the French artist's most famous paintings, including *The Gleaner* and *The Angelus*. Jean-François Millet's life was presented as "one great and dramatic adventure," said Blackwood, "and inspired me no end."[10] As a child he could relate to the story of the boy who grew up in a small village, drew on the stone floor of his cottage with pieces of charcoal taken from the fireplace and finally received the support of the community to go and study in Paris.

When he was thirteen, Blackwood discovered a book by a Mrs. Oliphant entitled *The Makers of Florence*, with an art nouveau gold-embossed binding.[11] It had chapters on "all the great Florentines: Boccaccio, Dante, Giotto, Brunelleschi, Michelangelo, Leonardo da Vinci, Savonarola," and it led him to realize that "some of the greatest people who

facing: David Blackwood outside his studio at Wesleyville, July 1957

ever lived had devoted their lives to art."[12] He read the book a dozen times, and before finishing school in June 1959 he "borrowed" the volume from the school library. It is still one of his most prized possessions. When he finally visited Florence years later, he felt as if he already knew the city inside out, thanks to the book's beautiful photogravures of the Duomo, the Pitti Palace and Santa Croce.

He found more information in the Wesleyville Regional Library. Displayed on several large tables were magazines such as *The Saturday Evening Post, Time* and *Life*, which contained articles on art, artists and exhibitions and introduced Blackwood to the cultural happenings in Washington, D.C., and New York. The library also subscribed to the *Canadian Geographical Journal* and *The Beaver*, in which he read articles about Tom Thomson and members of the Group of Seven, such as A.Y. Jackson. It was through these resources that Blackwood learned about the Ontario College of Art in Toronto, then the leading art college in Canada, and he decided to enrol.

Toronto

By 1959, when he entered OCA, his artistic imagination was all but fully formed. He knew that he wanted to work on Newfoundland subject matter but was obliged to follow the curriculum. He was taught to draw in the classical tradition: Eric Freifeld taught anatomy and life drawing; John Alfsen, drawing from the nude model; and Rowley Murphy, drawing from the costumed figure. He was taught painting in a traditional manner by Carl Schaefer and in an abstract style by Jock (J.W.G.) Macdonald. Although Blackwood was well aware of what was happening in contemporary circles and admired Willem de Kooning, Mark Rothko and Jackson Pollock, the art that he wanted to create "had no relationship whatsoever" to what they were doing.

There was only one place where he was allowed to do what he wanted at OCA: the printmaking studio. At that time, printmaking was focused almost exclusively on aesthetic issues. The most influential figure in the field of printmaking was Stanley William Hayter, who had founded Atelier 17 in Paris in 1927. Technical "cookery" had become its focus: as Blackwood put it, artists who worked there "played around with colour and lines, and so on." He considered a lot of the printmaking going on at that time largely "decorative," as the subject matter was considered of little or no importance. While technique is always "an underlying force," in Blackwood's work it never becomes an end in itself. It was in the printmaking studio in his second year at OCA (1960–1961) that he discovered the ideal medium in which to explore his Newfoundland subjects: the intaglio processes of etching, drypoint and aquatint.[13]

He also wasted no time visiting the Art Gallery of Toronto (now the Art Gallery of Ontario): "I arrived in Toronto the first week of September on a Wednesday. The following Saturday I took a Scarborough bus to the end

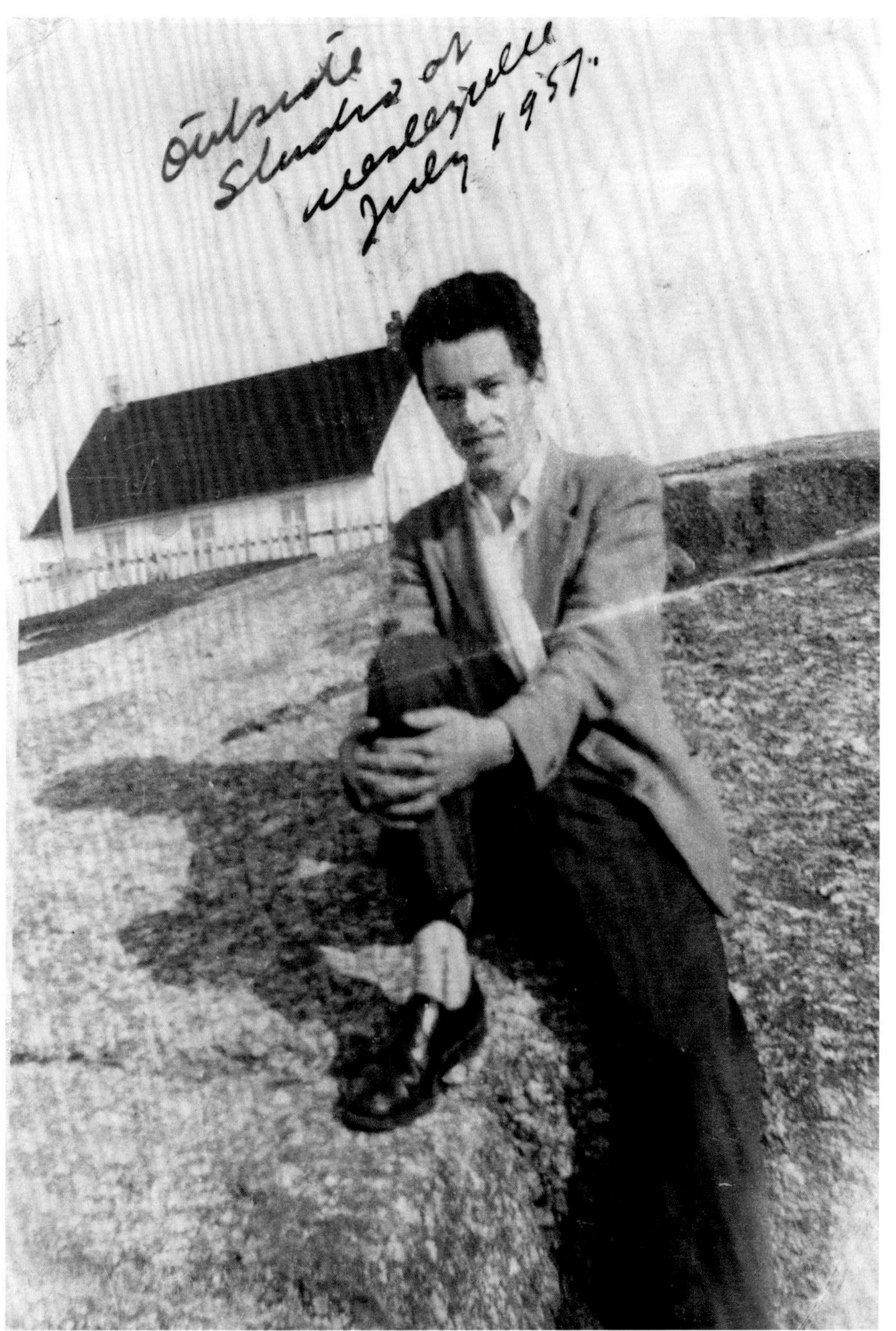
Outside
Studio at
Wesleyville
July 1957.

of the line where it met the Dundas Street Car—which took me to the front door of the Gallery. On entering the main entrance a series of connecting galleries in the west wing showed the great painting (Tintoretto, just acquired) hanging on the western end wall of the gallery. It was my first encounter with what the magazines describe as a great masterpiece—bought by public subscription. There were numerous outstanding exhibitions, the *Heritage de France*, a Delacroix retrospective, a major Picasso painting show—and in my final year at OCA a major Picasso print exhibition."[14] Blackwood spent many hours at the gallery during his years as a student at OCA (1959–1963).

At that time New York was seen as the centre of the art world, Canadian art was fighting for recognition at home, and Newfoundland had not yet made it onto the artistic map of Canada. When I first met Blackwood in the late 1970s, I remember thinking how brave he was to fly in the face of contemporary taste, to be so persistently independent in his exclusive focus on Newfoundland subject matter, in his use of the etching medium and a representational style. Of all the media he could have chosen, etching was the most austere and, along with other printmaking techniques, had been consigned to the bottom of the imaginary hierarchy of artistic media. As for style and content, formalist abstraction, which focused primarily on line and colour, was in vogue and narrative subject matter was dismissed as commercial. Painfully aware that his work "was so unfashionable," Blackwood became inured to seeing it routinely dismissed and classified as "illustration" by art world pundits. Fortunately this did not deter private collectors. Ironically, in the mid-1990s, after "storytelling" became fashionable in contemporary artistic circles, his work was vindicated.

One of the artists he most admired was the great fifteenth-century Italian fresco painter Giotto. Blackwood was attracted by Giotto's storytelling ability, the clarity of his compositions and the simplicity of his forms. He developed a working method based on the one used by Giotto and his followers. Alexander Millar, a former student of the great Mexican muralists Diego Rivera and David Alfaro Siqueiros, taught him composition at OCA. Millar showed the students how the muralists worked in the Italian tradition, developing a design for the whole composition, squaring it off by superimposing a grid, making outline drawings or "cartoons" for each square and transferring the cartoons to the wall so the final result could be executed section by section.

David Blackwood works largely from memory, seeing the distance from his subject matter in both time and space as advantageous to the process of gestation, enabling him to focus his feelings, pare down his narrative and simplify his imagery.[15] Once the idea takes shape, he draws his composition on a piece of paper, squares it off and works on one section at a time. For this reason the forms in his etchings, like those in Giotto's frescoes, appear locked together like pieces in a jigsaw puzzle. The figures are captured in deliberately simplified silhouettes: the men are frequently dressed in the heavy serge greatcoats that were scavenged from U.S. Army battleships that ran aground during the Second World War. They hung down to the feet of short Newfoundlanders. As Blackwood demonstrates in his etchings, these figures created "a very classic shape against the snow."

While at OCA Blackwood decided to make prints based on the sealing mythology of Newfoundland, which he believes "might well be the only Canadian mythology existing outside our native cultures."[16] The first etching, *The Lost Party*, was made in 1961, and the following prints were called the *Lost Party* series.[17]

Inspired by a scene from the SS *Newfoundland* disaster of 1914 (pp. 86–93), *The Lost Party* portrays a group of disoriented people who, lost in a storm, began arguing about which direction to take. In three etchings in the so-called *Lost Party* series, Blackwood included the figure of a bull because "it is at this point in the series that the men most clearly begin to emerge with the monolithic grace and nomadic anonymity which makes it possible, in describing them, to say that they are Neanderthal man or Newfoundland man; something about them transcends time."[18] In doing so he crosses cultures, referencing neolithic cave painting, Minoan mythology and Picasso's *Minotauro-machia* etchings, which he had seen at the AGO in 1964. He was also very taken at that time with a Plains Indian buffalo hide painted with battle scenes at the Royal Ontario Museum in Toronto.

Exposed for long periods on the icefields, sealers often became delirious and convinced that they saw strange things such as the spirits of family members and phantom ships. As Blackwood explained:

There's a local story here of people from this community. Down on Labrador, it was quite common to see whales encased. A whale would die from old age, and an iceberg would float down here with the carcass in it. But on one occasion, the people from this region must have encountered a mastodon encased in ice, because they had never seen anything like it. And they were very superstitious people. So everyone thought that they had seen the devil, and it was really some kind of great elephant. Of course, in the confusion it probably looked like an elephant, but it was covered in hair. They had never encountered anything like that. So that's a story, a folklore image that probably also crept into it.[19]

William S. Lieberman, then curator of prints and drawings at the Museum of Modern Art in New York and the leading expert on twentieth-century prints, was the one-man adjudicator of a juried Canadian biennial exhibition of works on paper that took place at the National Gallery of Canada in Ottawa in 1964.[20] He selected one of these prints

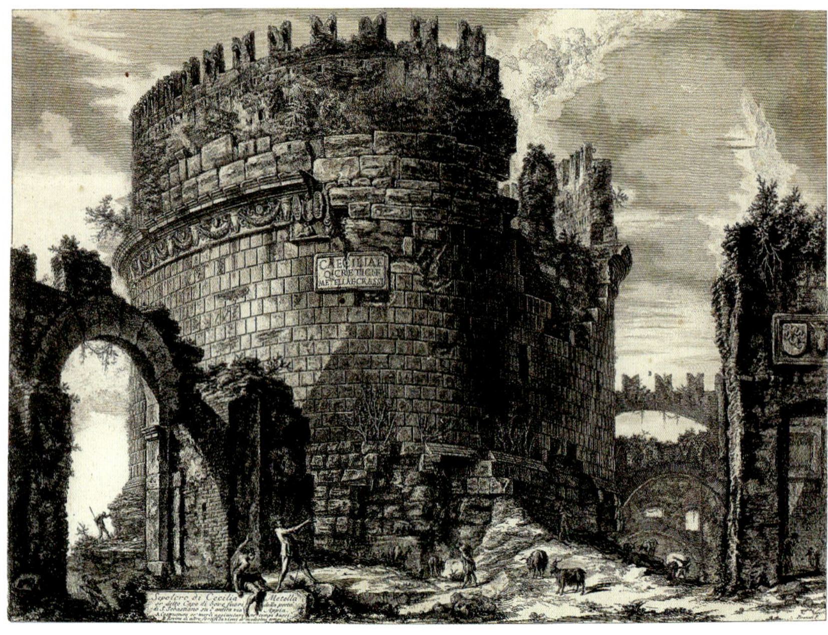

Giovanni Battista Piranesi, *The Tomb of Cecilia Metella* from *The Views of Rome*, 1762. Etching and engraving

for inclusion, *The Search Party*, reproduced it in the catalogue and recommended its purchase to the National Gallery of Canada. This became a source of controversy at OCA, since Blackwood was a student and work by the instructors was not selected for exhibition. Blackwood recalls that "there were only about two staff people who were thrilled" by his success. It was Lieberman's vote of confidence that established his career and led to the first acquisitions of his work by Ontario museums, in London, Sarnia and Hamilton.

Etchings

Blackwood's work can be read on several levels. Individual narratives act as points of entry into the underlying themes of man's loneliness, mortality, vulnerability and fate. His works deal with the human condition and human relationships within this context, and his focus has always remained on the men themselves, never their prey. Although inspired by the great *Newfoundland* disaster, the *Lost Party* series is a metaphor for a mankind that has lost its way. The frozen, icy world that he depicts in these and later etchings is not only one of the most inhospitable on earth, but it also recalls the sea of ice in Dante's *Inferno*, one of Blackwood's favourite pieces of literature. By incorporating imagery drawn from across millennia, from mythology, ancient human history, art history, photographic negatives and X-rays, he lends his work a timeless and universal character.

Blackwood thinks in darks and lights and expresses himself primarily in black and white. The power of black forms silhouetted against a white background was imprinted on his retina from childhood. As there was no electricity in Wesleyville, most of his early drawing and painting was done by lamplight. He says the move to Toronto was "magic to me at first—the whole business of electric lights, and street lights and all that."[21] As he notes, Bonavista Bay can be "a dark and lonely place" from January to July.[22] His etchings are conceived and set during the winter months, when there is little sun, the sky is heavy and opaque, and "everything really is black and white and grey." The light sources emanate from within his work: sky, snow, ice and sea are luminous.

The Newfoundland landscape has a "very restricted palette," especially in winter. "I've always been aware of the possibility of using colour," Blackwood says, "but never colour for the sake of colour—often colour would weaken the image." After experimenting he felt that, given his imagery, a more restrictive palette would be stronger. He believes in leaving something to the imagination and points out that "we don't need to tell people that the sky is blue."[23] Blackwood uses colour so selectively and idiosyncratically that when he does, it makes a tremendous impact.

At OCA David Blackwood was taught how to construct charts of warm and cool colours using the Bauhaus technique. While he primarily uses "earth colours"—browns, blacks, blues, reds, greens—he also employs complementary contrasts such as green and red, which create a melancholy tone and a naïveté that recalls hand-coloured photographs, early colour illustrations and postcards. Colour is generally used to indicate fire, torchlight or flowers on a coffin. It is generally applied to the copper plate *à la poupée,* although once in a while he applies it directly to the print using watercolour.[24]

Although his work is set in Newfoundland, Blackwood draws on his considerable knowledge of the great masters of printmaking. Soon after I met him, I asked whether he knew the work of the French artist and illustrator Gustave Doré. He thought for a minute and then said, "The only book we had in our house growing up was a family heirloom, a Bible that had passed down from my great-grandfather to my grandfather and then to my father. It was illustrated by Gustave Doré. And a very dramatic thing it was—a Bible with a wonderful chronology in the back, and pages in the front for family history."[25] The Bible now lives in Blackwood's studio, where it holds pride of place among photos and memorabilia that continue to inspire the artist. The illustration that influenced him most strongly is *Jesus Walking on the Sea.* He also owns other books illustrated by Doré, including Coleridge's *The Rime of the Ancient Mariner,* Milton's *Paradise Lost* and Dante's *Inferno.*

Blackwood was introduced to the great masters of printmaking by the OCA instructor and artist Fred Hagan, who was "an extremely literate man and was aware of just about everything that had happened in printmaking." Hagan pointed out that all great works of art have "some inexplicable inner mystery, something you can't quite put your finger on, that constituted a life of its own, a life force."[26] Among the printmakers Hagan most admired, "Piranesi was a god," followed by Rembrandt, Goya and Kollwitz.

Although Blackwood had his "own idea about stories and so on, things I wanted to do," he found in the works of certain Old Masters "great examples of what could be done with the medium, with the figure and with the landscape." His walls are hung with framed works by several of the printmakers he admires. These include some of the huge black and white etchings of Giovanni Battista Piranesi: although he "never dreamt of owning any," Blackwood managed to acquire three etchings from an elderly couple in Port Hope, of which his favourite is *Sepolcro di Cecilia Metella.*[27] Blackwood is attracted by the "great

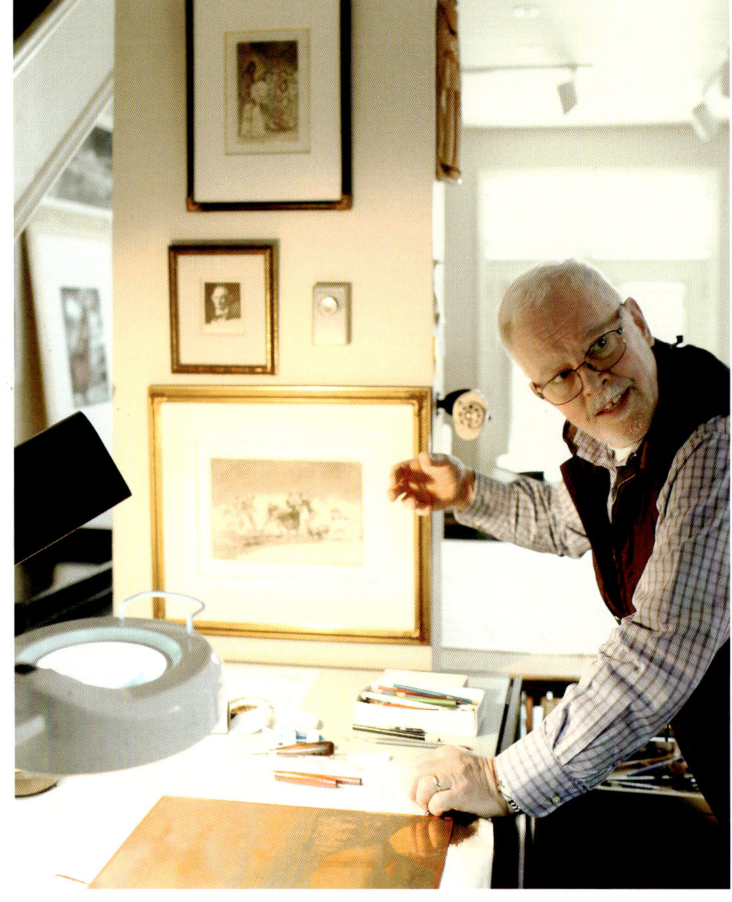

David Blackwood in the studio, Port Hope, Ontario, 2009

fantasy element," "psychological intensity" and "tremendous mystery" of the Piranesis, which have "a life of their own." Their large-scale, deeply bitten lines, powerful imagery and surreal quality are reflected in his own work.

Blackwood is an advocate of traditional etching and works directly on the plate "just like Rembrandt." He was taken by Clifford Ackley's "extraordinary exhibition catalogue," *Rembrandt: Experimental Etcher*, in which Ackley pointed out the way in which Rembrandt kept reinterpreting his etchings by making changes to the plate, varying the tone of the ink and the type of paper and films of plate tone.[28] Blackwood was impressed by the way in which this provided insight into "the creativity of Rembrandt's thinking." Blackwood also makes changes to the plate by scraping out and replacing parts of his composition, experimenting with different colours of ink and amounts of plate tone, and pulling experimental proofs before arriving at his *bon à tirer*, the final variation on which the edition will be based. When juxtaposed, the proofs have a cinematic effect that enables us to reconstruct his thought process.

Among the etchings that look down on the table in the studio where Blackwood inks his plates are Édouard Manet's *Head of Baudelaire*, plate 17 from Francisco Goya's *Tauromaquia* and Georges Rouault's *Bon électeur*, 1928. Other prints he sees every day include William Blake's *The Wrath of Elihu*, from *The Book of Job*, 1825, Käthe Kollwitz's *The Young Couple* and Marc Chagall's *The Shepherd and His Flock*, 1927–30. These are all strong, dark, powerful works, full of psychological or visionary intensity. To Blackwood they are living presences. This artistic dialogue across the centuries accounts in part for the timeless and universal element in his work and the power of his graphic style.

Themes

Although Blackwood felt compelled to make his Newfoundland etchings in order to convey his message, it required endurance to live within the darkness and

Francisco Goya, Plate 17 from *Tauromaquia*, 1816. Etching and drypoint

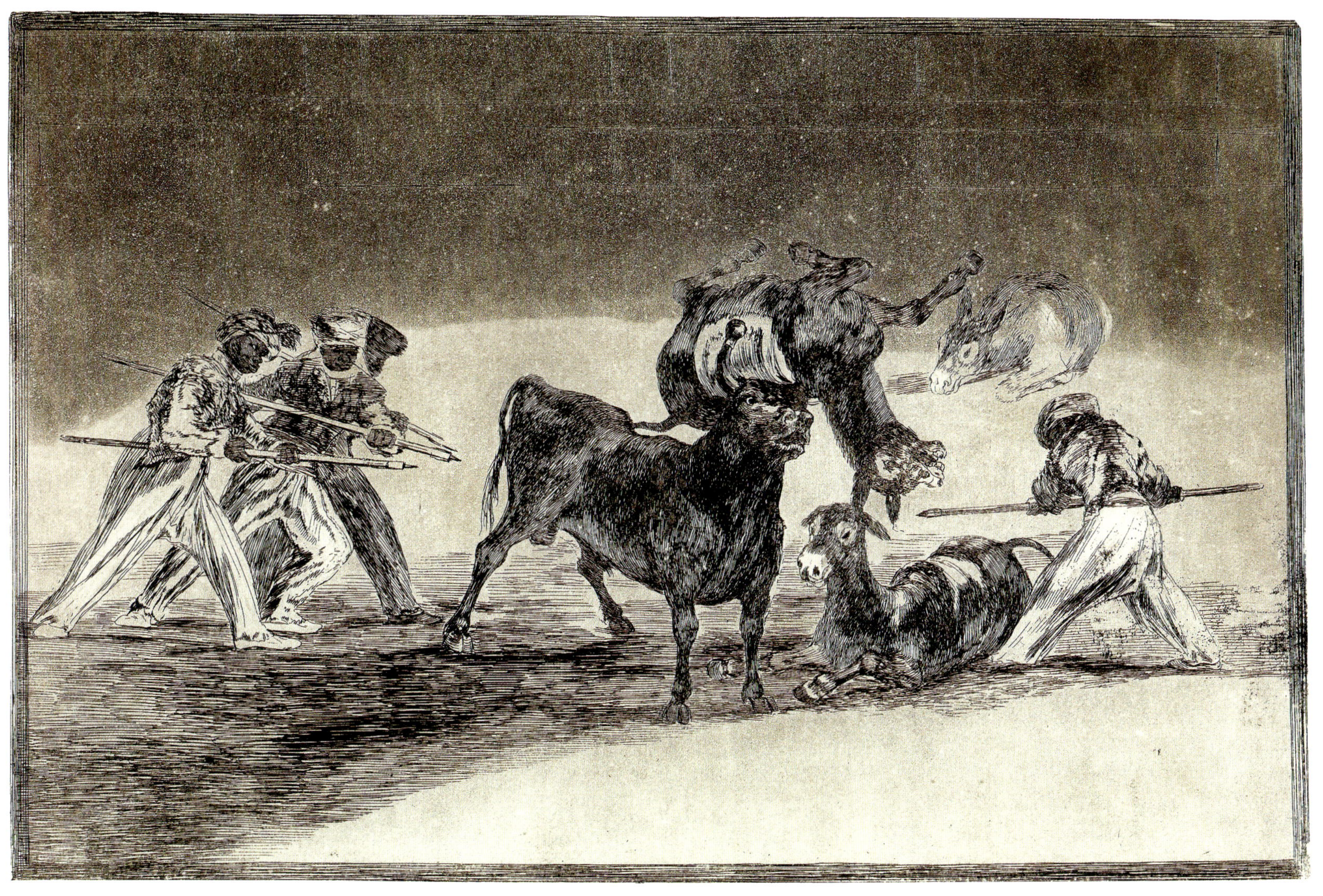

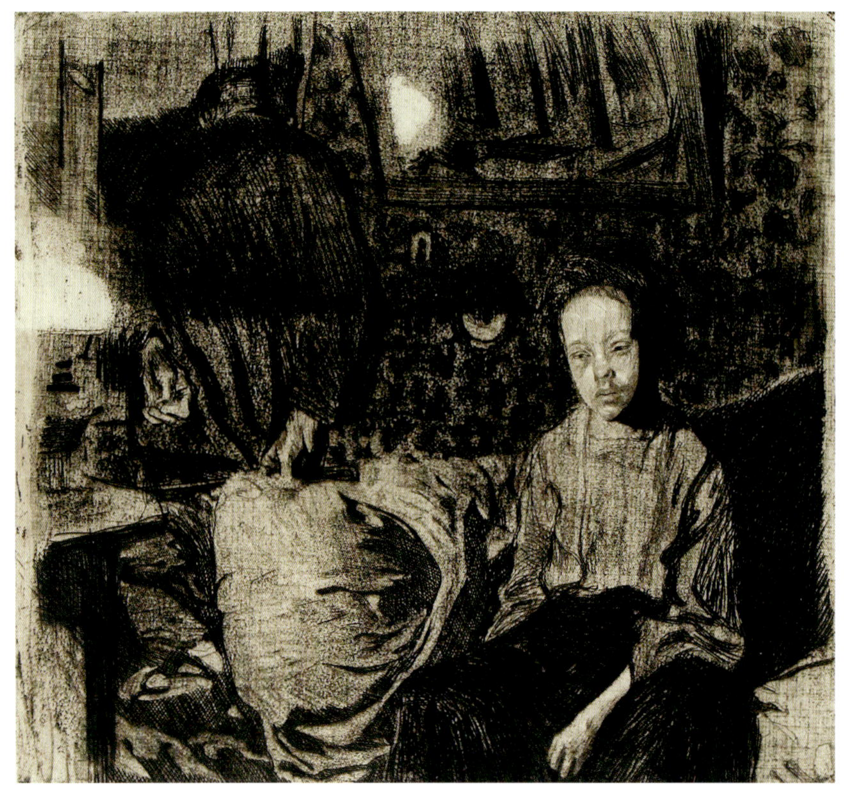

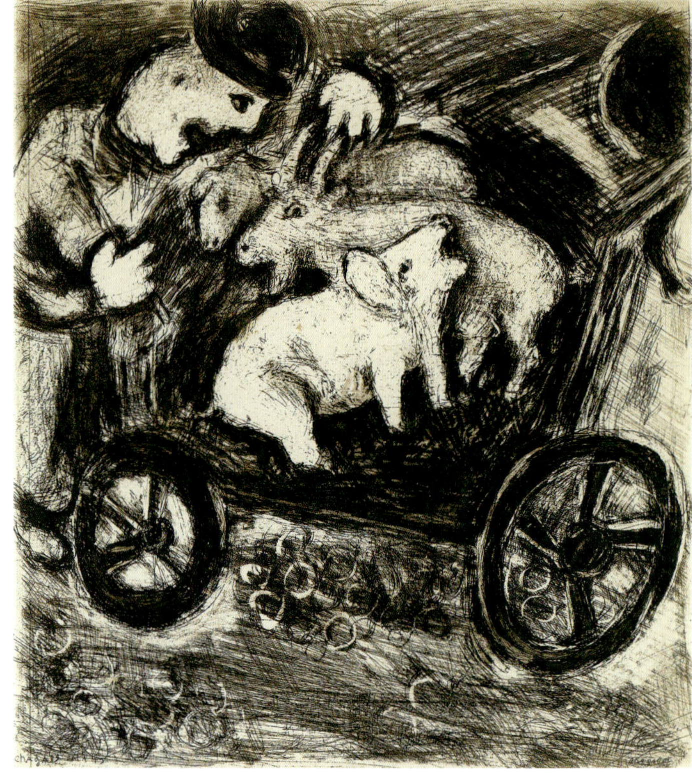

intensity of the subject matter for as long as it took to conceive and execute each print. He acknowledges, "There are a few prints that I have had great difficulty to even approach doing, because the subject matter is horrendous. Some of them are very dark and threatening to people, but that is a good thing."[29] He developed a set of survival techniques: like actors who perform nightly, he learned to step outside the narrative when he was not working on it. He also alternated between making figurative works with "difficult imagery" and landscape views. He makes prints in winter and looks forward to "the relief of escaping into watercolour painting" in summer, well aware that most people would find his etchings of Newfoundland hard, if not impossible, to live with.

His narratives are given exterior or interior settings. The two worlds could not be more contradictory: the exteriors are inhospitable, vast and freezing, whereas the interiors appear safe, cozy and warm. There is, however, an inherent paradox: while on the surface, the exterior dangers appear greater, the interiors hold veiled, even more serious, threats. White ice may be frightening but it is easy to see and avoid; black ice forms an invisible coating that frequently leads to fatal accidents. It is ultimately the unseen threats that are the most dangerous.

Blackwood's world does not end with physical reality: he taps into the realms of the subconscious, supernatural and paranormal and is familiar with the Celtic concept of the "thin space." His most celebrated image, *Fire Down on*

facing, left: Käthe Kollwitz, *The Young Couple*, 1904. Etching and soft-ground

facing, right: Marc Chagall, *The Shepherd and His Flock*, 1952, Plate 92 from *La Fontaine's Fables*. Etching

the Labrador, draws on both conscious and subconscious fears. A tiny ship in flames passes a towering iceberg while its crew, escaping in a Labrador fishing schooner, is unaware of the gigantic whale lurking below the surface. In this surrealist nightmare many things, seen and unseen, pose a threat to human existence, demonstrating both the fragility of the human psyche and the brittleness of human life.

Acts of God took on supernatural proportions in Wesleyville. Bonavista North is the site of severe electrical storms. On July 12, 1944, chain lightning struck the tall spire of the Methodist church, which was covered in zinc plates. There were no lightning conductors because it was taken as an article of faith that lightning would never strike a church. The spire, designed to inspire envy in neighbouring communities, could be seen from as far away as Newtown, eight kilometres up the coast. Because the steeple was a symbol of pride, it was widely believed that the lightning bolt and the destruction of the church were an act of God.

The houses in Blackwood's etchings have great presence and character, but they not only tell stories; they also guard secrets. The family home at Wesleyville was the setting for painful psychodramas. Left with four small children after the premature death of his first wife, Captain Blackwood did not waste any time finding and marrying David Blackwood's mother, Molly Glover (née Winsor), six

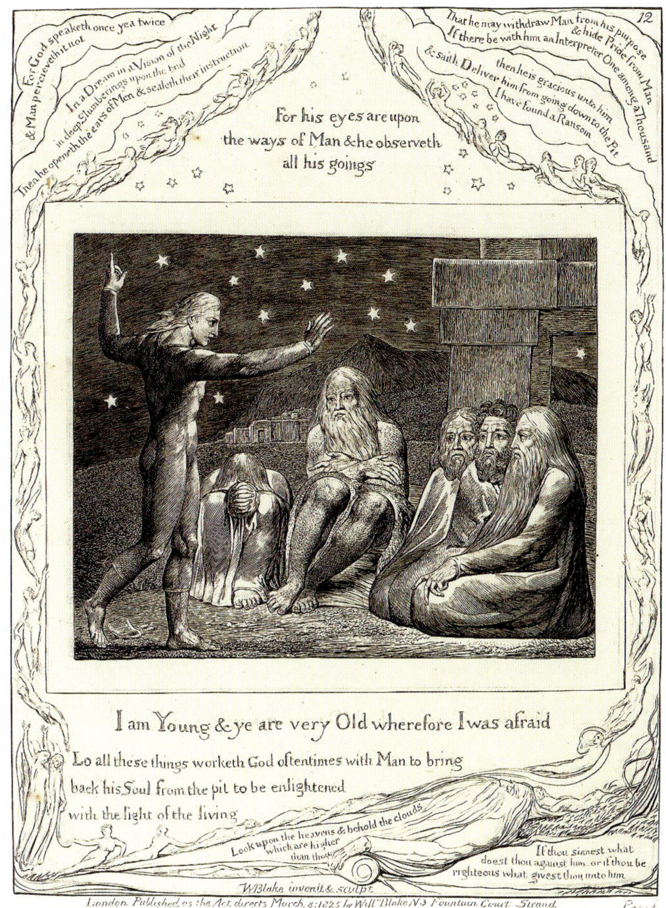

right: William Blake, *The Wrath of Elihu*, 1825, Plate 12 from *The Book of Job*. Engraving

months later. His mother rejected her new daughter-in-law, who "came from up in the bay" (a derogatory expression), and turned the children of the first marriage against her. Molly was marginalized by those in the community who were afraid of falling out with Mrs. Captain Blackwood, a merchant in her own right, who owned the business and the schooners on which many depended for credit.

Molly believed in ghosts. Blackwood recalls:

My mother always felt that the home was haunted and on stormy nights could hear things moving around between intervals of rolling

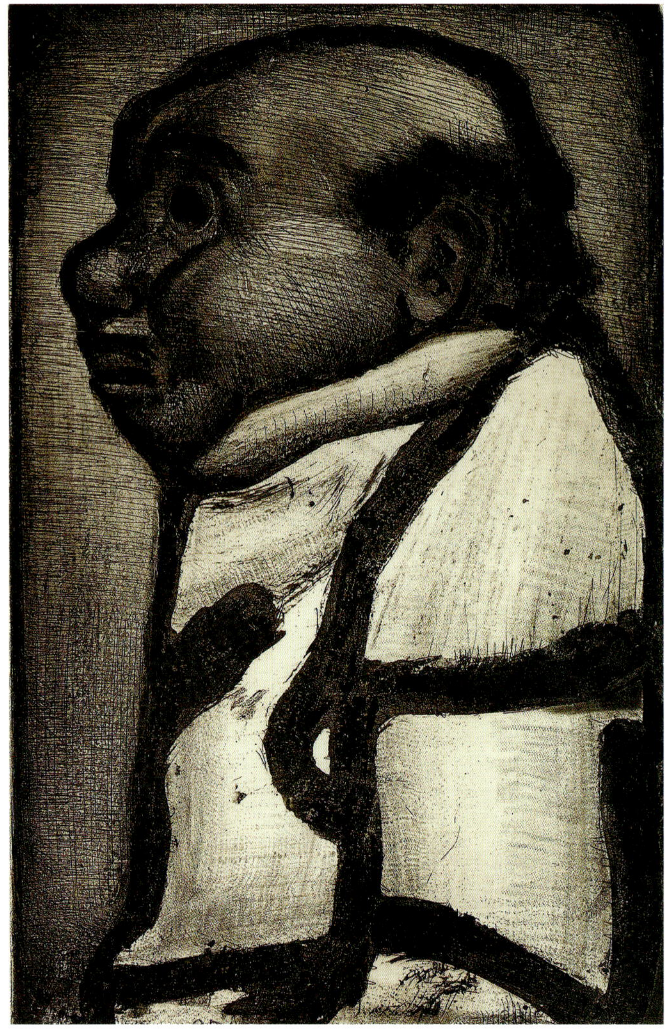

left: Georges Rouault, *Bon électeur*, 1928, Plate 5 from *Reincarnations of Père Ubu*. Etching, aquatint and roulette

facing: David Blackwood and Farley Mowat taking crab apart, 1985

thunder. When my father was away this was especially unsettling… It was during these periods that the house seemed to take on a somewhat sinister atmosphere, real or imagined. It was partly due to the attic. A narrow doorway high up in the peaked roof led to two wallpapered rooms in earlier days occupied by serving girls or young ladies in "service" to the household. By the late 1940s it was filled with the personal belongings of Captain Edward Bishop, my grandmother's uncle and my deceased grandfather.[30]

By degrees David's mother was pushed over the brink. She took a broom to the top of the house and, as she descended the staircase, broke every single pane of glass in the windows. She was taken away and institutionalized. Her husband took the children of his second marriage to live with their maternal grandparents on Bragg's Island. Although Blackwood remembers his grandmother's house as a "great oasis, very secure with a tremendous warm, loving atmosphere," Premier Smallwood's brutal resettlement scheme was to destroy this world as well, shattering the lives of the people who had lived there for generations like the windows that separated the safe interior from the threatening exterior. For Blackwood "it was a traumatic experience to watch the slow disintegration of these buildings… I still have dreams that all the buildings are standing and that I am busy with their reconstruction and restoration."[31]

It is the combination of emotional authenticity and psychological intensity that makes Blackwood's prints arresting and unforgettable. They encapsulate his childhood experiences within a dysfunctional family and a harsh environment. He sees Wesleyville as "Paradise Lost," Bragg's Island as "Paradise Regained" and "the destruction of the built heritage" as "Inferno." He finds the process of creation therapeutic, a way of coming to terms with his own past, and a requiem for a community that no longer exists. He continues to do his personal best to raise the

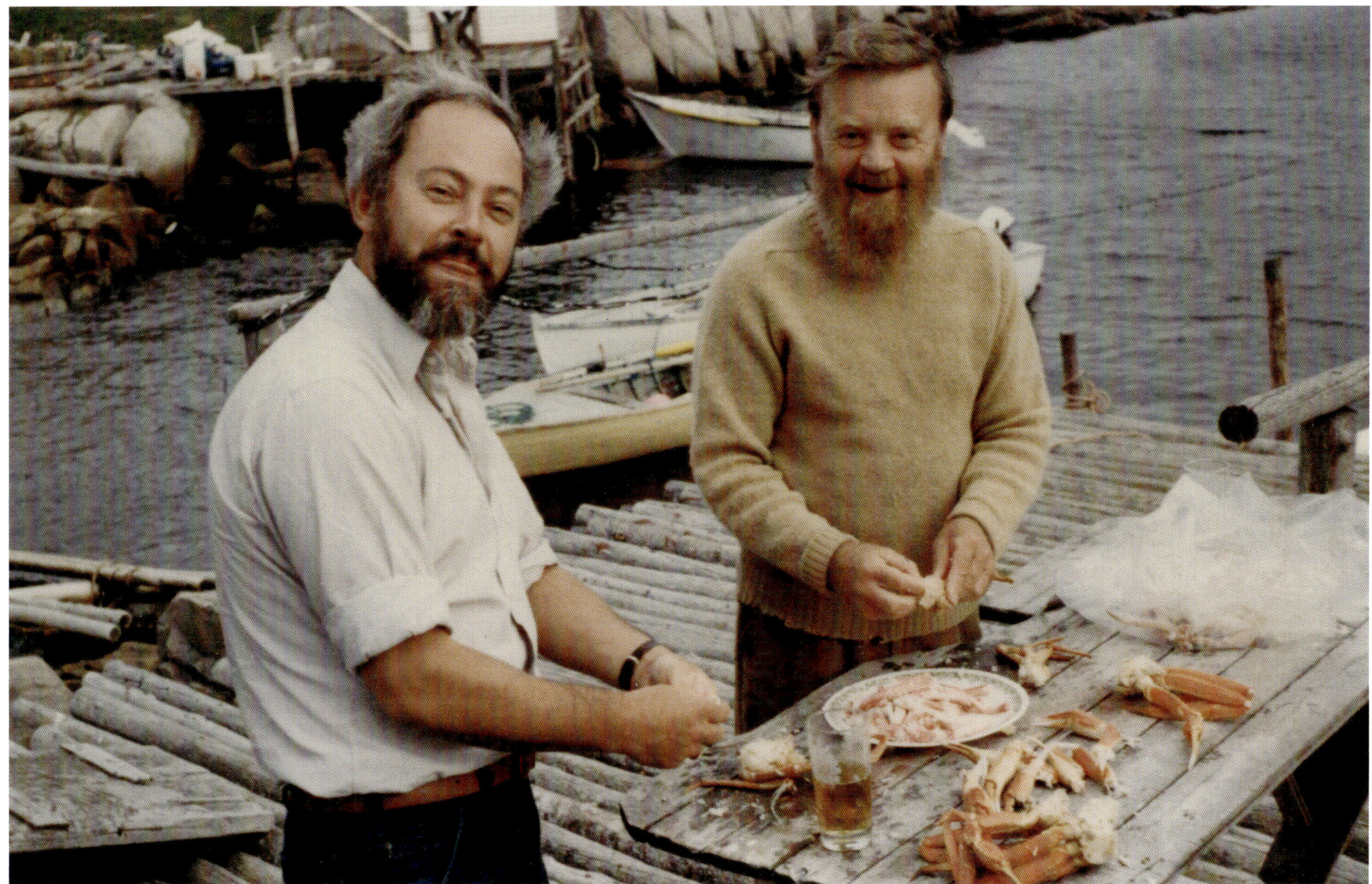

profile and protect and preserve the places that mattered to him as a child. Although those that are gone "exist only in memory and the occasional tattered photograph," they are brought back to life in his prints.[32] Blackwood points out that the etching *Captain Edward Bishop Home in Wesleyville* of 1978 was inspired by the total absence of any visual record. Taken as a whole, his etchings of Newfoundland constitute a self-portrait.

The power in Blackwood's etchings also comes from the fact that he addresses universal issues. No one has articulated his vision more eloquently than Farley Mowat:

Blackwood is a celebrant of essential man. He forces us to see that the antidote to the disease of the present lies in the past. He tells us that, if we are to survive, it is mandatory that we recover the attitudes and the abilities of primeval man, together with the understanding of man's true place and role in the natural world. He tolerates no embellishments which might soften his message and make it more palatable.

His thematic work is the Lost Party *series, and he makes it clear that the Lost Party is mankind—lost but not irretrievably doomed if, if, its members will awaken to the older truths... The figures in his works are the people out of time... They are not forgotten.*

They are essential Man. We need their councel [sic] and we need to understand the sources of their strengths and certainties as never before in human history.[33]

David Blackwood has achieved his goal: he has brought to life the culture of the Newfoundland of his childhood in his etchings. They are not only "rooted in granite" but grounded in the sweat and blood, hopes, fears and memories of a people and a way of life that no longer exist. In doing so, he has raised awareness of the things that he believes make up real quality of life: "community life, industry, spirit, independence, self-reliance, and self-confidence. These are the things Newfoundland had in great abundance prior to joining Canada in 1949."[34]

Blackwood has done this in a unique artistic voice that cannot be confused with any other in the history of art. His powerful images have "some inexplicable inner mystery, something you can't quite put your finger on," the quality Fred Hagan told him was to be found in all great works of art. He has not only made an unparalleled contribution to the history of Canada; he has given our modern world a message to outlive our times.

KATHARINE LOCHNAN *is Senior Curator and R. Fraser Elliott Curator, Prints and Drawings, at the Art Gallery of Ontario.*

Notes

1. This exhibition was at the Doris Pascal Gallery on Dundas Street West in Toronto, across the street from the Art Gallery of Ontario.
2. I would like to thank Professor Derek Wilton for explaining this complicated geological story for me with the help of maps at Memorial University. John Tuzo Wilson, who originated the theory of continental drift, was responsible for Blackwood's appointment as artist-in-residence at Erindale College at the University of Toronto and introduced him to his wife, Anita. Blackwood was fascinated by the man and his theories.
3. Many of the Irish would have been of Viking descent, as Waterford was founded by the Vikings. Fish was the staple of the Viking diet. They also hunted sea mammals.
4. The Ireland Newfoundland Partnership was founded in 1996 to facilitate scholarly collaboration and cultural exchange between Ireland and Newfoundland. I would like to thank Agnes Aylward, the former director of the INP, and her assistant, Kristy Clarke, for their help in contacting three INP grant recipients who are contributors to this book—Derek Wilton, Martin Feely and Caoimhe Ní Shúilleabháin—and for assisting me in many ways with this project.
5. Michael Scott, "Life in Isolation: A Talk with David Blackwood," *Vancouver Sun*, March 21, 1998.
6. I would like to thank Professor Martin Feely for demonstrating this by showing me comparative rock samples from Ireland and Newfoundland in his office at National University of Ireland, Galway. To read more about the geological links between Newfoundland and the west of Ireland, see *The Limestone Barrens Project* by Charlotte Jones, Sean McCrum and Stuart Reid (Owen Sound, ON: Tom Thomson Memorial Gallery, 2004), which received funding from the Ireland Newfoundland Partnership.
7. Charles Mandel, "Portrait of the Artist," *Edmonton Journal*, November 6, 1998.

8. David Blackwood. MS. Blackwood Biography Memorial, 3, Blackwood Papers.
9. Farley Mowat, "The Survivor: David Blackwood," January 1970, Blackwood Papers.
10. David Blackwood. Handwritten notes. Blackwood Papers.
11. Mrs. Oliphant, *The Makers of Florence* (New York: H.M. Caldwell Company, n.d.). Inscribed on title page: "The School, Wesleyville, Newfoundland, June 1937." David Blackwood's private collection.
12. David Blackwood. Handwritten notes. Blackwood Papers.
13. Blackwood has used Stanley William Hayter, *New Ways of Gravure*, (New York: Watson-Guptill), 1981.
14. David Blackwood. Handwritten Notes. Blackwood Collection. The Tintoretto was Jacopo Robusti Tintoretto, *Christ Washing His Disciples' Feet*, 1545–1555, oil on canvas, 154.9 × 407.7 cm, Gift by General Subscription, 1959, acc. no. 58/51, Art Gallery of Ontario. For the other exhibitions Blackwood describes, see Lee Johnson, *Eugène Delacroix* (Toronto: Art Gallery of Toronto and National Gallery of Canada, 1962); Jean Sutherland Boggs, *Picasso and Man* (Toronto: Art Gallery of Toronto and Montreal Museum of Fine Arts), 1964.
15. Blackwood believes that the poet E.J. Pratt also had to work at a distance, and that is why he wrote his Newfoundland poems in his office in Victoria College, Toronto. David Blackwood. MS. Blackwood Biography Memorial, 3. Blackwood Papers.
16. David Blackwood. MS. Blackwood Biography Memorial, 11.
17. That title was assigned not by Blackwood but by the art market.
18. William Wilson, MS, 1964. Blackwood Collection.
19. David Blackwood, interview by Katharine Lochnan, Wesleyville, Newfoundland, September 2009.
20. William S. Lieberman, *Canadian Watercolours, Drawings and Prints* No. 3 (Ottawa: National Gallery of Canada), 1964.
21. David Blackwood, interview by Katharine Lochnan, Wesleyville, Newfoundland, September 2009.
22. Michael Scott, "Life in Isolation: A Talk with David Blackwood," *Vancouver Sun*, March 21, 1998.
23. David Blackwood, interview by Katharine Lochnan, Wesleyville, Newfoundland, September 2009.
24. Coloured inks applied to the copper plate directly using a rolled-up piece of rag known as a poupée ("doll"), as in *The Kite*.
25. Michael Scott, "Life in Isolation: A Talk with David Blackwood," *Vancouver Sun*, March 21, 1998.
26. David Blackwood, interview by Katharine Lochnan, Wesleyville, Newfoundland, September 2009.
27. The other two are *Veduta del tempio della Sibilla in Tivoli* and *Veduta di un Sepolcro*.
28. Clifford Ackley, *Rembrandt: Experimental Etcher* (Boston: Museum of Fine Arts), 1969.
29. David Blackwood, interview by Katharine Lochnan, Wesleyville, Newfoundland, September 2009.
30. David Blackwood. Handwritten notes. Blackwood Papers.
31. Ibid.
32. Ibid.
33. Farley Mowat, "The Survivor: David Blackwood," January 1970. Blackwood Papers.
34. Joan Murray, "Blackwood's Newfoundland: An Interview with David Blackwood," *Canadian Forum*, May 1978, 12.

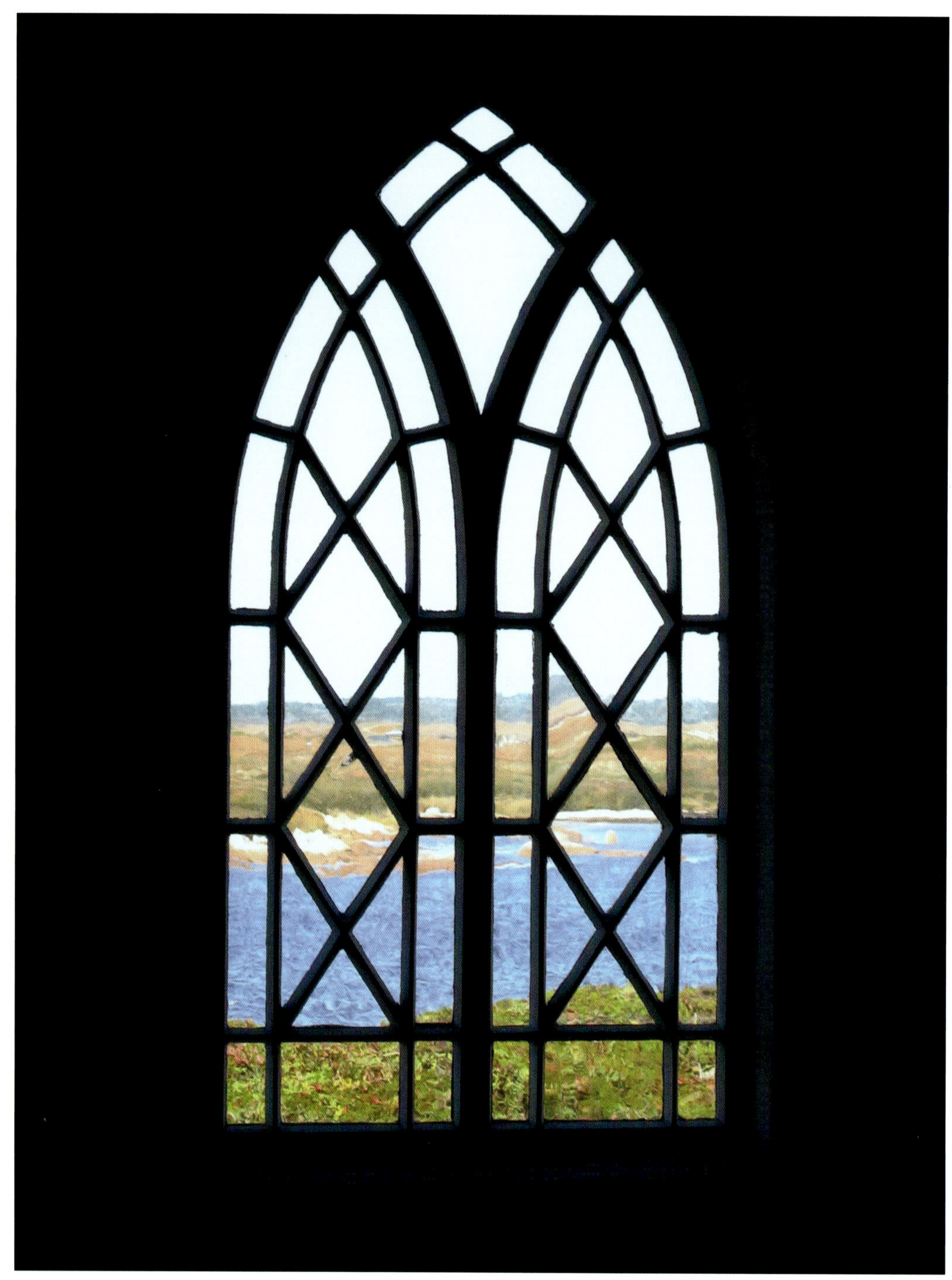

View through window of St. Luke's Anglican Church, Newtown, Newfoundland, September 2009

WILLIAM WHITING

BRITISH · 1825–1878

Eternal Father, Strong to Save · 1860

. . .

Eternal Father, strong to save,
Whose arm hath bound the restless wave,
Who biddest the mighty ocean deep
Its own appointed limits keep;
Oh, hear us when we cry to Thee,
For those in peril on the sea!

LINES 1–6

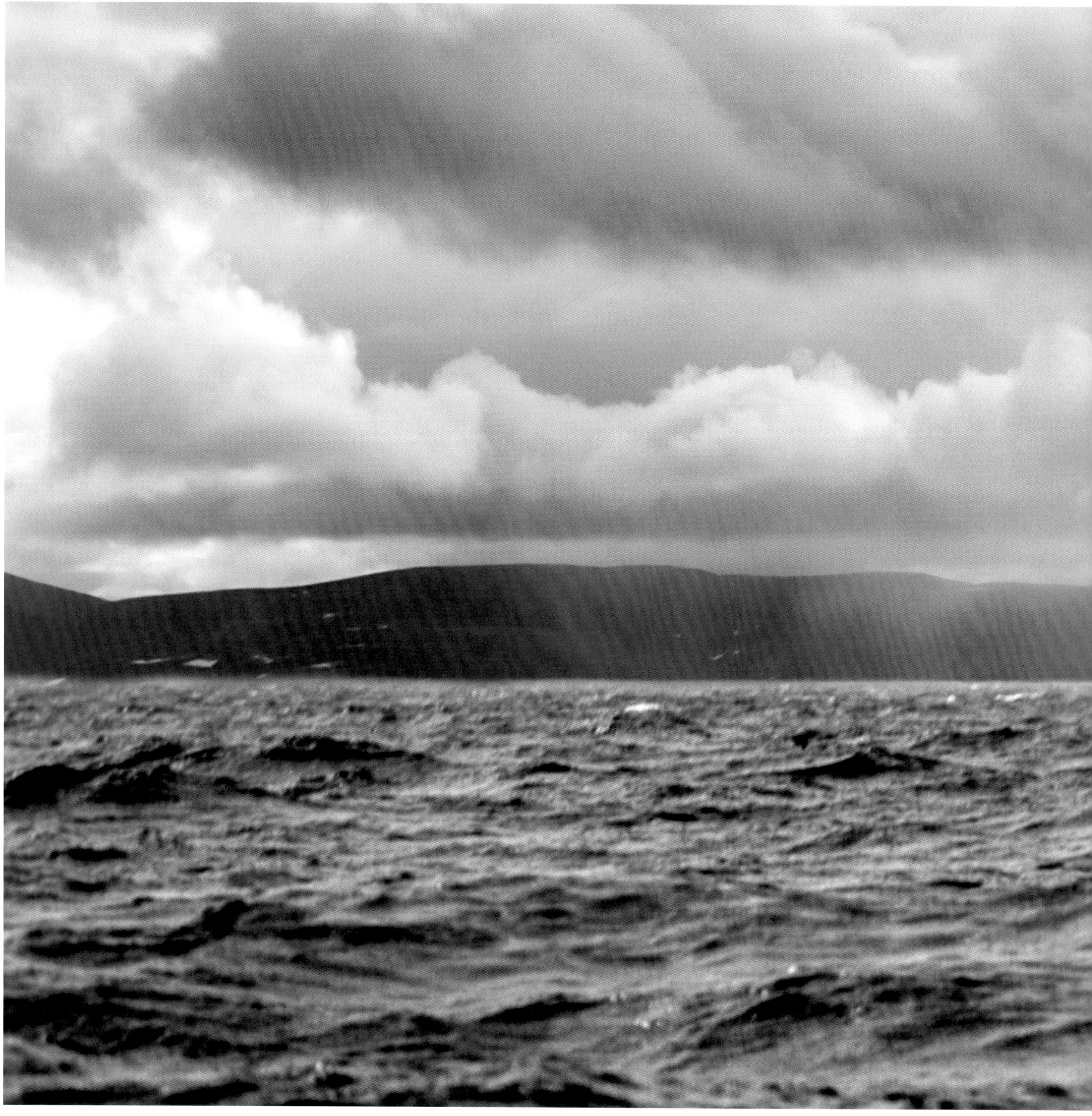

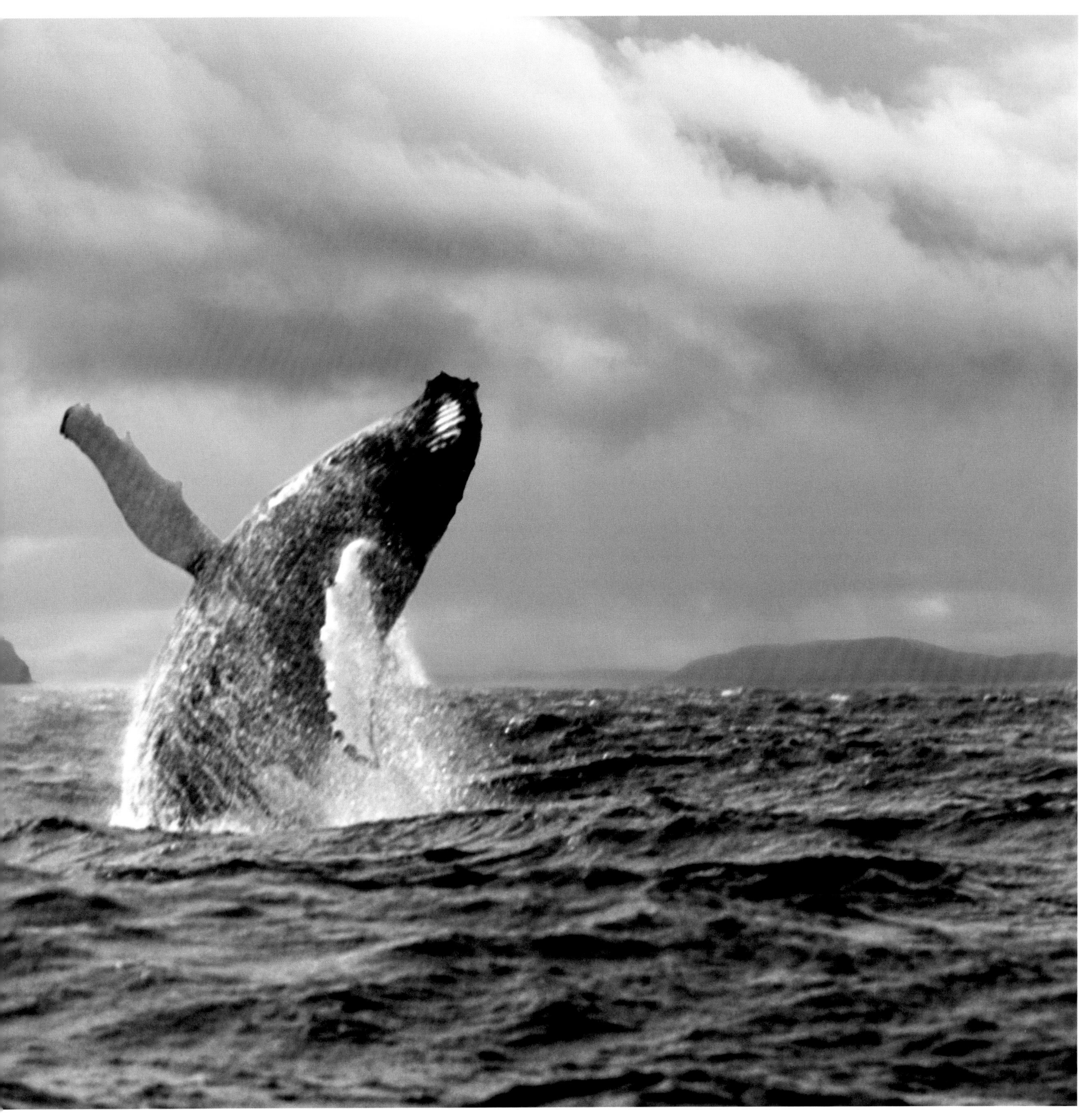

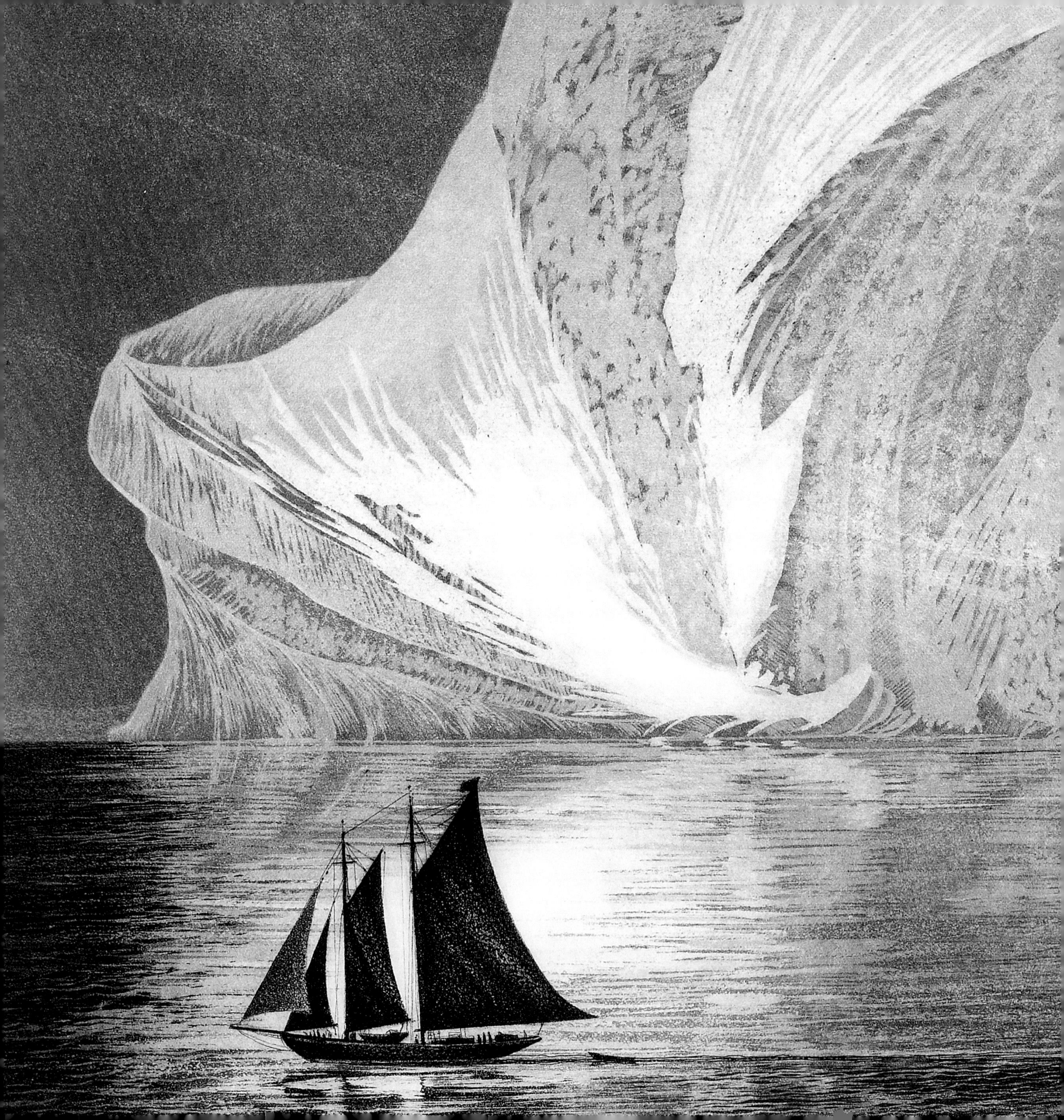

Ice and Fire

AN INTERVIEW WITH DAVID BLACKWOOD

Gary Michael Dault

This interview took place the afternoon of Sunday, August 1, 2010, at David Blackwood's studio in Port Hope, Ontario.

GARY: I'm wondering if there is any truth in the idea that your career as an artist took you through three distinct but interrelated stages: it seems to me that in the beginning, you must have seen yourself as a kind of documenter, a role that may well have evolved into your seeing yourself, next, as essentially a historian—as you moved physically farther from your Newfoundland home, from Wesleyville. And then it seems to me that you may well have modulated, in the latter part of your career, into the inhabiting of a third role—that of mythologist, a maker of palpable memories of a powerful but bypassed culture. Do those three stages seem right to you?

facing: Detail from **Flora S. Nickerson Down on the Labrador**, 1978 (plate 24)

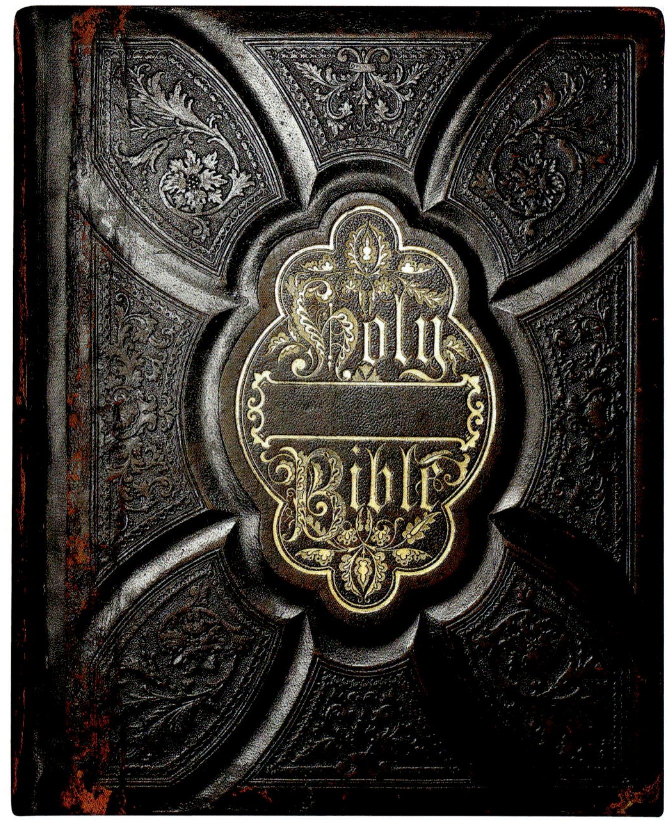

David: Very much so, but, you know, there was no conscious attempt to do any of this. It all just happened. You were there, and you were a part of it, and you simply carried on. The rich, vivid environment you were brought up in, the storytelling in the community... well, you just simply lived it.

Gary: But so did everybody else, and they didn't end up becoming artists.

David: It's true, there were of course specific influences on me. There was a teacher who presented Shakespeare to us in a dramatic way that always stayed with me, and his reading of Coleridge's "The Rime of the Ancient Mariner" left a permanent impression. Also, we had a small regional library in Wesleyville, which had among its holdings Romain Rolland's *Life of Millet* from 1902—which had a huge influence on me, partly because of the parallels (as I saw them) in our lives, his being born in a tiny village, and so on...

Gary: You have mentioned the influence on you, too, of the preachers and guest speakers at the Jubilee Methodist Church in Wesleyville, the sound of the great rolling prose—from the King James Bible—that would come from them, that kind of language that rolled like the sea. It must have been like organ music. That must have had a profound effect on you.

David: With its great emphasis on the Old Testament.

Gary: Blood and thunder and lightning and dire threats of retribution?

David: All that greatly affected who we were and how we behaved. In recent years, a Jewish gentleman I know pointed out to me a number of resemblances between Methodism and Judaism. And it's true, even to the point where Newfoundlanders would not eat certain kinds of seafood—shellfish, such as lobster and crab. And those taboos are clearly part of the Jewish tradition as well.

Gary: Really? Newfoundlanders would simply export those products?

David: Yes. There was never, never any eating of lobster, crab or flounder.

Gary: Why not flounder?

facing: Edward Churnside
Bishop Bible, King James version

below: Gustave Doré, *Jesus Walking on the Sea*, Plate facing p. 705 in *The Holy Bible* (Philadelphia: A.J. Holman & Co., 1874). Wood engraving

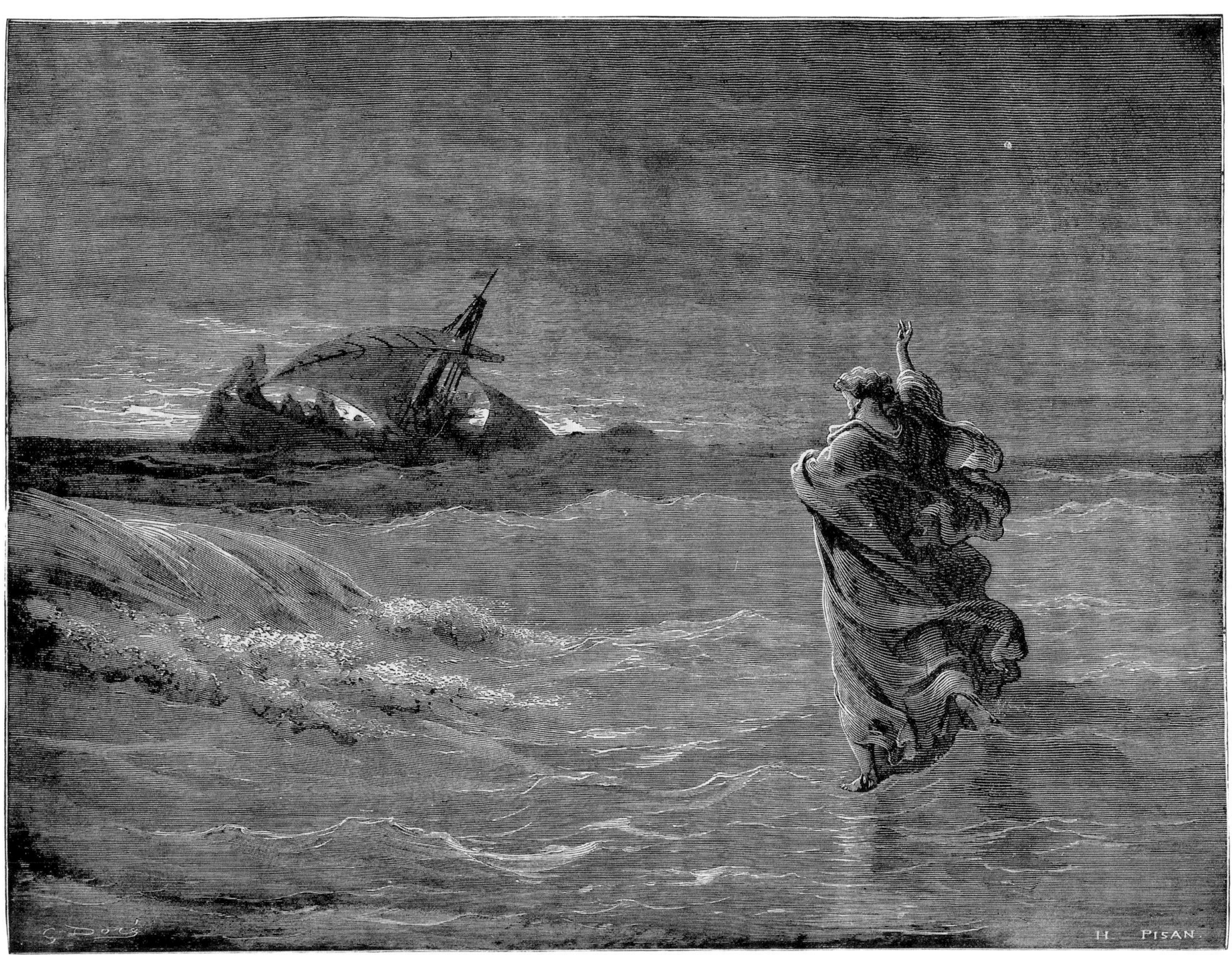

facing: The hearse at a funeral in Wesleyville, 1929

David: You didn't eat anything that sort of crawled on the bottom of the ocean. It all came out of the all-prevailing Old Testament.

Gary: I remember your mentioning how much force the Gustave Doré illustrations for the Bible exerted upon you, too.

David: Oh, Doré was a profound influence! His drama!

Gary: As I recall, Doré illustrations tend to be toweringly dramatic...

David: And shot through with shafts of light. Light was a big factor in the work, streams of light.

Gary: And this is clearly a profoundly important part of your work.

David: Yes, and this was also a part of the Methodist philosophy: Daybreak. Dawn. Light was a big factor.

Gary: As a moral category?

David: Yes, very much so. The idea of light was woven not only in the preaching in the church, but it permeated everything... It was what the people responded to—to nature. That was part of the preaching, part of the philosophy of the Wesleyans: the overwhelming goodness of light. To seek light. Enlightenment, in all its senses. There's a great hymn in the Methodist church, "Lead, Kindly Light, amid the Encircling Gloom." They even put it in inscriptions and quoted it on headstones.

Gary: Can we take those meanings that appear to live in the light and the dark and shift them around into another dichotomy—the idea of what is above and what is below? That is, what's above the surface of the ocean, and what's beneath it? The emblematic etchings of yours here might well be pictures like *For Ishmael Tiller: The Ledgy Rocks, Fire Down on the Labrador, Loss of Flora S. Nickerson* and *Wesleyville Fleet in Labrador Sea*. It just seems to me that much of the power of your depictions of those prodigious whales lurking beneath the surface of the sea might derive from the idea of the submerged as the realm of the unconscious. Is that something you felt when you were making those pictures?

David: I suppose we can see in it the presence of the unconscious—unconsciously. But I also think all that had a great deal to do with living intimately, every day, with life and death. As small children, of course, we were very much aware of any new baby being born into the community. Every single man, woman and child would go and see that new baby. Then when Uncle John passed away, every man, woman and child in the community would go to the house to see him in his coffin, laid out. Little children would come and knock on the door and say, "Can I see Uncle John?"

Gary: Really?

David: They would be brought into the house and led into the parlour. They weren't tall enough to peer into the coffin, which would be up on two chairs, so they'd be lifted up so they could look into it. I remember—probably I was two or three years old—going to see my great-grandmother

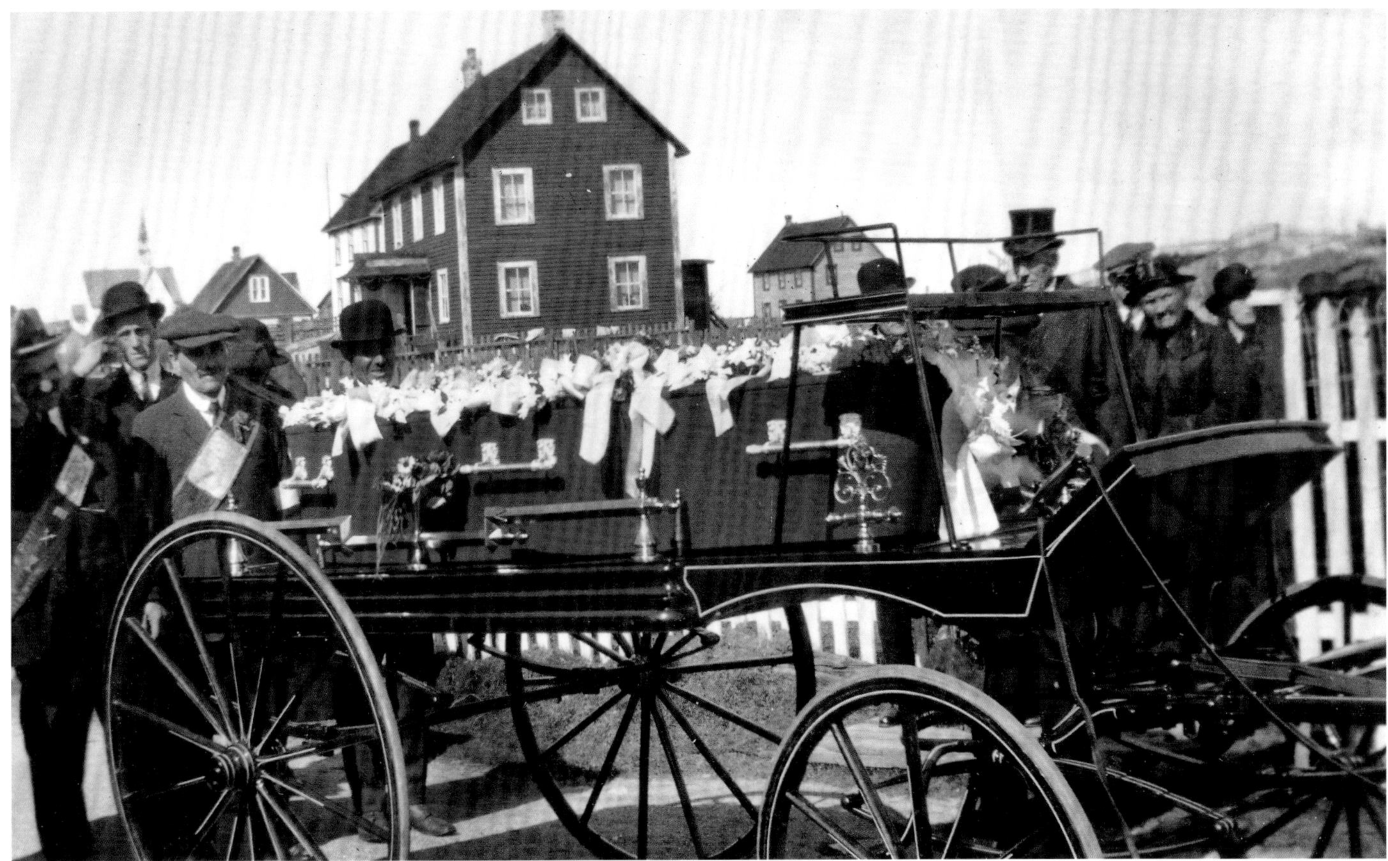

in the same circumstances. I, too, wasn't tall enough to see. And so I was lifted up so I could look into the coffin—and there would be Nana Bishop, with her whiskers—ninety-nine years old. We were very much aware of the mysteries of life and death, even at a very early age. Children today are protected from all of this sort of thing.

Gary: I guess we're profoundly sanitized now, compared to all that—which cannot be good for our cultural lives.

David: No. And then, of course, there were the elemental aspects of life in Newfoundland. Today, we certainly don't worry too much here about wind and great storms. But at home, we were so much aware of all that. Perhaps that deeply felt knowledge constitutes part of the unconscious you're talking about.

Gary: Did you feel anything of the deep past when you were eight years old walking the deck of your family's schooner, the *Flora S. Nickerson*?

David: Yes, I was already aware of the drama of it all.

Gary: Even as a child?

David: Oh, indeed. Absolutely. It came about as a constant replay of the ordinary, the everyday.

Gary: Did you read *Moby Dick* as a young man? It'd be pretty hard not to see a kind of Melvillean sensibility in your work.

David: Not in school, but I did read it shortly afterwards, because its subject matter led me into reading it, absolutely—Melville's rapture and despair about the dark, unknowable side of the seas.

Gary: When you started to make your work seriously, did you just know that you had hit upon your great subject, which would be the Newfoundland past?

David: As a student at the Ontario College of Art, where I came to study in 1959, I learned that every artist needs a subject. And yes, I quite quickly realized that mine would be Newfoundland.

Gary: It has seemed always to nourish you.

David: I grew up in that narrative tradition and just carried it on. I didn't pay any attention to fashion or trends in art…

Gary: Well, I think that required a lot of grit, because the art community is incredibly sensitive to change of valence and change of style, and it takes a lot of stamina to withstand the latest aesthetic flavour of the month…

David: It's the steadfastness, the tenacity of Newfoundlanders.

Gary: They must have really been a tough group of people.

David: And they did not have the luxury of nice big ocean liners to bring them across the Atlantic. Some of those people came in small boats. They knew how to build small boats that were very, very strong.

Gary: Tell me, when you live that close to nature, do you begin to develop—I don't mean to sound mystical here—but do you begin to develop some incredibly sensitive understanding of coming changes in weather, in lurking dangers…?

David: Oh yes… fear of the ocean! My father was a sea captain from the age of seventeen. He took command. He had gone to sea up the coast of Labrador, which was the big fishing ground for the northeast coast of Newfoundland. To push beyond the territories of the "inland fishermen," who would be going out in small boats, they'd push on in their schooners to fishing grounds much farther afield, heading for the Labrador. And my father started going to the Labrador when he was only ten. By the time he was seventeen, he took charge of a schooner under the watchful eye of a relative who was all of forty! But no problems developed, and he carried on. My father had a tremendous fear of the ocean—which is another way of saying he had tremendous respect for it.

Gary: Remarkable.

David: Because he knew the unpredictability of the tides and winds and, of course, they were working without modern navigational aids, without all the modern technologies. Fog was a factor, wind, tide, the Arctic ice they would encounter as they were moving north to the Labrador. Of course, they encountered an extraordinary phenomenon, the Arctic icefields moving south. And they were

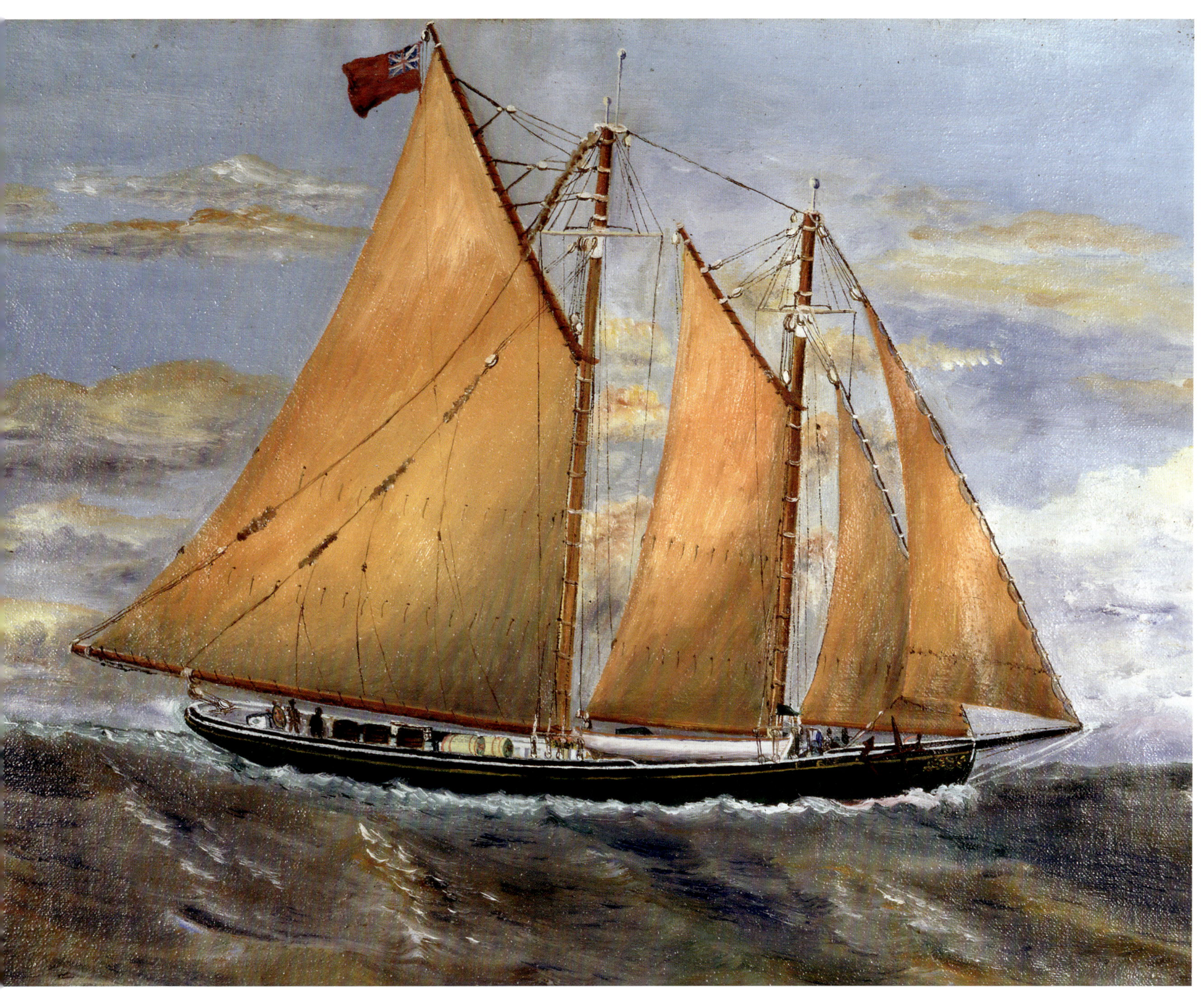

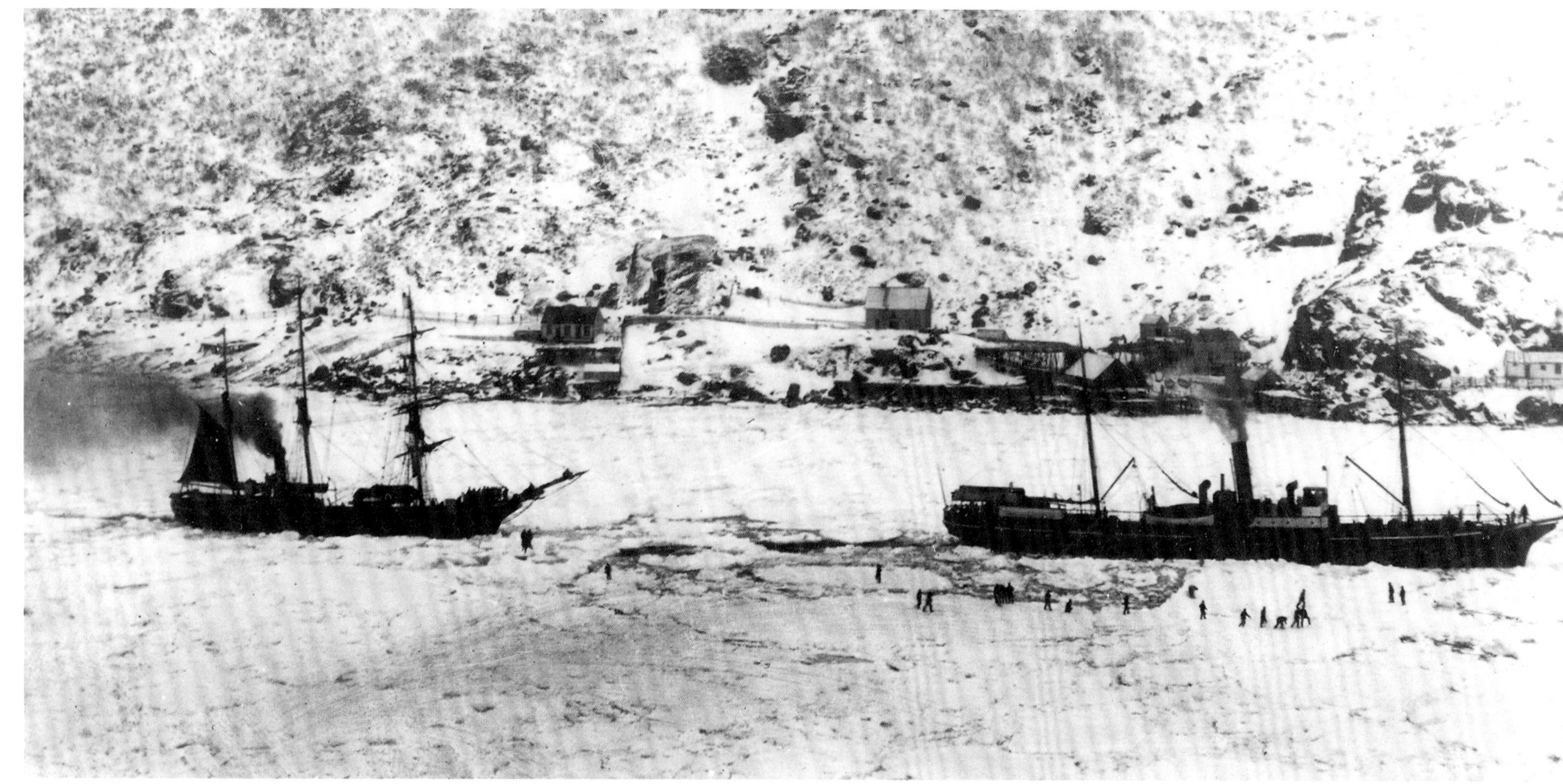

navigating through all that, against the wind and tides, so there is no doubt that they were to become great ice navigators. Admiral Perry depended on those same men to take them to the South Pole and the North Pole.

Gary: It's almost as if such men grew to be semi-aquatic, as they came to develop the kind of senses an animal would have for its environment . . . a remarkable sensitivity to it.

David: My grandfather, Captain A.L. Blackwood, was a well-known sealing captain. And he could actually smell the seal herds at a great distance—on the wind. He could tell, for example, that there were seals fifty miles out—and how many of them there were! These men were very much in tune with nature, and had huge respect for it.

Gary: And that has been imported wholesale into your pictures, it seems to me.

David: I would agree, yes.

Gary: I want to ask you about ice. I've looked at a lot of your etchings, and ice is a big factor in them. Ice is almost like a *character* in your pictures. This is astonishing to me, because we think of icebergs as occasional and picturesque. But the ice in your pictures is almost oppressive.

David: It's because of the northeast coast, and the Labrador current bringing that icefield down . . . It made for a horrendous climate in that area. That is where all the fog is actually made, off in the northeast coast. The icefield there is incredible—January, February and March—and then

facing: SS *Kite* of Bowring Brothers, Ltd., and SS *Grand Lake* of A.J. Harvey & Co., St. John's, Newfoundland, 1903–1908

the other extra element, the Arctic icefield coming down, filling in the entire Bonavista Bay, and staying for long periods of time. You could very easily count fifty big icebergs at a time in the region. Some of them were so huge that they would embed themselves in the ocean floor. And they would change shape daily because of tides and winds and so on. Some of them were lodged a great distance off shore, and they were gigantic!

Gary: They also seem troublingly unpredictable, volatile almost.

David: Certainly they would affect the climate. Because of them, it could be very, very cold, if the wind was blowing in the right direction—even though it might seem to be a bright sunny day.

Gary: Some of the most terrifying of your etchings have to do with the horrifying, claustrophobic business of being trapped in the ice. And this was not uncommon, I guess—parties, ships enclosed in the shifting ice…

David: The boats would become jammed and then the direction of the wind would create a tremendous pressure. If you were lucky, the boat would simply pop up onto the ice!

Gary: Really?

David: Or if you were unlucky, it would be crushed. And then the other great fear was fire.

Gary: Well, I was going to say that your etchings seems to me—of course I'm simplifying a bit here—to be essentially black, white and blue, cold blue. But then there are these red bits, and the reds are quite scary, because even though there are sometimes celebrational reds in your pictures—in the kite etchings, for example—for the most part, the reds indicate fires.

David: Well, there are flowers in some of them…

Gary: But only very occasionally.

David: Yeah, yeah.

Gary: But what sticks in my mind are these horrifying fires on the horizon, ships burning. That terrible red glow in the sky.

David: Fire was a big factor. It destroyed houses, churches, boats…

Gary: Because of wood stoves?

David: There were chimney fires, wooden buildings burning down, churches struck by lightning…

Gary: That's a bit ironic, surely?

David: Well, the big Methodist church in Wesleyville was a testament to the strength and power of the village's fishermen and sea captains and was considered strong and inviolable, and when a lightning bolt actually did strike it, it was profoundly humbling to the people in the community.

Gary: Because they interpreted it as some kind of Old Testament retribution?

David: Very much so, for it was seen to be a blow directed at what was taken to be their pride and particularly the pride they were taking in material things—the fine *facing:* Wesleyville, with icebergs, c. 1990

church building. They finally came to the conclusion that it was almost inevitable that the church would be destroyed, you see?

Gary: Thinking more about fires, tell me something: How on earth could a ship, a schooner, catch fire on the open sea?

David: The galley.

Gary: A grease fire?

David: Well, you know, absolutely. Every now and again, especially later on when gasoline was introduced, there would be a galley fire. Normally, the cooking fire would be put out before nightfall. Nobody would ever allow the fire in the stove to burn all night. But every now and again, of course, because something was being fried (and everything was fried), there might suddenly be a big fire. And then you'd be facing the worst possible scenario, the thing that was the greatest fear of all—to be caught in the Labrador Sea all alone, and having to abandon.

Gary: How horrifying!

David: Nowhere to go, no one to go to. So that was the dreadful image that was always in everyone's mind, having to abandon your schooner.

Gary: Dreadful, because you'd either drown or freeze to death.

David: Oh yes, absolutely. So in my print *Fire Down on the Labrador,* it's the ultimate disaster that I'm depicting—to be caught in that environment, and having to abandon ship.

Gary: Just as a sort of momentary relief from disaster at sea, let's talk for a moment about your kite pictures. Tell me, were kites a kind of overcompensation for, a corrective to, that very earnest, dangerous life you've been so vividly describing?

David: It was one of the community activities, like mummery. Certainly, kite building and kite flying gave you some respite from the ongoing severity of life. In Wesleyville, kite flying was only in March, by the way.

Gary: Only March?

David: Only March. During no other time of the year.

Gary: Not later in the summer?

David: No, no, no, no. It was solely a March activity.

Gary: Why? Because of the winds?

David: Yes, because of the constant prevailing winds.

Gary: And I take it that kites were not toys, but rather a serious activity.

David: Well, they weren't toys, no. It was really quite a serious business. It wasn't play.

Gary: Was it tough to get that big kite up there?

David: It took two or three people to make it stay up there.

Gary: Did you make kites?

David: Oh yes, indeed. There are three types. There was the loop kite, and the diamond-shaped kite, and the big box kite—which can be quite a challenge to get off the ground [see *Uncle Cluny's Kite over Wesleyville,* 1989]. It was very

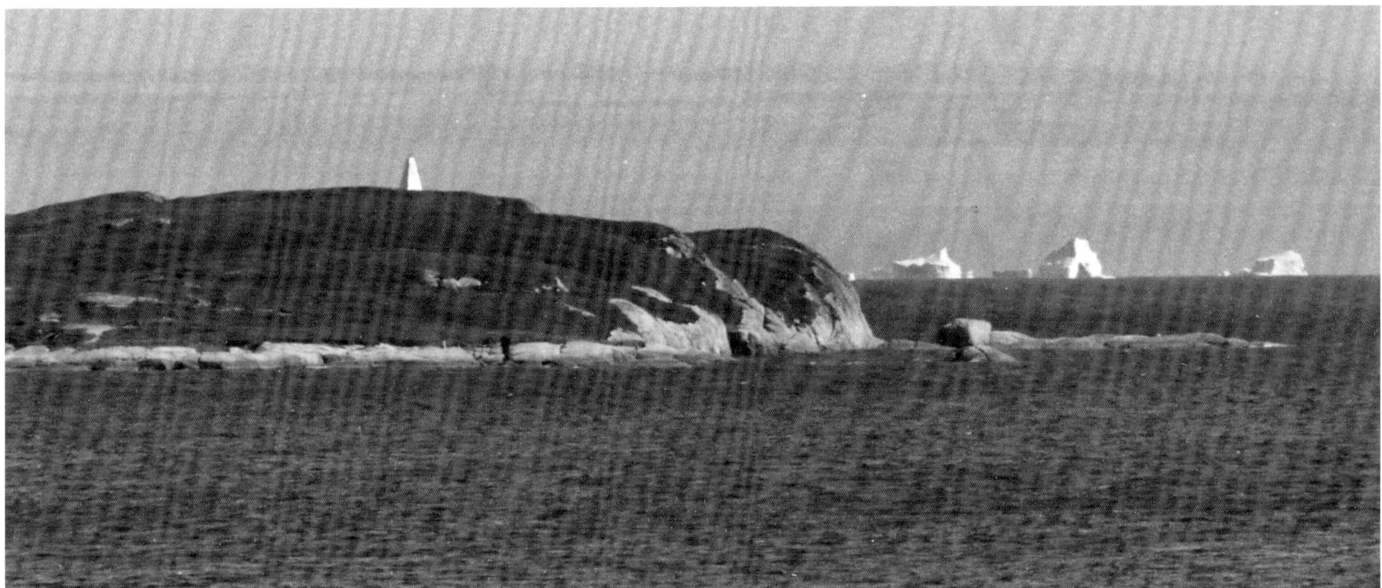

complicated. If you were extremely adventuresome and ambitious, you could attempt the big box kite.

Gary: And mummery, was that a part of your youth? Do you remember the mummers?

David: Oh yes. The twelve nights of Christmas. Mummery came from medieval England, from the eras of Kings Richard I, II and III. Mummers were part of their court entertainment. But it was older even than that, apparently originating with the Druids. When the early settlers came from England to Newfoundland in the 1400s and 1500s, they brought those customs with them. Eventually, mummery stopped in England but carried on in the isolation of the Newfoundland outports. And of course it gradually changed. Certain towns would develop their own unique ways of going about it. My father would tell me stories of how, when he was a child, the system of mummery was very much an English medieval one... in that people would wear antlers and fur.

Gary: You've done some wonderful pictures of the costumes.

David: But in my own time, an evolving kind of mummery resulted in the disappearance of all the animal materials. And it became more a matter of wearing veils and dressing up.

Gary: Sounds like more of a Halloween.

David: Yep. Very, very much like what we would be referring to as Halloween over here.

Gary: Did it end? The mummery tradition, I mean?

David: It did.

Gary: It ended with relocation?

David: Well, in my region, and in my home town, it was definitely not being practised in 1975. I remember the National Film Board of Canada wanting to do a film about mummery. They came to Wesleyville, but there were no mummers that Christmas. Television had come and taken over. People no longer wanted all these unruly, outlandish

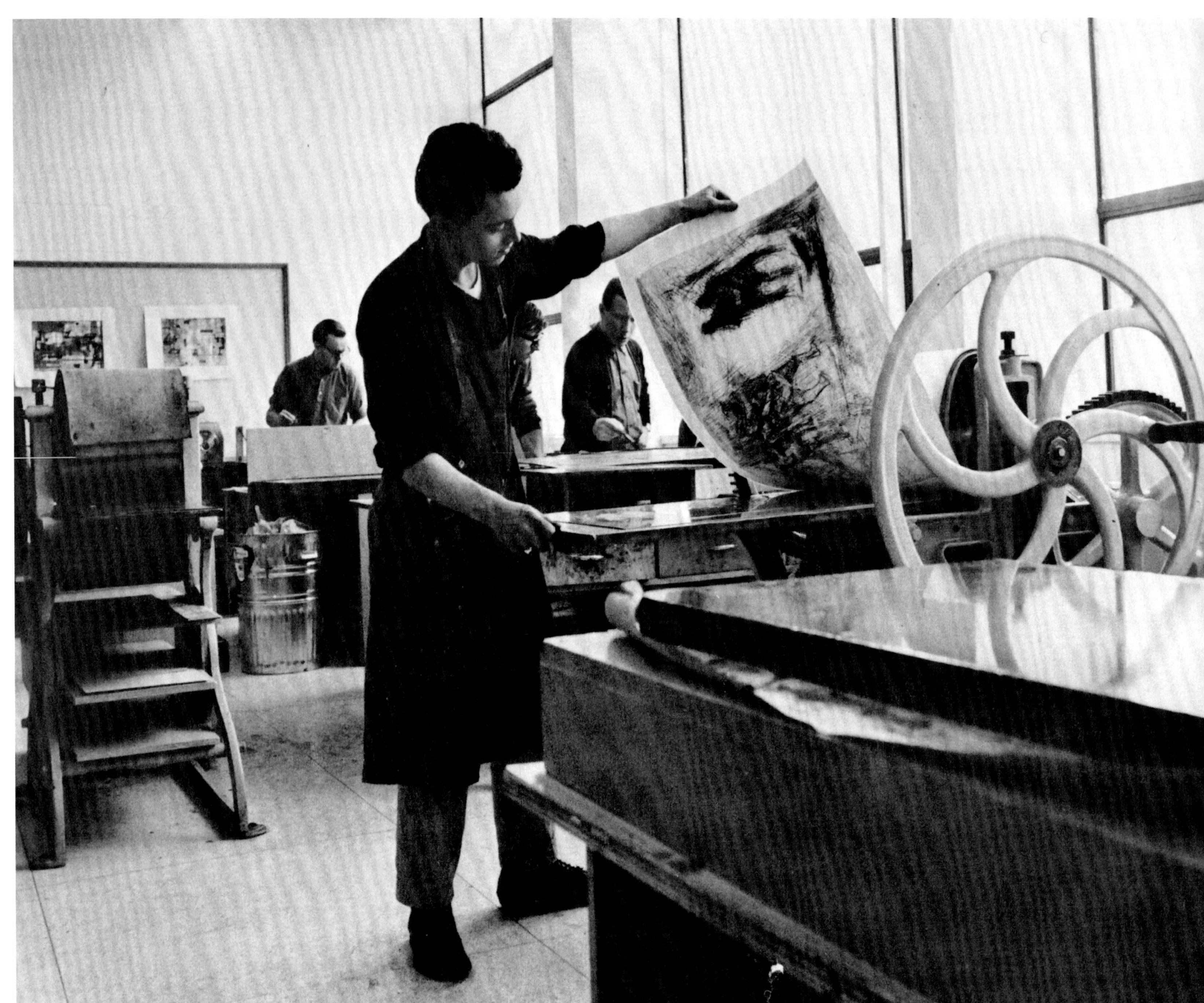

facing: David Blackwood pulling an impression at OCA on the big press, Toronto, Ontario, 1963

strangers coming through the house. And it all stopped. So the National Film Board decided, "Well, you know, what can we do to create some mummers?" And all the townspeople then got very excited and dressed up, and went through the motions.

Gary: Pseudo mummers.

David: Yes. And they had so much fun doing it that the next year, they decided, "Well, why don't we do that again?"

Gary: Even without the NFB!

David: It was a small rebirth of mummery. Now, it has been carried on for the tourists. And they're doing it in the summer!

Gary: But that's absolutely pointless, isn't it?

David: Well, it's no longer "the twelve nights of Christmas"!

Gary: So much has changed. That's what I meant by saying that your work seemed to go from documentary to history, to mythology. It's all like a dream now.

David: The Newfoundland that we knew is no longer there. Perhaps one of the only connections with it would be the prints. So there's the mythology you were mentioning earlier.

Gary: It seems that your prints, your etchings, are, in a sense, related to the literary. It's as if they're scripted, in a way. They not only tell an effective story, but they seem to exist as a kind of cuneiform or sign making. It's as if there's actually a language you've developed. Would you agree?

David: Yes, but it's never been intentional.

Gary: The subject matter of your etchings seems so specific, it's almost difficult to believe that you're not somehow on site, rapidly sketching what is there before you. It's hard to see it as recollection, because it's all so incredibly detailed and accurate. Normally, when somebody recollects something, what they get as a result is impressionistic.

David: That's true.

Gary: But you are the very opposite of the impressionistic art.

David: Well, the other thing, Gary, is that I have a tremendous archive here.

Gary: Here in the studio, you mean?

David: Yes. And going back a long time. A lot of the material we've collected is Victorian. So there's a useful and powerful visual record there.

Gary: And you frequently avail yourself of this source material?

David: Absolutely. Around 1900, a very unusual thing happened in Wesleyville. There arrived in the community a man—his family name was Oakley—who had fallen totally in love with photography. He had all the necessary photographic equipment and was passionately photographing everything in and around our village. If you go to Wesleyville today, there's nothing there. People drive through it. They turn around. They come back. They can't find Wesleyville. It's been almost completely erased—indeed, through the process of amalgamation, even its name was changed. It's now called New-Wes-Valley—which rather clumsily incorporates the names of several small villages.

Gary: Oh, dear.

David: But this photographic gentleman, Mr. Oakley, provided visual proof of what the village was once like. Because of his photographs, I can prove, for example, that in 1900, there were sixty schooners in the harbour and that there were twenty-seven big merchant sea captains' houses built there. Now there's only one.

Gary: But how would you have access to his photographs? Wouldn't this Mr. Oakley have taken everything with him?

David: As a matter of fact, an old lady, a member of the Oakley family—who was actually a distant relative of mine—once asked me to come and see her. I went, and during the visit she said, "Mr. Blackwood, what am I going to do with all this?" and got out all of these unbelievable photographs for me to take away.

Gary: I take it you still have them?

David: I have all of the material.

Gary: That's wonderful. So you really are an archive.

David: Yes. The culture of the Newfoundland I knew is all gone now—except as documentary record.

Gary: And the stuff of your prints. And so you're constantly working with equal amounts of archival material, and your harvesting of your own memories.

David: That's right.

Gary: Tell me something about etching. It seems to me that etching is laborious, labour-intensive, exacting. Now, I'm no doubt being naive here, but etching would not seem to me to be the ideal medium with which to capture the delicacies of memory, the violence of storms, the unknowability of ice, the violence of human drama. Etching is slow. One might almost have expected you to be a vigorous sort of action painter or something...

David: I suppose so.

Gary: The exacting nature, the specifically demanding nature of etching seems miles away from the immediacy of your subject. How were you led into etching? Why did you become so totally involved in it?

David: I came to Toronto from Newfoundland in 1959, as I said, to study, and in my first year, at the Ontario College of Art, there was a drawing instructor—Fred Hagan—who was on the lookout for students that could draw. And that was because he was also the director of the printmaking department. And having started into printmaking, I then became aware of the work of the great narrative artists—of Rembrandt, Daumier, Käthe Kollwitz. At OCA, as it was then, you had a choice, of course, of media—you could work in lithography, etching, woodcutting, silkscreen. But I was powerfully drawn to etching. It struck me as a combination of drawing, carving and metalwork. It was very tactile.

Gary: Did you feel at home with it right away?

David: I felt tremendously at ease with it. And of course, prior to my arrival at the college, which had been there for a hundred years, nobody had worked on anything larger than an eight-by-ten-inch etching press. We all used this tiny antique press and made tiny little prints. Then, one day, they brought in a new press from New York that could take a plate twenty by thirty inches. As a result, I made the first large etching at the college. I got into trouble for it, too, because in printmaking, there were set rules about what you could do and what you couldn't do. For example, etchings had to be made with a needle, and so not with the wire brush—as I was doing. Fred got very upset. "What do you think you're doing?" he'd ask me. "What do you think you're doing?!" Because he had very particular ideas about what you did in first year, in second year, in third year: there was Problem One, then Problem Two, then Problem Three, and so on. But I was very impatient with that. So, I went on working in my own way.

Gary: How old were you when your etchings began to get respectful attention?

David: Nineteen or twenty. A curator from the Museum of Modern Art in New York, William S. Lieberman, had been invited to Ottawa to adjudicate an exhibition, the National Gallery's biennial of Canadian prints, and was quite taken by one particular large etching of mine called *The Search Party*. He put it on the cover of the catalogue and recommended that the National Gallery acquire this for their collection.

Gary: So you were in the National Gallery at age twenty!

David: It got me into all sorts of trouble.

Gary: Why? For insufficient modesty?

David: Oh, my God! You weren't even allowed to *sign your work* at the Ontario College of Art back then.

Gary: But now, it's been a long time from your boyhood in Newfoundland, and since your apprenticeship in printmaking at the Ontario College of Art, and yet you've never run out of subject matter—a subject matter that feels, in your hands, perpetually urgent. The profundity of all of your early experiences in Newfoundland seems clearly to have provided you with subject matter for a lifetime.

David: It fed the imagination, you see, forever. And exactly how that happens is a mystery. It's an utter and total mystery.

GARY MICHAEL DAULT *is a writer, art critic and painter.*

top: Cod-splitting knife

bottom: Fisherman's mittens

facing, top: Brass bell from the SS *Imogene*

facing, bottom: Model of SS *Imogene*, 1990

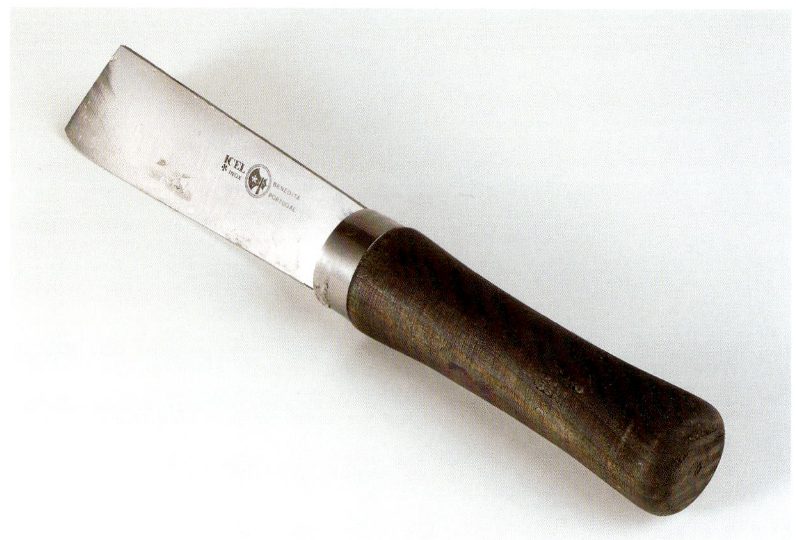

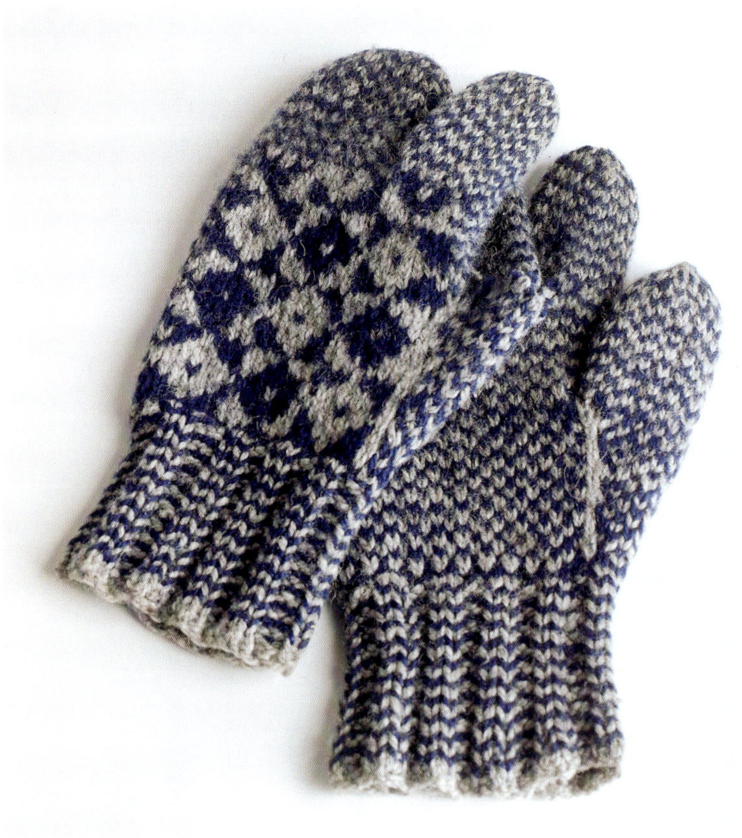

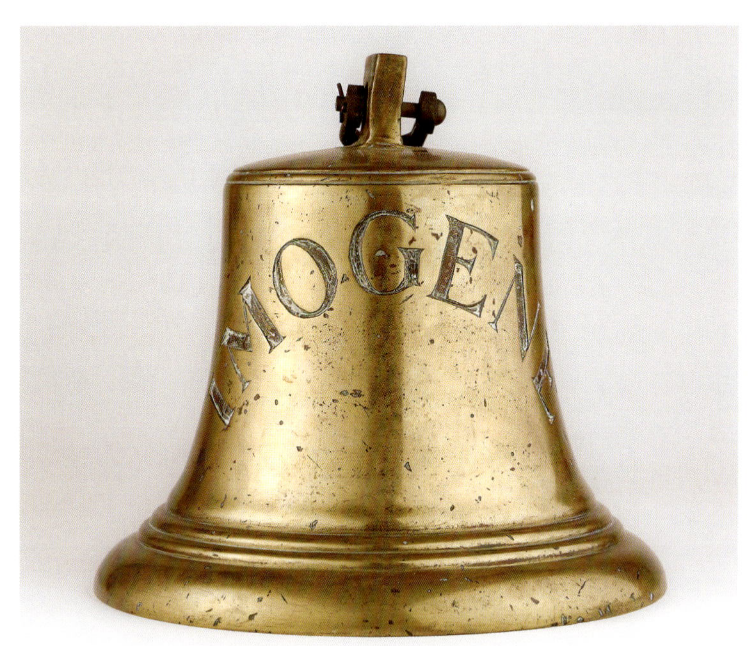
IMOGENE

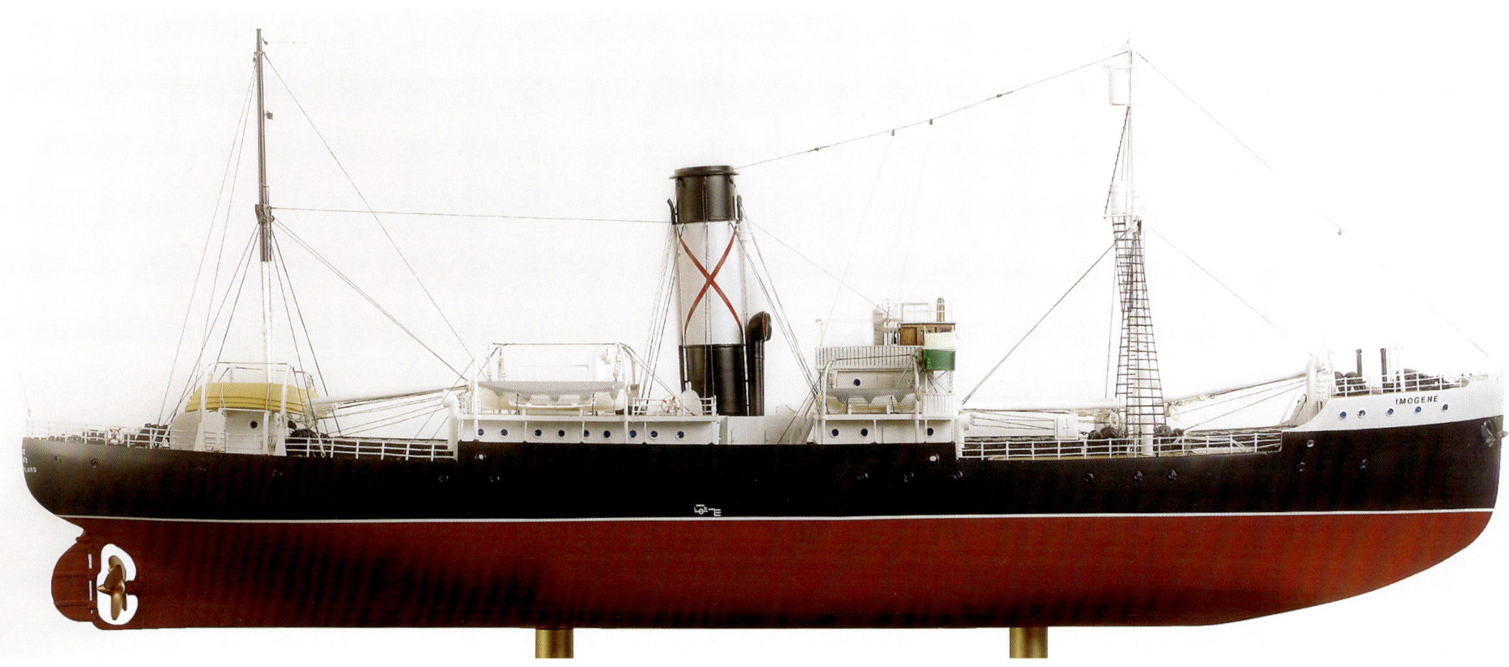
IMOGENE

top: Flora Nickerson in Grenfell dry dock, St. Anthony, Newfoundland, 1948

bottom: Nameplate from the schooner *Flora S. Nickerson*

facing, top: Flag of the Society of United Fishermen

facing, bottom: Bowring flag from the SS *Imogene*

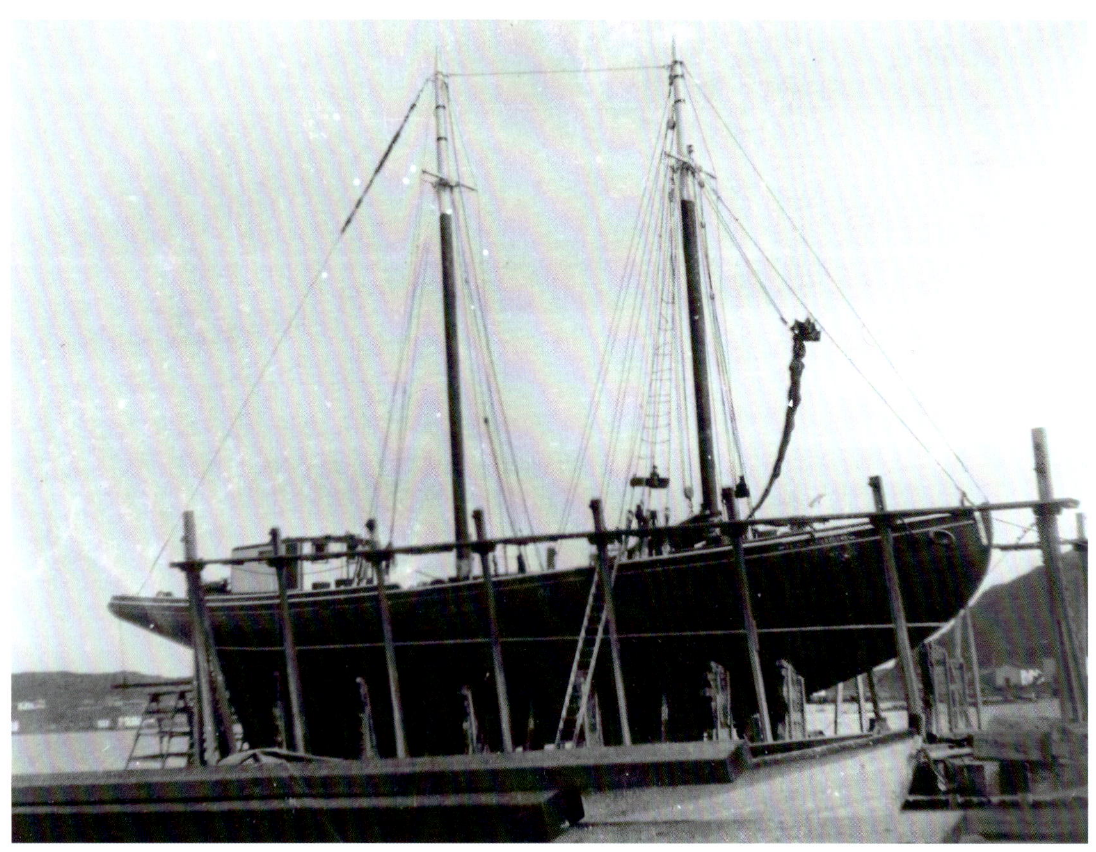

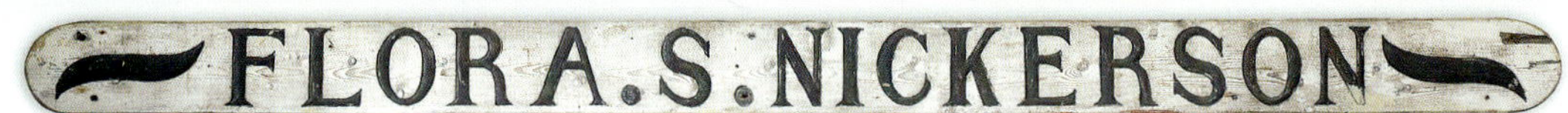

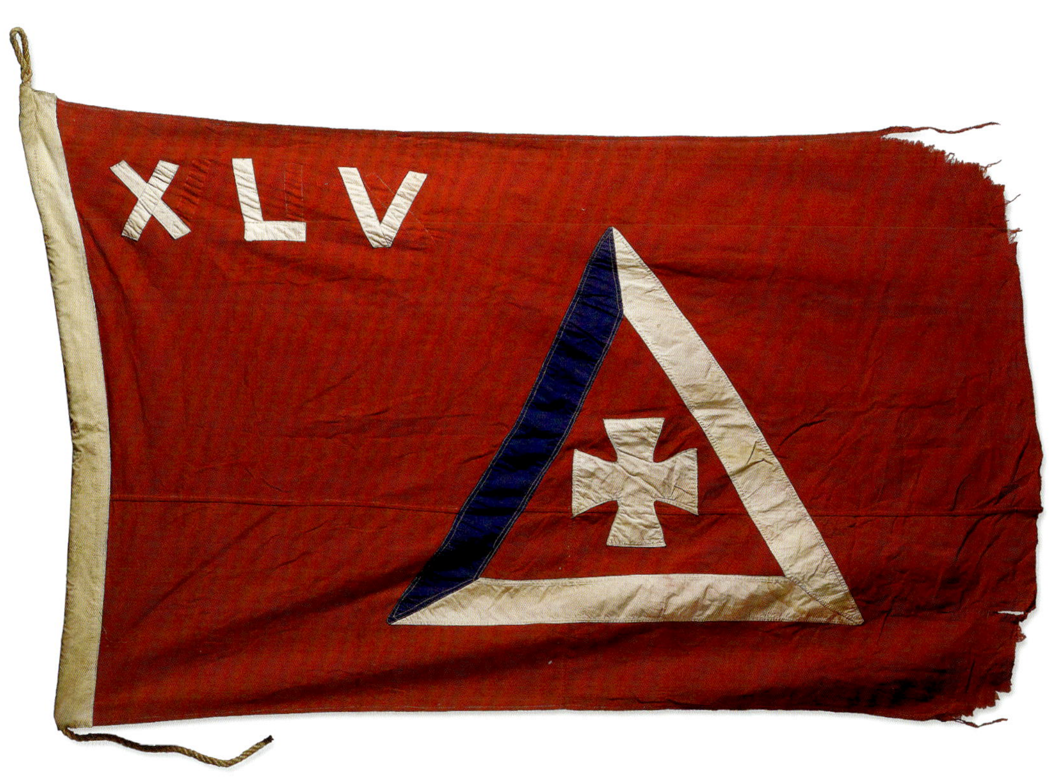
XLV

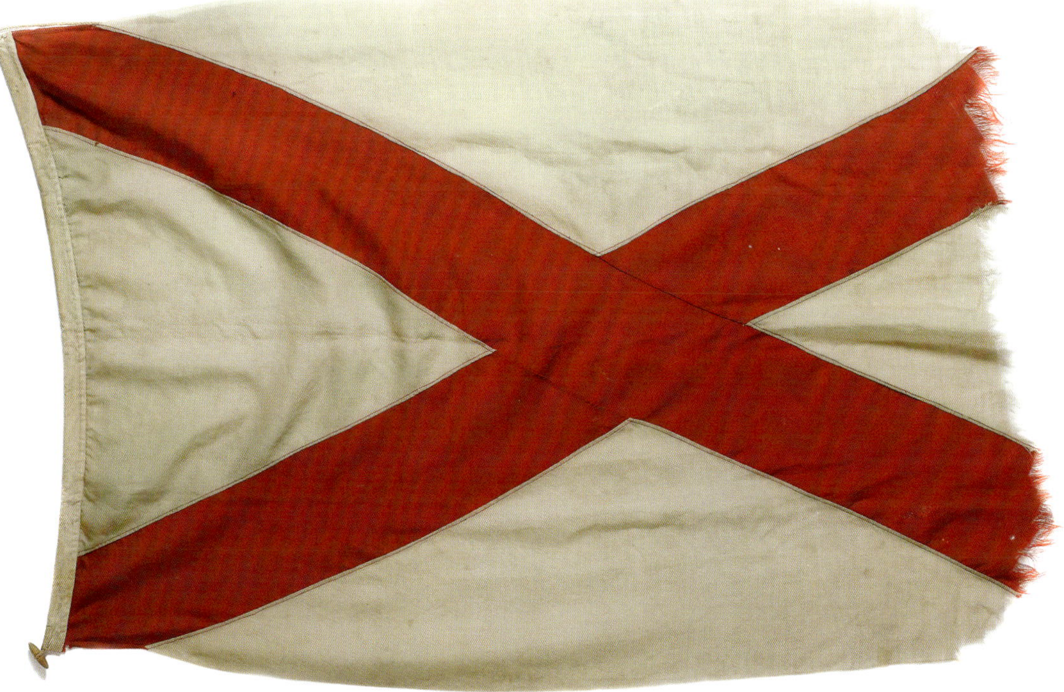

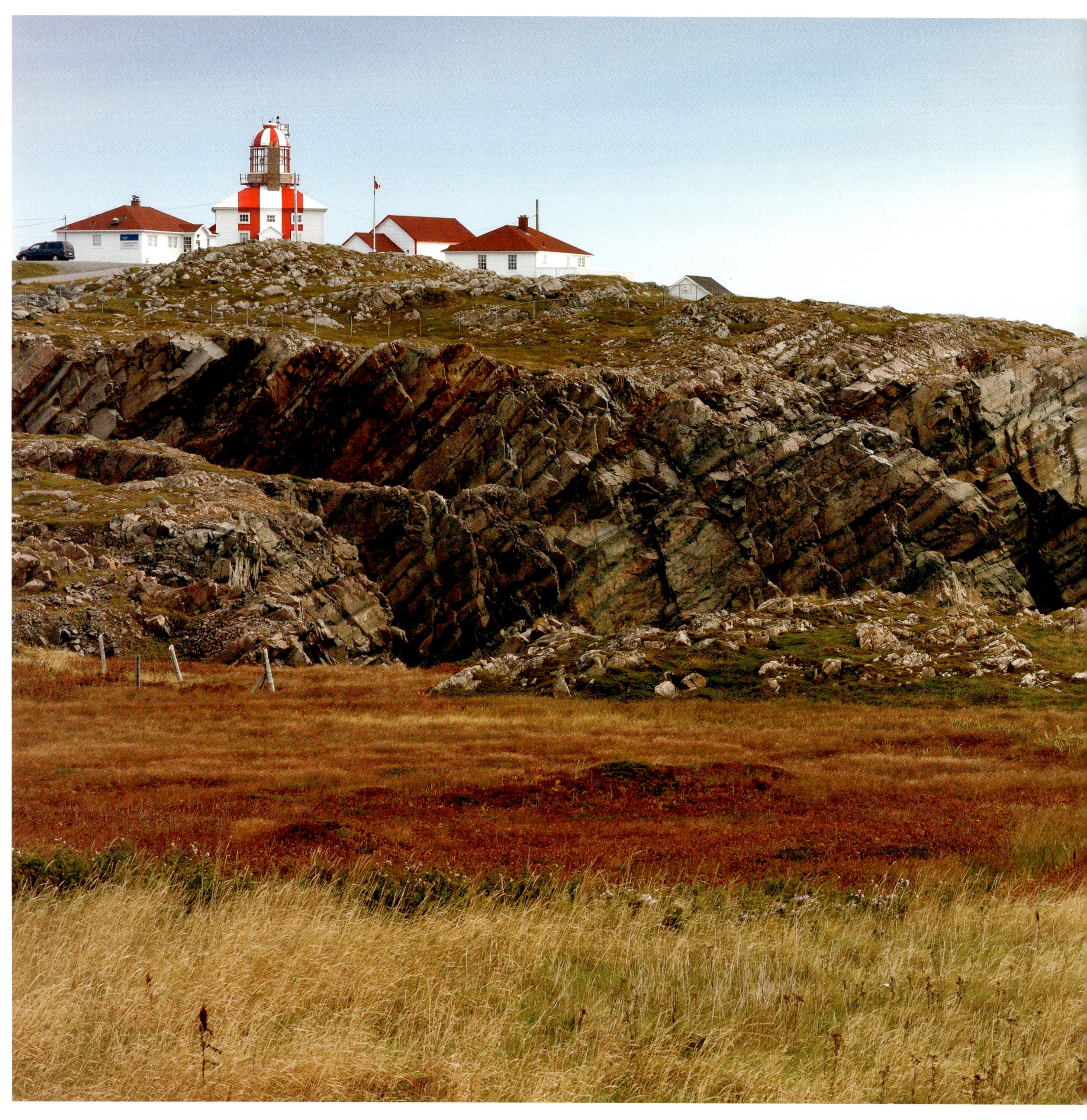

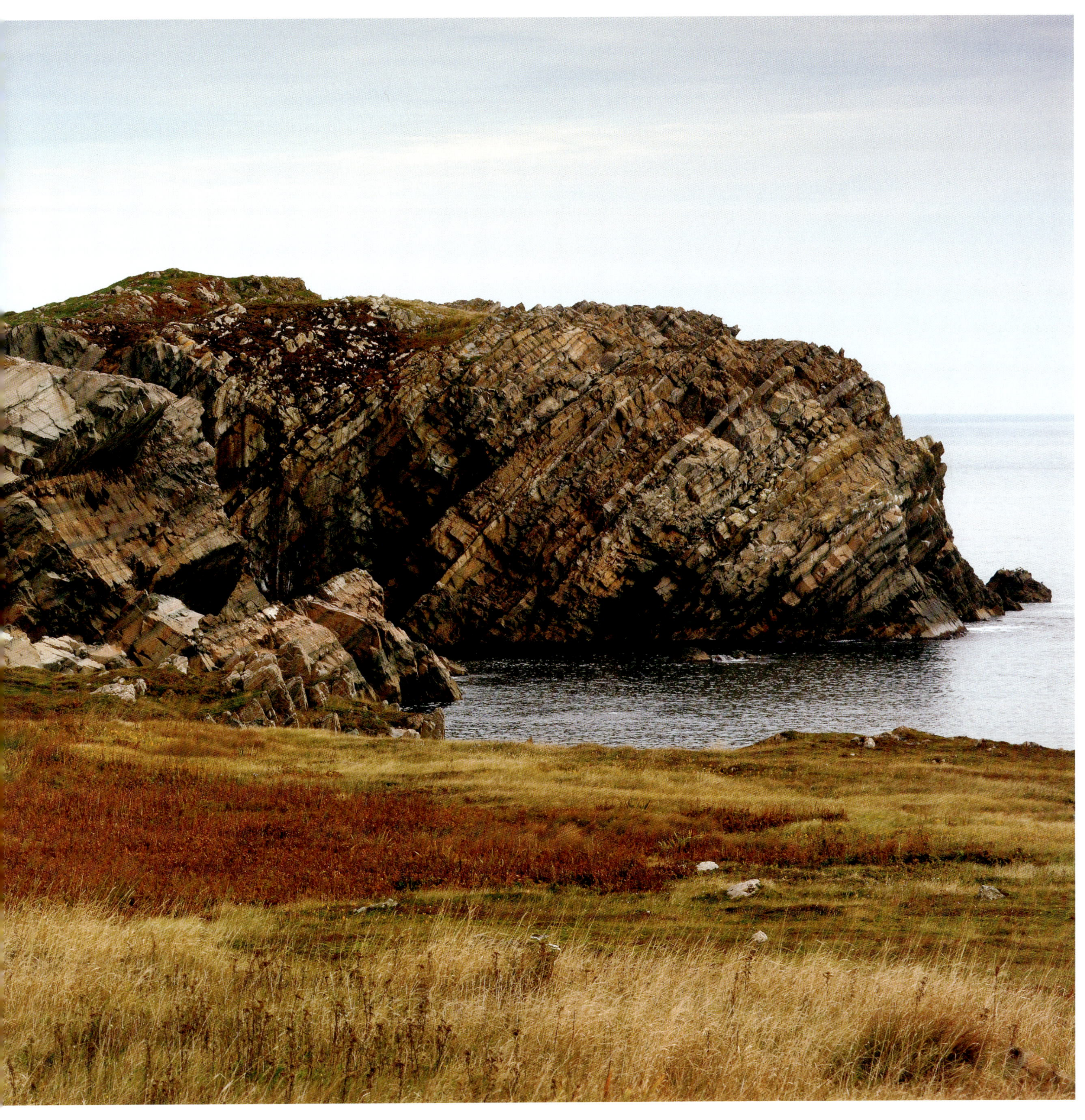

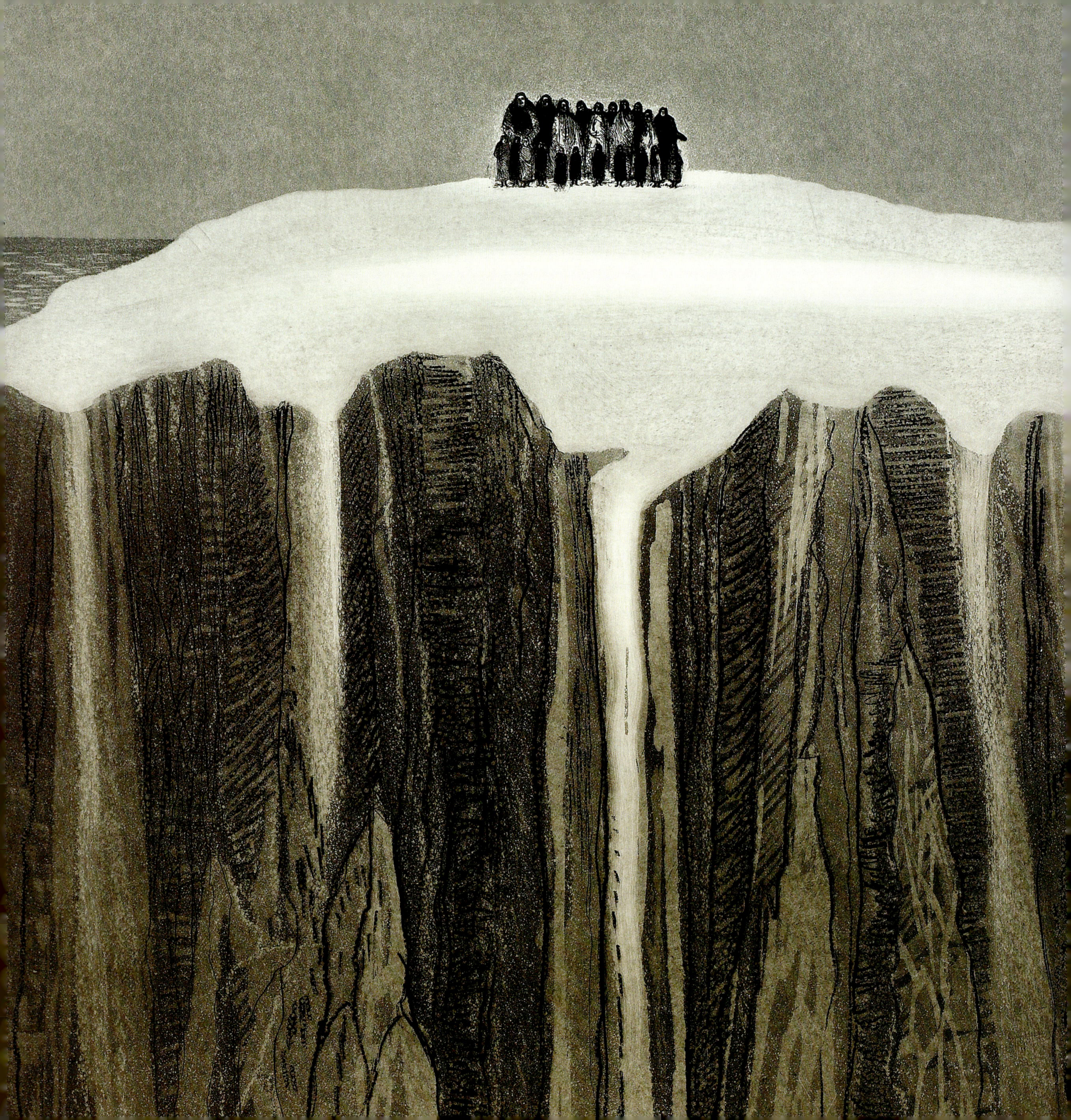

Rooted in Granite

THE TOPOGRAPHY AND GEOLOGY OF DAVID BLACKWOOD'S ART

Derek H.C. Wilton and Martin Feely

THE ISLAND OF Newfoundland, termed "the Rock" by some (though others find the term pejorative), represents the northern terminus of the Appalachian mountain belt, an ancient stretch of mountains perhaps once as high as the Himalayas, now broken and worn down by the forces of nature. The milieu for David Blackwood's art is the coast of the Cape Freels Peninsula centred on the village of Wesleyville, an area of early conversion to Methodism in North America. This is the storied northeast coast of Newfoundland. Framed on the northwest by the Straight Shore and on the southeast by Bonavista Bay, it resembles a spear tip of the Appalachian mountain belt jutting out into the North Atlantic.

facing: Detail from **Cape Islanders Waiting**, 1967 (plate 11)

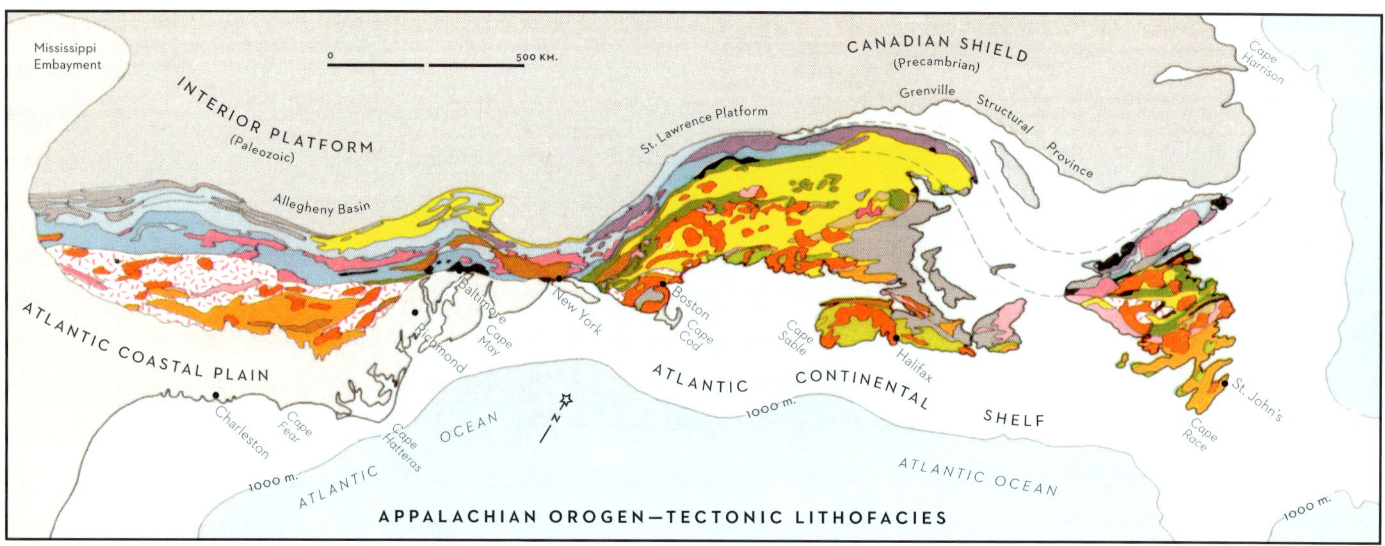

above: The Appalachian Mountain Belt (or Orogen) · *facing:* A general chart of the island of Newfoundland, 1775

On a northeastward trajectory from Newfoundland, the island of Ireland forms the first landfall across the Atlantic Ocean. Shaped by the same forces of nature, Ireland is Newfoundland's long-lost geological twin. The two were separated by the opening of the "new" Atlantic Ocean and share the same rocks that record earlier primeval oceans. Just as the Appalachian Mountains end in Newfoundland, so the Caledonian mountain chain begins in Ireland. The Appalachians stretch from Newfoundland to Georgia in the southern United States. The Caledonides stretch from Ireland through Scotland into western Scandinavia. Once, over 400 million years ago, the Appalachians and the Caledonides formed a continuous mountain belt.

Geographers classify the region around Wesleyville as part of the great Canadian boreal forest, which encompasses a broad swath of Canada—35 per cent of its land mass—from British Columbia and the Yukon in the west to Newfoundland in the east. This forest is fundamental to Canadian concepts of self; according to *The Atlas of Canada*, "This northern forest, named after Boreas, the Greek god of the North Wind, is an inevitable and unavoidable part of who we are."[1] However, the northeastern coast of Newfoundland, including Wesleyville, is more finely classified as the Eastern Hyper-Oceanic Barrens Ecoregion of the middle boreal zone of Newfoundland, meaning that the ocean has had an immense impact on the local environment. Thus, David Blackwood's home is part of the Canadian landscape, but at the same time it is different, as it constitutes the unique edge of that landscape. His art likewise stands out as familiar, but with an edge sensibility.

To the human beings who populate David Blackwood's art, descriptions of their home as "hyper-oceanic barrens" would seem like vacuous intellectual rhetoric; these people are actually part of their landscape. And what a landscape it is. It is an edge region, in some Celtic traditions a "thin place" where "spirit and matter meet" and where one is "exposed to the full forces of nature."[2] It is a borderland between land and sea but not really part of either, a piece

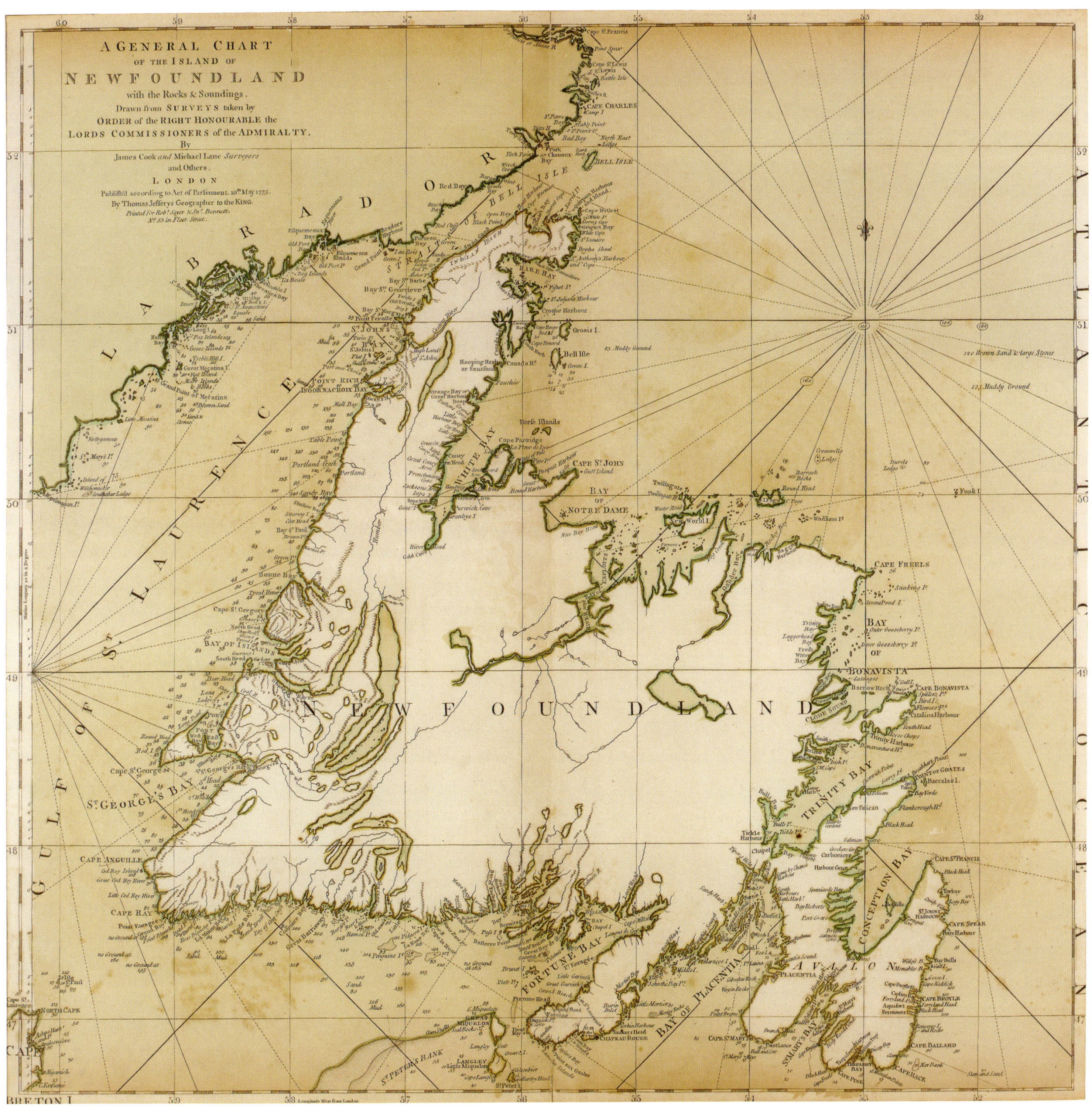

A GENERAL CHART
OF THE ISLAND OF
NEWFOUNDLAND
with the Rocks & Soundings.
Drawn from SURVEYS taken by
ORDER of the RIGHT HONOURABLE the
LORDS COMMISSIONERS of the ADMIRALTY.
By
James Cook and Michael Lane Surveyors
and Others.
LONDON
Publish'd according to Act of Parliament. 10th May 1775.
By Thomas Jefferys Geographer to the KING.
Printed for Robt. Sayer & Jno. Bennett,
No. 53 in Fleet Street.
LABRADOR
GULF OF St. LAURENCE
NEWFOUNDLAND
ATLANTIC OCEAN
BELL ISLE
CAPE CHARLES
BAY OF NOTRE DAME
WHITE BAY
CAPE St. JOHN
CAPE FREELS
BONAVISTA BAY
CAPE BONAVISTA
TRINITY BAY
CONCEPTION BAY
CAPE St. FRANCIS
CAPE SPEAR
CAPE BALLARD
CAPE RACE
AVALON
PLACENTIA
BAY OF PLACENTIA
St. MARY'S BAY
FORTUNE BAY
St. PETER'S BANK
MIQUELON
LANGLEY
St. Peter
CAPE RAY
CAPE ANGUILLE
St. GEORGE'S BAY
Cape St. George
BAY OF ISLANDS
POINT RICH
Bonne Bay
Sandy Bay
Portland Creek
Bay St. Genevieve
HARE BAY
Groais I.
Bell Isle
Horse Islands
Cape Partridge
Twilingate
CLODE SOUND
Baccalao I.
POINT OF GRATES
NORTH CAPE
BRETON I.
Funk I.
Longitude West from London

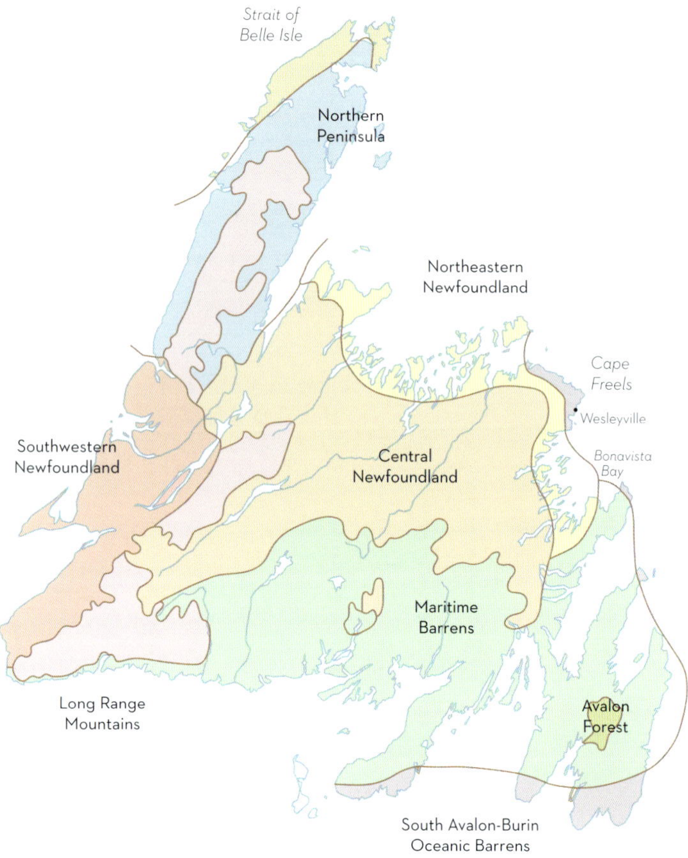

The Ecoregions of Newfoundland

of land battered by a cold ocean that constantly tries to break it apart, a collision/combat zone where the sea tries to reclaim the land and all of Blackwood's people. Blackwood's land, the Wesleyville area, receives the full brunt of the ocean's wrath and the Labrador Current: it sticks its head out into the ocean, daring it to beat it down. Blackwood's people are also like that.

The fundamentals that define this edge region and Blackwood's art are water, ice and land; together they form a troika of planetary elements in the Cape Freels region that leaves nowhere to hide from the wrath, and sometimes the beneficence, of nature. The land itself comprises the bones of an ancient mountain belt unearthed in the Wesleyville area. The ice is both a contemporary element that offers life and sustenance, but only at great peril and personal danger, and a force that sculpted and reshaped the land. And of course, the water is represented by the vast cold northern sea, as deep, dark and cold as death, that stretches across to Ireland. That ocean is the product of profound primordial forces from deep within the Earth.

Moving Continents and Transient Oceans

To the modern geologist, the crust of the Earth, the part upon which we live and play out our existence, is not a fixed, rigid foundation but actually consists of disparately sized blocks (or continent-sized plates) that are constantly moving over the underlying hot and plastically behaving mantle. The people in Blackwood's art are similarly not rigid and fixed but move across the sea and land. As the Earth's plates move apart, new oceans are created and continents separate from one another. Since the Earth's girth is not expanding, as plates move apart, other parts of plates must crash together. The sites of these collisions, where one plate crumbles into or beneath another, are what geologists call mountain belts or orogens.

The formation of the Newfoundland and Irish land masses is really a meandering tale of rifting (continental plates moving apart) and mending (plates coming

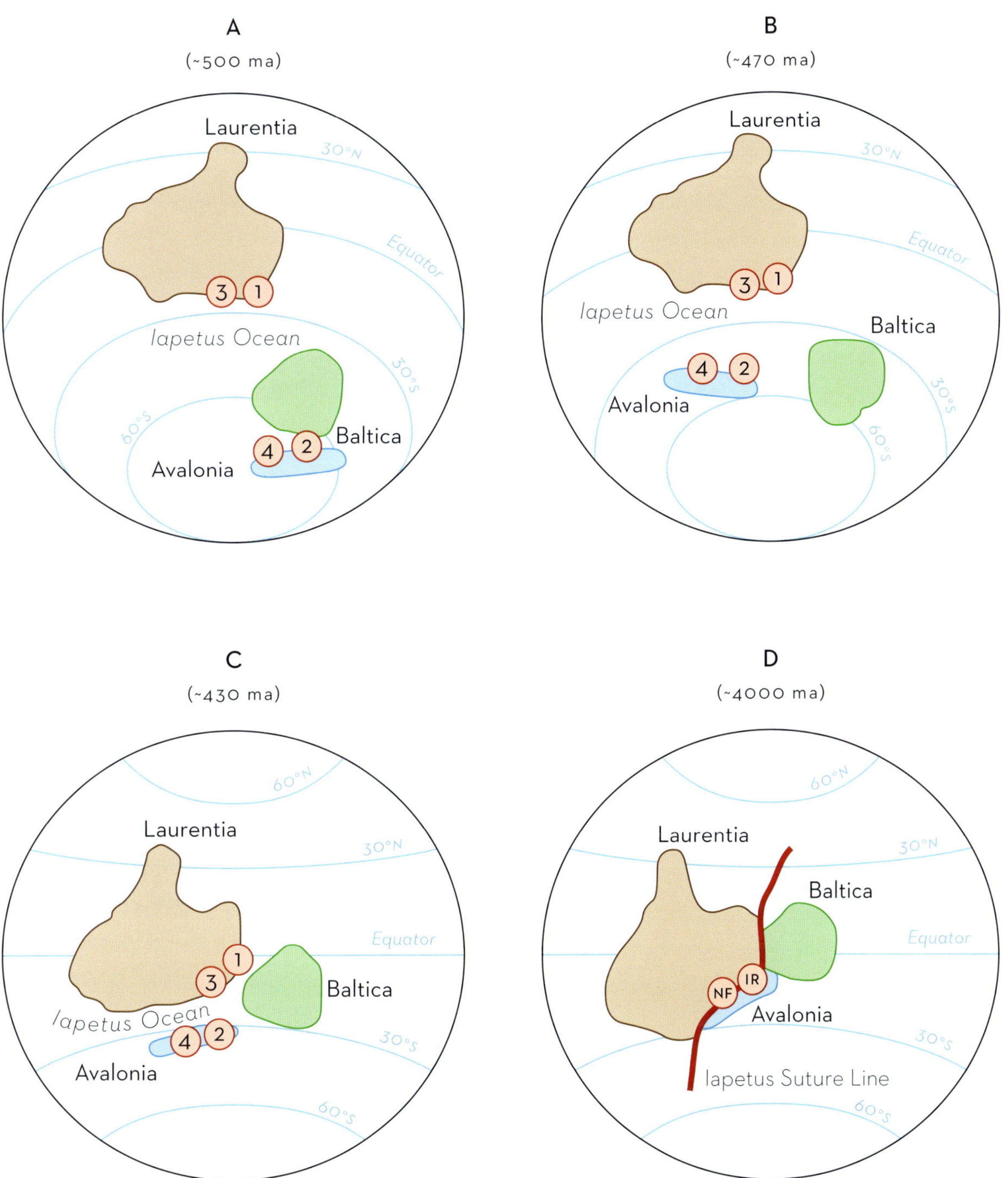

The distribution and eventual joining of the Newfoundland and Ireland land masses (ma stands for megayears)

A to C: The relative postions of northwest Ireland and Scotland (1) southwest Ireland and England (2) to north Newfoundland (3) between ~500 and 400 ma.

D: The relative positions of Ireland (IR) and Newfoundland (NF) after closure (suturing) of the Iapetus Ocean at ~400 ma.

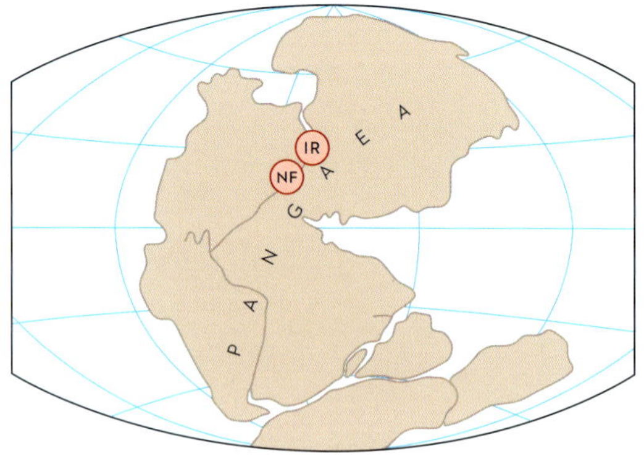

PERMIAN 225 ma

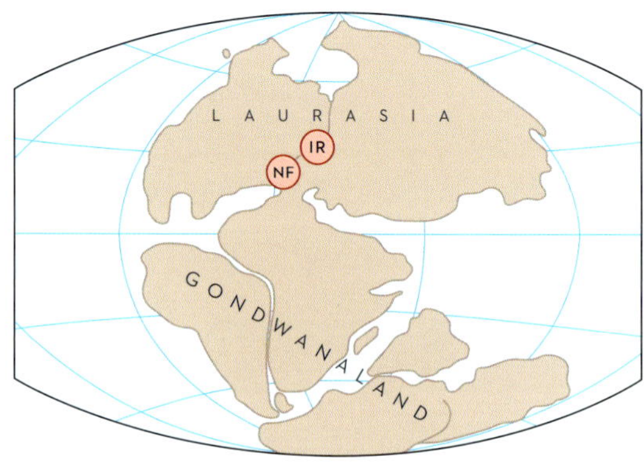

TRIASSIC 200 ma

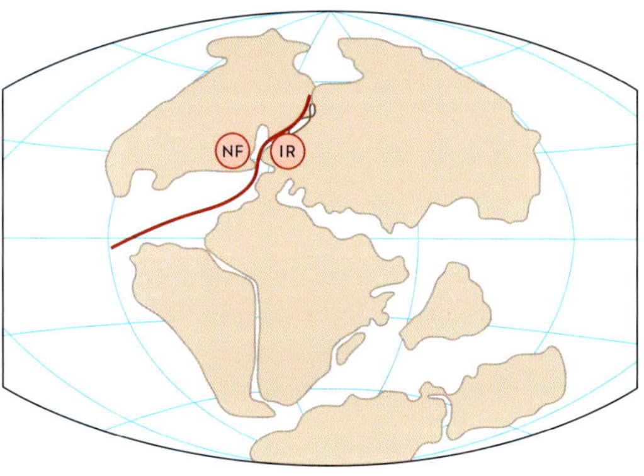

JURASSIC 135 ma

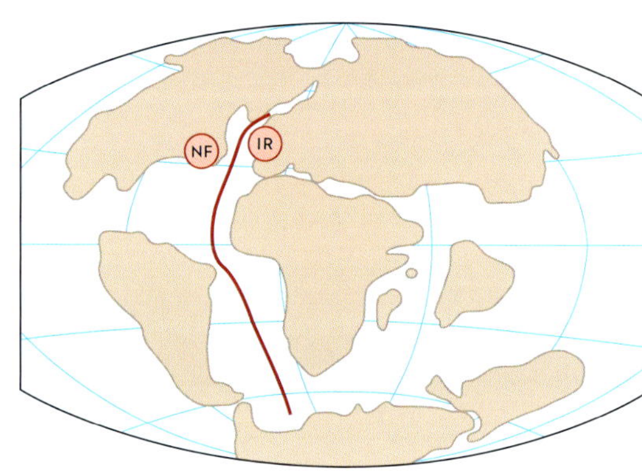

TERTIARY 60 ma

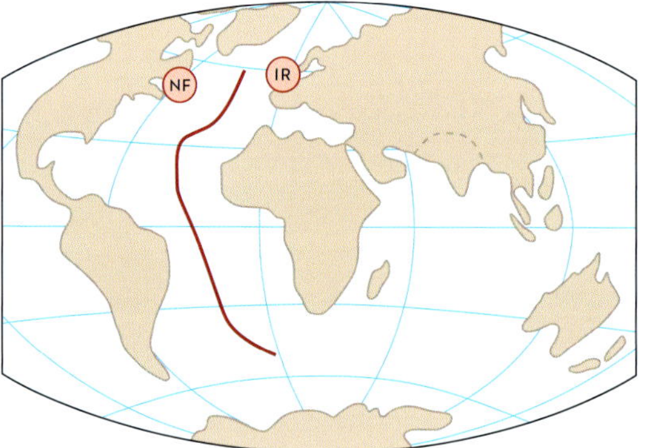

PRESENT DAY

The opening of the Atlantic Ocean and the distribution of Newfoundland and Ireland from 225 million years ago (225 ma) to today

470-million-year-old marble bands, Maam Valley, Connemara, Ireland

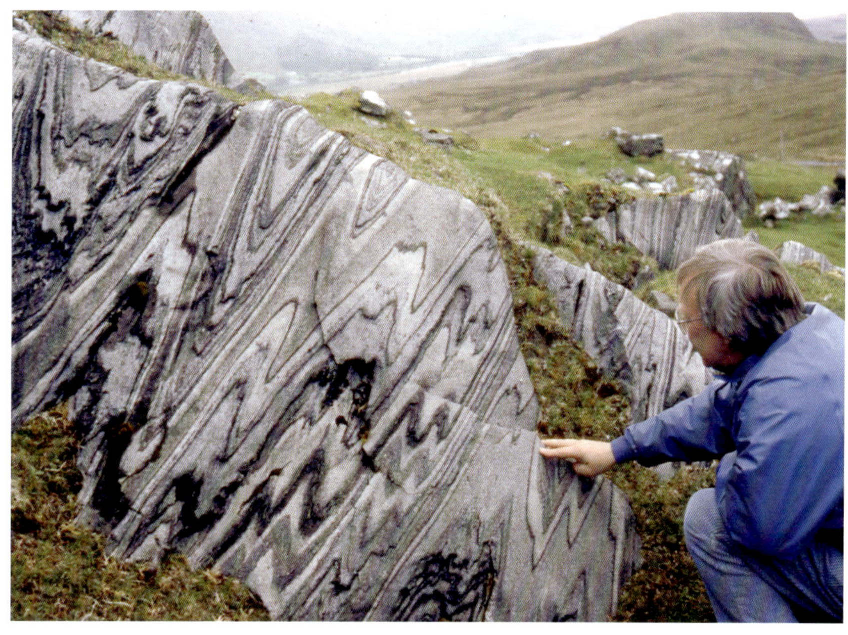

together) during the unremitting evolution of the Earth over the last 600 million years. The saga involves the colliding, crumpling and melting of continents or plates on a gigantic scale, during which copious quantities of melted rock (magma) from the middle of the Earth either flowed over the Earth's surface or pooled into slowly cooling molten masses deeper in the crust.

Phantoms underlie David Blackwood's art and likewise are present in Newfoundland geology. Around 600 million years ago, northeastern Ireland and England and western Newfoundland were juxtaposed as the coastline of a large continent straddling the equator. That continent, called Laurentia, has long since broken into pieces; parts of Laurentia now constitute what geologists term the Canadian Shield, the ancient core of North America. The land masses that are now eastern Newfoundland and southern Ireland and England, in contrast, were part of a phantom microcontinent named Avalonia.

Six hundred million years ago, Avalonia and Laurentia were separated from each other by the Iapetus Ocean, a phantom ocean that disappeared before reappearing as the modern Atlantic (in Greek mythology, Iapetus was the father of Atlas, after whom the Atlantic is named). There was also a third continent called Baltica (now part of Fennoscandia, the Baltic region and portions of eastern Europe), extant on the edges of the Iapetus. The Iapetus Ocean spread apart for over 100 million years, further separating Avalonia from Laurentia. Around 500 million years ago, this ocean spreading stopped, then reversed, and Laurentia and Avalonia, along with Baltica, moved closer and closer to each other, until they collided around 400 million years ago, suturing and forming the Appalachian and Caledonide mountain belts, and the supercontinent Pangaea. Thus, the disparate parts of Newfoundland and Ireland came together as the Iapetus Ocean closed, and the crumple zones, where the rocks were subject to deformational forces, generated spectacular folds in the rocks. The grand new continent, called Pangaea (meaning "one earth"), comprised the welded continental plates of Laurentia, Baltica and Avalonia. The parts of this continent that are now Newfoundland and Ireland were still south of the equator, close to 30° south latitude. With time, the Appalachian-Caledonide mountains eroded, and during the Carboniferous period (350 to 300 million years ago) both Newfoundland and Ireland were submerged

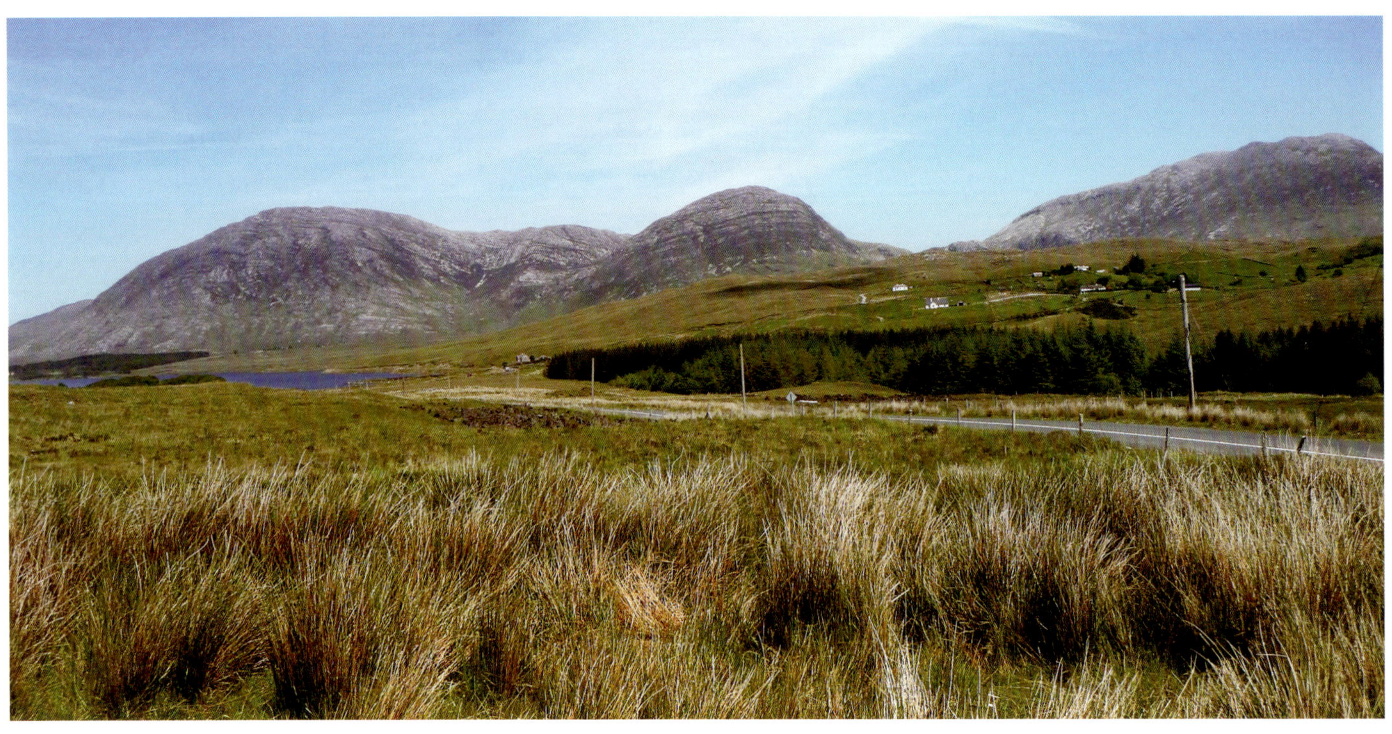

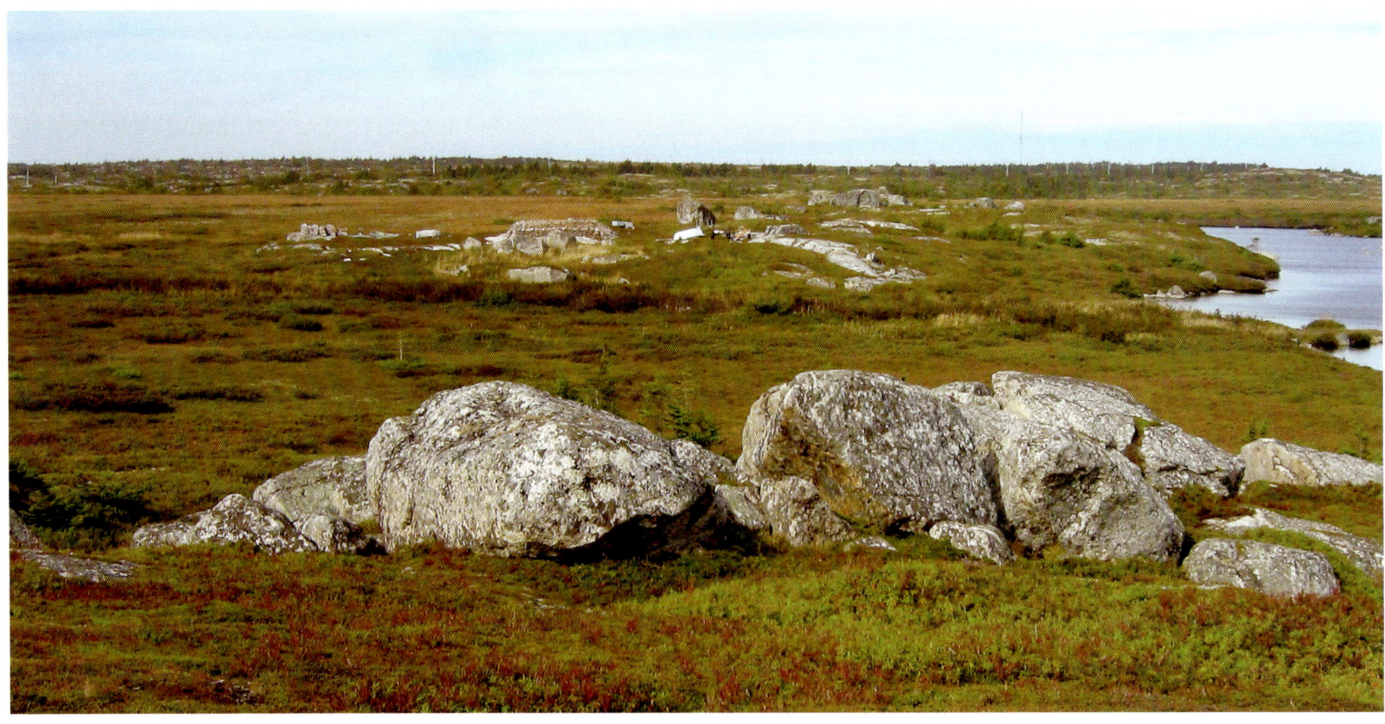

facing, top: Ten-thousand-year-old glaciated landscape of Connemara, Ireland

facing, bottom: Typical granite landscape near the Wesleyville graveyard. David Blackwood nicknamed these the "Cowboy Rocks."

below: Granite outcropping, Wesleyville, September 2009

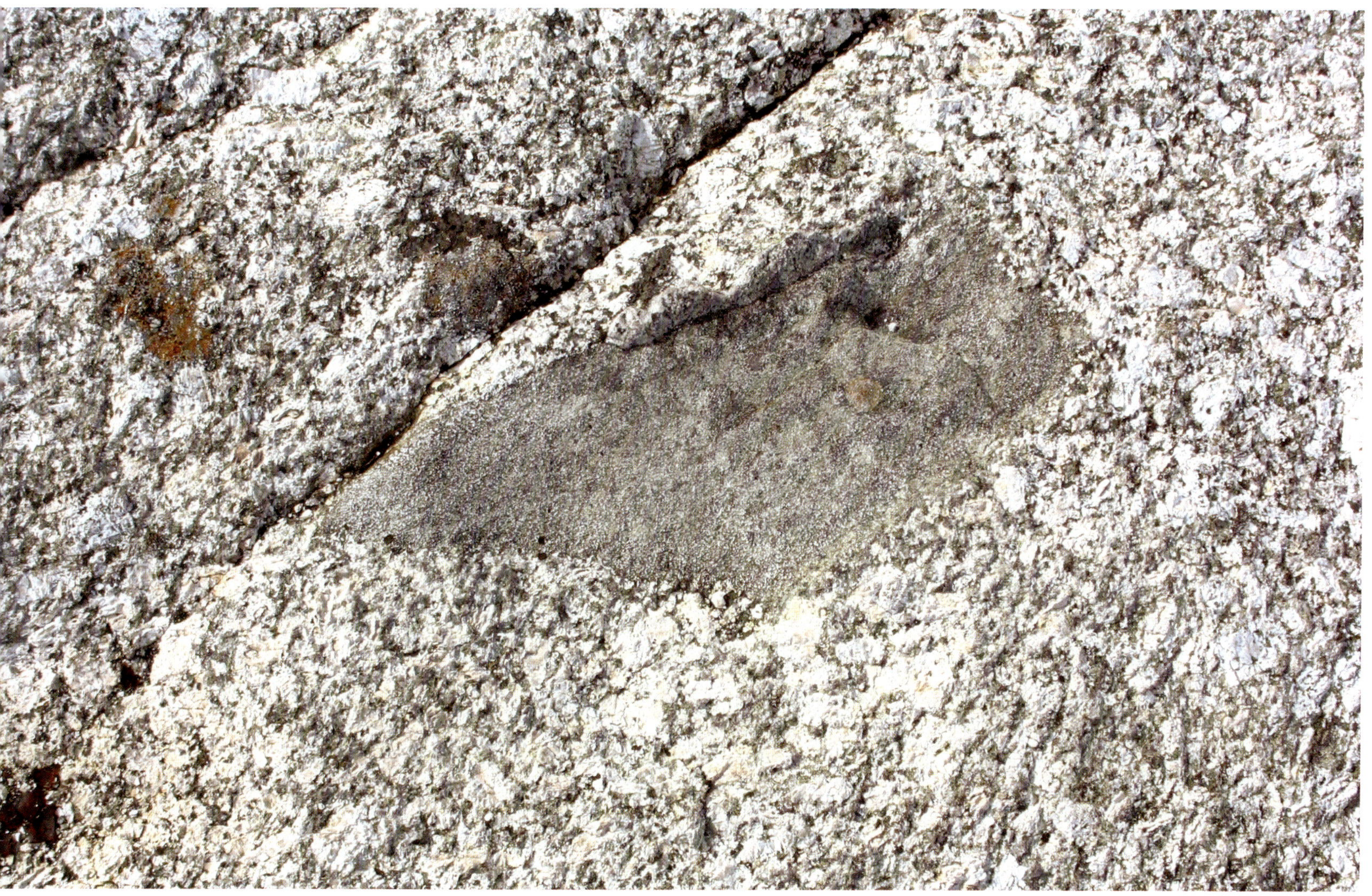

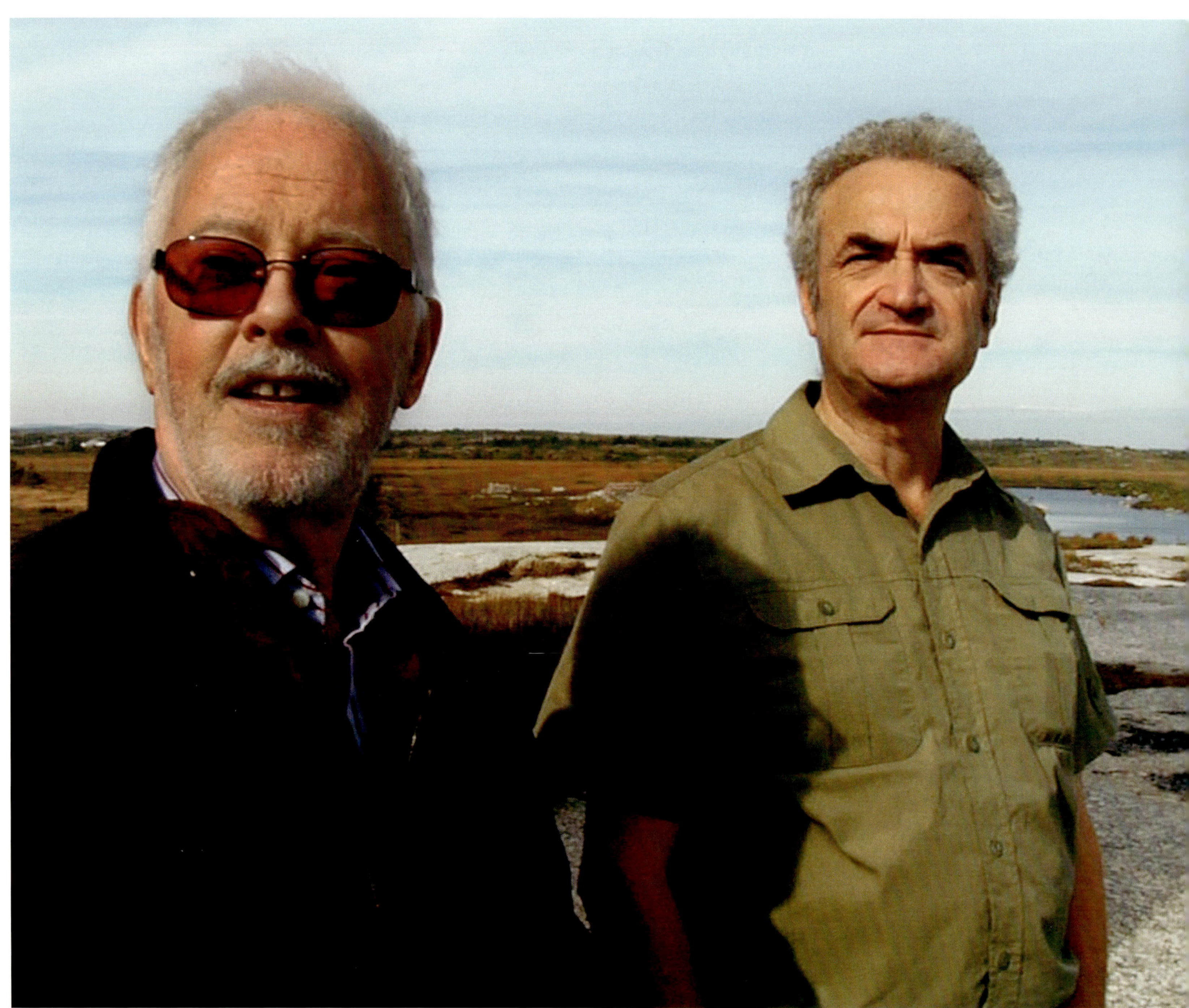

facing: David Blackwood and Derek Wilton at Wesleyville, September 2009

beneath shallow tropical seas; it was a time of very warm temperatures because the land masses were near the equator, and enhanced carbon dioxide was in the atmosphere. Evaporation of ocean waters in landlocked basins on proto-Newfoundland and proto-Ireland produced halite and gypsum deposits as well. It was perhaps the warmest times that these land masses had ever experienced; there were certainly no icebergs or sea ice.

But the Earth and the forces of nature proved restless and relentless. By about 178 million years ago (the beginning of the Middle Jurassic period), the crust of the Pangaean supercontinent was riven by cracks as hot magma from the mantle rose to the surface. The crust began to break apart along these rifts, and the modern Atlantic Ocean began to form. As the ocean opened up, it severed North America from Europe, at least in part, along the Newfoundland and Irish coasts. The Atlantic Ocean continues to open to this day, at a rate of approximately 25 millimetres per year, with Newfoundland moving westward on the North American plate and Ireland moving eastward on the Eurasian plate. The region's youngest rocks, Jurassic and Cretaceous (from 145 to 65 million years ago), were deposited in offshore basins that stretch from Newfoundland to Ireland. These basins have a variety of esoteric names such as Jeanne d'Arc, Porcupine and Orphan, and some of them are very important to the economy of Newfoundland, and potentially that of Ireland, as the hosts to offshore oil fields.

There is a certain irony that oil riches derived from ancient dead organisms buried deep in the ocean floor now provide the economic salvation for many people who inhabit the Wesleyville area, replacing the living creatures that swam in the ocean or rode on the ice that succoured their forebears and that we see in Blackwood's work. The fear that many of these ancestors had of ocean depths is clear in *Fire Down on the Labrador.* Perhaps in light of the recent Gulf of Mexico disaster, theirs was a prescient vision.

Granite Plutonism

Water and ice, liquid and solid phases of the same material, are essential components of Blackwood's landscape. Rocks in the Wesleyville area are now quite solid but have been, at least in part, liquid in Deep Time. As the Iapetus Ocean closed and associated rocks were crushed, crumbled, deformed and folded, heat built up deep in the Earth's crust. Eventually the heat became so intense as to melt rock and form liquid magma. The first melting of the crustal rock happened at around 750 degrees Celsius, and the magma that formed was enriched with silica and alkali elements (potassium and sodium). Magma with this composition is defined as granitic, and the resultant rock that forms when the magma cools is granite.

Granite is not just a compositional term, however, but also a textural term: the rock's texture is defined by coarse-grained mineral crystals, generally large enough to be identified by the naked eye. The large crystals in the rock imply that the parental magma did not rise to the Earth's surface; it cooled slowly far below the surface, almost as ponds of liquid. Because granite forms from the melting of rocks, the magmas typically engulf older rocks, sometimes linking disparate plates, which geologists call stitching plutons. Though now separated by the Atlantic Ocean, many granites in Newfoundland and Ireland are of the same age and composition, further indicating that the two land masses at one time were contiguous.

Much of the bedrock underlying the Cape Freels Peninsula and Wesleyville is granite; in fact, there is a distinct rock unit classified as the Cape Freels granite. Near Lumsden, on the Straight Shore, a particularly striking granite unit called the Deadman's Bay granite is exposed and has been used as a facing stone at Memorial University in St. John's. But that very term "exposed" tells an important story. The granites formed well below the Earth's surface, and the fact that they are now exposed implies that a substantial amount of rock erosion and removal has occurred.

Granites are beautiful rocks, and because they're silica-rich they're very hard and don't easily break apart. Consequently granite does not readily produce the constituents for soil, and even when it does break down the silica and alkalis do not support the growth of vegetation. In the Cape Freels Peninsula area, the region of David Blackwood's art, the final result of the Iapetus Ocean activity was the production of a granitic bedrock, a hard substrate that inhibited the growth of vegetation but provided a solid shore base from which one could launch into the sea.

The Ice Ages

By the beginning of the Quaternary period (2.588 million years ago), both Ireland and Newfoundland had assumed their present shapes. It was during the earliest part of this period, the so-called Pleistocence epoch (2.6 million to 10,000 years ago), that the landscapes of both land masses were profoundly transformed and sculpted by ice. Through this epoch, the northern hemisphere—including Newfoundland and Ireland—was subject to cycles of widespread continental glaciation during which the land was covered by ice sheets up to three or four kilometres thick. The last glacial period was 110,000 to 10,000 years ago, when there were a number of glacial advances and retreats over the Newfoundland and Irish landscapes. The last maximum was 18,000 years ago, when both islands were completely covered by ice. The ice finally left about 10,000 years ago, revealing a rockscape of virtually barren scraped bedrock covered here and there by mounds, aprons and taluses of broken, glacier-transported boulders, gravel and sand. In the case of the Cape Freels area in particular, all remnants of soil and softening vegetation were essentially bulldozed out into the ocean by the glaciers.

Sketches and photographs of Ediacaran fossils from the Port Union–Catalina area of the Bonavista Peninsula

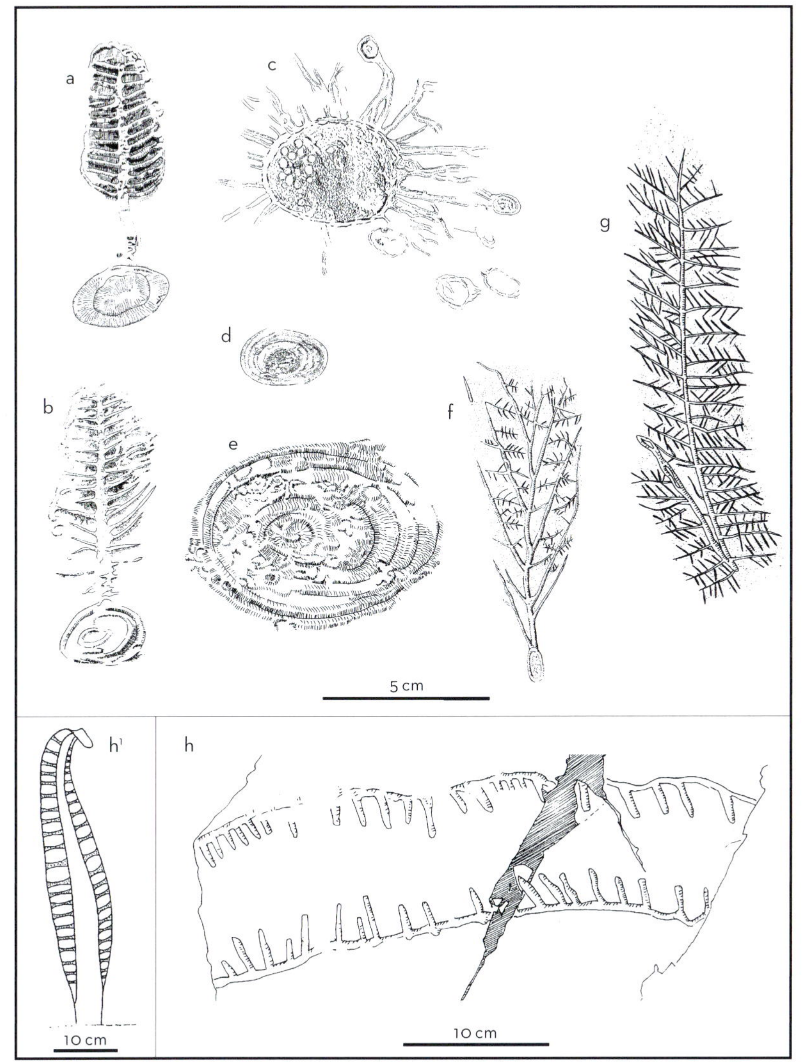

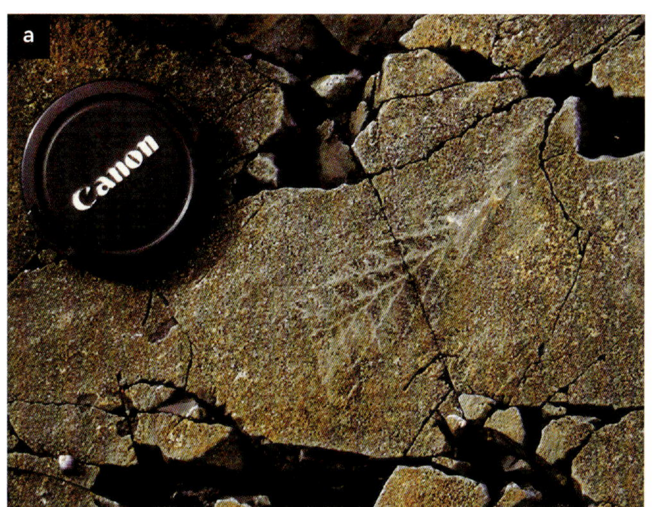

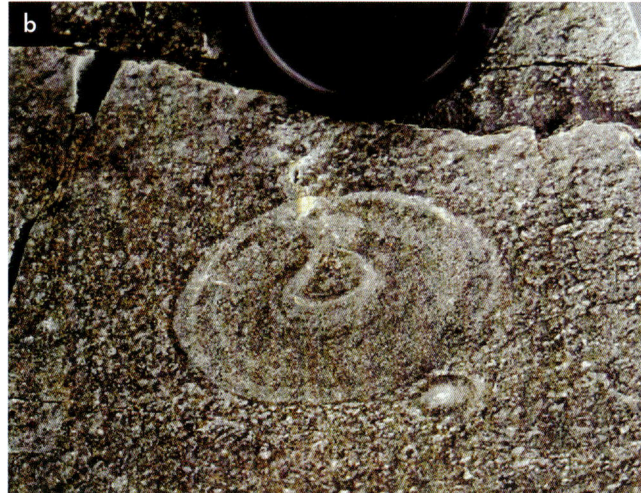

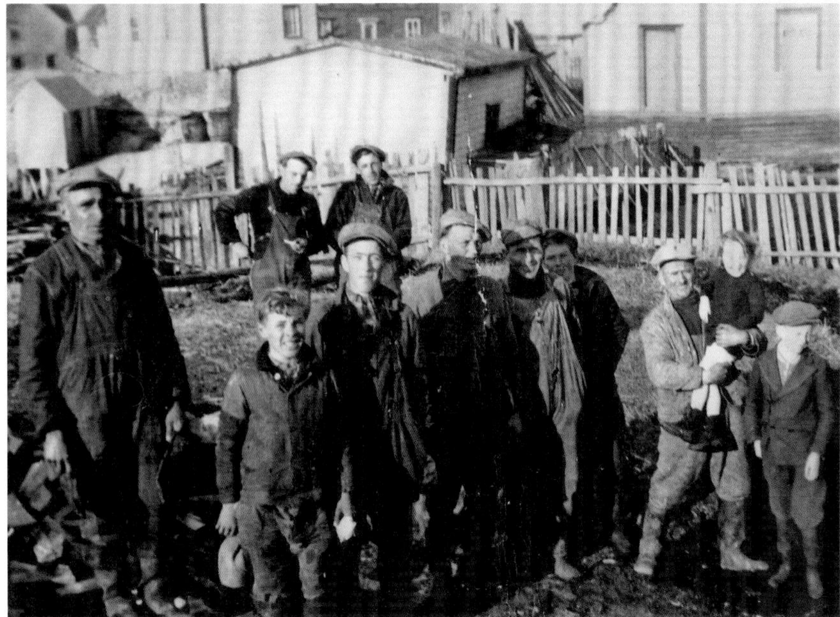

Blackwoods in Brookfield, c. 1939–1940

The mass of these omnipresent glacial sheets weighed heavily on the underlying land surface, pushing it down. Furthermore, the frozen water tied up in the ice sheets effectively removed water from the oceans, lowering sea level by up to 120 metres. When the ice melted, there were two contrasting consequences. First, the land rebounded upwards, but not at even rates; hence the coast of Labrador is still rising as the land recovers but the shore and land near Wesleyville are sinking slightly. Second, with the rise of sea level, the land masses of both Ireland and Newfoundland were cut off from their respective mainlands, forming islands. Humans had not yet ventured to the newly unglaciated Newfoundland and Ireland surfaces, so they would eventually have to cross water to reach them.

The permanent ice sheet of Greenland is the remnant of these continental glaciers and represents the potential source from which new ice masses might arise to once again cover the northern hemisphere, if the Earth's surface temperature cools again in one of the long-term climatic cycles of the Quaternary. As the cold essence in the heart of David Blackwood's art, the Greenland ice sheet still has a great impact on the people, if not the landscape, of Newfoundland and the Cape Freels Peninsula. The icebergs that terrorize crews and sink ships calve from the Greenland ice sheet and are transported around Cape Freels by the Labrador Current. The continental glaciers from the Pleistocene epoch have a much weaker grasp than at their peak 18,000 years ago, but they are still stretching their icy fingers from the past into the Blackwood present.

The west coast of Ireland, in contrast, has completely escaped the wrath of the cold Labrador Current and icebergs. Ireland is bathed in the warmth of the Gulf Stream, which flows from the Gulf of Mexico across the Atlantic Ocean, producing a climate in which vegetation works much faster at recovering the landscape than in Newfoundland. The Gulf Stream is deflected away from the Cape Freels Peninsula by the southern end of Newfoundland.

The Tenacity and Fragility of Life

As so succinctly illustrated by Blackwood's art, life on the northeast Newfoundland coast is tenacious but fragile at the same time. An instructive allegory can be found in the old rocks on the other side of Bonavista Bay from the Cape Freels Peninsula. Here geologists have recently discovered fantastic fossils of a life form called Ediacaran biota. These creatures lived about 580 million years ago and were the first multicellular organisms to appear on Earth; they were life at its most complex for the time. They appeared following a major global glaciation and were anchored to the sea floor of the Iapetus Ocean, that ancient ancestor to the Atlantic. Shortly afterwards they disappeared from the Earth, leaving no modern descendants. In fact, they appear to be unlike any other group of multicellular organisms such as plants or animals, and some even suggest that they may actually have been "failed experiments" in the evolution of life. In their time, in that shelf area of the Iapetus Ocean, they tenaciously clung to the sea floor.

Similarly, in their time, David Blackwood's people cling tenaciously to their place on Earth. They and the land they inhabit are rooted in granite, but that is a most difficult medium to securely attach oneself to. Bedrock to the region, granite is a hard rock that provides no good nutrients for the growth of vegetation. The granite is so hard and extensive in Blackwood's Newfoundland that it is difficult to find ground to even bury people in; there is nowhere to hide from the forces of nature, even when you're dead. And when Cape Shore people can find a patch of bog for burials, the granite-based acid soils dissolve their very bones; thus their impact on the landscape can be quite minuscule in the end.

Grinding glaciers stripped away the vegetation of that land and exposed the ancient granite crust. The ocean carries still the offspring of continental glaciers from Greenland, bits and pieces of ice that victimize the coastal edge and can bring death and destruction to those who venture out to sea. But ice also brings life to the edge in that strange creature the seal, born of ice, sea and land; more at home in the water than on land, it is the opposite of Blackwood's people.

Though Blackwood's art roars with the intensity of the forces of nature, its final conclusion is that people can triumph, if fleetingly, and forge a home for themselves on the edge. Their joy of companionship and fellowship, the bright colours of their homes, the subtle beauty of their lovingly tended gardens and the tenacity of their toil show the strength and faith of their fight. Their spirit and essence, along with the strange beauty of the landscape and the immense, ancient power of the forces of nature, live on through David Blackwood's art.

DEREK H.C. WILTON *is a professor in the Department of Earth Sciences at Memorial University of Newfoundland.*
MARTIN FEELY *is Senior Lecturer in Earth and Ocean Sciences at the School of Natural History, National University of Ireland, Galway.*

Notes

1. Natural Resources Canada, *The Atlas of Canada*, atlas.nrcan.gc.ca.
2. Coffey, M., *Explorers of the Infinite* (New York: Jeremy P. Tauchar/Penguin, 2008), 26.

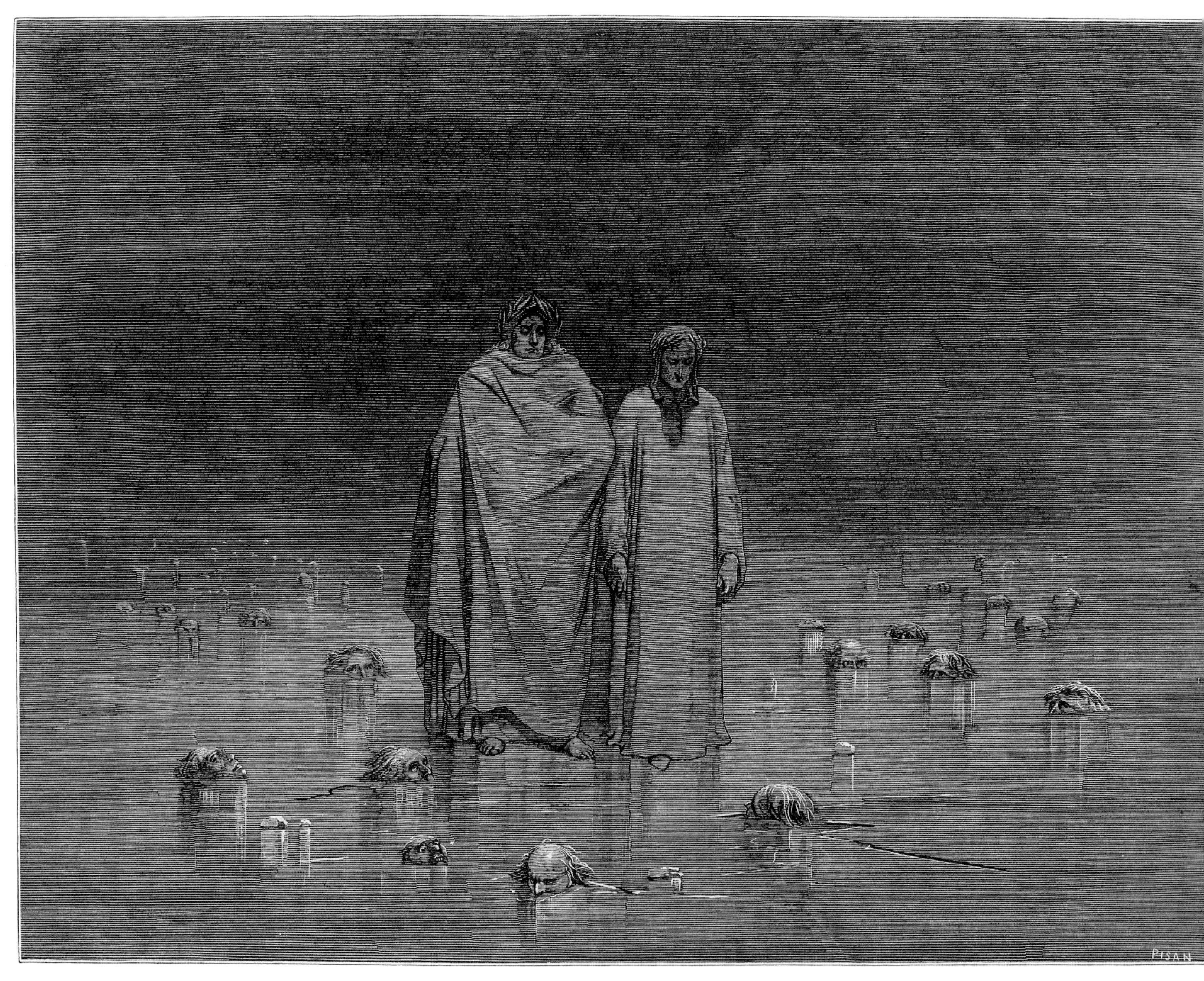

Gustave Doré, *Dante and Virgil*, Plate 68 from *The Vision of Hell by Dante Alighieri*, translated by Henry Francis Cary (London: Cassell, Petter, and Galpin, 1866). Wood engraving

DANTE ALIGHIERI

ITALIAN · 1265–1321

"Inferno," from *La Divina Commedia* · 1308–1321
(trans. Hollander)

. . .

At that I turned to look about.
Under my feet I saw a lake
So frozen that it seemed more glass than water.

Never in winter did the Austrian Danube
Nor the far-off Don, under its frigid sky,
Cover their currents with so thick a veil

As I saw there. For had Tambernic fallen on it,
Or Pietrapana, the ice would not
Have creaked, not even at the edge.

And as frogs squat and croak,
Their snouts out of the water, in the season
When peasant women often dream of gleaning,

So shades, ashen with cold, were grieving, trapped
In ice up to the place the hue of shame appears,
Their teeth a-clatter like the bills of storks.

Downturned were all their faces, their mouths
Gave witness to the cold, while from their eyes
Came testimony of their woeful hearts.

Canto XXXII · LINES 22–37

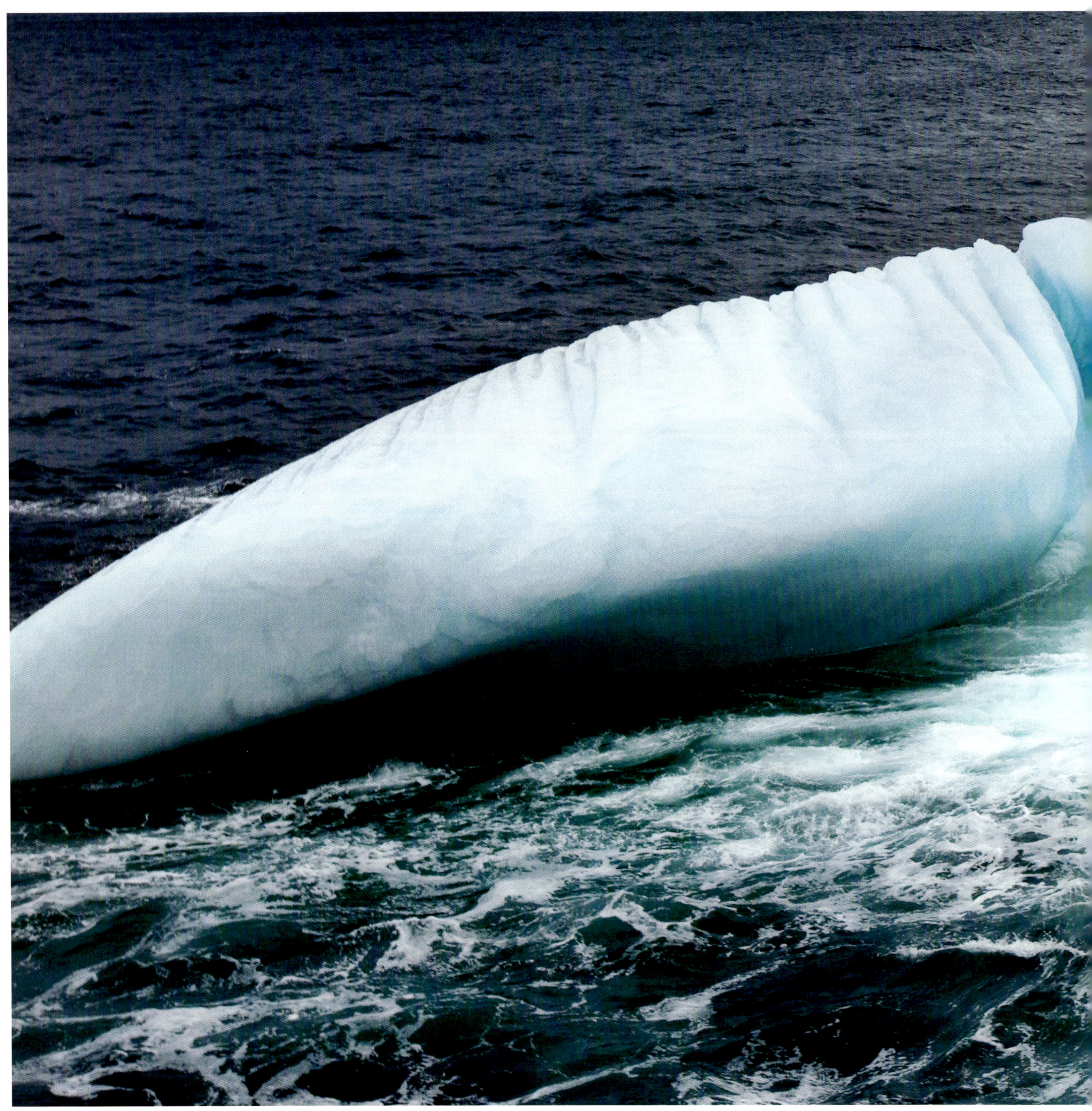

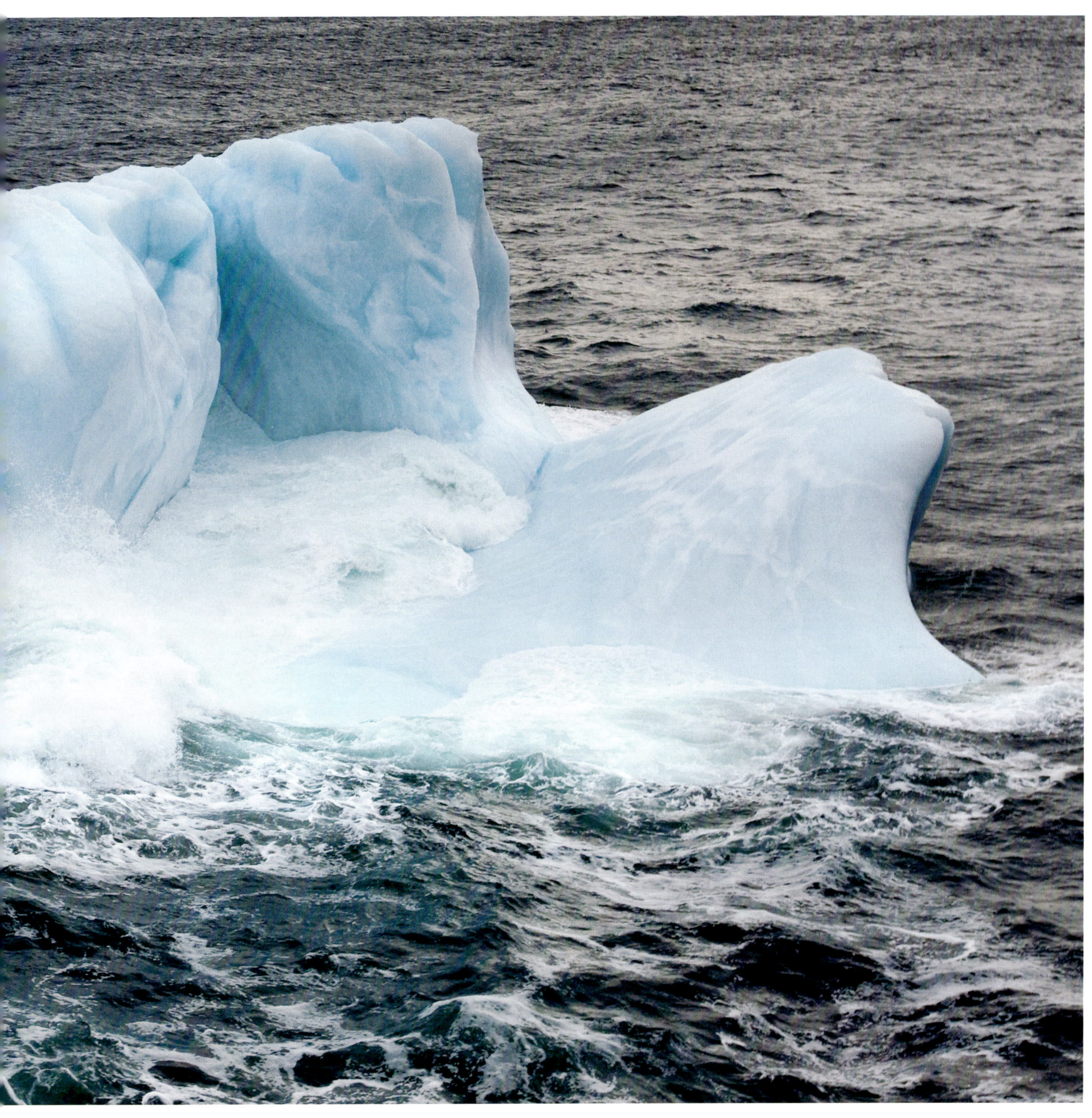

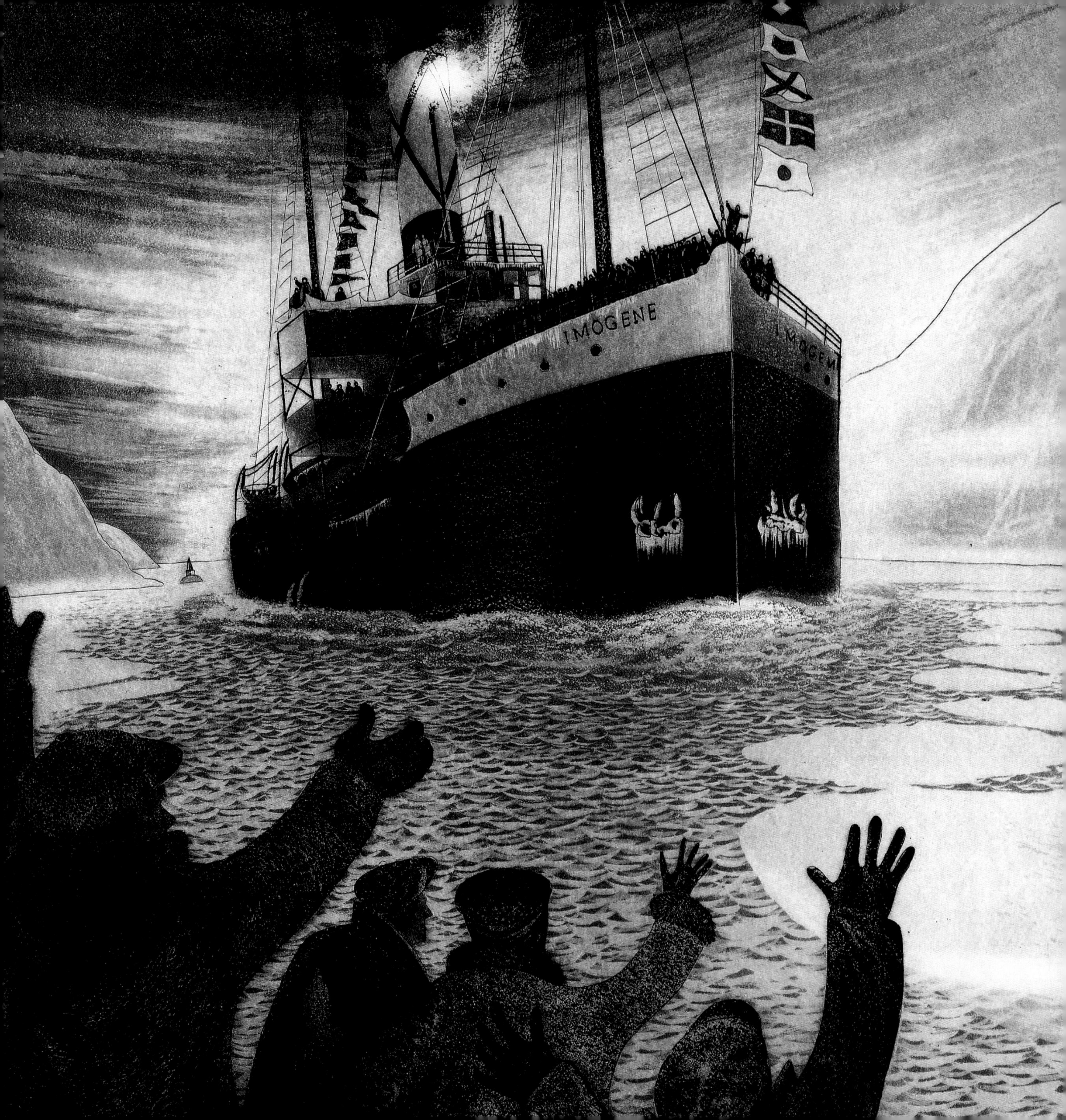
IMOGENE

The Newfoundland of David Blackwood

A HISTORICAL SETTING

Sean T. Cadigan

DAVID BLACKWOOD comes from Wesleyville, which was once an important outport for the cod fishery and seal hunt on the north side of Bonavista Bay, Newfoundland. The North Atlantic shaped the lives of the original settlers of Bonavista Bay. The conditions that provided rich fisheries—the meeting of the frigid Labrador Current and the warmer Gulf Stream off the Grand Banks—meant that Newfoundland experienced tremendous precipitation and a short growing season. Rain, fog and melting snow eroded and leached the soil, leaving it shallow and infertile. That climate and soil supported limited boreal woodlands but severely limited farming, except of root vegetables and livestock, particularly goats. Settlers had to earn their living from the sea by fishing for cod in the summer and hunting seals in the spring.

facing: Detail from **SS Imogene Home from the Icefields**, 1972 (plate 23)

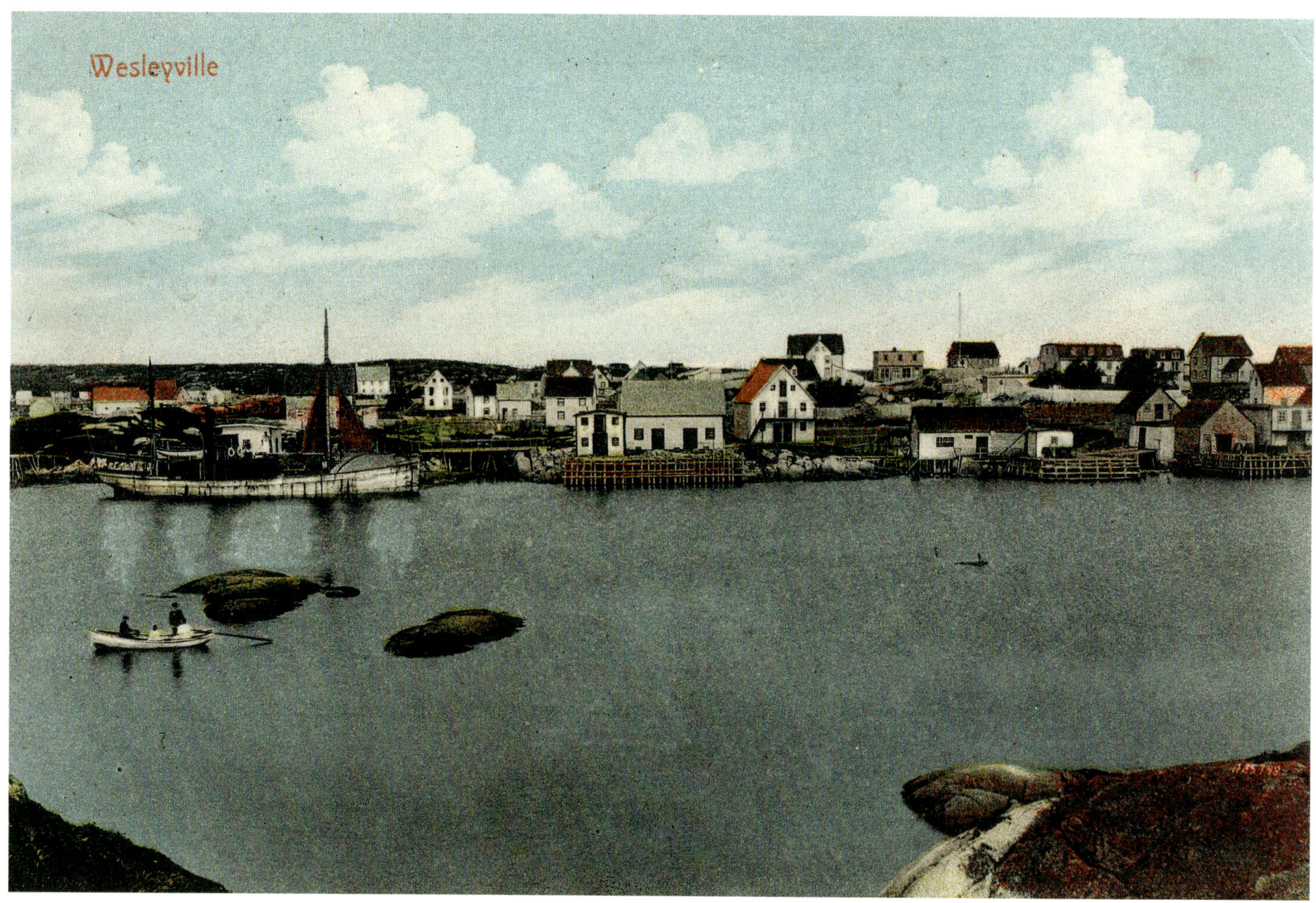

Within the constraints of a cold-ocean coastal environment, the relationships between fishing households and merchants defined outport society. The international value of salt cod declined after 1815, forcing settlers to create smaller household fisheries instead of using bigger vessels such as schooners. Most settlers used small boats and family labour, supplemented occasionally by servants. Settlers relied on fish merchants to import almost everything they needed to survive. Merchants supplied goods on credit against the settlers' fish and fish oil using truck credit practices, a form of largely cashless trade. Merchants took salt fish, cod oil, seal oil, pelts and smaller quantities of other products from their clients. Once they had assembled enough of such produce in their storehouses, they shipped it to markets in Europe, the Caribbean and South America.

By extending credit to fishing households, merchants avoided the costs of participating directly in the production and marketing of salt fish. They also used truck to minimize the financial risk of giving fishers credit at the

facing: Coloured postcard of Wesleyville, 1907

beginning of the fishing season, long before they knew the quantity and quality of fish and fish oil they would get in return for export and, more importantly, before they knew what the eventual prices for these products would be. Once they knew what markets would be like, merchants set the prices for fishers' purchases and produce. Fearful of overextending credit, merchants advanced as little money as possible.[1]

Fishing people often resented truck, feeling that merchants charged them too much for their goods. However, truck provided them with access to imported necessities. In addition to making salt fish, outport households engaged in woodcutting, berry picking and supplementary farming. They did all the work associated with building, equipping and maintaining their own homes and fishing premises, in part to limit the amount of credit they required from merchants in exchange for fish and seal products. People exchanged labour, goods and services with one another in the informal markets of the local community, where considerations of kin and mutual obligation were as important as supply and demand.[2]

Paternalistic relationships existed between fishing households and fish merchants. People expected that merchants would behave ethically, and they could take action against merchants who overcharged them or dealt with them arrogantly. Such actions might draw on old English or Irish customs such as mummering, a yuletide ritual that happened from Boxing Day to Old Christmas Day (January 6) in which householders would entertain their masked neighbours, who spoke in disguised voices. David Blackwood recalled that mummering, while usually festive, could serve as "a vehicle for meting out a sort of rough justice to transgressors at year's end. If a slight had been given, someone wronged, or an obligation not met, collective disapproval might be expressed by the mummers coming round to 'straighten a person out.'"[3]

Fishers could also take direct action against merchants they felt to be unfair. Some took legal action, but others used extrajudicial measures such as assaulting merchants, taking fish to competitors or throwing agents or bailiffs into the harbour over disputes about court proceedings instigated by merchants. Such acts might force merchants into more paternalistic credit practices, ones that cloaked exploitation in a superficial mutuality and forestalled open conflict. Most fishers wanted to believe that they were being treated fairly by merchants; they could be loyal to a local merchant who lived up to their expectations, and might defend one threatened by court action for debts to larger mercantile firms in St. John's.[4]

Merchants allowed some clients credit as an investment in better fishing gear and larger boats. The inshore fishery on the northeast coast followed a ruinous cycle: fishers discovered new fishing grounds, depleted their local cod stocks, then either failed to repay their merchants

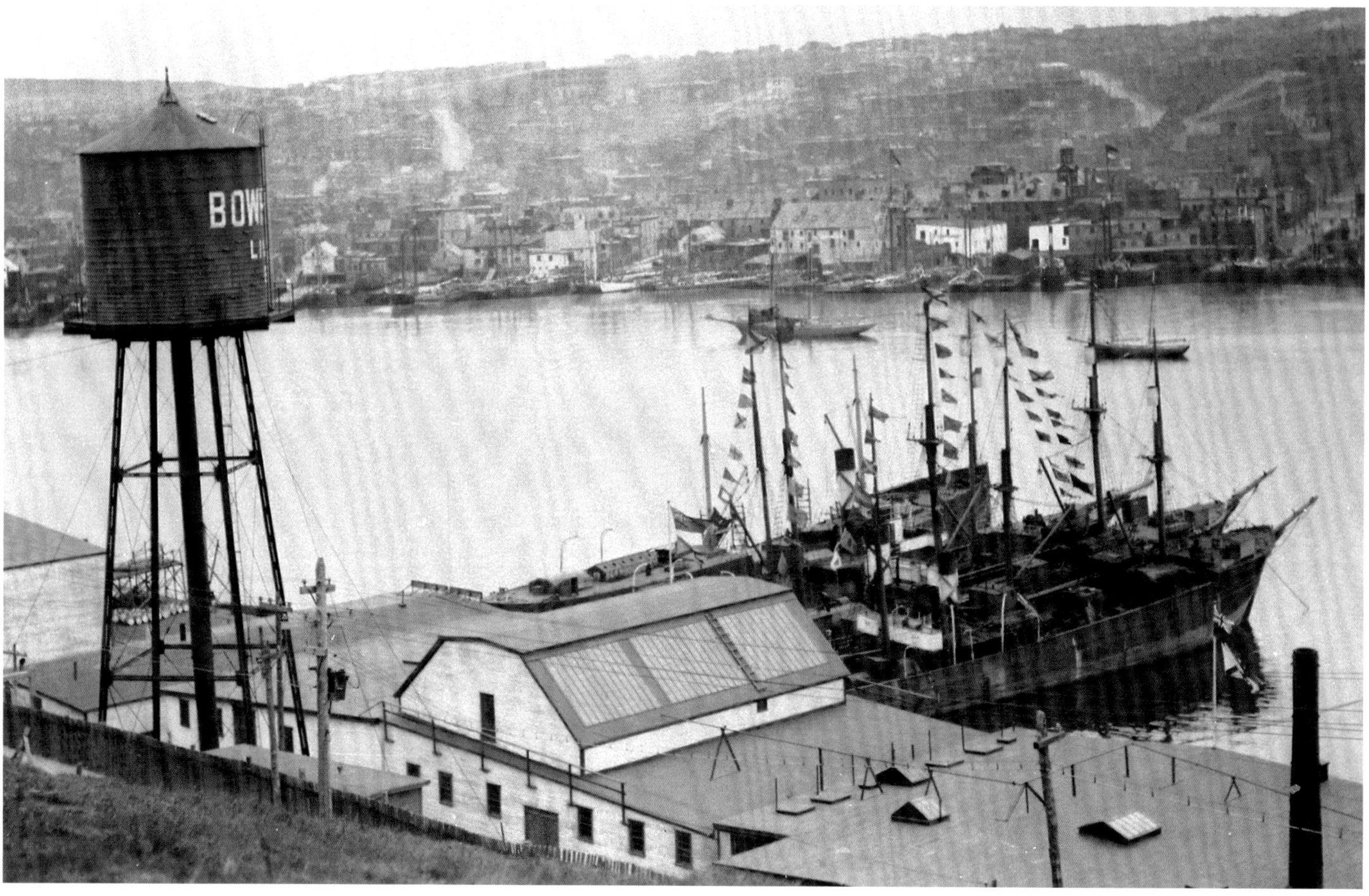

or invested in more efficient but costly fishing gear and vessels to move on to new fishing grounds. They would trek ever farther northward searching for new fish stocks to exploit in the cold waters and ice off the Labrador coast each summer. The most successful fishers operated schooners and might act as dealers for fish merchants or, rarely, go to Labrador as merchants themselves. To keep their schooners occupied at Labrador while waiting to carry back passengers and catches, captains had their crews fish as well, paying them a share of the catch. Jesse Winsor, one of the great Wesleyville captains in the Labrador fishery and seal hunt in the early twentieth century, was such a trader. He took over his father's business in 1907, serving as master on a schooner in the Labrador fishery, but he also carried supplies for other schooners and operated a sawmill at home.[5]

The Labrador fishery gave birth to Wesleyville. The ancestors of the people of Wesleyville first settled in about 1810 on small islands just off shore from what is now the town. These little islands, the most important of which was Swain's Island, were close to rich inshore fishing grounds, had good places to catch seals and had fine harbours

facing: Sealing ships alongside Bowring Brothers, Ltd., St. John's, Newfoundland, c. 1910–1935

right: Samuel Tiller's Store and Flake, Wesleyville, 1917

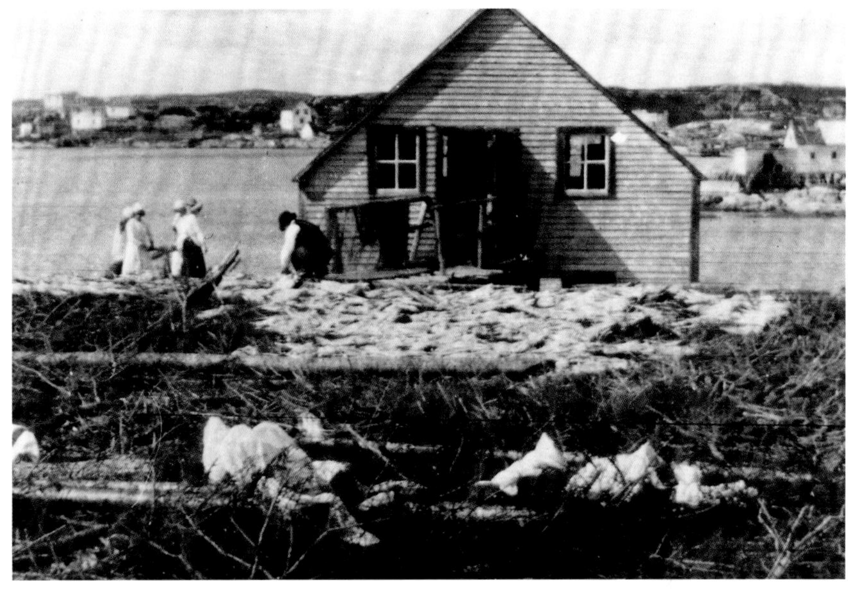

for securing small boats. By the early 1850s, a number of Swain's Islanders were running large schooners in the Labrador fishery. These schooners required larger and deeper harbours than could be found on Swain's Island, and the islanders needed larger fishing premises—including wharves, flakes and stages—because they would bring fish back from Labrador for curing. As a result, from 1870 to 1930, many islanders gradually relocated to Wesleyville, which also bore the name of Swain's Island until 1884.

Over the course of Wesleyville's involvement in the Labrador fishery, about 175 men served as captains of ships, mostly schooners, that plied the waters off Labrador. Such was the calling of David Blackwood's grandfather, Captain Albert Blackwood, and his father, Captain Edward Blackwood, with whom David Blackwood sailed to Labrador as a young man on their schooner, the *Flora S. Nickerson*. Each year, many of the community's men left for Labrador. Once they procured enough fish to fill the holds of their vessels, the crews returned to unload in Wesleyville, where the women and children would dry the fish for export. If conditions were good, schooners might be able to return to Labrador for another load.[6]

Paternalism bound together the masters of fishing schooners and their crews. On larger vessels, skippers drew on the household organization of the fishery for their authority, acting as patriarchal masters of the men under their command. On smaller vessels, skippers required the consensus of their crewmates. In larger vessels, especially those of the seal hunt, captains were more autocratic. They took all the credit for successful hunts as if they personally killed the seals yet they earned the loyalty of their crews by dispensing favours and patronage rather than simply disciplining crew members who were disobedient or disrespectful.[7]

Paternalism at sea drew on the notion that skippers were like fathers to their crews, but in reality family life ashore rarely allowed men the authority they might enjoy as skippers. For example, David Blackwood's grandfather commanded from the deck of his fishing schooner, but "the actual power" in the family "lay in the strong matriarchal control of Mrs. Blackwood," his grandmother.[8] Women dominated the shore work of curing fish and doing their households' supplementary farming. Women also stayed behind to manage the affairs of their households and communities while the men went away to the Labrador fishery during the summer.

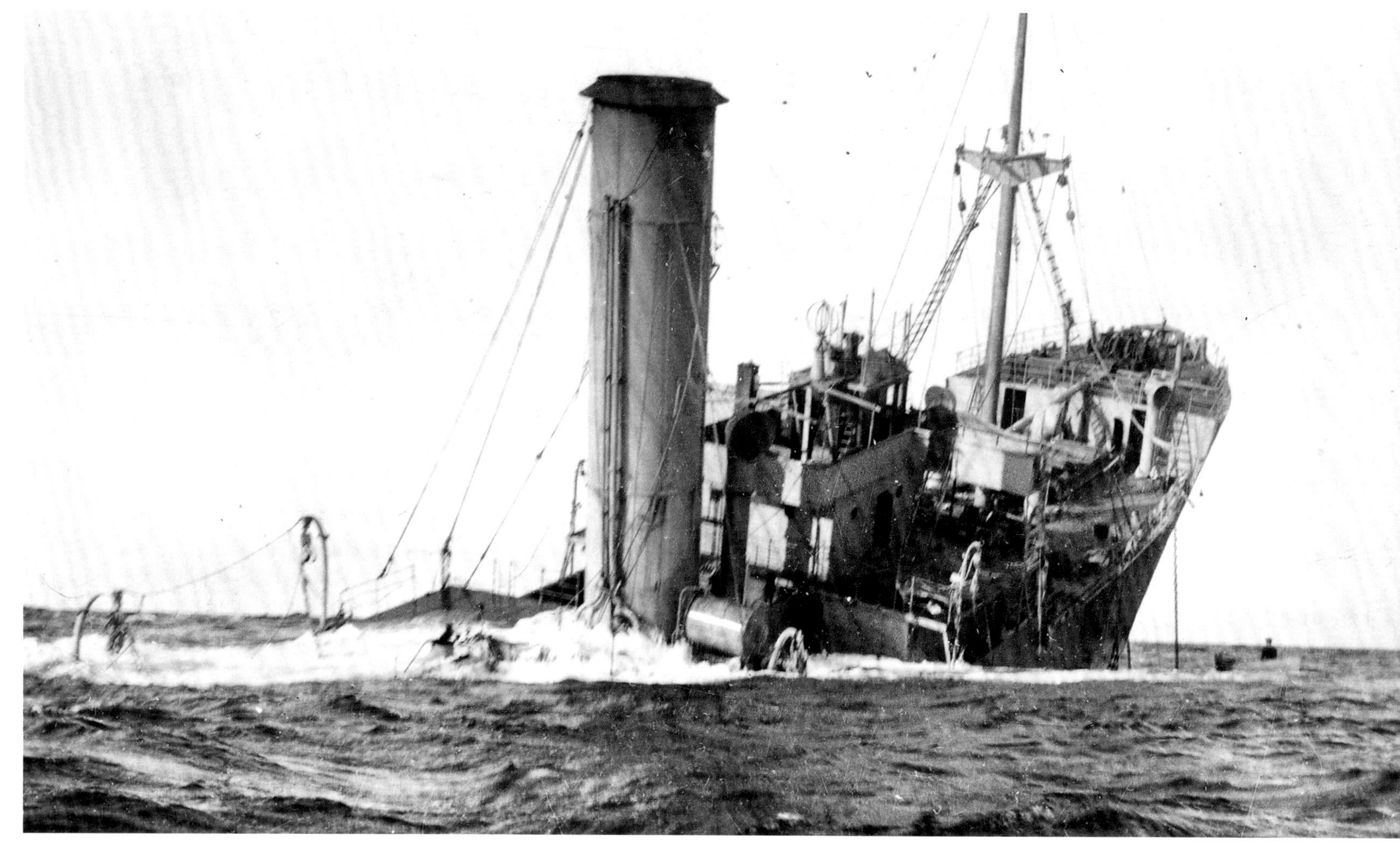

Kinship and the sea were important to outport people, and so was a rich, church-centred spiritual life. Methodism was the most important faith on the north side of Bonavista Bay, and nearly everyone in Wesleyville in the late nineteenth and early twentieth centuries could be counted among its adherents. In 1906, the people of Wesleyville decided to build a church that would be a testament to their faith, and in 1912 they dedicated the Jubilee Methodist Church. Church services and meetings were essential to social life. During the late winter, the most important service was held on Sunday evening for the three hundred or so men from Wesleyville and the surrounding area who went to the seal hunt. "We sang 'Eternal Father strong to save . . . O hear us when we cry to Thee for those in peril on the sea,'" remembered one of the town's best known ministers. "When the sealers returned the church was filled again every Sunday night until our schooners left for the Labrador fishery, in late May or early June."[9]

facing: SS *Imogene*, c. 1910–1935, sinking in the Strait of Canso, Nova Scotia, 1940

Paternalistic community bonds could not prevent all social and economic conflict, as seen in the rise of the Fishermen's Protective Union (FPU) under William Ford Coaker. Born in St. John's in 1871, Coaker had worked as a fish handler on the waterfront as a boy, and led his fellow handlers in a successful strike for better pay in 1884. As a young man, Coaker had moved to Notre Dame Bay to manage a fish cannery and to operate a small shop. His business failed in the bank crash of 1894, and Coaker developed a strong sympathy for his neighbouring fishing people, who he felt were ruthlessly exploited by the fish merchants of St. John's.

By the early twentieth century, credit restrictions alongside truck had begun to stir fishers' resentment towards merchants, especially the St. John's firms that often supplied the Labrador fishery. It was disheartening for schooner crews to bring fish to St. John's in the fall, only to learn that low prices meant poor earnings and hardship for their families during the winter. Skippers shared in their crews' misfortunes because they too received their pay as shares of half the schooners' earnings, with the other half going to the vessel's owner, who was rarely a skipper.

By 1908–1909, Coaker was proclaiming "To each his own," the FPU motto. He organized fishers into a co-operative organization that attempted to eliminate merchants as brokers in the marketing of fish.[10] In Wesleyville, the FPU organized a local council in 1910. Coaker attended a public meeting there in 1911, and the local FPU council opened its own hall in 1925. For more than twenty-five years, local members of the FPU came together to sing:

We are coming Mr. Coaker from the East, West, North and South,
You have called and we're coming to put our foes to rout;
By Merchants and Governments too long we've been misruled,
We're determined now in future that no longer we'll be fooled,
We'll be brothers all and freemen, and we'll rectify each wrong.
We are coming Mr. Coaker and we're forty thousand strong.[11]

The FPU concentrated on improving fish marketing, but it was also concerned about the general conditions of outport Newfoundland, including work in the seal hunt. The days of schooners from places such as Wesleyville participating in the hunt were over, as St. John's firms—the only ones able to afford to do so—invested in new steaming vessels that alone could force their way deep into the offshore ice pack to search for new herds of seals to kill. These firms relied on communities such as Wesleyville to supply captains for their vessels. Along with Jesse Winsor, Edward Bishop was a prominent Wesleyville captain in the hunt between 1906 and 1926, as was Llewellyn (Lew) Kean, who commanded his first sealing ship, the *Ranger*, from 1939 to 1941.[12]

Although the seal hunt operated largely from St. John's, it continued to employ many of the men of Wesleyville.

Ships in harbour, St. John's, Newfoundland, c. 1877–1885

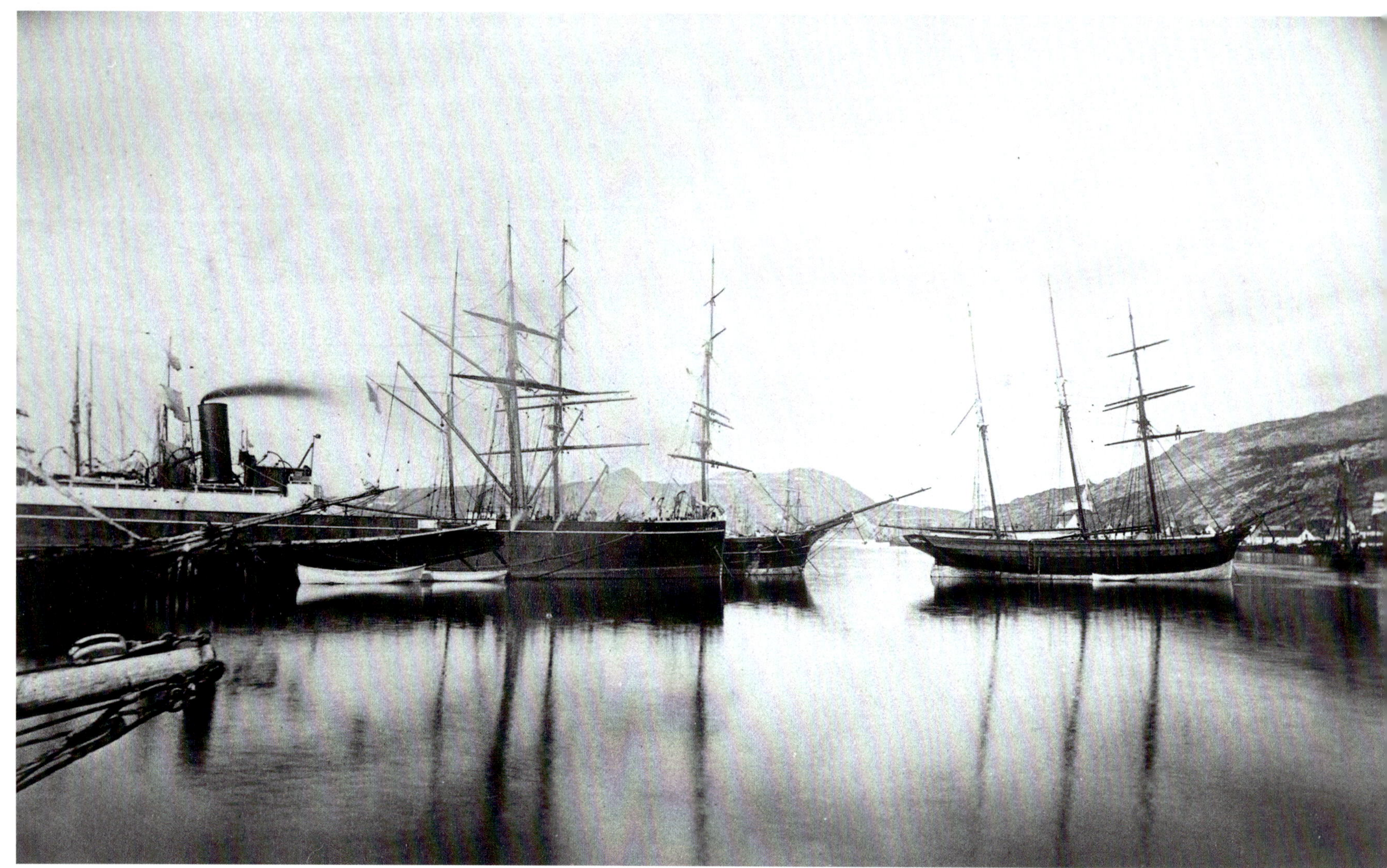

For many, the spring hunt was their first opportunity to earn some cash after their credit and stores from the previous summer and fall had been all but exhausted through the winter. The hunt was dangerous. The crushing ice floes, icy waters and unpredictable gales of freezing rain and snow that mark spring in the North Atlantic always claimed ships and men. By the late nineteenth century, outport men faced an additional challenge. Men from Wesleyville, for example, had to make their way to St. John's, trekking about a hundred kilometres over frozen water and barrens as they hauled sledges with their equipment to the nearest railroad station, at Gambo. From there, they would take the cheapest passage available to St. John's.[13]

The steamer hunt challenged the paternalistic relationships between sealing captains and their crews. The higher overhead costs of steamers, combined with the increasing difficulty of finding seals, led the captains to take greater risks in order to have successful voyages. Sealing skippers divided their larger crews into four watches that they would send onto the pack ice to kill patches of seals. It was rare to find enough seals in one patch to keep all of the watches busy, so captains often dropped a watch in one place and then steamed to another patch of seals to drop more men over the side. Sometimes the steamer would return to collect a watch, but often the captain expected his men to walk to the vessel, towing seals behind them. However, if bad weather or ice conditions changed for the worse, there was a danger that the sealers might become stranded. Such was the case in 1898, when Captain George Barbour of the SS *Greenland* lost forty-eight men in a blizzard, one of whom was from Wesleyville.

The *Greenland* disaster provoked public outrage about the dangers of the hunt, but little else. Men continued to go to the ice, often introducing their younger relatives to it. Paid in shares, the sealers were happy to join the vessels of skippers with reputations as "real seal killers," or as men who could find the "main patch" of the seal herds, thereby assuring a successful hunt for all. The most famous was Captain Abram Kean, and sealers vied with each other to get a berth on his vessels. Likewise, men hoped to join the vessels captained by Kean's son Westbury or Kean's nephews. The Keans often went to the ice together in a fleet of steamers.

Together, Abram and Westbury Kean played a key role in the most infamous of sealing catastrophes, the SS *Newfoundland* disaster of 1914. That spring, Abram took the steamer SS *Stephano*, belonging to Bowring Brothers, to the ice, while Westbury took the *Newfoundland*, which belonged to a competing firm, Harveys. Although the firms were in competition, Abram helped his son find the main patch of seals. The *Newfoundland*, an older wooden steamer, had difficulty navigating through the pack ice, so on the last day of March Westbury decided to send his crew over the side to walk to the *Stephano*. Abram Kean brought many of the

facing: Landing a badly frostbitten man, St. John's ambulance corps, c. 1910–1935

crew to a patch of seals, although they had already struggled over the ice for more than four hours to reach his ship.

The weather grew stormy and they became lost. Each Kean thought the men were safe aboard the other's ship, and they had no way to contact each other because the *Newfoundland* didn't have a wireless radio. The men of the *Newfoundland* wandered in a raging storm for fifty-three hours. Improperly clothed and with little food, many succumbed to hypothermia and exhaustion. A few survivors eventually struggled to a nearby steamer, the SS *Bellaventure*, which began a rescue operation.

Seventy-eight men died as a result of the tragedy, provoking political furor throughout the colony. William Ford Coaker of the FPU took up the sealers' cause against Abram Kean and the People's Party government, which Kean supported. St. John's came to a standstill when people heard of the tragedy. The declaration of war against Germany cut short the outcry, and Kean's career as a successful sealing captain continued.[14]

The political controversy surrounding the *Newfoundland* disaster scandalized St. John's, but it did not appear to be as strong in places such as Wesleyville. No one from Wesleyville had been lost, although some of its men had been on the ship. Residents of the town later reflected that it "seems to be a miracle" that, although Wesleyville men had been going to the ice for more than 130 years, only about six had lost their lives in the dangerous hunt.[15] Local people may have taken a more individual approach to tragedy and personal loss that was grounded in their religion. Methodist spirituality saw a profound sense of tragedy every day in the bitter winds, cold seas, looming rocks, daunting ice, meagre soils, tight-fisted merchants and remote government. The world was hostile, but the measure of true Methodists was the "varying degrees of humility and nobility" with which they bore their hardships.[16]

The outport life contemplated in David Blackwood's work came to an end in the 1940s and 1950s. Commentators often associate the change with the disappearance of communities such as Bragg's Island, the home of Blackwood's maternal grandparents, the Glovers.[17] The Labrador fishery was important to the people of Bragg's Island, but it had a prosperous inshore fishery too. While people followed the seasonal round of the fishery much as in Wesleyville, the men of Bragg's Island often went to Glovertown, Gambo or Hare Bay to seek work as loggers in the growing forestry industry of the main part of Newfoundland. The economic boom of the Second World War, combined with the development of the pulp and paper industry, meant that many of these seasonal migrants were attracted to the greater amenities of the logging towns.

With Newfoundland's entry into Confederation in 1949, it became harder for small places like Bragg's Island, unlike the larger and less remote communities such as Wesleyville, to attract good teachers. If families wanted

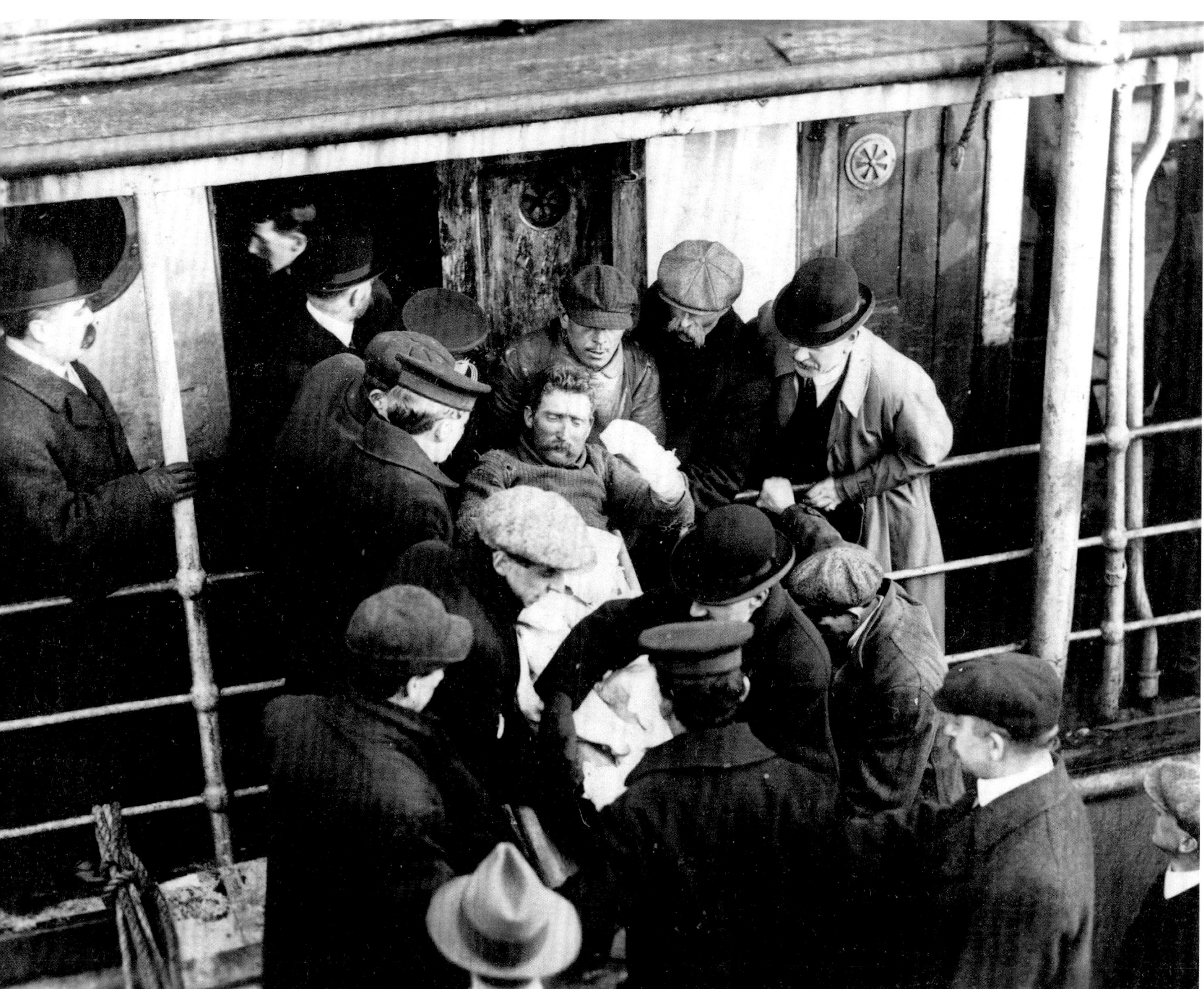

below: Sealers from Wesleyville en route to St. John's aboard the schooner *Winifred Lee*

facing: House belonging to Mr. Malcolm Rogers being towed by a 40 HP motorboat during relocation from Fox Island to Flat Island, Dover, Newfoundland, August 1961

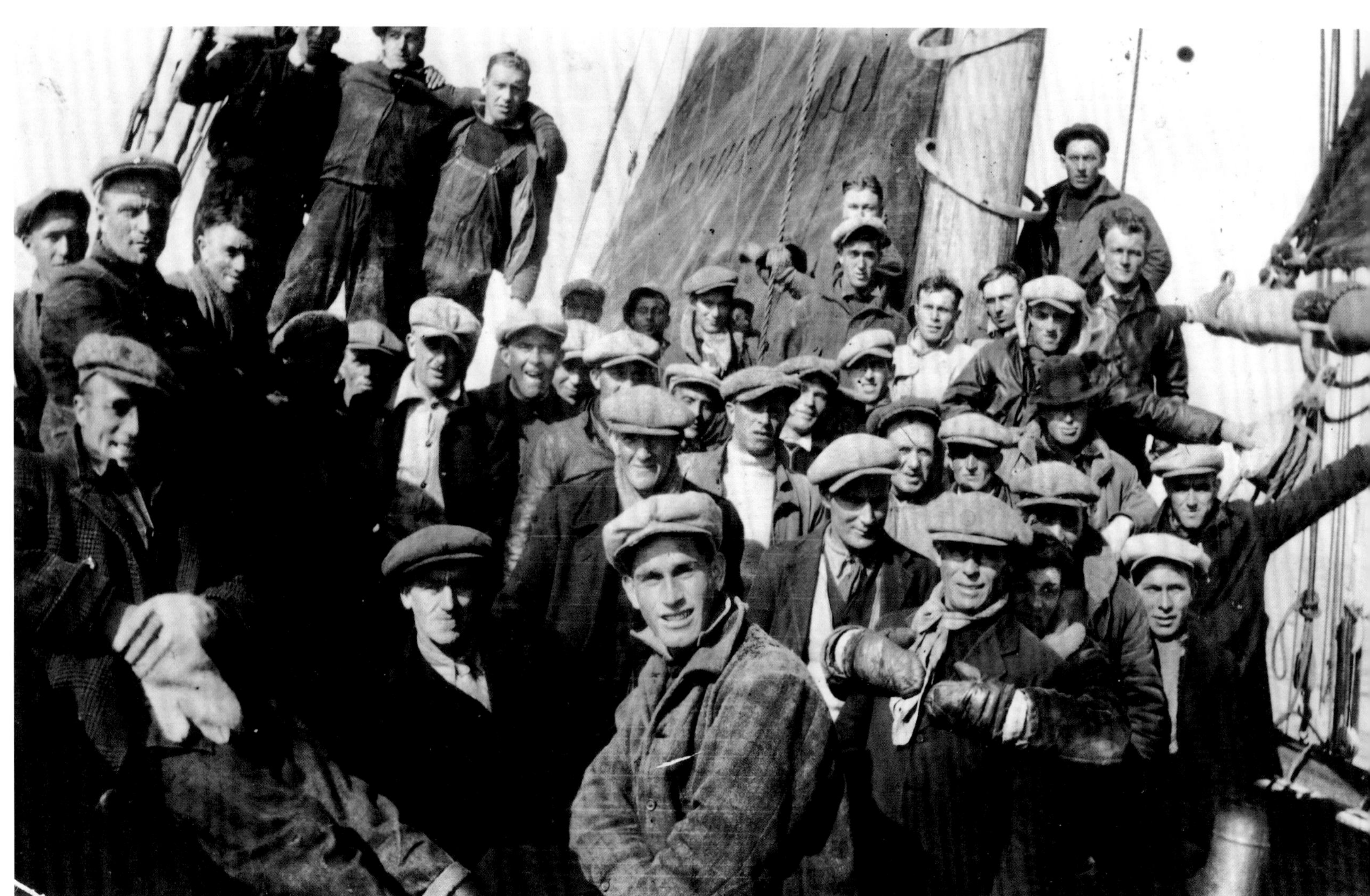

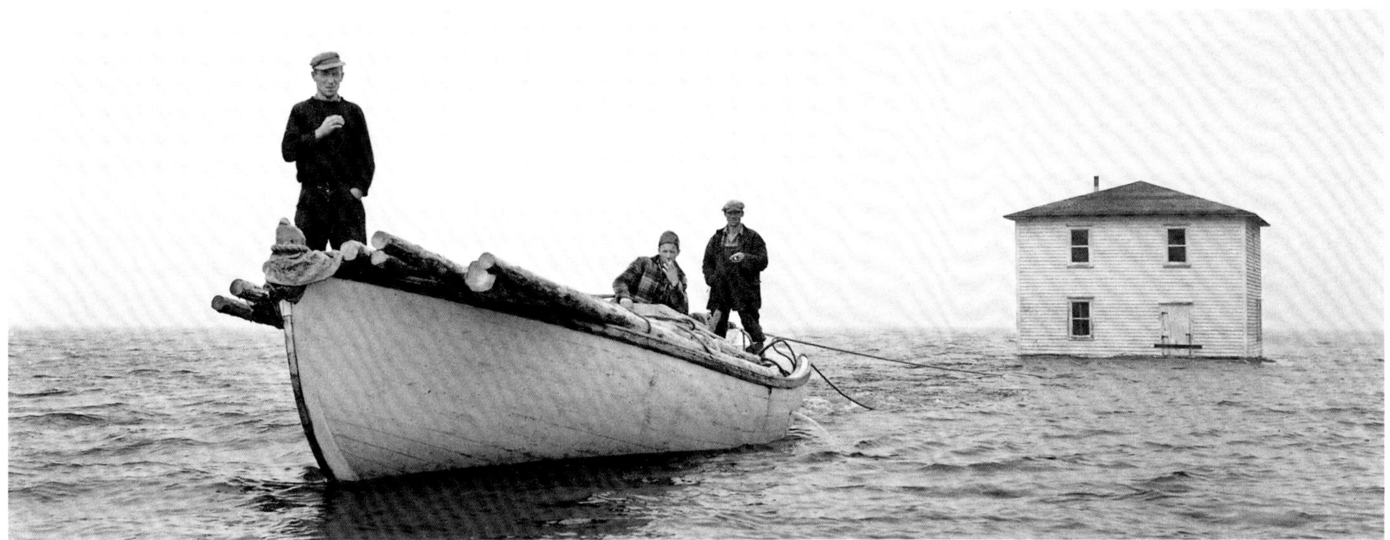

their children to have quality educations, they faced the prospect of sending them away. People began to drift away; by 1953 the local merchant, the minister and a minister from a neighbouring island decided to move. The merchant negotiated an agreement with the provincial government that provided limited financial support for resettlement. The residents of Bragg's Island took the assistance when the merchant moved in 1954.[18]

That same year, the provincial government had begun resettling coastal communities around Newfoundland to provide better and more cost-effective public services. Disillusionment quickly set in among the resettled people. Outport people had always resettled—the foundation of Wesleyville had been an act of relocation—but for their own reasons and at their own pace. The government resettlement schemes of the 1950s and 1960s were poorly planned, insufficiently funded and socially divisive. Financial incentives for relocation often required that all members of a community agree to leave, which placed unbearable pressure on those who may have wished to stay. People who left found themselves dispersed among strangers, cut off from the comforts of kin and church. There were new public amenities, but too often the industrial employment that was supposed to appear in centralized communities did not.[19]

The consequent underemployment and demoralization were a far cry from the days when people felt that they had struggled heroically through a hard life, with tight-fisted merchants and uninterested governments, to build communities founded on kinship and fellowship. Many outport people initially wanted resettlement, but its disappointments appeared to justify the misgivings that many others, including David Blackwood's maternal grandparents, had about leaving Bragg's Island. Ironically, the pain of resettlement brought forth a terrible beauty through its contemplation in Blackwood's art.

SEAN T. CADIGAN *is Head of the Department of History at Memorial University of Newfoundland.*

Notes

1. Sean Cadigan, *Hope and Deception in Conception Bay: Merchant-Settler Relations in Newfoundland, 1785–1855* (Toronto: University of Toronto Press, 1995), 37–50, 109–11, 148–50.
2. Cadigan, *Hope and Deception*, 37–63.
3. David Blackwood, "Mummering in Newfoundland," in *David Blackwood: The Mummer's Veil* (Oakville, ON: Abbozzo Gallery, 2003), 34. See also Herbert Halpert and G.M. Story, eds., *Christmas Mumming in Newfoundland: Essays in Anthropology, Folklore and History*, 2nd ed. (Toronto: University of Toronto Press, 1990), 34–61, 165–85.
4. Cadigan, *Hope and Deception*, chap. 6.
5. Sean T. Cadigan and Jeffrey A. Hutchings, "Nineteenth-Century Expansion of the Newfoundland Fishery for Atlantic Cod: An Exploration of Underlying Causes," in Poul Holm, Tim D. Smith and David J. Starkey, eds., *The Exploited Seas: New Directions for Marine Environmental History* (St. John's: International Maritime Economic History Association/Census of Marine Life, 2001), 31–65; "Winsor, Jesse T.," *Encyclopedia of Newfoundland and Labrador* (St. John's: Newfoundland Book Publishers, 1994), 5: 586.
6. Naboth Winsor, ed., *The Sea, Our Life-Blood: A History of Wesleyville, Newfoundland: A Project of the 'Ocean View' Senior Citizens* (Gander, NL: BSC Printers, 1984), 15–19, 26–34, 68–74; William Gough, *The Art of David Blackwood* (Toronto: McGraw-Hill Ryerson, 1988).
7. Shannon Ryan, *The Ice Hunters: A History of Newfoundland Sealing to 1914* (St. John's: Breakwater, 1994), 65–105, 213–63; Eric W. Sager, *Seafaring Labour: The Merchant Marine of Atlantic Canada, 1820–1914* (Montreal and Kingston: McGill-Queen's University Press, 1989), 44–51.
8. Gough, *Art of David Blackwood*.
9. Naboth Winsor, "'By Their Works': A History of the Wesleyville Congregation, Methodist Church—1874–1925, United Church—1925–1974," privately printed, 1976, 4–18.
10. Eric Winsor, "History of Wesleyville," unpublished undergraduate paper deposited at the Centre for Newfoundland Studies, Queen Elizabeth II Library, Memorial University of Newfoundland, 1975, 32–35; Ian D.H. McDonald, *"To Each His Own": William Coaker and the Fisher-men's Protective Union in Newfoundland Politics, 1908–1925*, ed. J.K. Hiller (St. John's: Institute of Social and Economic Research, 1987), 34–47.
11. Naboth Winsor, *The Sea, Our Life-Blood*, 112.
12. Naboth Winsor, *The Sea, Our Life-Blood*, 77–79.
13. Eric Winsor, "History of Wesleyville," 26–27.
14. Ryan, *The Ice Hunters*, 306–17.
15. Naboth Winsor, *The Sea, Our Life-Blood*, 80.
16. Sandra Beardsall, "Methodist Religious Practices in Outport Newfoundland" (ThD thesis, University of Victoria and University of Toronto, 1996), 59, 88.
17. Gough, *Art of David Blackwood*.
18. Lorne Goulding, "Settlement Study of Bragg's Islands," unpublished undergraduate paper deposited at the Centre for Newfoundland Studies, Queen Elizabeth II Library, Memorial University of Newfoundland, 1978, 5–51.
19. Noel Iverson and D. Ralph Matthews, *Communities in Decline: An Examination of Household Resettlement in Newfoundland* (St. John's: Institute of Social and Economic Research, 1968, 1979).

THE NEWFOUNDLAND SEALING DISASTER OF 1914

top: Roll call after Newfoundland Sealing Disaster of 1914. SS *Bonaventure* nearest camera at right

bottom: Sealing fleet assembled for consultation off the coast of St. John's, Newfoundland, 1914

facing: Newfoundland Sealing Disaster of 1914

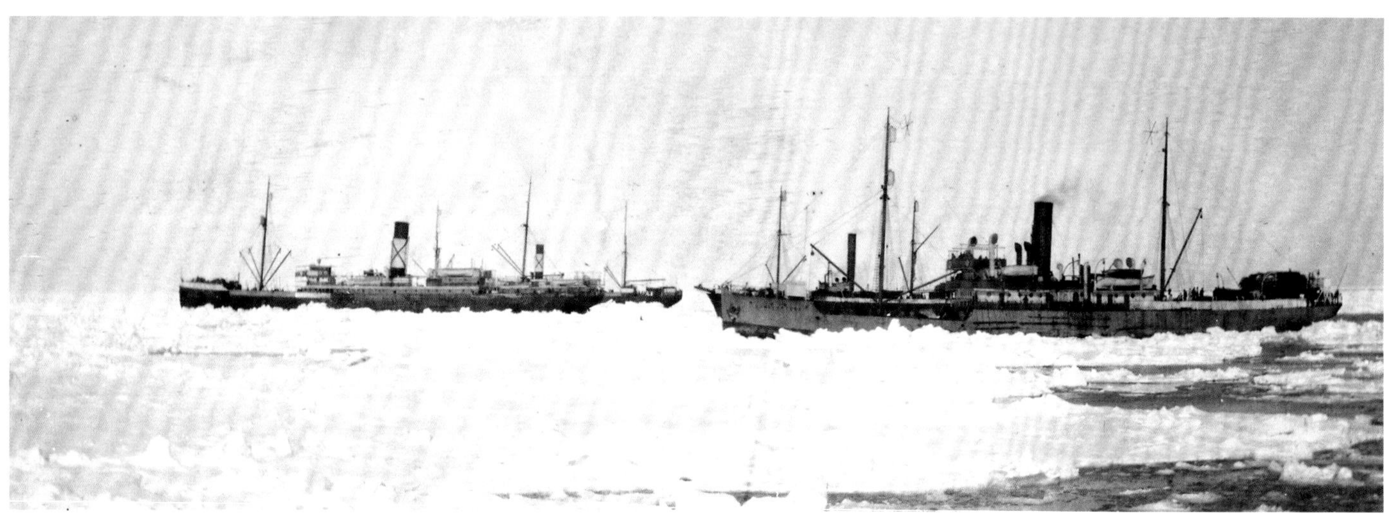

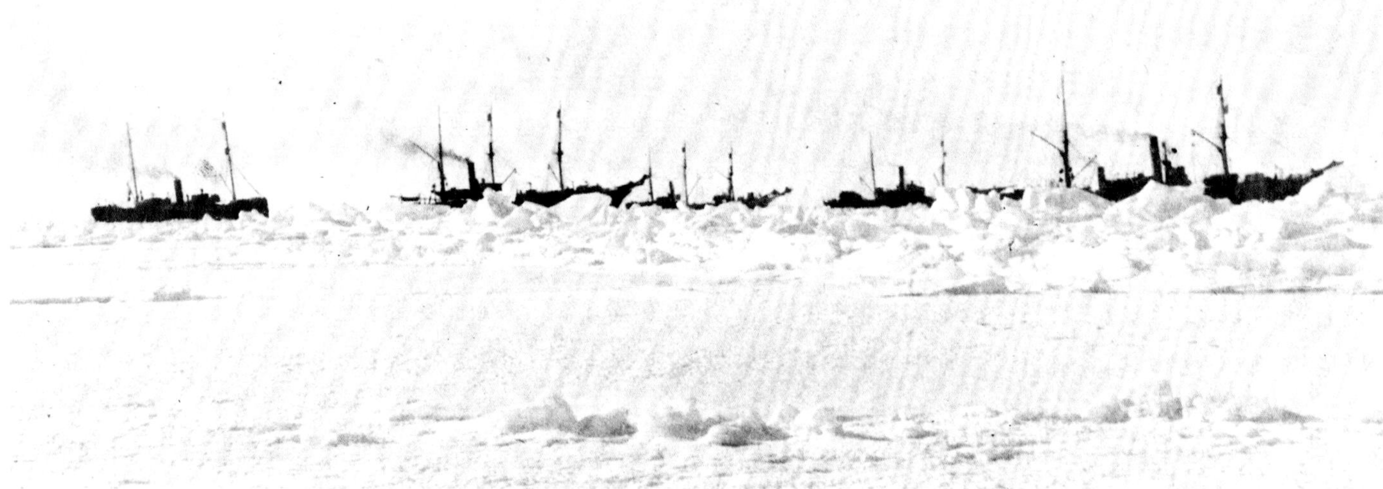

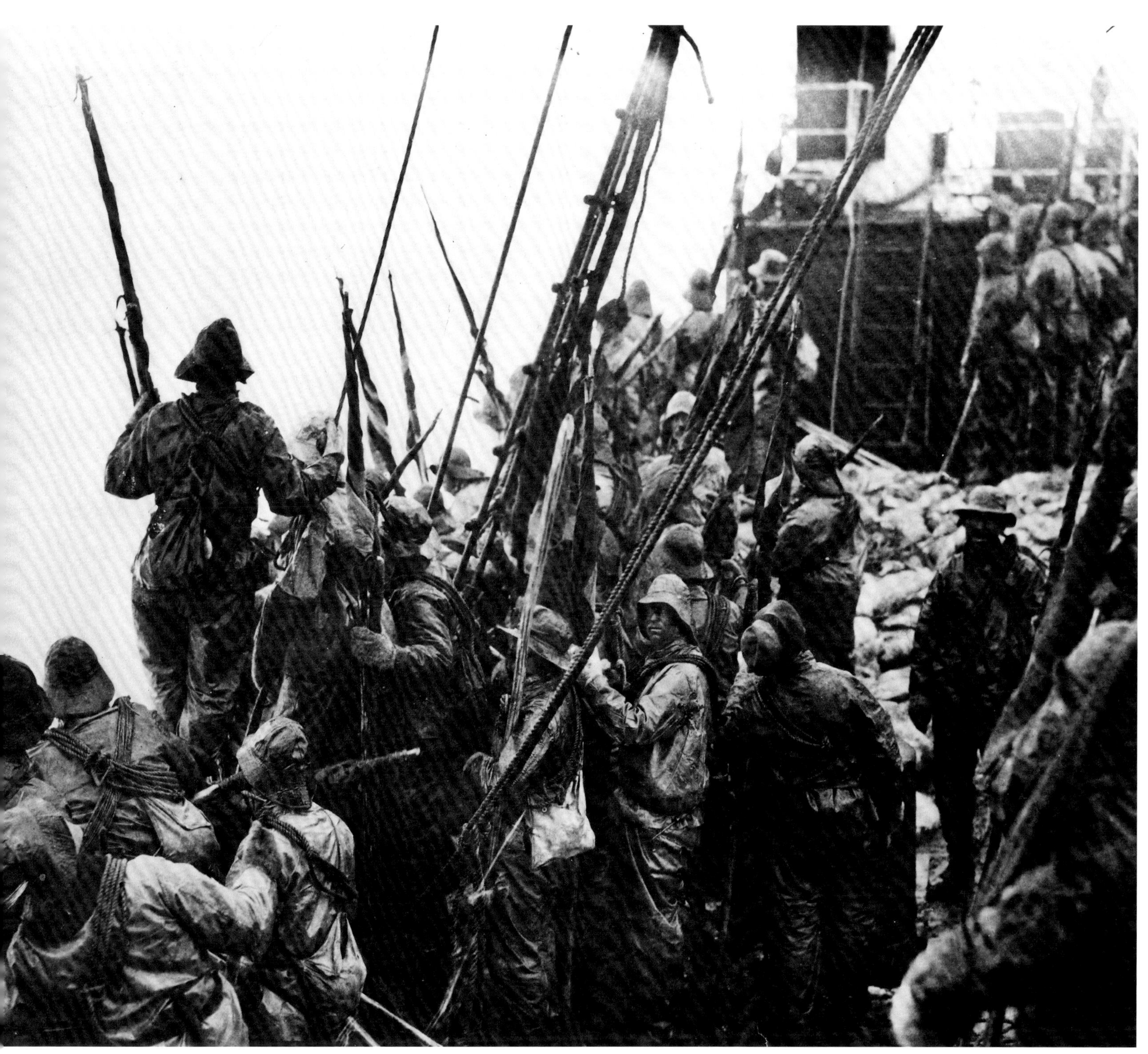

facing and below: Search party going out from the rescue ship, the SS *Bellaventure*, 1914

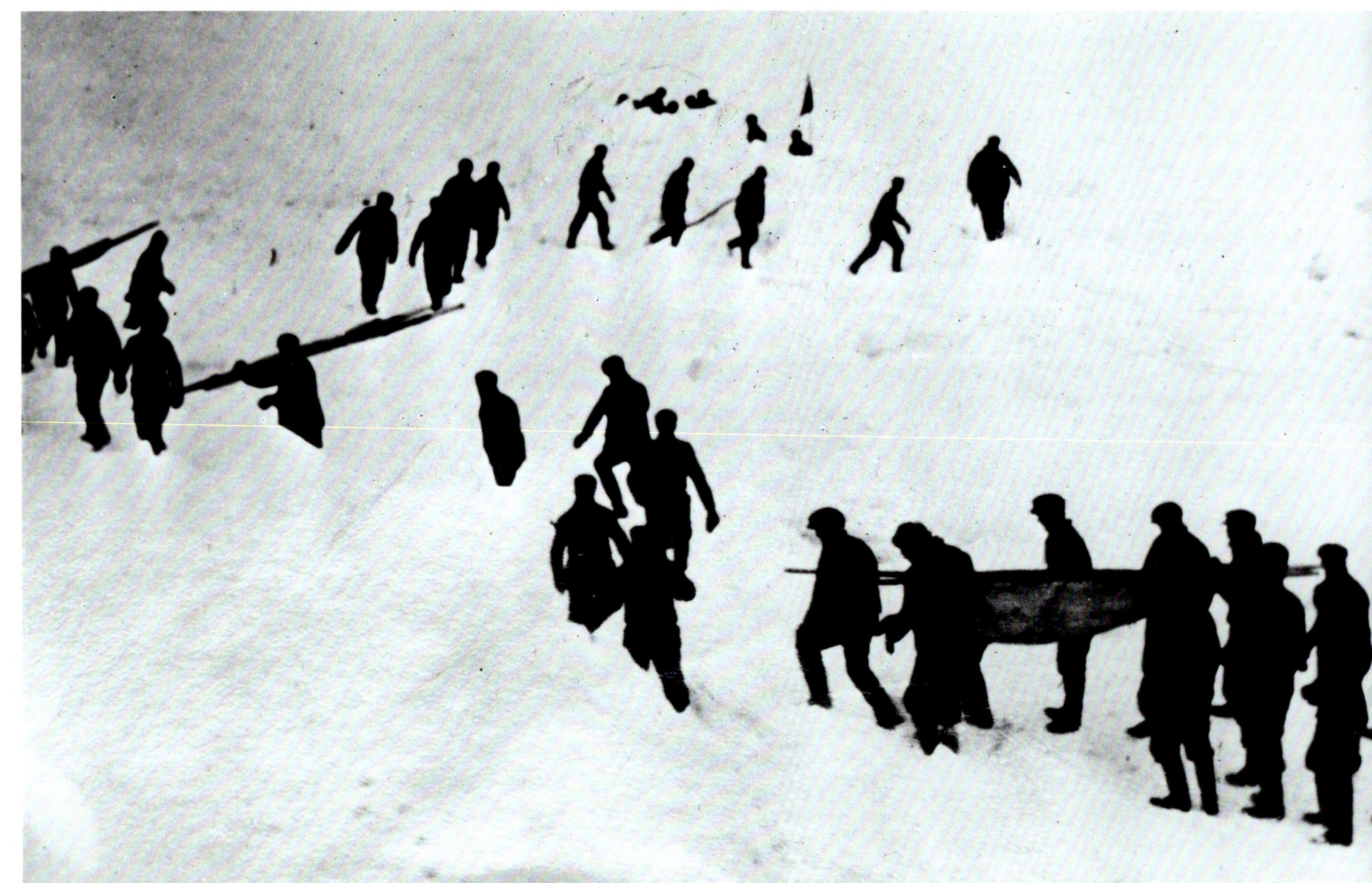

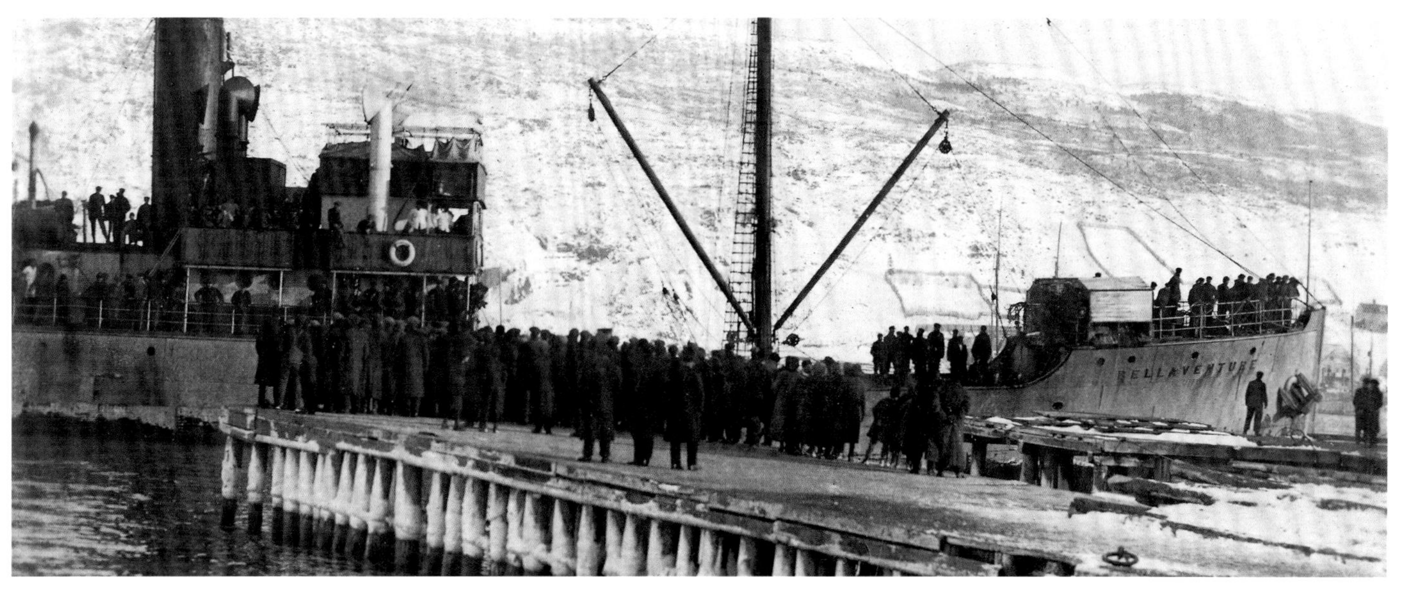
BELLAVENTURE

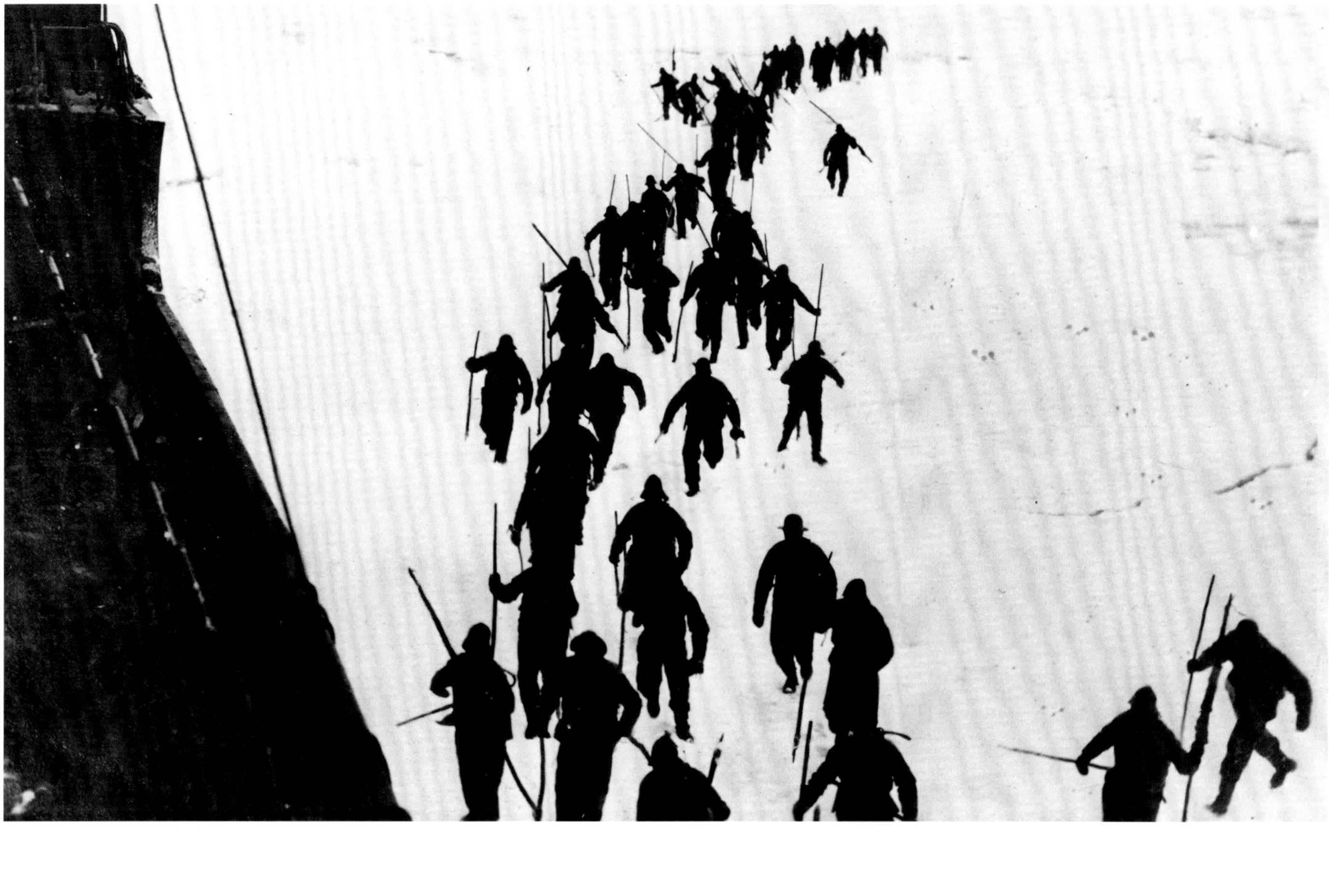

facing and below: SS *Bellaventure* crew bringing bodies and survivors of the Newfoundland Sealing Disaster aboard the ship, April 2–3, 1914

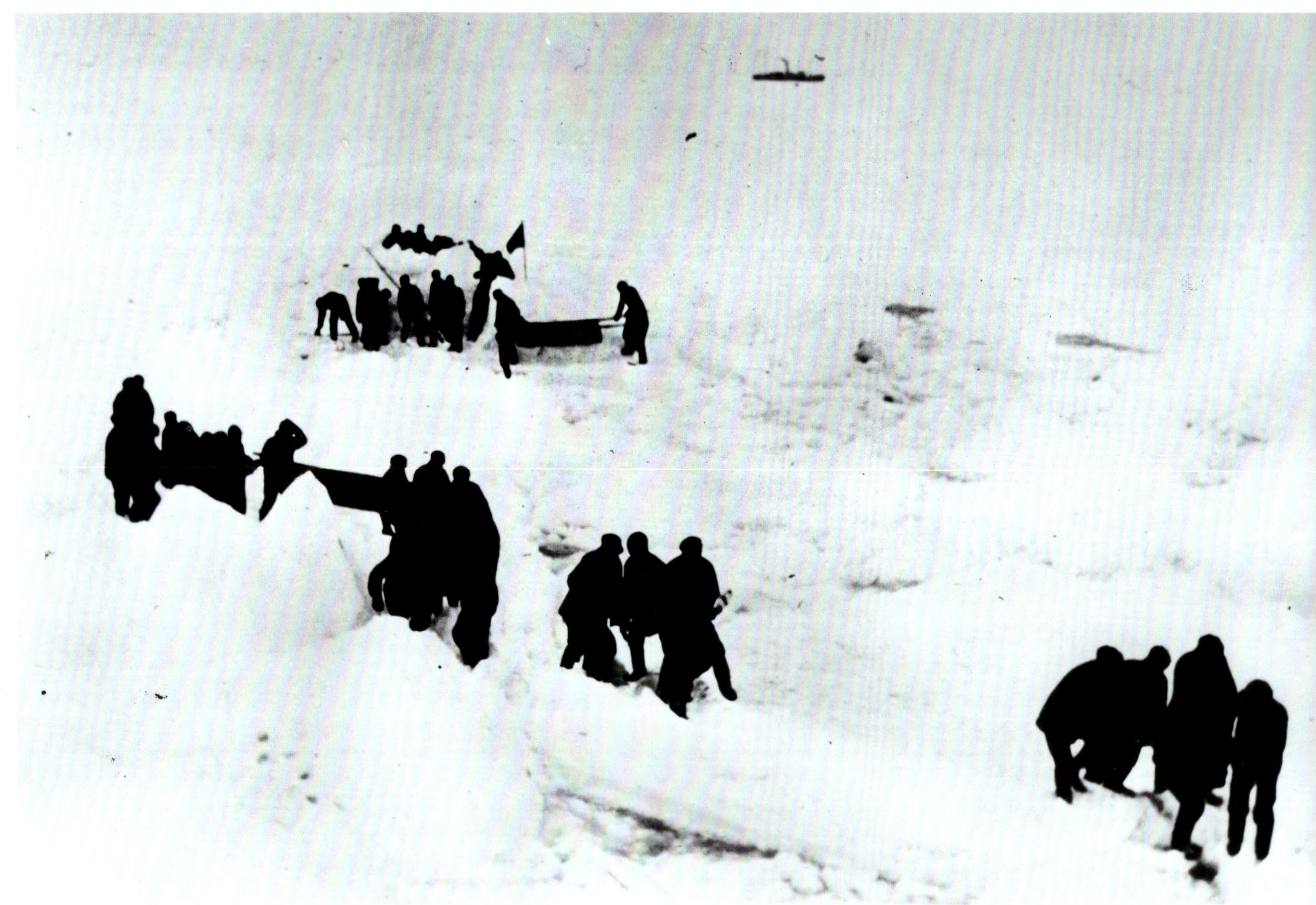

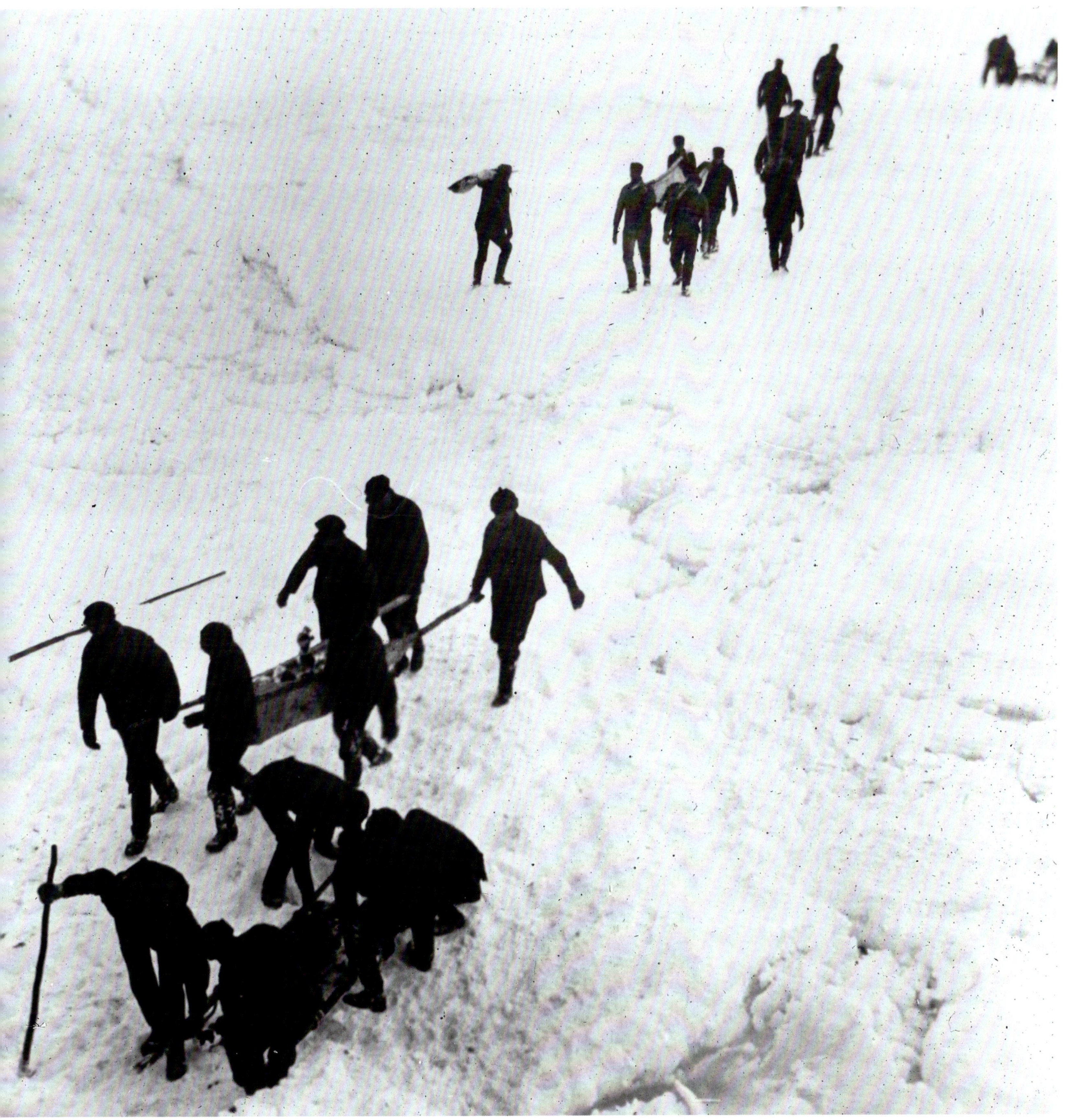

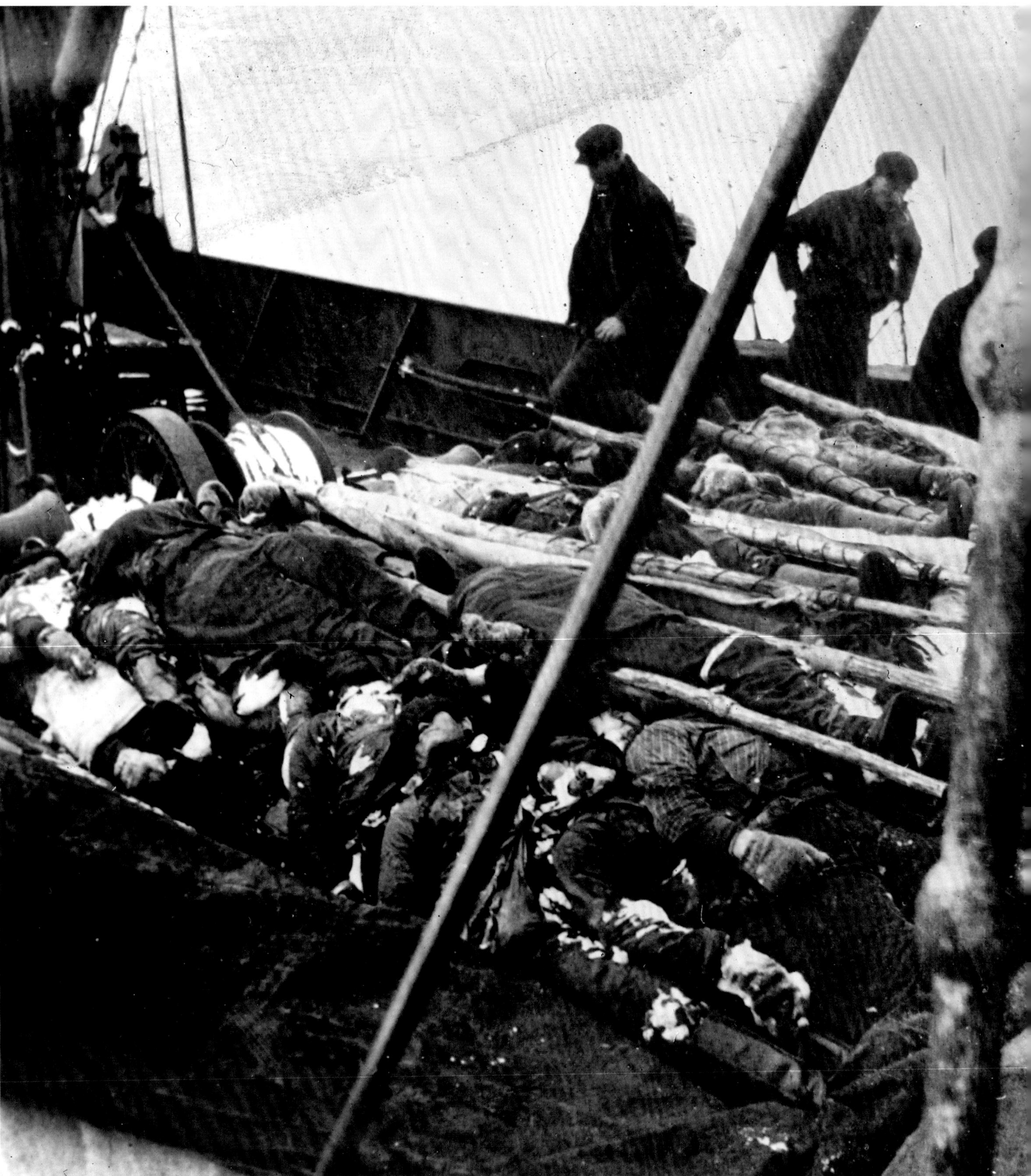

facing: Bodies from the Newfoundland Sealing Disaster stacked on the decks of the SS *Bellaventure*

below: Coffins, Newfoundland Sealing Disaster, April 1914

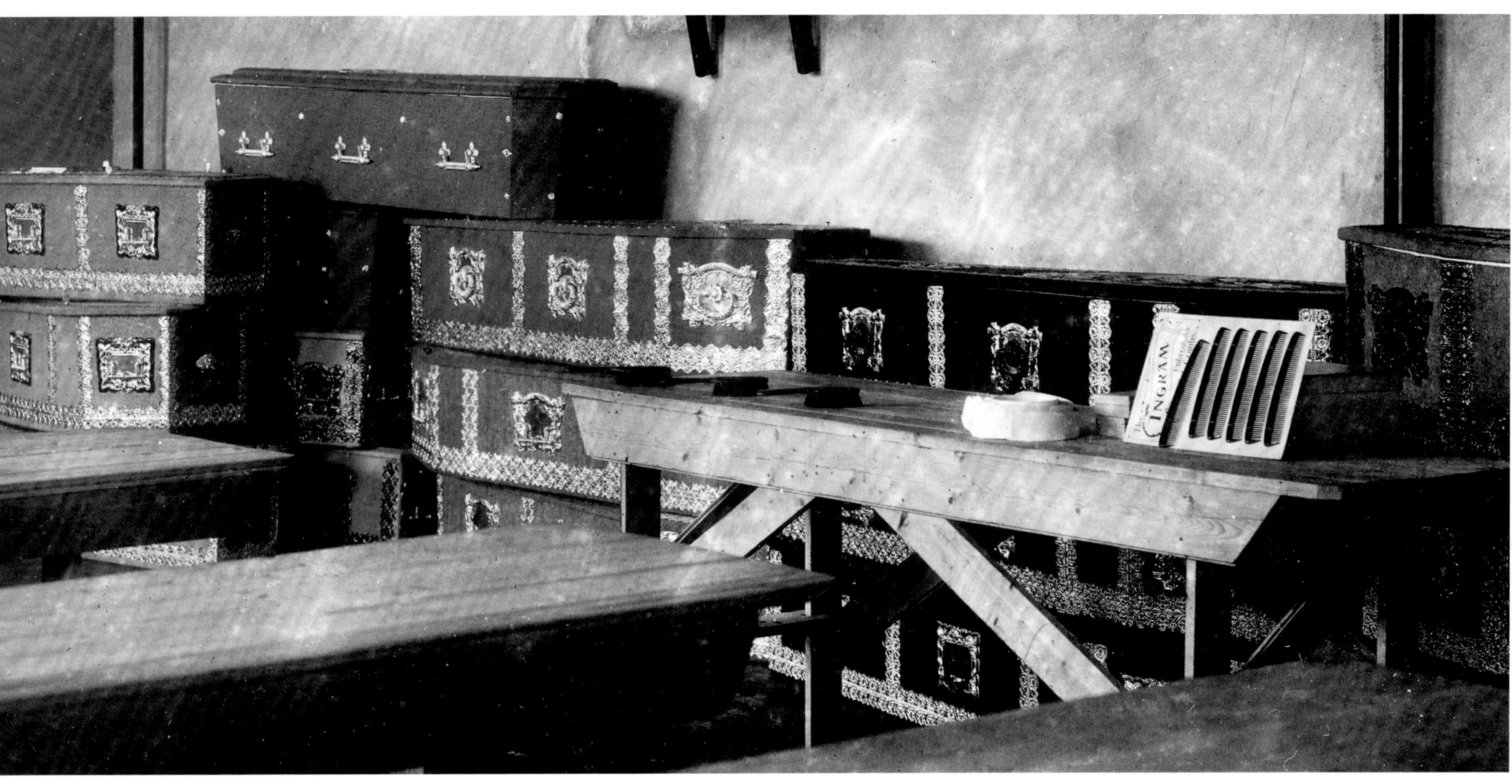

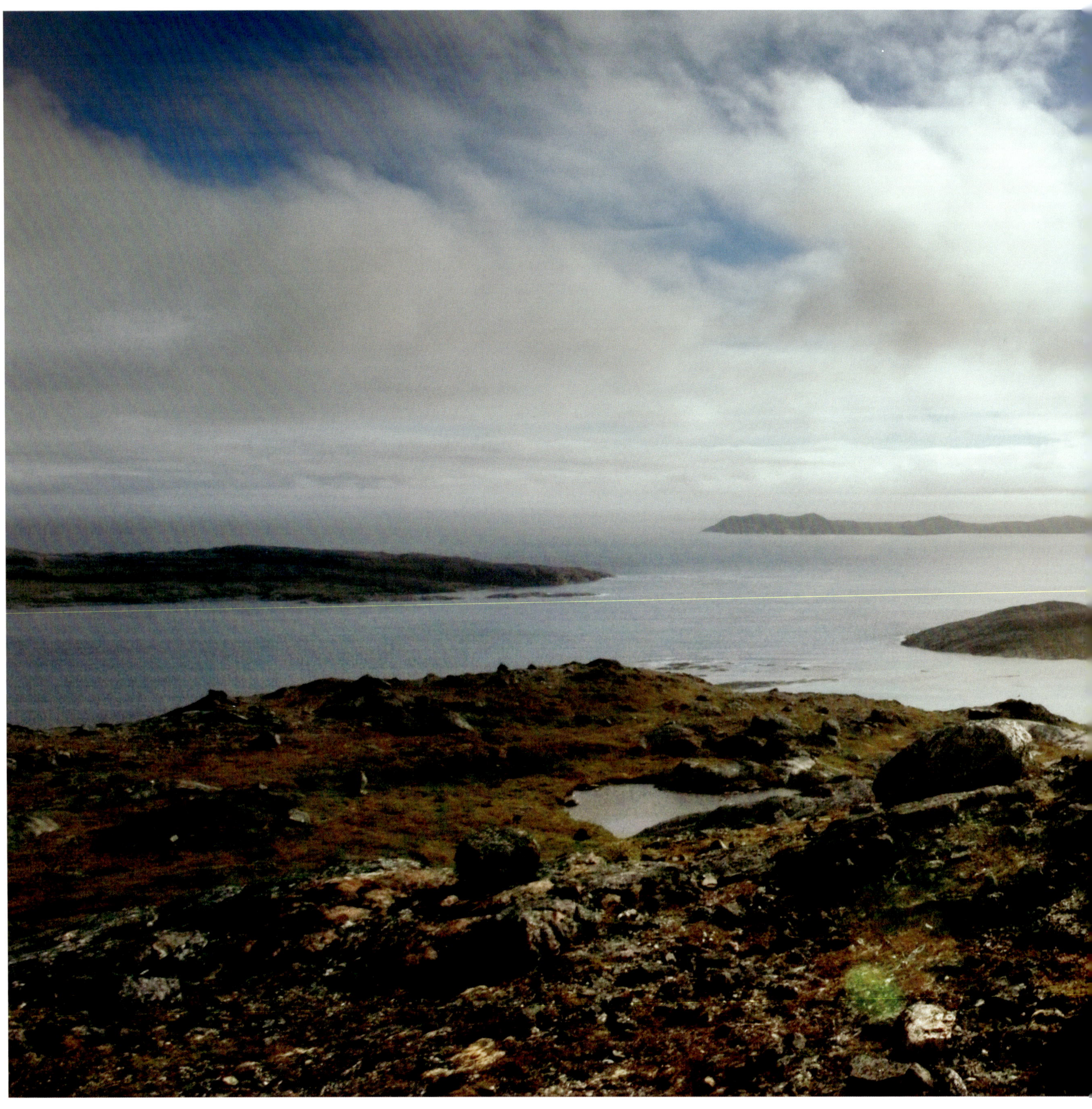

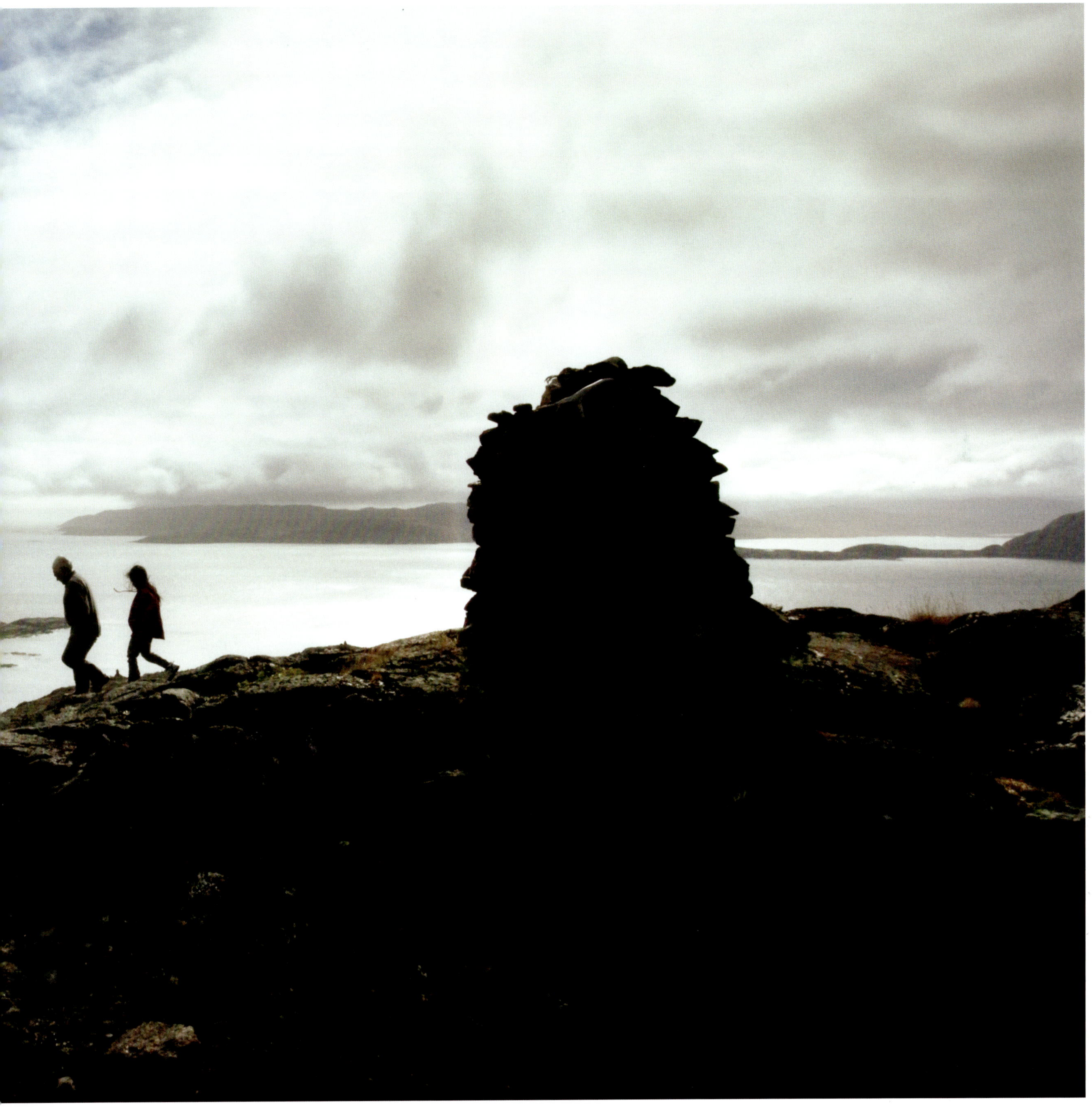

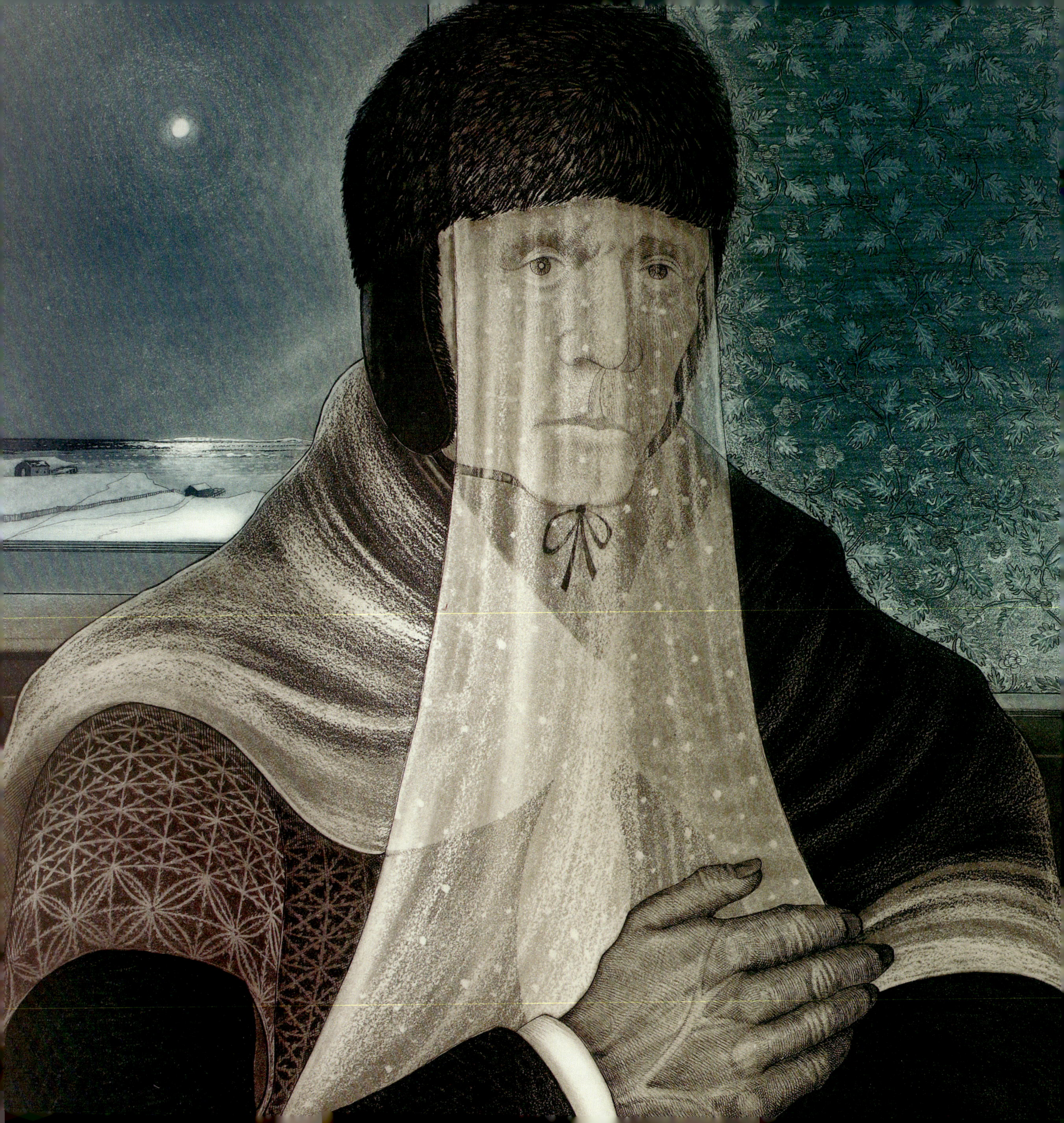

Oft on a Moonlit Night

THE STORY OF MUMMERS IN NEWFOUNDLAND

Caoimhe Ní Shúilleabháin

How oft' some of us here to-night
Have seen the "mummers out,"
As thro' the fields by pale moon light
They came with merry shout,
In costumes quaint, with mask or paint.

THE TERRA NOVEAN EXILE'S SONG
(quoted in *Dictionary of Newfoundland English*)

THE KNOCK ON the door in the still moonlit night silenced the chat in the kitchen. It was an unfamiliar sound; neighbours didn't knock before entering. Then a voice was heard, "Any mummers allowed?" and the family burst into nervous chatter. The mummers were here!

When the Irish and West Country English settled Newfoundland in the eighteenth century they brought with them the customs and dialects of their

facing: Detail from **Lone Mummer Inside**, 1979 (plate 35)

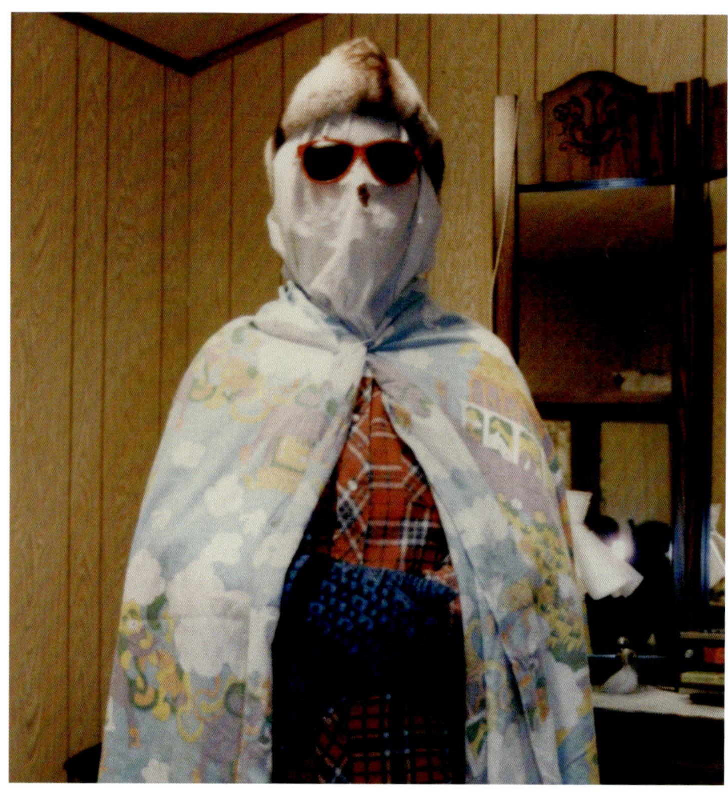

Wesleyville mummer, 1986

home countries, strong remnants of which can still be found in the province today. One tradition that still survives is that of mummering. During the twelve days of Christmas, people disguise their appearance and visit the houses of their neighbours, who must attempt to guess who these "mummers" are. After their identities are revealed, the mummers are expected to provide entertainment through music or song, and the hosts will usually reward the mummers in the form of food and drink. Of all the calendar customs (traditions built around significant dates) that these settlers introduced, mummering is one of the few examples to survive. Why is this? And why has mummering come to be such an important and iconic element of Newfoundland culture as a whole?

The Visiting Tradition in Newfoundland

Visiting has long been an integral part of Newfoundland culture, for several reasons. Given the isolation of outports, entertainment options were extremely limited; thus visiting became one of the most significant social activities in traditional society. Furthermore, land was of far less importance than the sea upon which most people's livelihood depended; thus there was little demarcation of boundaries between properties, and houses were built close together, which was conducive to visiting. The proximity of households also promoted co-operation between neighbours, a vital element for survival in these isolated communities.

Visiting neighbours were welcomed without ceremony into a kitchen warmly lit by a blazing stove. The kitchen was not considered a private space in the houses of Newfoundland outports, and anyone could—and would—enter unannounced. The rest of the house, however, was seldom accessed by those outside the family, save for the rare occasions when strangers or important visitors were entertained in the "room" (the formal parlour, which was used only under special circumstances).

Visiting intensified at Christmas, when all the men in the community were home from the fishing grounds, and indeed there was a certain obligation to visit at this time of year. In David Blackwood's hometown of Wesleyville the Christmas period preceded the men's spring departure for the Labrador fishery and was therefore an important opportunity to catch up with neighbours and friends. Mummering is part of this long-standing tradition of house visiting in Newfoundland.

The History of Mummering in Newfoundland

Mummering constitutes only one part of a large body of seasonal house-visiting customs that existed in Britain and Ireland. House visits traditionally formed part of the festivities at significant times such as at Christmas and on the quarter days marking the beginning of the seasons; many house-visiting customs, such as the Biddy Boys (February 1) and the May Doll (May 1), were linked to important events in the pastoral calendar. Few of these customs survived among Newfoundland settlers, perhaps because the economy and society were very much fishery-based rather than land-based. As the celebrated Irish folklorist Kevin Danaher observed, "Calendar Custom is deeply influenced by environment... It is intimately connected with the daily and yearly routine of work."[1]

Newfoundland's mummering tradition appears to have existed in both Irish- and English-settled communities throughout the province. There were two types of mummering: the house visit and the mummers' play, a type of folk play performed in people's homes, involving combat between two main characters and the subsequent revival of the slain victim by a doctor, always a comic figure. The house visit was the more common of the two and is the form that exists today. Until recently the house visit was presumed to be a degeneration of an older and more complex visiting tradition, such as the mummers' play, but now scholars believe it to be an independent and pre-existing tradition. The mummers' play, with its echoes of pre-Christian ritual in its theme of death and revival, appealed strongly to antiquarian scholars, which may have caused the house visit to be overlooked by earlier academics and researchers.[2] This is one of the reasons why it is impossible to determine how long mummering has existed in Newfoundland. However, it appears to have been well established by the mid-nineteenth century, and the earliest known written reference is an 1842 account in a book entitled *Excursions in Newfoundland*.[3]

The mummers' play is believed to have its origins in Britain and to have spread from there to Ireland and Newfoundland. It served as a method of gaining access to the houses of the better-off and is thought to have been strongly motivated by the desire of working-class people to raise money at Christmas, as traditionally money would be sought in those houses where the play was performed. This motivation would have been redundant in the essentially egalitarian Newfoundland outport society, however.[4] In most outports there simply was no upper class, so the mummers' play was likely an urban phenomenon in Newfoundland.

facing: David Blackwood and Carl Barbour in his kitchen, Newtown, Newfoundland, c. 1979

There is evidence for the Christmas house visit in West Country England—but it does not appear to have existed in Ireland, though several Irish customs are similar.[5] (The Wren Boy tradition, for example, is an Irish visiting custom that takes place on December 26. Groups of people visit homes in the community carrying an effigy of a wren and reciting a specific verse. This custom still exists in some Irish-settled communities in Newfoundland.) The house visit, unlike the mummers' play, took place among social equals, and its main purpose was the visiting of neighbours, the reaffirmation of social bonds and the sharing of "Christmas cheer."

The typical Newfoundland mummers' house visit shares many characteristics with other kinds of house-visiting traditions in both Ireland and Britain, including the visitors' attempts to hide their identities through cross-dressing, with clothes turned inside out, faces blackened and voices disguised. The visitors' activities—knocking and requesting entry, sometimes playing pranks on the householders—are also common to these types of traditions.

Newfoundland mummers were not collectors, which is probably the biggest difference between Newfoundland mummering and other home country house-visiting traditions.[6] Hospitality in the form of food and drinks was anticipated at each house visited, but the mummers did not expect to be given anything to take away with them. This was likely an adaptation to the non-cash society of outports, whose economies were based on truck (a non-cash system of credit and debit operated by merchants and fishermen).

Mummering in Practice

Mummers in Newfoundland, moving in groups of various sizes, did their rounds during the twelve days of Christmas. Central to the visit was the guessing game, where the hosts attempted to work out the identity of the visitor. Disguise was of the utmost importance, because in such small, tight-knit communities individuals could be recognized just as easily by their hands or their gait as by their faces. Therefore, hands were kept covered, voices disguised, clothing was stuffed to try to hide body shape, and many mummers even attempted to alter their gait.

A typical method of covering the face was to wear a veil, fastened behind the head or secured by headgear, and made from muslin, lace, net curtain, cotton or any other similar fabric.[7] David Blackwood's mummers are generally represented in their veiled state, with their faces visible through the veil. In some images—such as *Lone Mummer Inside* and *Lone Mummer with Cat*—one hand is exposed, indicating that the identity of the mummer was probably known.

Once one mummer's identity was determined, guessing the identities of the accompanying mummers became a vastly easier task. To escape such detection by association, people sometimes chose to mummer with others outside

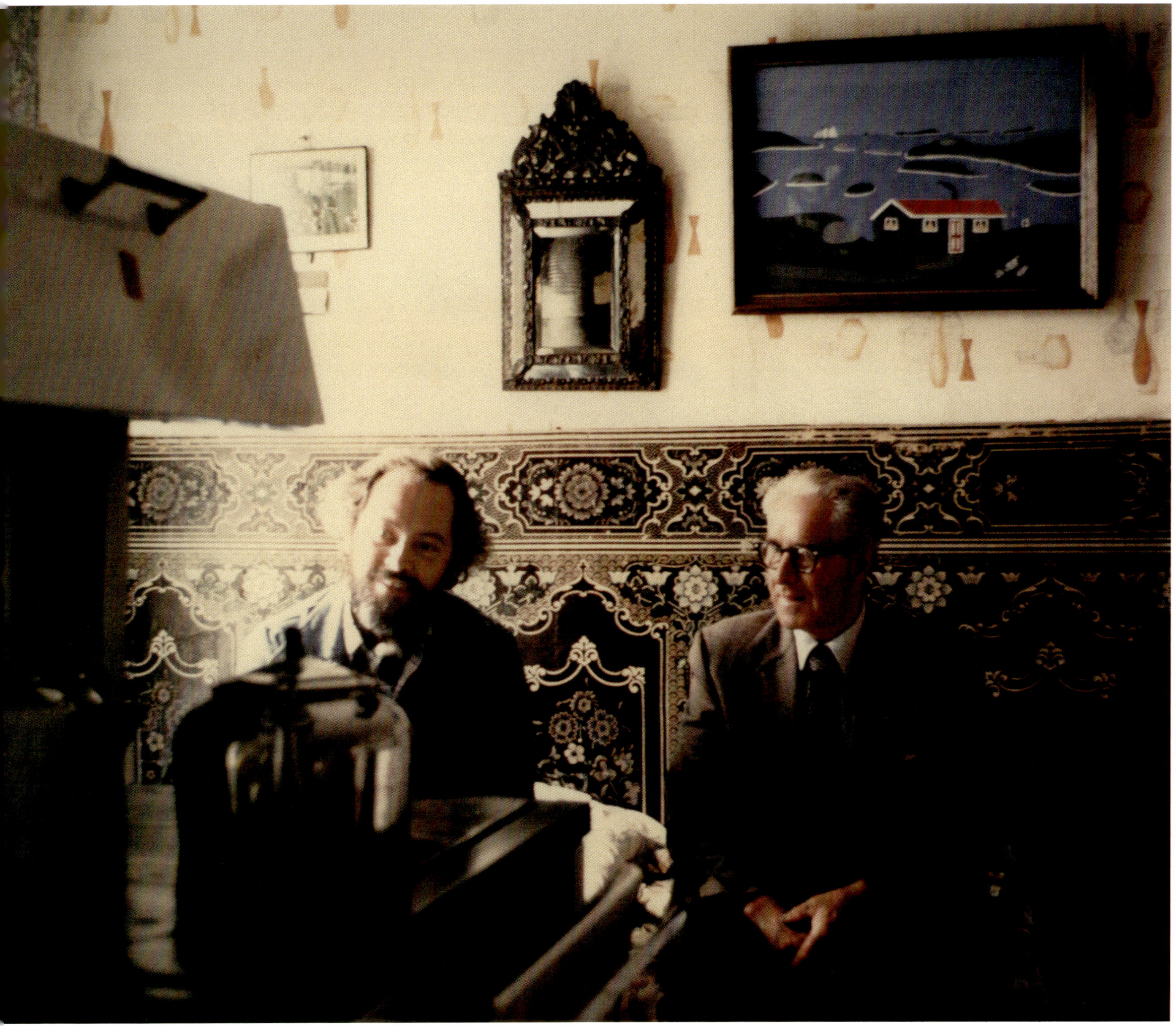

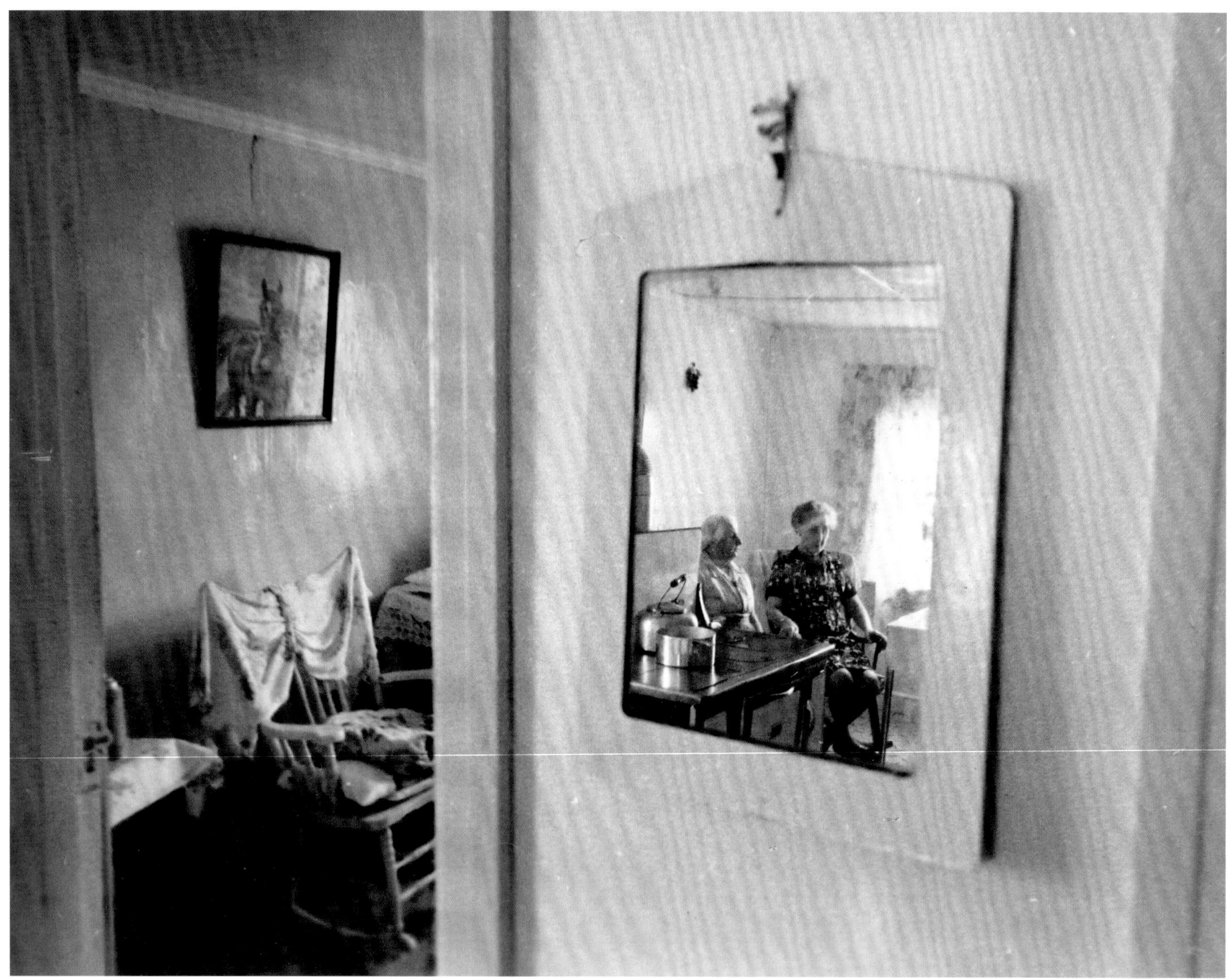

their immediate friendship group. However, families did mummer together, as represented in David Blackwood's print *Mummer Family at the Door.*

When the mummers arrived at a door they would knock, thereby setting the stage for a visit that was out of the ordinary. In *Mummer Family at the Door,* the family is waiting on the threshold for permission to enter—unusual in outport Newfoundland, where neighbours would walk into the kitchen without ceremony or invitation. These visitors often looked quite frightening, and the protection offered by their disguise gave them licence to act out of character—or in the character of their temporary identity. Behaviour

facing: Aunt Mary Fifield and visitor reflected in a mirror, 1969

often departed from what would normally be expected of a visitor to another's home. Mummers might "carry on" with the hosts in an overly familiar manner or behave aggressively towards those present.

In the majority of cases the mummers would eventually unmask. This unmasking was an important part of the visit, as to remain unidentified would be to interfere with the hospitality and reciprocity central to the notion of visiting, and would violate acceptable social behaviour.[8] Once the mask was removed, visitors reverted to their normal social roles and the social order was, in a sense, restored.

Strangers and the Lone Mummer

Mummers appeared as strangers to their own society during the visit.[9] In an isolated and close-knit outport community such as Wesleyville, the figure from the outside—the stranger—was a fearful character who brought with him the unfamiliar and the unknown. In these intimate communities the behaviour of neighbours was predictable, and the behaviour of strangers, as of mummers, was not.

When mummers announced their visit with a knock on the door, those inside reacted with apprehension, similarly to how they would react to strangers, testifying to a fear of the unknown. Until a mummer was unmasked and the face of a neighbour revealed, an uneasy undercurrent marked the visit, with the household unsure of how to behave around these strange figures whose behaviour did not fit with societal norms. The disguised figure was particularly frightening to children. Indeed, punishment by a mummer was often used to threaten children should they step out of line. As John Widdowson explains in his equating of mummers with strangers: "A stranger has something of the aura of many supernatural/invented figures in that his origins and intentions are unknown, he lacks definite location and positive identification, his behaviour is unpredictable (and therefore less controllable) and he is potentially malevolent and dangerous."[10]

The mummer often claimed to be from far away, as a stranger would be, perhaps from a distant outport or even from the North Pole. This idea is represented in David Blackwood's print *Lone Mummer Approaching,* which gives the impression that the mummer is journeying from afar.

The strangeness and the otherworldliness of these visitors has been captured by David Blackwood in many of his striking prints. The transparent veils on Blackwood's mummers suggest the border between the real and the supernatural, between that everyday civilized behaviour necessary for the successful functioning of a community and those darker, more threatening aspects that can be present in such a community, those that lurk beneath the surface and to which the mummering tradition gives an opportunity for release. With moonlight reflecting off the ghostlike figures, Blackwood's representations of the mummers evoke an atmosphere that is almost otherworldly.

This notion of stranger was accentuated in the visit of the lone mummer. Although the phenomenon of a lone mummer was relatively rare, the individual male adult is classified as one of ten different groupings of mummers.[11] The lone mummer might speak little, would refuse any hospitality in the form of food or drink, and might leave without revealing himself. He therefore functioned outside community norms and, to a certain extent, outside the norms of the mummering tradition.

Even as he acknowledged the rarity of lone visits, David Blackwood represented this strange visitor in a significant number of his works. The lone mummer was strange, fascinating, threatening. Even in comparison with the usual mummering visit, an occasion when people behaved out of character and one that could be marked by a certain disquietude, the visit of the lone mummer was extremely disconcerting. Blackwood himself describes how the lone mummer in Wesleyville was seen as an ominous sign, a harbinger of death. These visits were therefore undoubtedly a source of unease to the hosts.

Mummering's Dark Side

When disguised as mummers, house visitors overcame their usual inhibitions, with the disguise offering a release from normal roles in society, allowing participants to act out of character without risking the censure of the community.[12] In some instances mummers punished members of the community who had acted unacceptably on some occasion or in a manner that could have disrupted the delicate equilibrium of tightly woven outport communities. This punishment often took the form of a physical beating. The interdependence of such communities required that conflict and hostility be avoided, and mummering provided a socially accepted means of dealing with conflicts that did arise.[13]

Mummering may also have been an important release for those living in strict Methodist societies such as Wesleyville. The Methodist tradition in Newfoundland was quite conservative and retained a strong evangelical streak; thus pastimes such as drinking, card playing and dancing were discouraged.[14] Mummering may have offered a culturally acceptable opportunity to overcome these restrictions.

Mummering and Society

Mummering served a variety of functions distinct from those described above. The social aspect of the visit was hugely important, and at a time of year when members of the community were expected to visit every house in the area mummering was a way of fulfilling the obligations of Christmas visiting. New settlers had an understandable desire to hold on to some remnants of the life they knew in their home country, and through this a sense of home and community in the new country was developed. The process of disguising and recognizing also served to test and confirm existing relationships in the community.[15]

After Newfoundland joined Confederation in 1949, the province gradually began to open up to external influences. Modernization crept in and with it came an inevitable erosion of the traditional way of life. Mummering faded in many places across the province.

However, in more recent years the tradition has experienced something of a revival, and today it has to an extent become symbolic of the uniqueness of Newfoundland culture, epitomizing what differentiates the province from the rest of Canada. The demise of the cod fishery in recent years has forced many Newfoundlanders to leave the province in search of employment, and for many of these emigrants mummering has nostalgic associations with all that makes Newfoundland and Christmas special and memorable.

Life in outport Newfoundland may have changed immensely since David Blackwood observed the mummers in his own household in Wesleyville, but even in this much-altered society this form of ritual visiting has a place at the heart of the province's culture.

CAOIMHE NÍ SHÚILLEABHÁIN *is a translator in the Irish Unit of the Directorate General of Translation at the European Commission.*

Notes

1. Kevin Danaher, *The Year in Ireland* (Cork, Ireland: Mercier Press, 1972), 11.
2. Martin Lovelace, "Christmas Mumming in England: The House-Visit," *Folklore Studies in Honour of Herbert Halpert*, ed. Kenneth S. Goldstein and Neil V. Rosenberg (St. John's: Memorial University of Newfoundland, 1980), 271–81.
3. J.B. Jukes, *Excursions in Newfoundland* (London, 1842), 1:220–21.
4. Lovelace, "Christmas Mumming," 271.
5. Ibid.
6. Herbert Halpert, "A Typology of Mumming," in *Christmas Mumming in Newfoundland*, ed. Herbert Halpert and G.M. Story (1969; repr., Toronto: University of Toronto Press, 1990), 38.
7. J.D.A. Widdowson and Herbert Halpert, "The Disguises of Newfoundland Mummers," in *Christmas Mumming in Newfoundland* (see note 6), 149.
8. Caoimhe Ní Shúilleabháin, "The Wren Tradition and Other Visiting Customs in Newfoundland and Ireland" (MA diss., Memorial University of Newfoundland, 2004), 42.
9. Melvin Firestone, "Mummers and Strangers in Northern Newfoundland," in *Christmas Mumming in Newfoundland* (see note 6), 75.
10. Widdowson, J.D.A., *If You Don't Be Good: Verbal Social Control in Newfoundland* (St. John's: Institute of Social and Economic Research, 1977), 70.
11. Louis Chiaramonte, "Mumming in 'Deep Harbour': Aspects of Social Organization in Mumming and Drinking," in *Christmas Mumming in Newfoundland* (see note 6), 93–94.
12. John F. Szwed, "The Mask of Friendship: Mumming as a Ritual of Social Relations," in *Christmas Mumming in Newfoundland* (see note 6), 113.
13. Faris, "Mumming in an Outport Fishing Settlement," in *Christmas Mumming in Newfoundland* (see note 6), 139.
14. Liza Piper, "Newfoundland Methodism," Newfoundland and Labrador Heritage, 2000, www.heritage.nf.ca/society/methodist.html.
15. *Encyclopedia of Newfoundland and Labrador*, ed. J.R. Smallwood (St. John's: Newfoundland Book Publishers, 1984), 2:264.

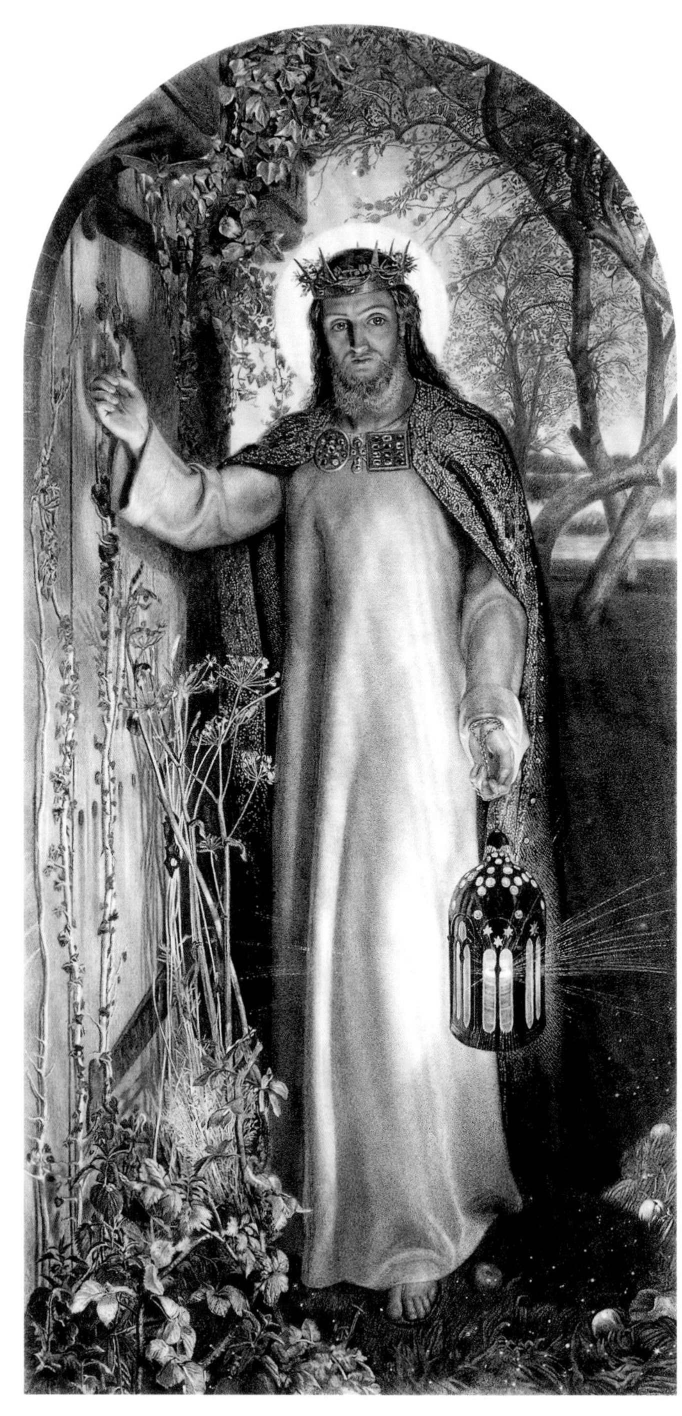

William Henry Simmons after William Holman Hunt, *The Light of the World*, 1860.
Engraving and stipple engraving on chine collé

John Henry Cardinal Newman

BRITISH · 1801–1890

"Lead Kindly Light" · 1833

. . .

Lead, kindly light, amid the encircling gloom
Lead Thou me on!
The night is dark, and I am far from home—
Lead Thou me on!
Keep Thou my feet; I do not ask to see
The distant scene–one step enough for me.

I was not ever thus, nor pray'd that Thou
Shouldst lead me on.
I loved to choose and see my path, but now
Lead Thou me on!
I loved the garish day, and, spite of fears,
Pride ruled my will: remember not past years.

So long Thy power hath blest me, sure it still
Will lead me on,
O'er moor and fen, o'er crag and torrent, till
The night is gone;
And with the morn those angel faces smile
Which I have loved long since, and lost awhile.

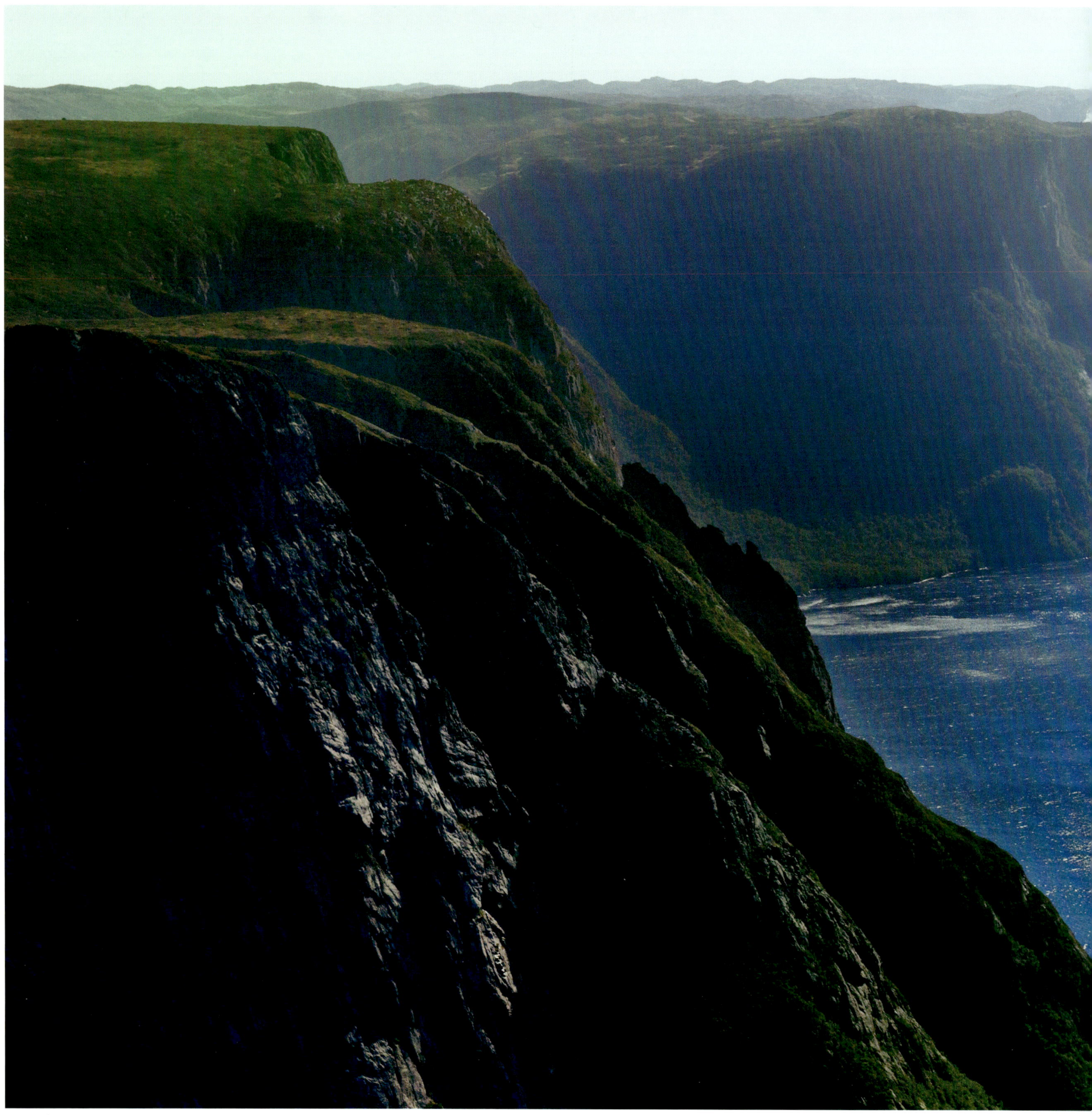

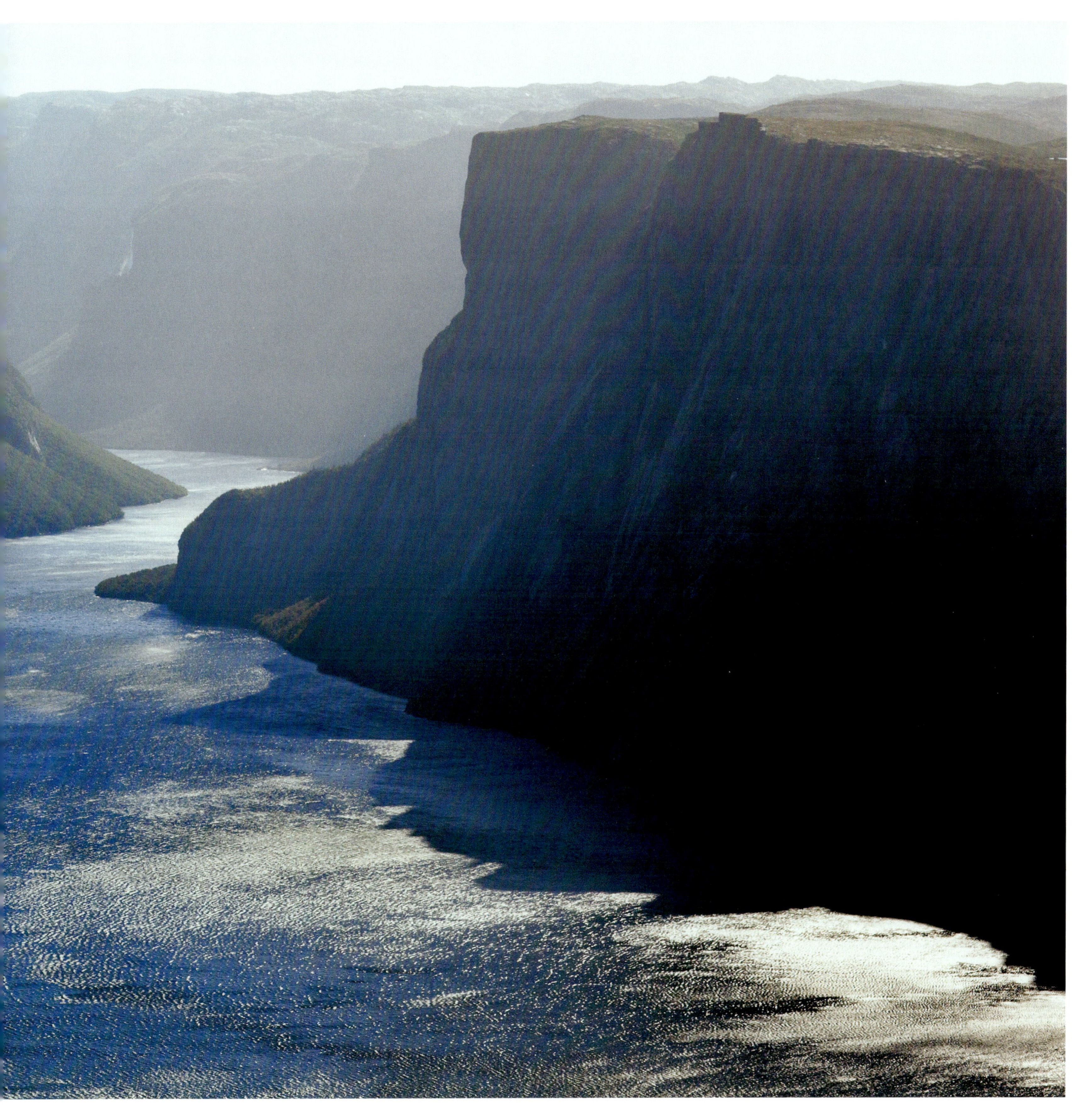

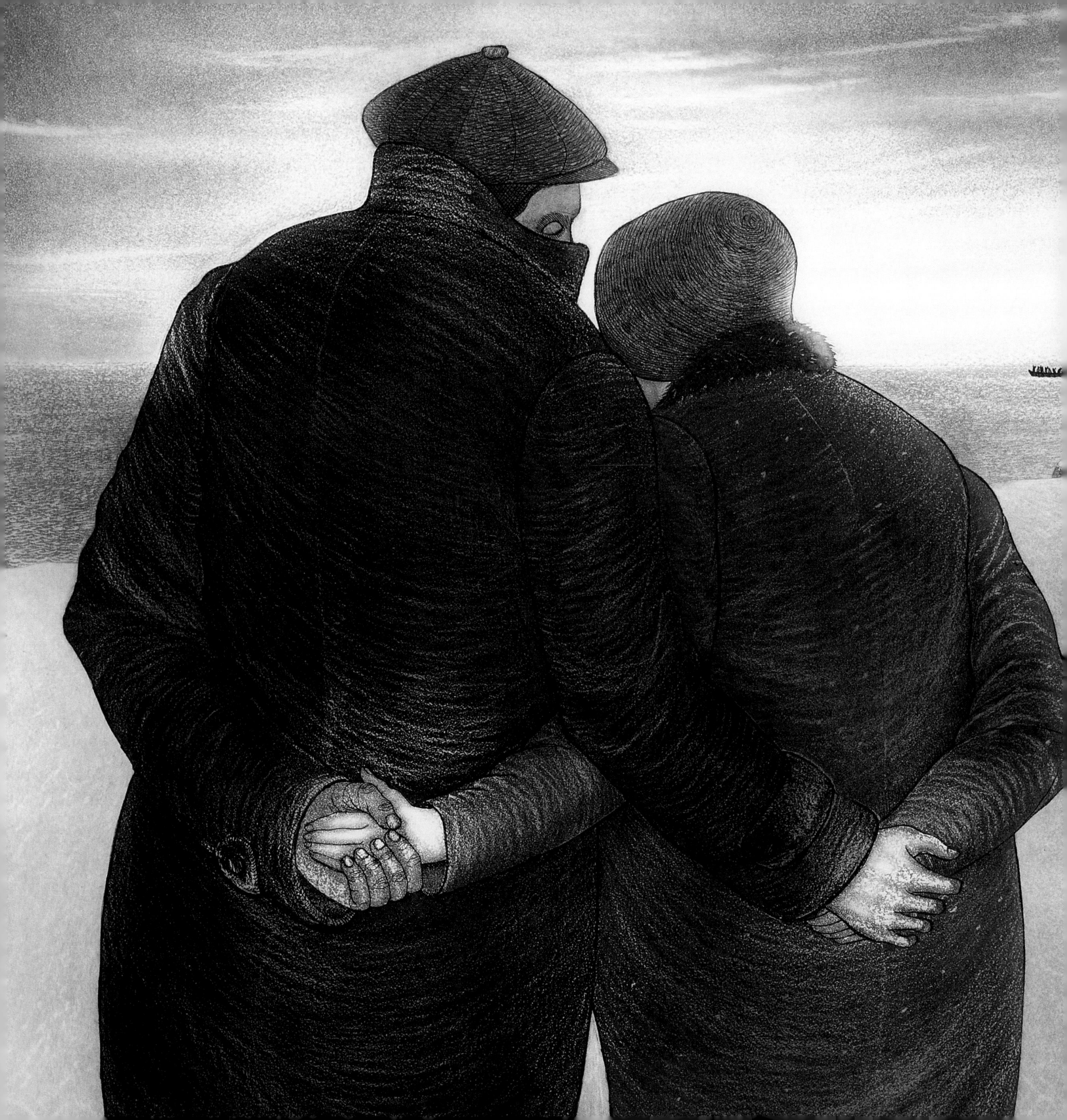

Candles in the Dark

Michael Crummey

THERE'S A DISTANCE in the work of David Blackwood that has always felt like home to me.

It's the distance between Blackwood himself and the gone world of outport Newfoundland he portrays so obsessively in his etchings—the growing gap between Newfoundlanders like myself and the lives of those who came before us. To my eyes at least, that distance is one of the things that make his art so resonant, so beautiful and haunted and eerily alive.

Five years ago my wife and I bought a summer house in Western Bay, a small outport on the north shore of Conception Bay. The house was built eighty years ago and it was still in the Dalton family when we purchased it from two elderly brothers. Both men had long ago moved to St. John's and were reaching an age where they felt incapable of looking after the property anymore, but they were there with their wives when we first went to look at

facing: Detail from **Aunt Mag and Uncle Elias Feltham**, 1976 (plate 28)

facing, top: The Dalton House in Western Bay, Newfoundland

facing, bottom: The North Shore of Conception Bay from the South Side Road, Western Bay

the house, a white two-storey with a pantry added on at the back. There's a well in the pantry that provides the place with water, and the brothers told us about helping their father dig all thirty feet of it and boxing the walls with shale when they were boys. I had never met the Daltons before, but they told me my grandmother was a good friend of their mother. Nan and my Aunt Helen, when she was a teenager, spent many afternoons drinking tea in the kitchen we now own. We didn't make the highest offer on the house, as it turned out, but they sold it to us because of the family connection. They liked the idea of having someone they "knew" living in the place.

At the end of the south-side road is the site of the first Methodist cemetery in the community, dating from the early 1800s. My great-grandfather is buried there, though there's no headstone or marker to identify the exact location. No one seems to know if the man was born in Newfoundland or where he might have arrived from otherwise, but either way he's as far back as I can trace the family ancestry. The name is Irish, a fact I discovered while giving a reading in Belfast a decade ago. There are still plenty of Crummeys in and around Belfast, though there was a significant migration from the north of Ireland to the English West Country several centuries back, and Dad's family could have come from either place.

My father left Western Bay at the age of seventeen to work the ore mills in Buchans, the mining town in central Newfoundland where I was born. Before we bought the Daltons' house I'd never spent more than a week-long summer vacation here, back when I was a youngster, and I had come through for only brief visits after Nan died in the early 1970s. So this particular community was never my home by any practical definition. But there is nowhere I experience a deeper sense of belonging, a feeling that I'm standing at the doorstep of everything that's made me who I am. In fact, I get a certain satisfaction from not knowing where the family came from originally. Whatever country those first European settlers left behind is irrelevant to my sense of myself and my place in the world. *Newfoundlander* is as complete a description as I seem to need or want.

I feel the same flush of recognition whenever I encounter David Blackwood's artwork. His Newfoundland, too, is a kind of self-enclosed universe—isolated and independent, barely touched by the outside world and quite unlike anywhere else on God's green earth. Except for the occasional appearance of a Union Jack atop Job Sturge's house or at half-mast outside Aunt Gerti Hann's, there is virtually no external referent or context for Blackwood's Wesleyville or Bragg's Island, for the schooners on the Labrador or the men working on the ice floes off the coast. Or else the external referents are so distant and vague as to be largely meaningless. English, Irish, a dash of Welsh, French and Scots, along with a handful of other minor influences

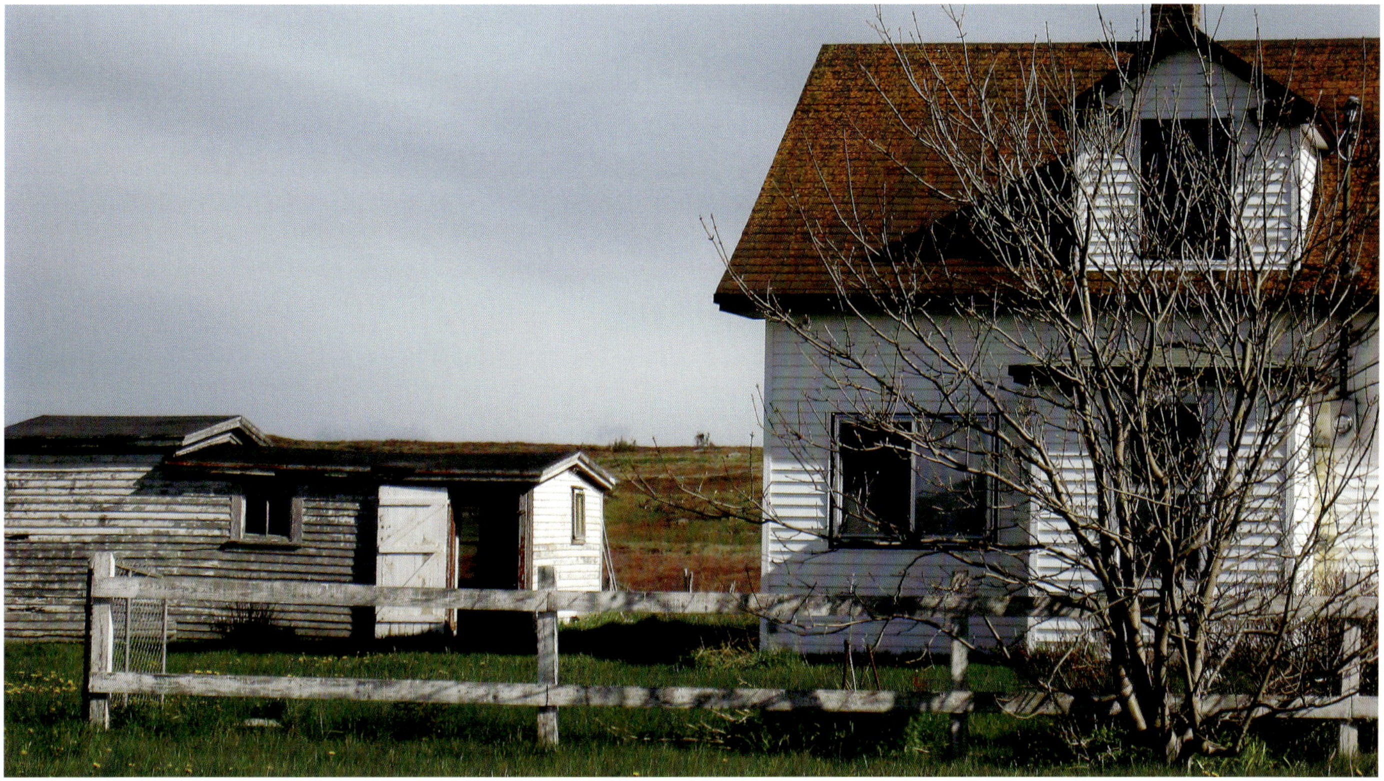

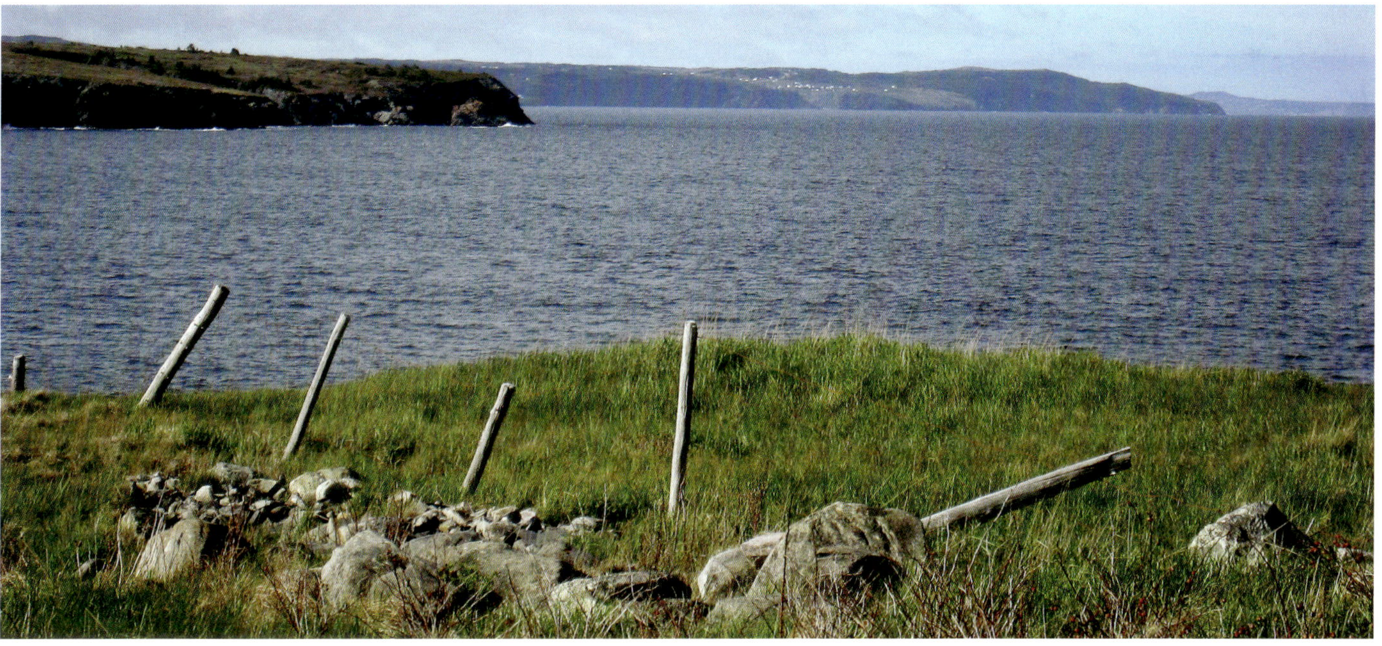

David Blackwood, Wesleyville, June 1957 (left); Arthur Crummey, aged 15 (right)

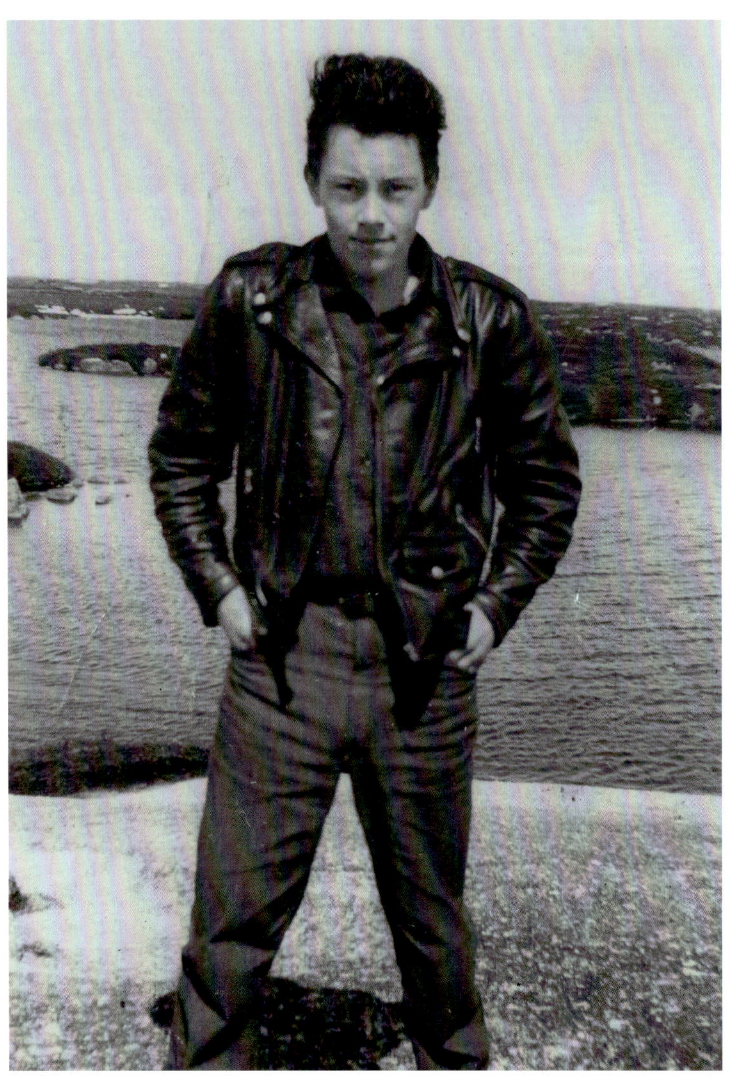

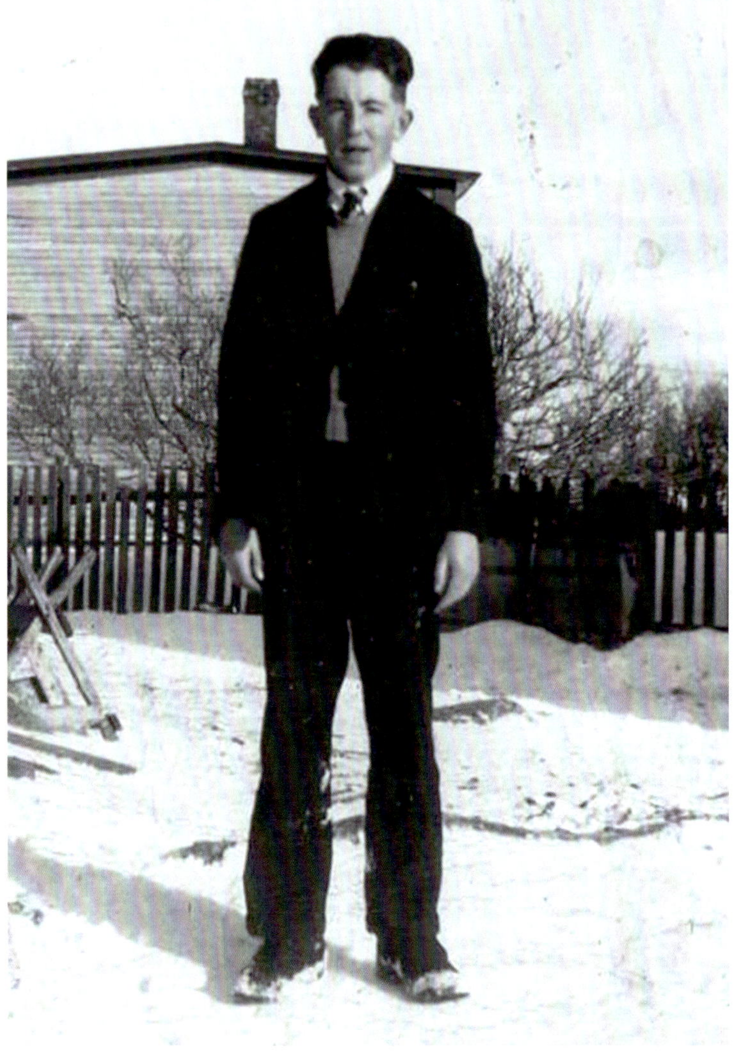

in the mix—you can tease out the individual strains if you care to. The fact is that nothing adequately explains who these people are but the place itself.

JUST BEYOND THE Methodist cemetery in Western Bay there's a path to the lighthouse, a dirt road that winds through pasture and the outlines of old farm gardens framed by stones picked from the ground and tossed clear of the decent soil. Here and there a depression marks the location of a house or root cellar from back in the days when fishermen lived along this entire stretch of road. From the lighthouse you can see across the water as far as the tip of Conception Bay, and at night the North Shore is dotted with the lights of a dozen tiny communities all the way to Baccalieu. Just over the headland to the south is Bradley's Cove, which was a fishing village in its own right before it was abandoned in the early sixties and now is used as a community pasture through the summer months.

If I needed reminding of the fact, Western Bay makes it abundantly clear that the Newfoundland my father knew is worlds away from my own experience of the place. And that is more or less true for just about everyone living in the province now. Dad was born into a pre-industrial society that had persisted unchanged in most respects for several hundred years. In the span of his lifetime, Newfoundland underwent a transformation that much of the rest of Western society dragged out for two centuries or more. Many of the particular circumstances that made Newfoundlanders so distinct are no longer the defining forces they were fifty years ago. The isolation of outport communities, both from one another and from the larger world, the dearth of formal education, the economic dependence on the inshore cod fishery and seal hunt, the vulnerabilities resulting from exposure to extreme weather and lack of medical care—all of these things we know only through stories now, through the memories of those fewer and fewer still alive who experienced them. And though no one in their right mind could wish those times back, I've always felt a curious homesickness watching the last of that world settle into displaced memory, into myth. I've spent my entire life as a writer trying to bridge that distance. Or, at the very least, to point across it towards the lights of those tiny communities winking along the shoreline.

Years before I had any notion of writing as a vocation, before I had any conscious sense of what I was up to, I was drawn to Blackwood's depiction of a lost Newfoundland that feels ancient and somehow timeless. I've always felt a kindred impulse, an obsession with a time and place that is gone and yet manages to be, improbably and vibrantly, very much with us.

In the 2001 Douglas & McIntyre collection *David Blackwood: Master Printmaker*, there's a picture of the young Blackwood taken in Wesleyville in 1956. It shows a teenager in a leather bomber jacket and black shirt, jeans with wide turned-up cuffs, a slightly unkempt James Dean haircut. Hard to imagine him on the deck of the family schooner, the *Flora S. Nickerson*, or cleaning fish in that getup. He would have looked more at home at a Bill Haley concert. It's only the barren landscape behind the youngster that gives away where he's from.

Blackwood was born a decade after my father, and less than ten years before Newfoundland joined Canada. He grew up in Wesleyville, surrounded by people who made their lives in the Labrador fishery and the annual spring seal hunt. The presence of old-world Newfoundland in the rhythm of daily lives and in the obsessive round of stories told in kitchens and on fishing stages would have been palpable. But, as that black and white picture suggests, the times were about to be changing. The influx of American popular culture through the huge U.S. military presence in Newfoundland during the Second World War and the sea change about to be unleashed by Confederation were barrelling down the pipe. And though by all appearances he adopted the new fashions as they arrived, it's the world the artist knew as a child that has preoccupied him ever since.

In some metaphorical way, I like to see myself standing in that photograph with Blackwood, dressed in the fads of modern days, though the landscape that frames us is something of another order altogether. Something enduring and forbidding, and missed easily enough if all that interests you is the foreground.

THERE'S AN IDEALIZATION in Blackwood's portrayal of outport Newfoundland that a passing appraisal might dismiss as mere romanticism. The perfect picket fences and tidy buildings of Wesleyville and Bragg's Island, the weathered and wise faces of sea captains and grandmothers haloed with a kind of unearthly light might seem, outside of the larger context, to be part of the burgeoning genre of tourist art: bucolic pictures of dories and kitchen stoves and mummers in outlandish costumes and hand-stitched quilts hung on a line. It's inevitable, I expect, that the predominant response to the kind of wholesale cultural change that Newfoundland has experienced recently is nostalgia. Many writers and artists over the last half century have given in to that temptation, depicting outport life as a simpler place and a simpler time, less complicated and therefore somehow purer. Blackwood's take is more nuanced and complex, and far closer to the truth. As he presents it, those days were simpler only in the sense that the complications in one's life were, by and large, less convoluted. Yet they were starker and the consequences usually more dire. That fact, more than any other, I think, is what made Newfoundlanders who they were.

It's difficult these days to have a real sense of how close to the edge people in these pre-Confederation outports—even bustling, successful communities like Wesleyville—were living. Most of the graves in the Methodist cemetery down the road from our home in Western Bay

Arthur Crummey with his parents, brother and sister, c. 1945

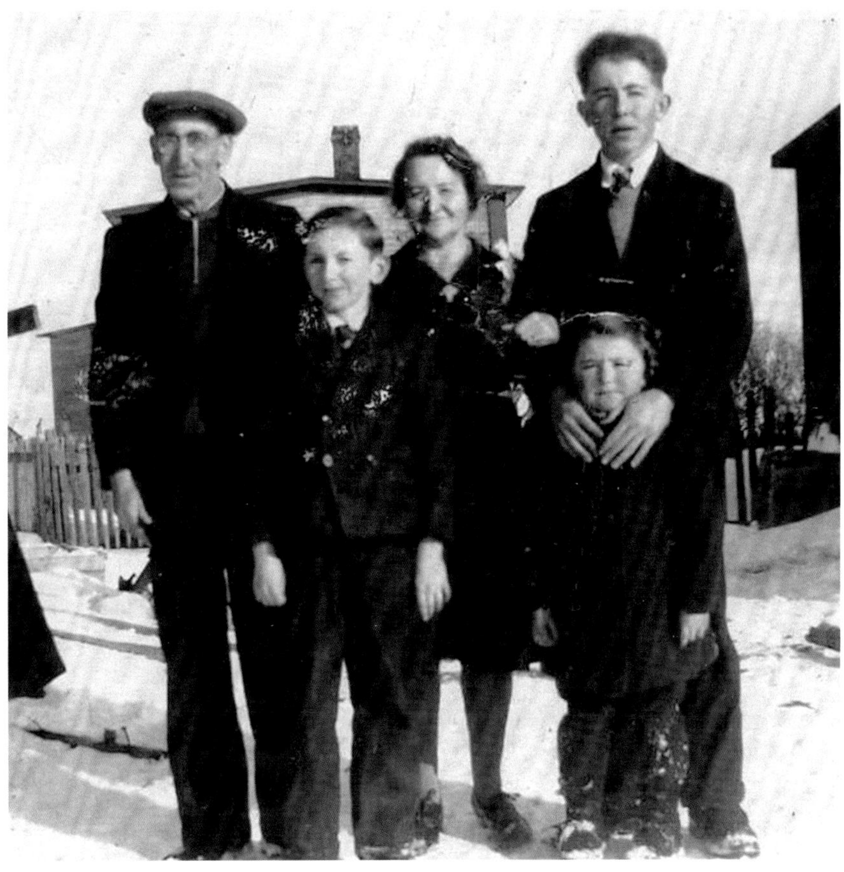

are anonymous now, though there are still a handful of ancient headstones legible enough to read. The largest standing stones mark the graves of two brothers and a sister buried side by side, all of them dead before the age of twenty-five through one calamity or another. Anyone familiar with Newfoundland graveyards will tell you this isn't an especially unusual configuration to come upon.

In Brake's Cove, on the island's west coast, there are two tiny graveyards tucked away on a hill at one end of the beach. At its height, Brake's Cove was home to seventeen families, many of them with ten to twelve children. The beach is occupied now by a row of summer houses, all of them owned by families who left for the "growth centre" of Cox's Cove in 1966 and 1967 under the Smallwood government's controversial resettlement program. The path to reach the graveyards winds up a steep hill and back into the woods. In spots you have to grab tree branches to keep your feet on the slope, and it's difficult to imagine how a body was carried up to its final rest. But all the decent ground closer to the houses was set aside for cultivation, planted with the potatoes, turnips and cabbage, carrots and parsnips that kept people fed through the winters. At the smallest of the two cemeteries, four headstones lie on the grass, the broken marble pieced together like jigsaw puzzles—a husband and wife, the husband's sister and one of the couple's sons, who drowned as a young man, lying there. In the clearing above the headstones you can see the outline of a rowed potato garden set beside the graves for years before the cove was abandoned.

That knife-edge—how much of a life was given over to simply keeping body and bones together, how suddenly and unpredictably people could be stripped of all that their knowledge and work and care had set in store—is apparent everywhere in Blackwood's work. The starkest examples of this are the *Lost Party* prints, which first made his reputation, of sealers wandering helplessly or freezing to death on the icefields. But it's a strain that runs through all his work. Look at the huddle of figures perched atop the cliffs in *Cape Islanders Waiting*. There's nothing else human on

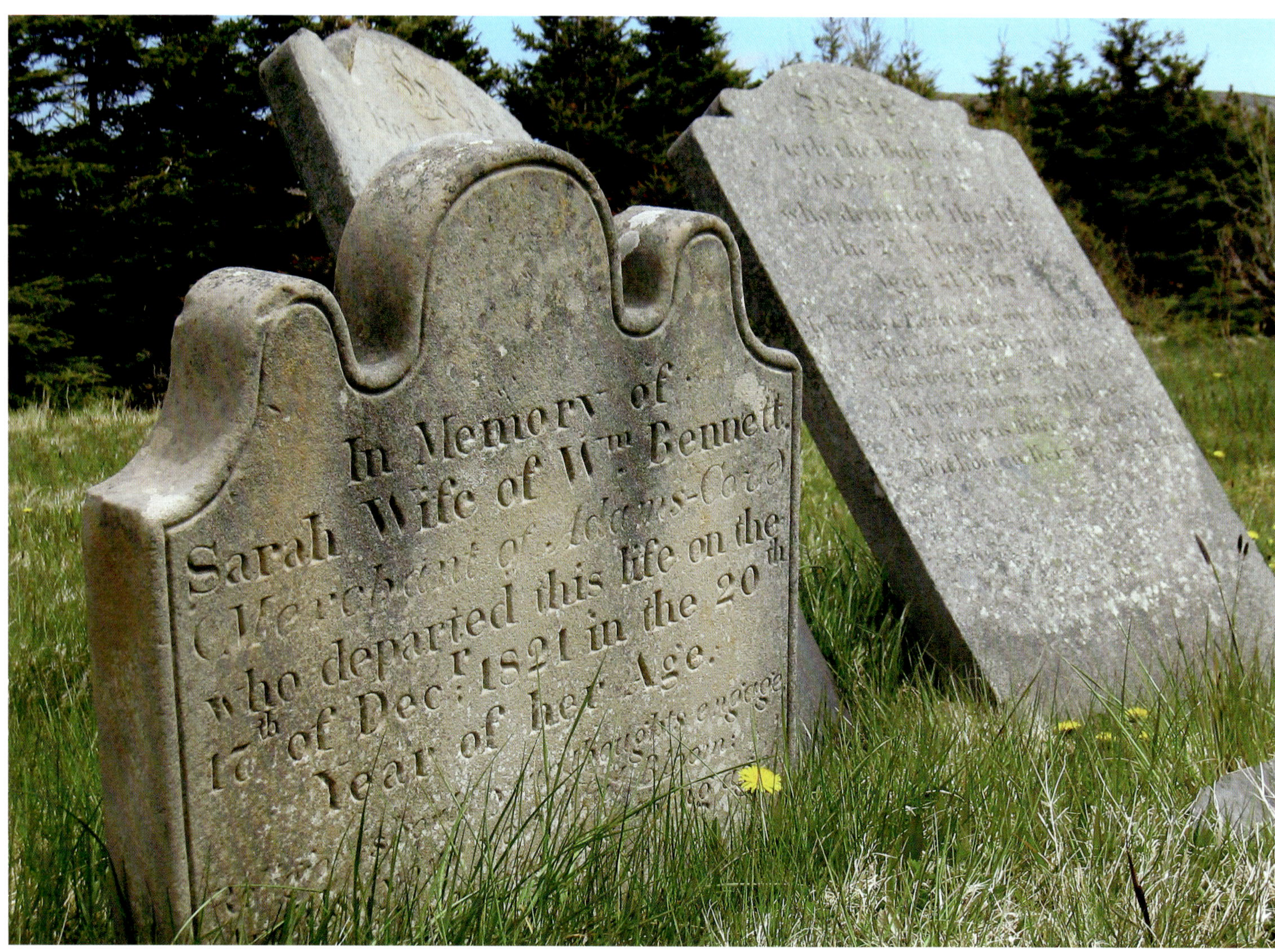

Methodist cemetery on the
South Side Road, Western Bay

the scene, no sign of settlement or habitation, of paths or tools or utensils, nothing to offer shelter or comfort. They are stripped of any sense of safety, even identity. They've circled together, instinctively it seems, and they look displaced somehow, lost. It's as if the group had been dropped onto this barren shoreline out of the heavens and abandoned there. There's only the implacable rock of the island, and beyond it the ocean, and that tiny vulnerable congregation dwarfed by it all.

In *April Iceberg off Bragg's Island* my eye is always drawn to the forlorn line of people on the headland. Those figures, in the context of the sheer sea cliffs and the enormous iceberg, are almost invisible. They have the look of the last surviving posts of an ancient fence that has long since fallen and disintegrated. And that fragile line of figures appears over and over in Blackwood's prints—often as witnesses to or participants in some disastrous event: the helpless audience on the ice in *The Burning of the ss Viking*, those ant-like columns of people departing Bragg's Island in *Gram Glover's Dream* or the lost sealers in *Great Lost Party Adrift*. Even in the celebratory *Wedding on Bragg's Island*, the guests trail out behind the newlyweds like a ragged wedding train, the line dipping across the winter barrens behind them as far back as the distant church. It's as if the only human marks on the landscape of any significance are the people themselves. And even they seem fragile, evanescent. Candles in the dark.

Blackwood's idealization of his Newfoundlanders is born of seeing them in the context of the challenges they overcame in simply subsisting. He's expressing admiration, the kind of respect for the accomplishments of his elders he was taught as a child. The neat picket fences, the handmade boats and nets and tools, the complex knitting patterns of sweaters and trigger mitts, the fastidiously kept houses—all the signs of civilized human society are marks of a community's success in establishing itself in a capricious, almost malevolent world. In Blackwood's work, that success is no small victory. And it is never more than provisional.

IN THE FALL OF 2008 my wife and I had the chance to sail along Newfoundland's south coast, a stretch of shoreline that is in some ways most reminiscent of the Newfoundland that was. There are only a handful of outports dotting the hundreds of kilometres between the Burin Peninsula and Rose Blanche on the southwest corner of the island. All of them are fishing communities established in the early 1800s, many of them still accessible only by sea. On a deceptively warm fall afternoon we anchored off an unoccupied cove called Little Garia Bay and were ferried ashore in Zodiacs and let loose for a couple of hours. A handful of cabins lay across the cove, including one with a satellite dish, but there was no one around. For miles along the south coast there wasn't a sign of human presence. The only trees lay in sheltered arms on the south sides of bays.

facing: Flora S. Nickerson

Out of the wind, the weather was unseasonably warm, and some passengers sat in their shirtsleeves to enjoy the sun while Holly and I and a handful of others hiked into the backcountry. It was a steep ascent through the brambles, but above the crest the countryside was bald stone and standing water, the land stripped of topsoil and scraped almost level by retreating glaciers. Erratics—large stones dropped on the landscape as the glaciers moved off—dotted the surface. There were sightings of ptarmigan, an osprey and a bald eagle, but the hundreds of square kilometres within view gave the impression otherwise of being completely empty. It was a gorgeous, almost apocalyptic landscape. It felt like a glimpse of how the world might have looked a hundred million years ago. Of how it might look a hundred million years on. There was something in the size and implacable wilderness of the place that seemed to diminish the human, to highlight how small we are in the grand scheme of things, how inconsequential and insignificant. It made me want to stay close to Holly as we wandered inland, to have her within arm's reach.

Blackwood has always set the human element in his art within that same looming scale, of ocean and headland and relentless night. In *The Great Peace of Brian and Martin Winsor*, their "great peace" is dwarfed by the massive sickle blade of the whale curving over the lost hunters, by the iceberg that dominates the background. In *Loss of Flora S. Nickerson* and in *Fire Down on the Labrador*, the human disasters are happening in the wings, barely registering against the vastness of the north Atlantic and its creatures. I've always been struck by how often light is a peripheral presence in Blackwood's best-known work, whether in the torches of sealers adrift in the cavernous winter night, the helpless ship ablaze in *Fire Down on the Labrador*, or the tangential gleam of sunrise or sunset just offstage in his many seascapes. Even the brilliant sun in *Hauling Job Sturge's House* feels more like the cold glow of ice and stars that frequently illuminates Blackwood etchings. In his prints, the red light of a torch or a kerosene lamp set against the monumental indifference of the natural world seems both ephemeral and heroic.

And it's here that he comes closest to the truth of the place, to the reality of my father's world, which I've been trying to express in my own obsessive way for twenty-five years now. At the heart of David Blackwood's art is a sense of awe, in all meanings of the word. The sheer scope and the eerie beauty of the landscape he depicts inspire both wonder and dread in equal measure. The cumulative effect of his work is to make the history of settlement on this island—and all human endeavour beside it—seem impossibly fragile and fugitive. And heartbreakingly tenacious and honourable.

MICHAEL CRUMMEY *is a writer and poet.*

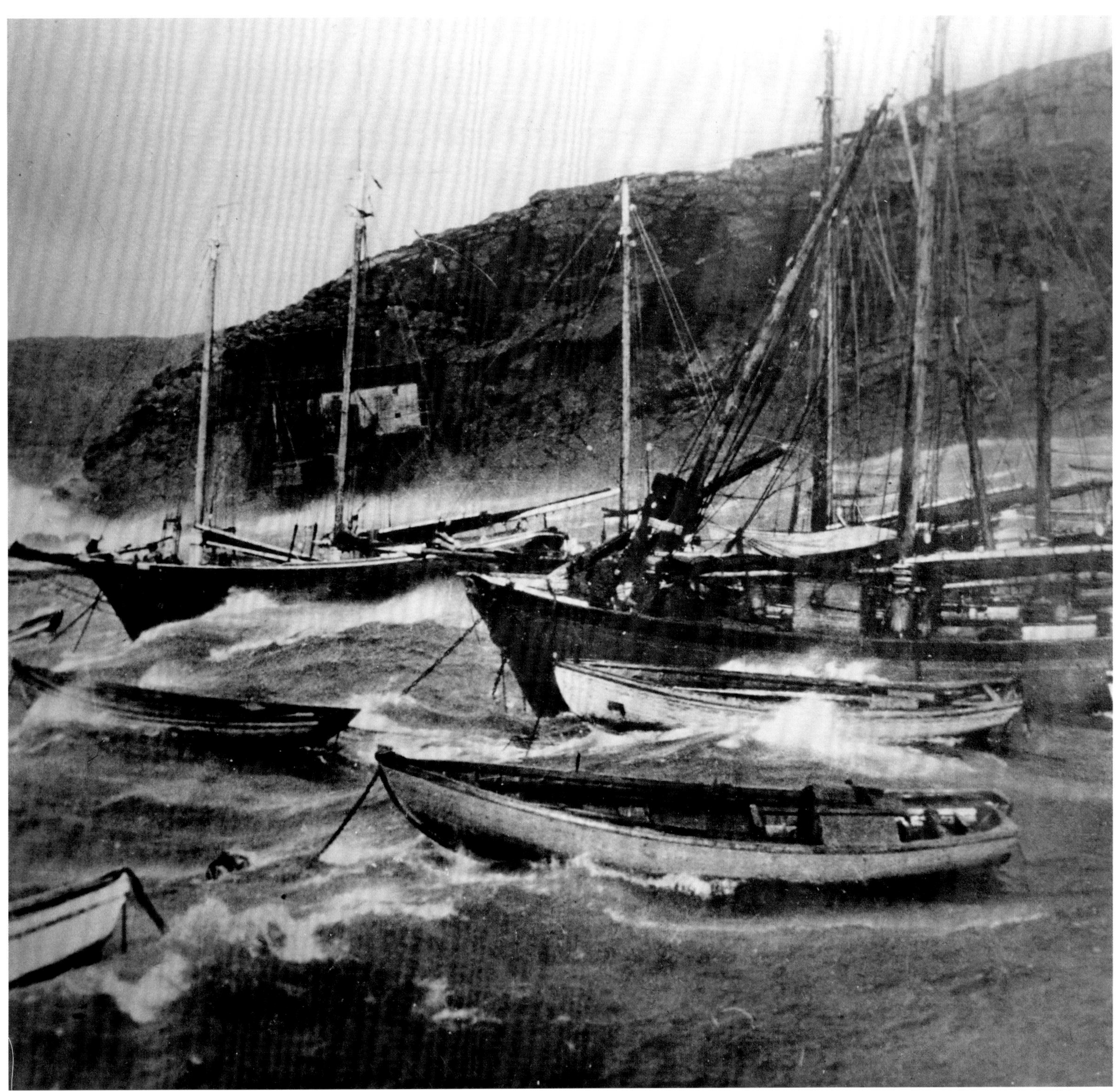

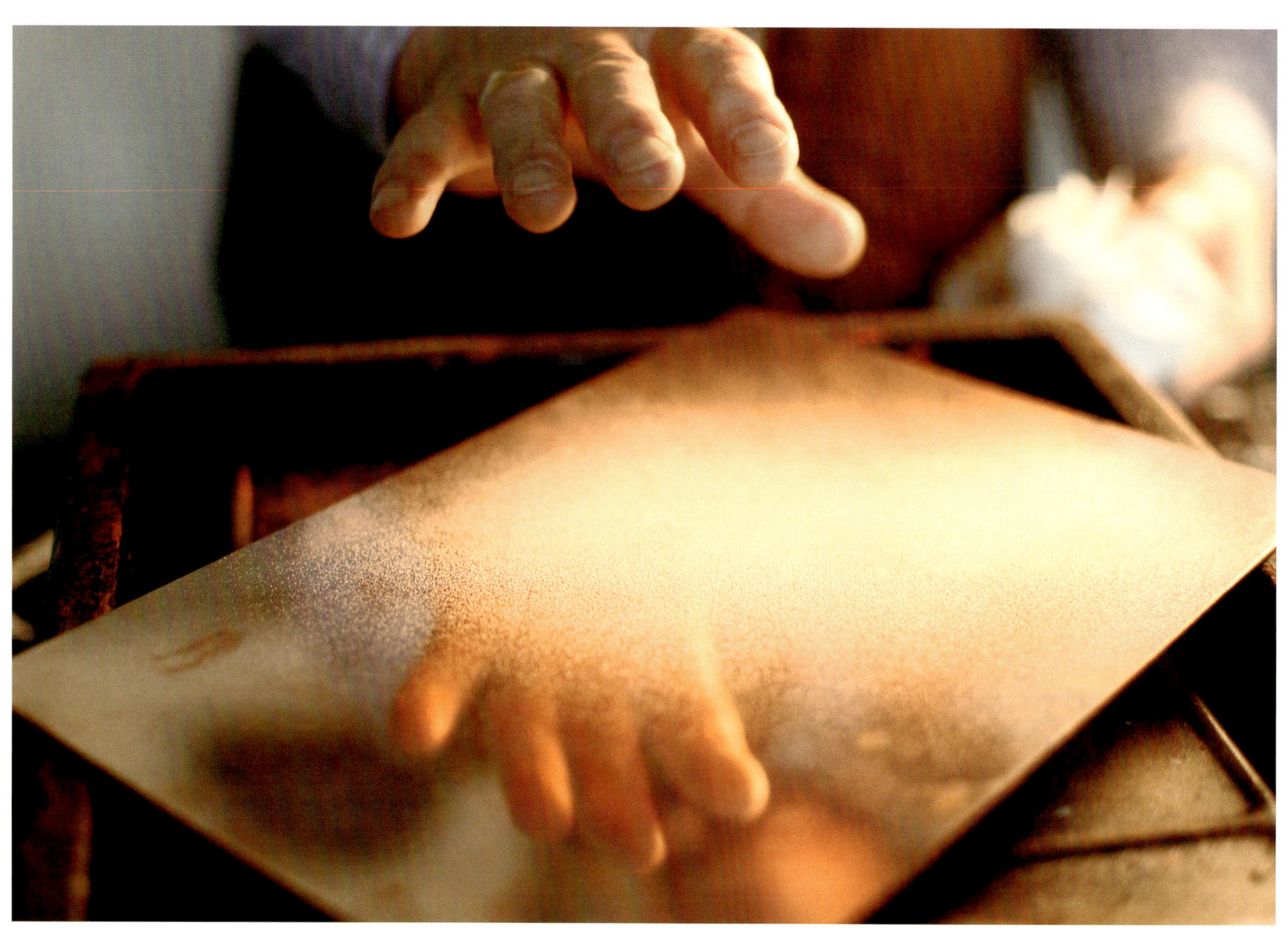

David Blackwood applying resin ground (aquatint) to a copper plate, 2010

PLATES

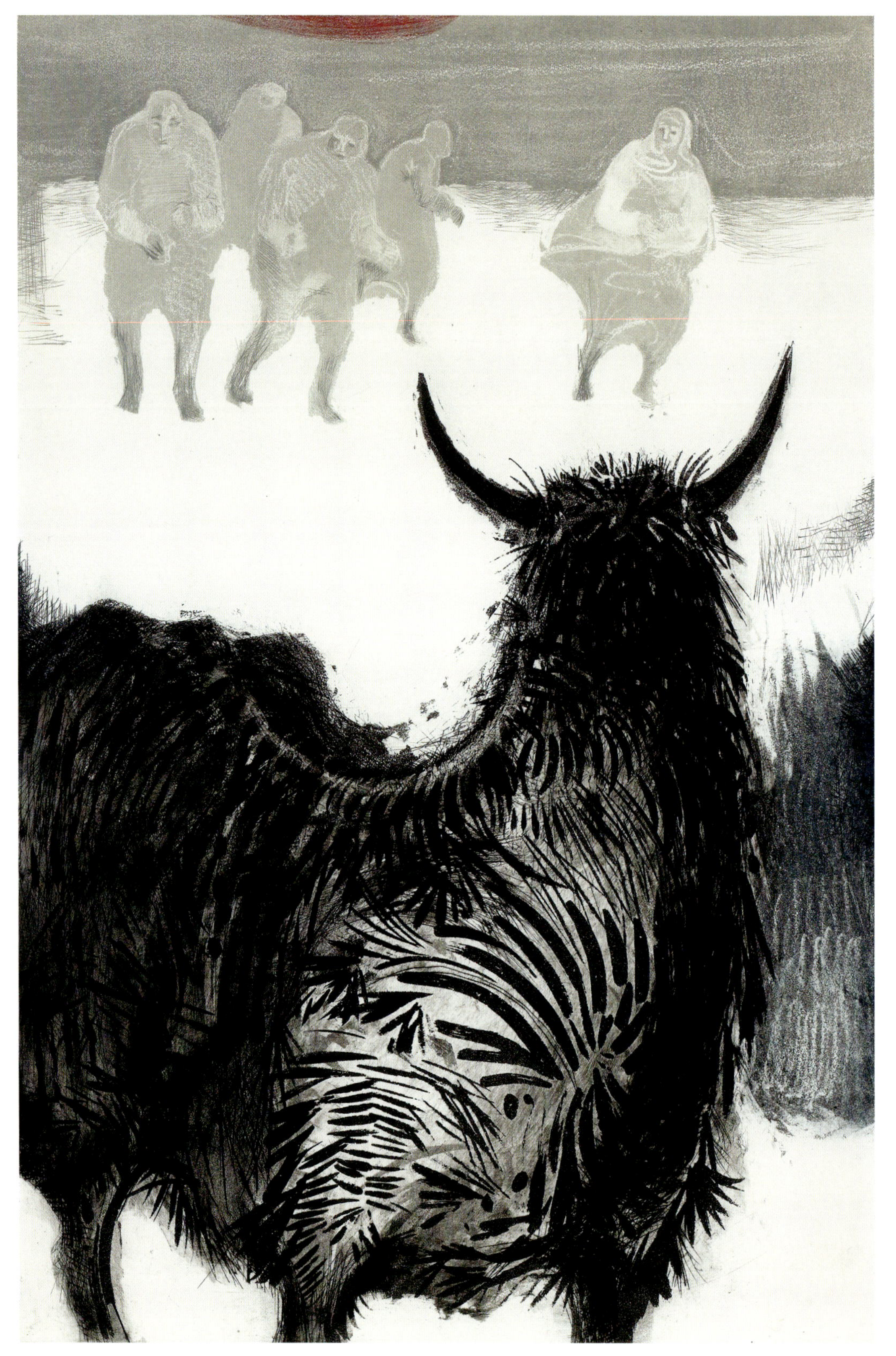

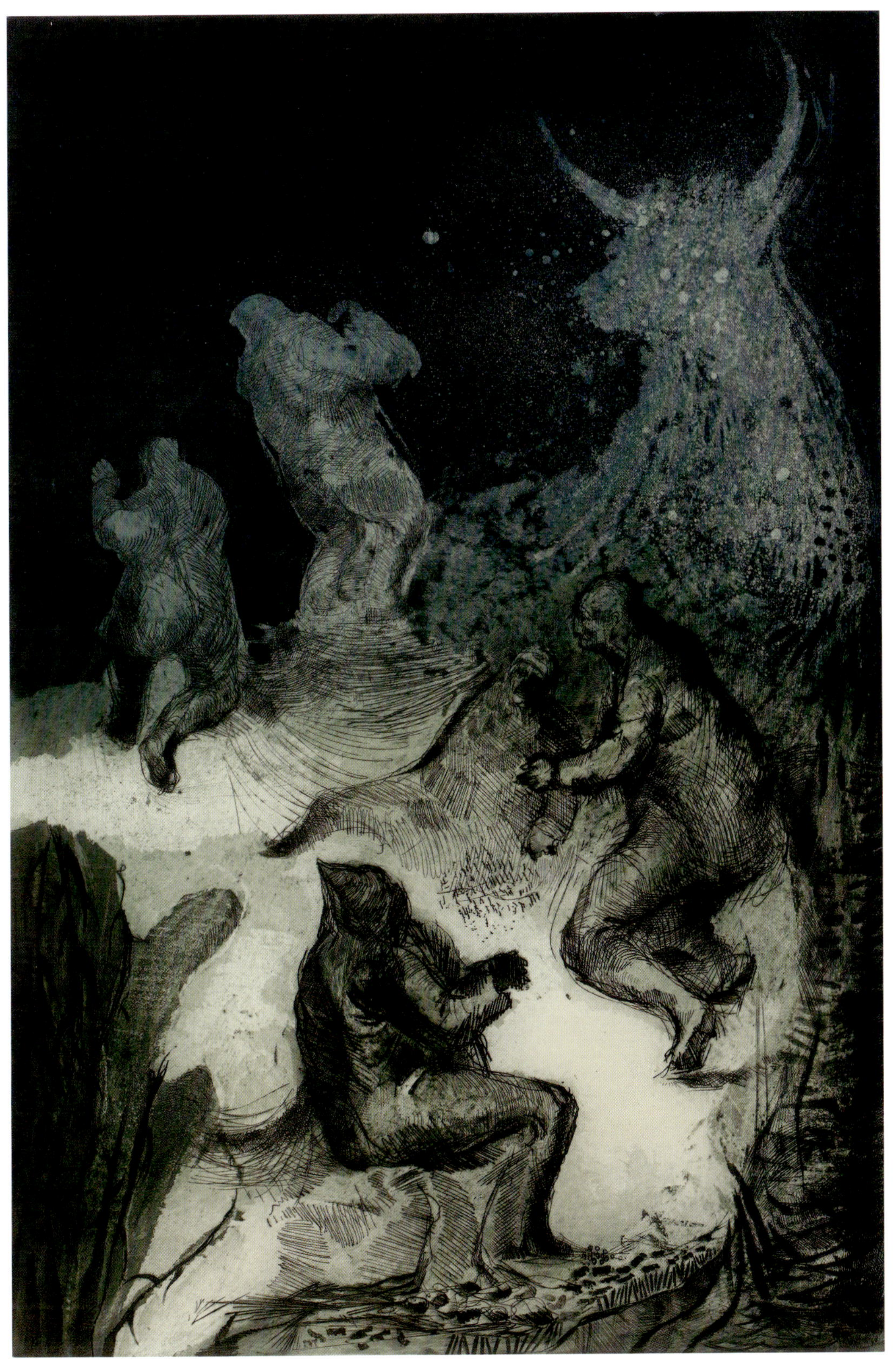

facing: 1. **The Search Party**, 1963

left: 2. **Vision of the Lost Party**, 1964

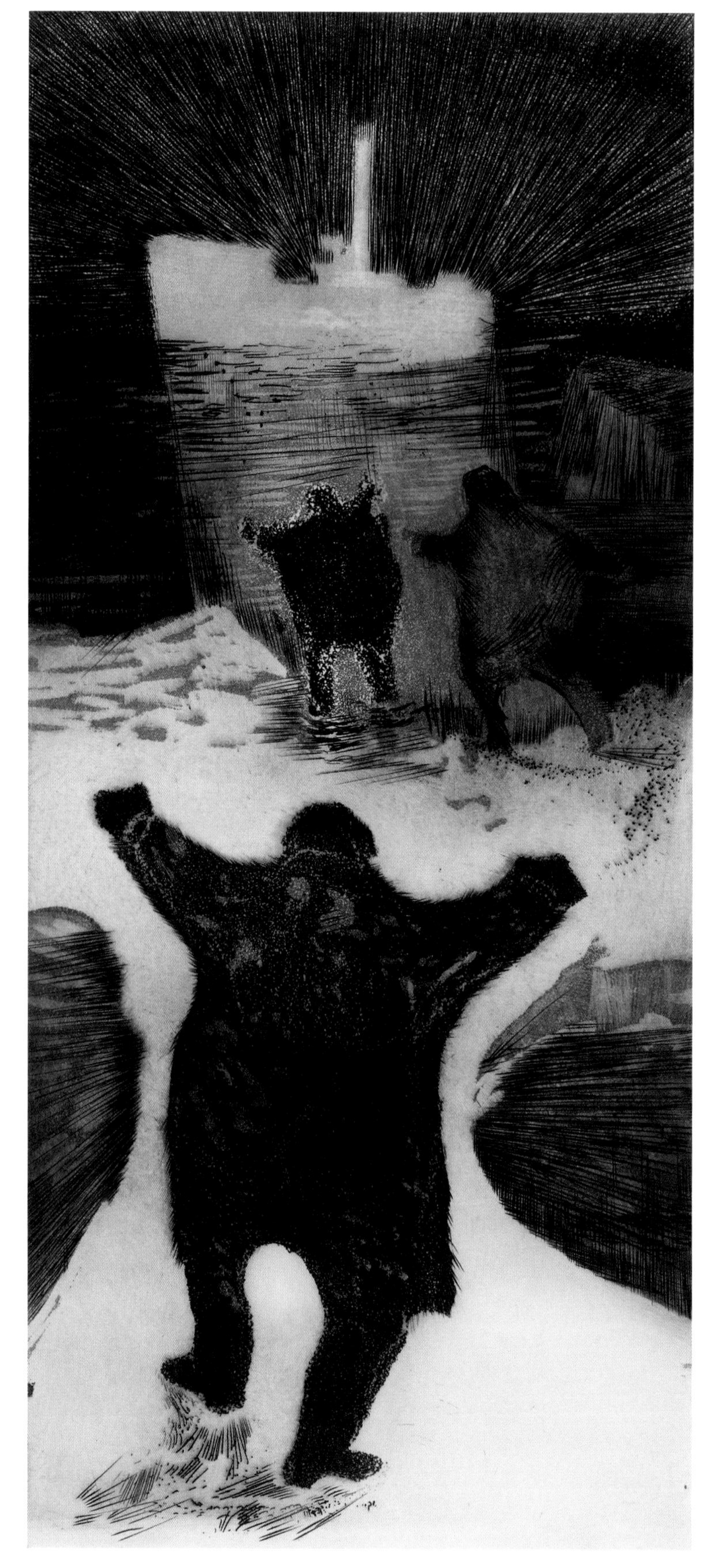

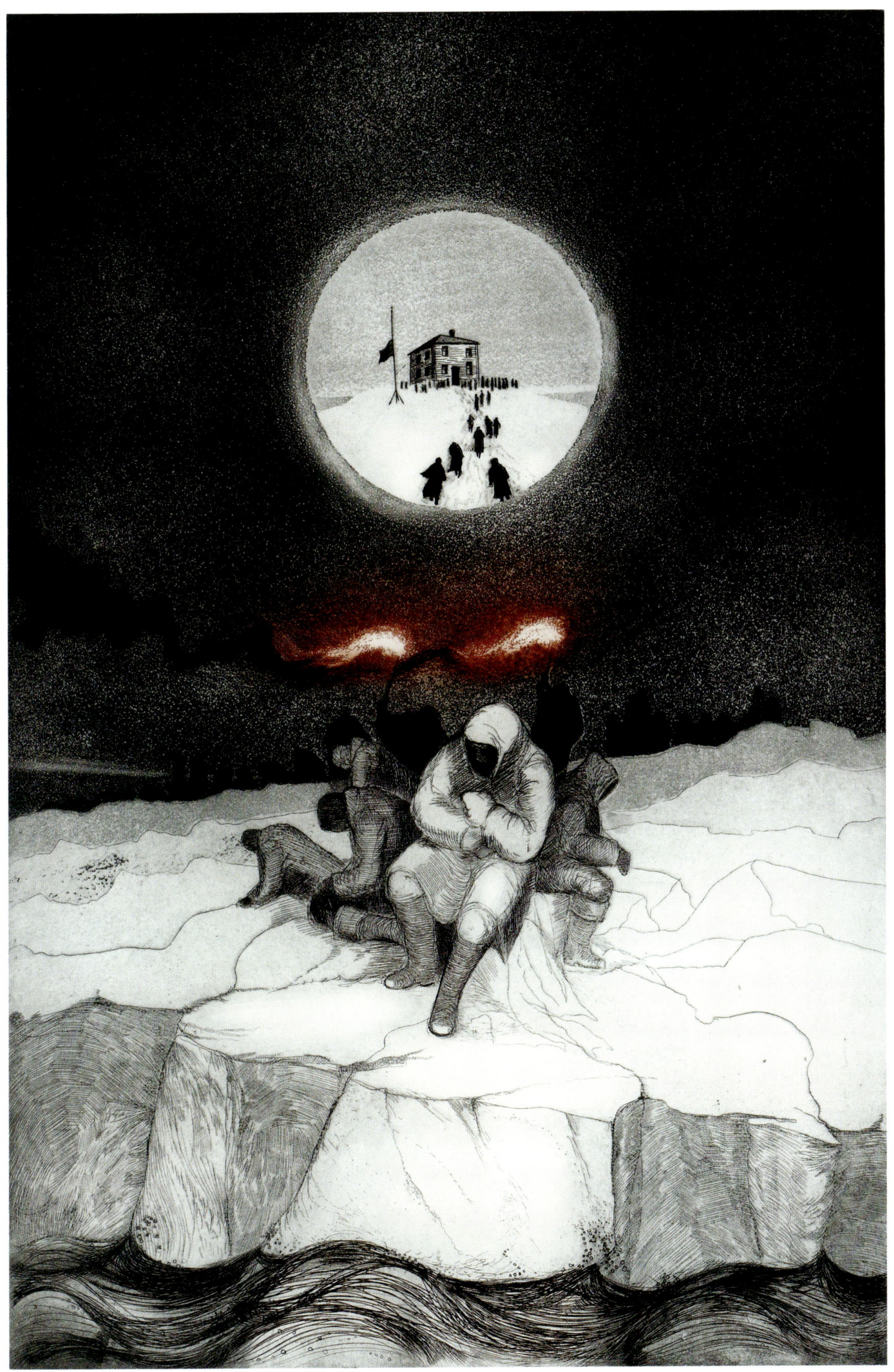

facing:
3. **The Mirage**, 1965

left: 4. **Vision of the Lost Party: Outport Funeral**, 1967

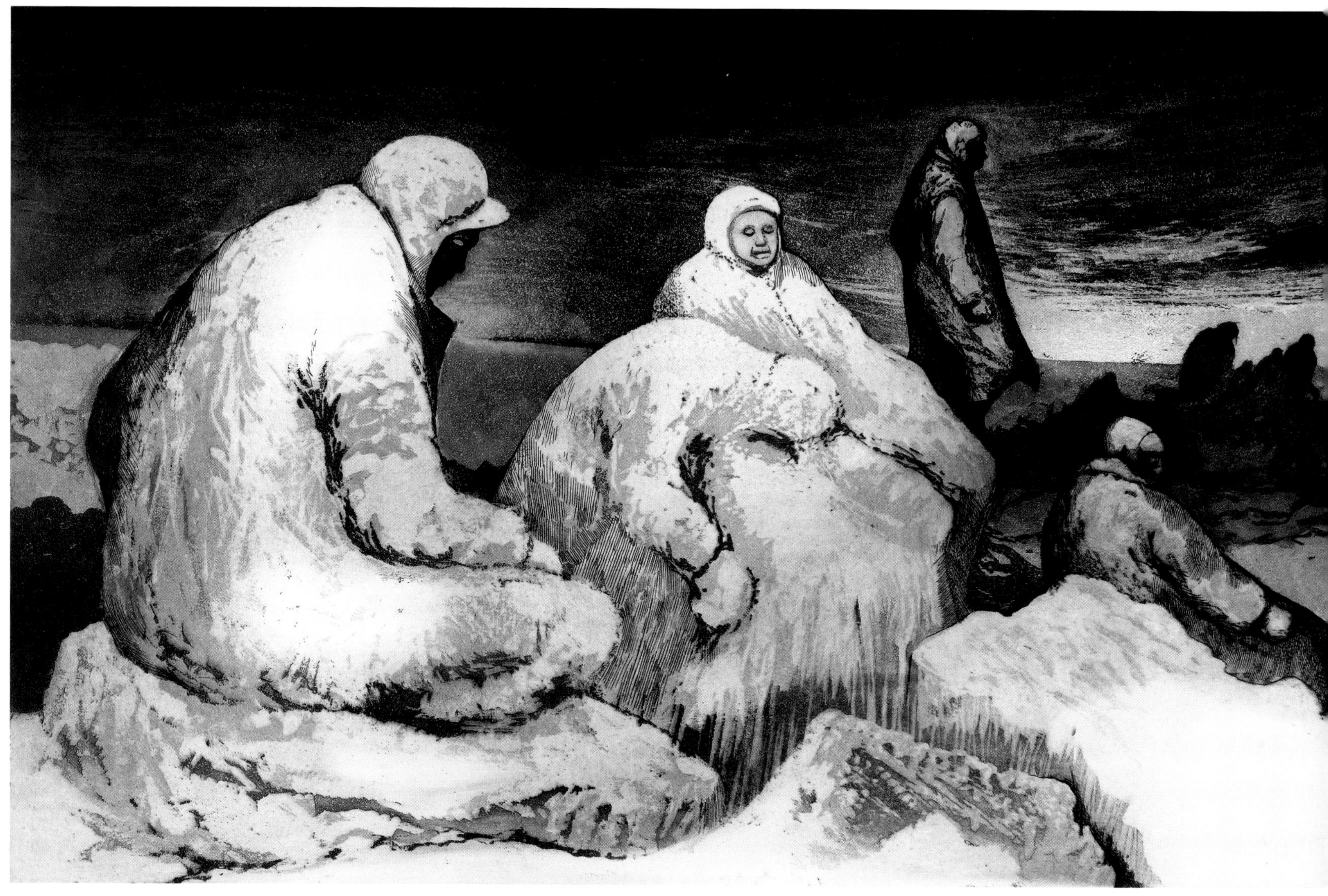

above: 5. **Kean's Men Waiting for the SS Bellaventure**, 1968

facing: 6. **Spirit Departing: Once Told Tale**, 1968

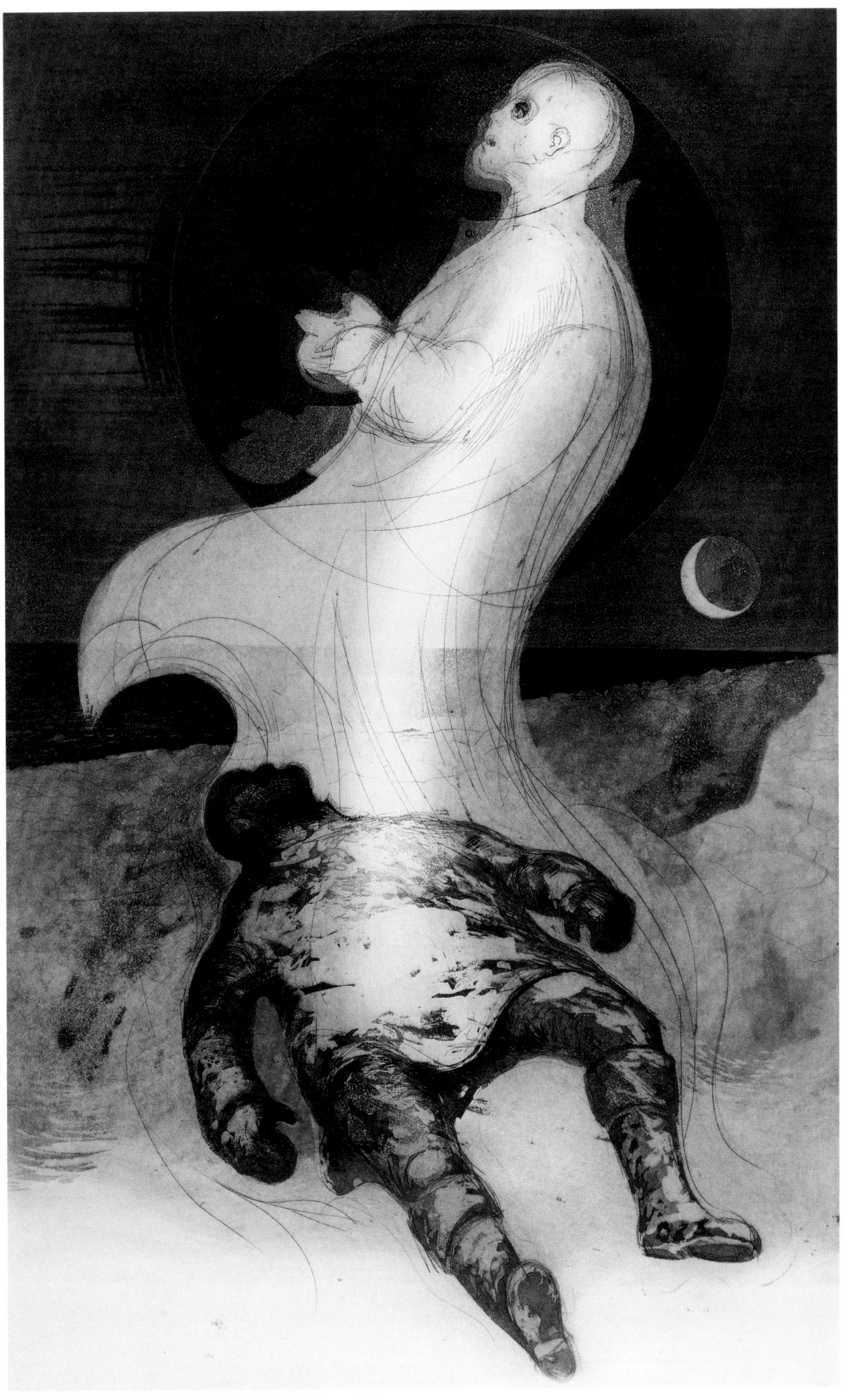

7. **Great Lost Party Adrift**, 1971

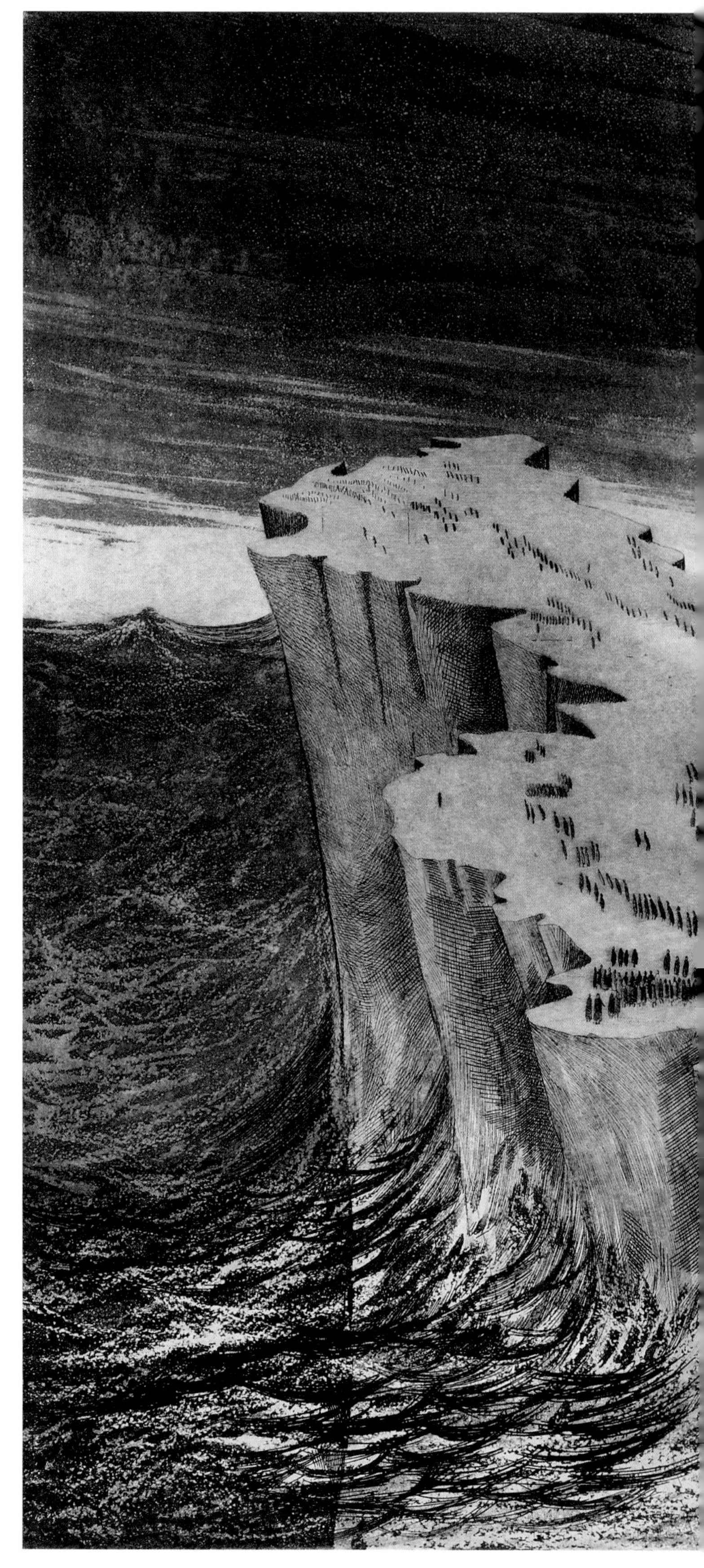

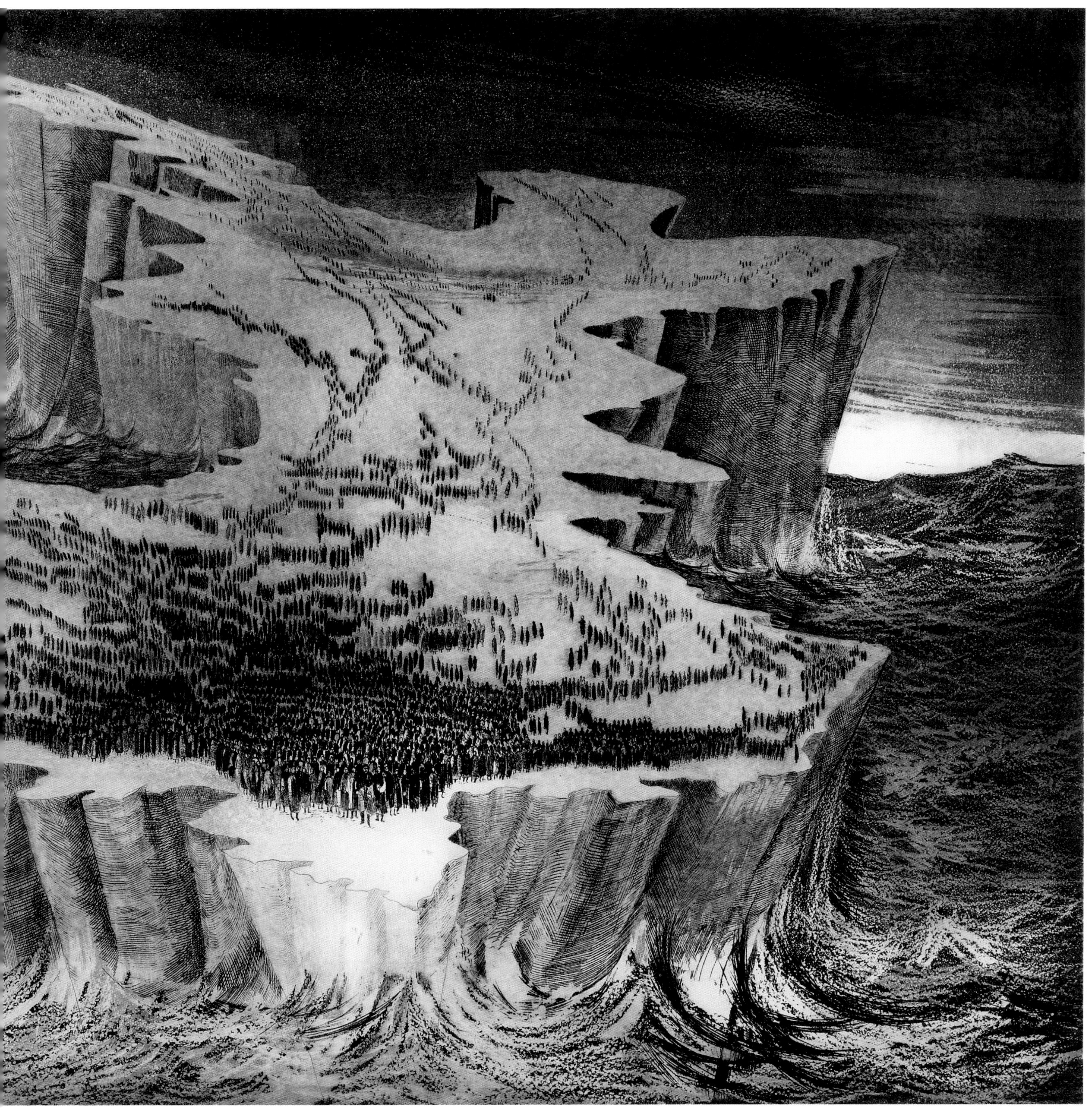

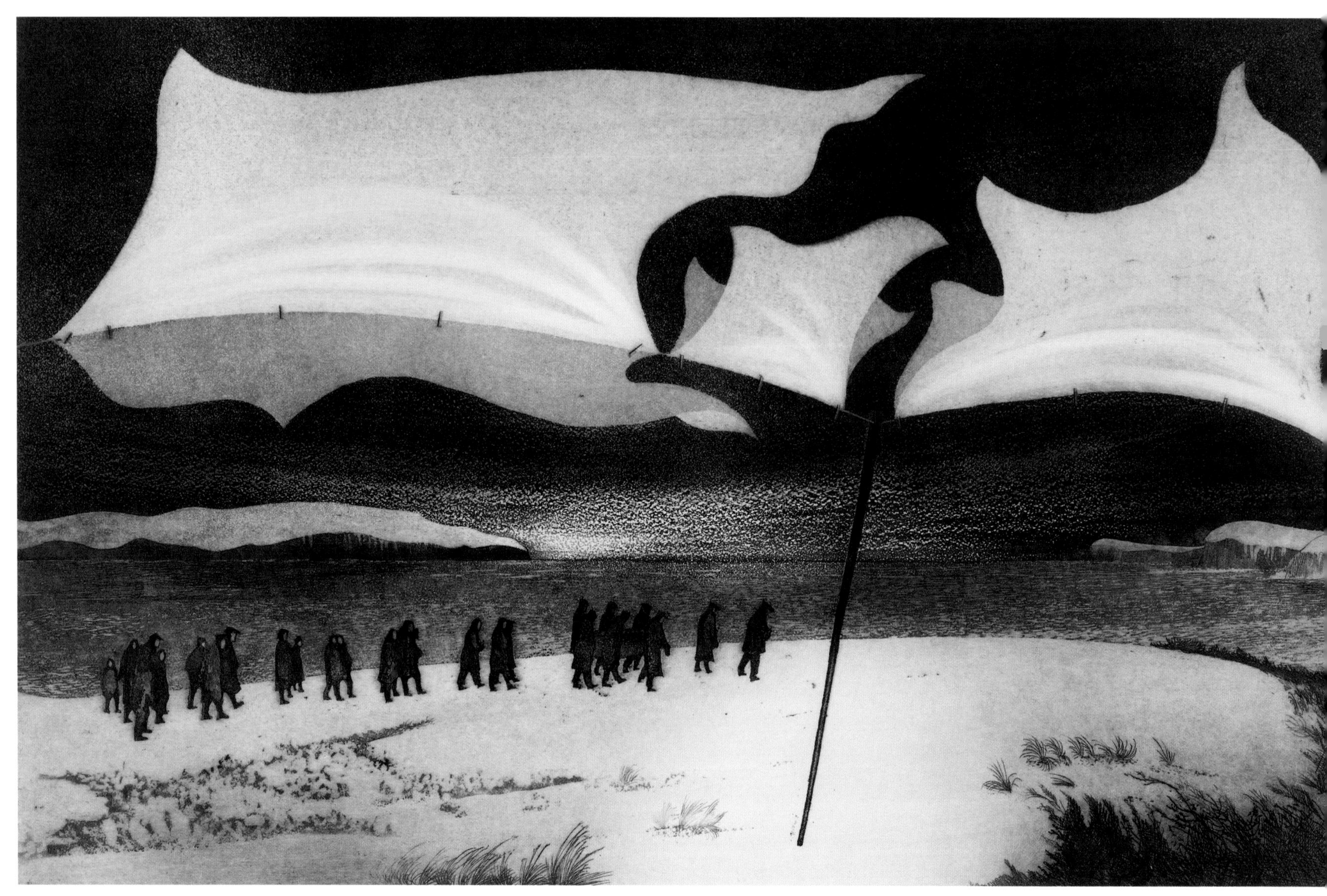

8. **Monday Morning, March 1**, 1968

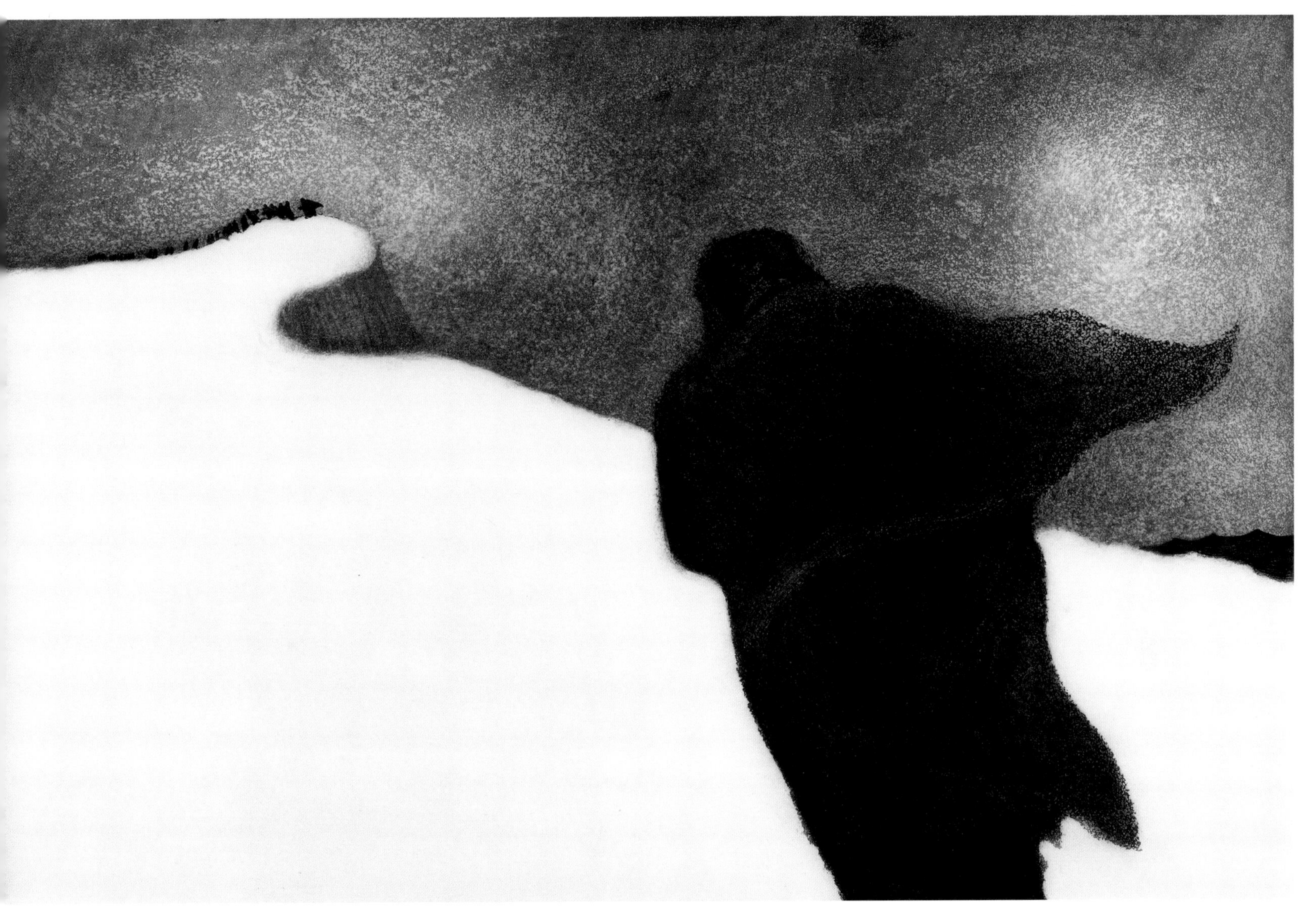

9. **Wreck off Bragg's Island**, 1967

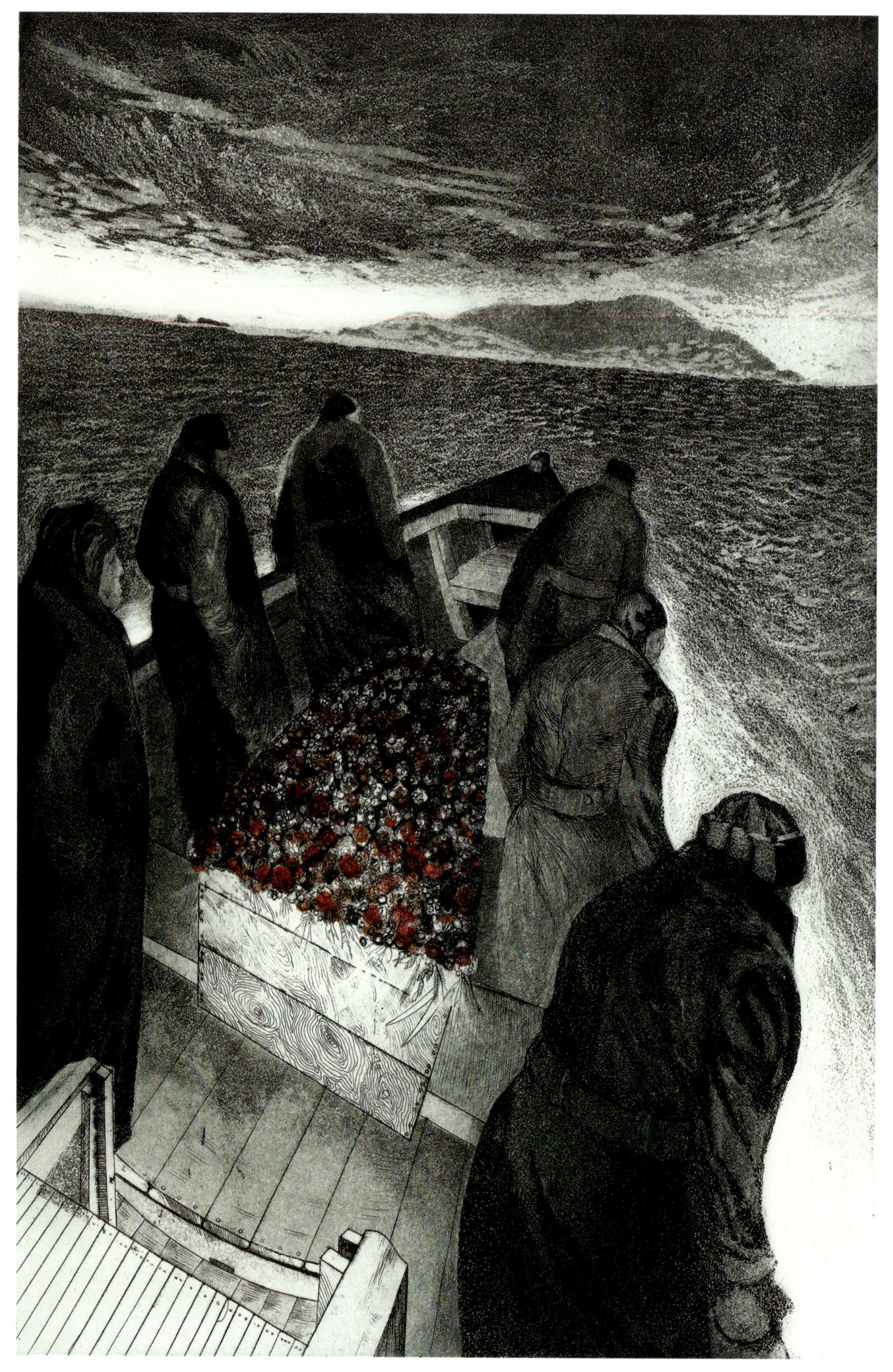

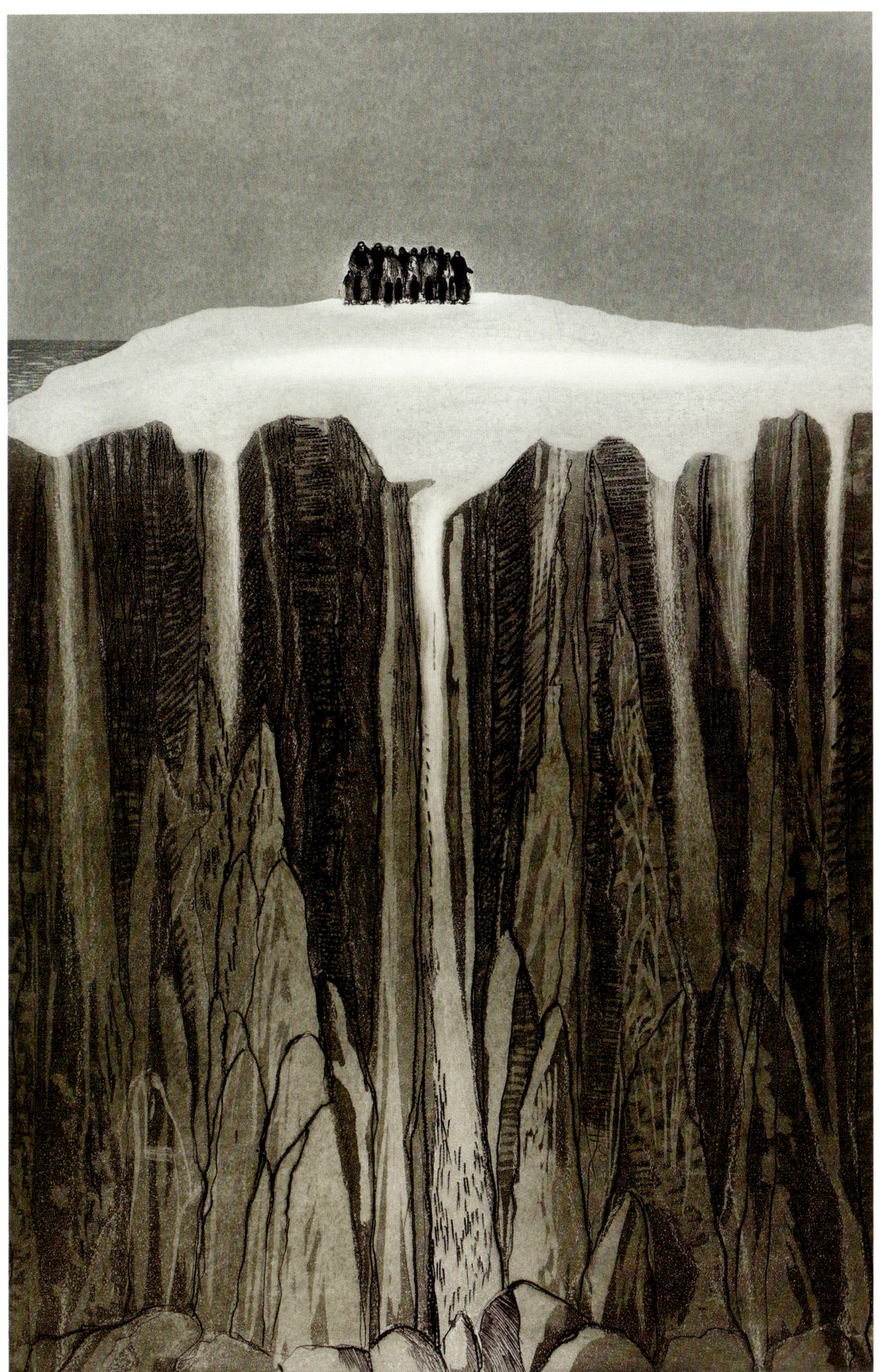

facing: 10. **Island Funeral**, 1967

left: 11. **Cape Islanders Waiting**, 1967

right: 12. **Survivor Wandering**, 1968

facing: 13. **Sealer's Dream**, 1968

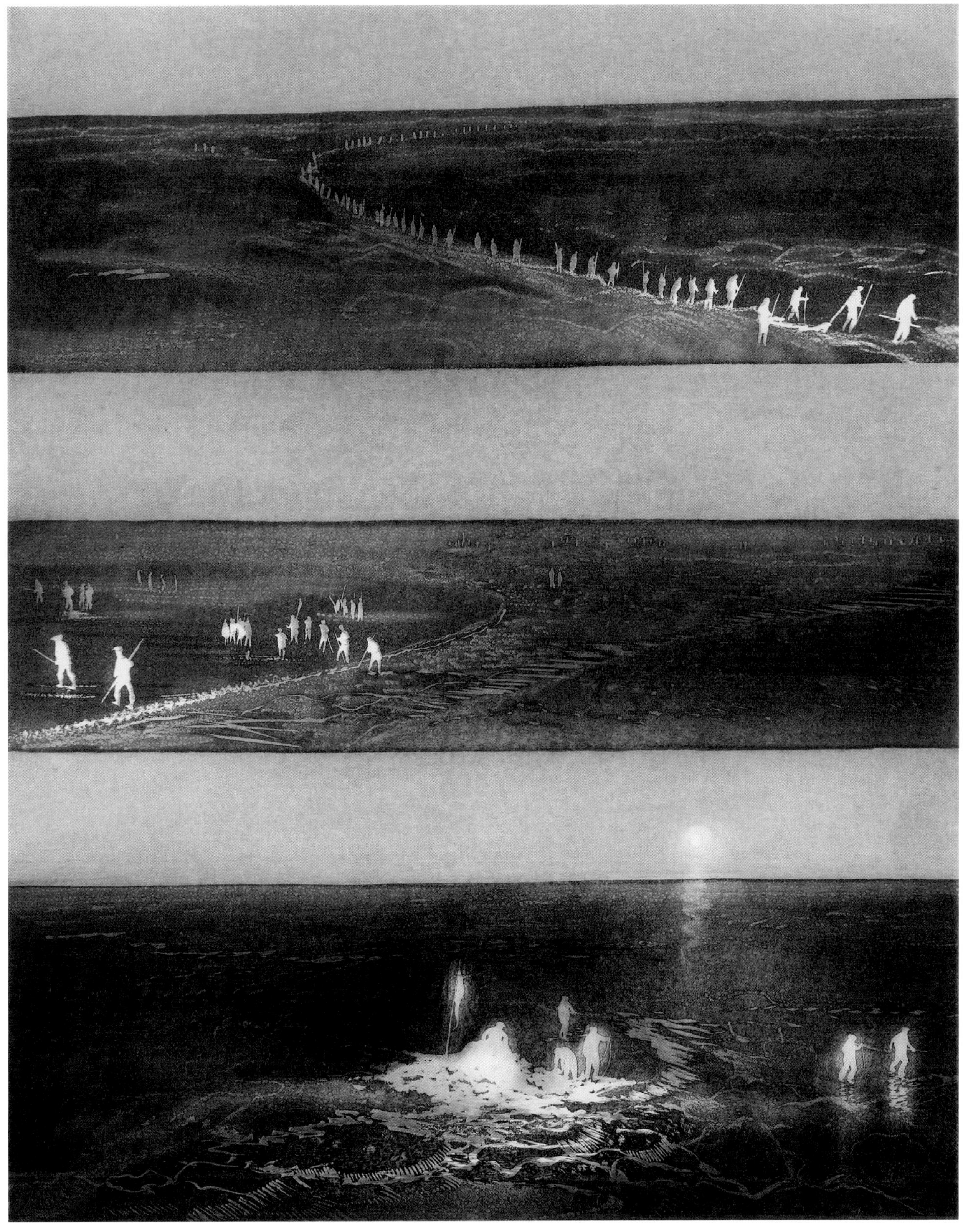

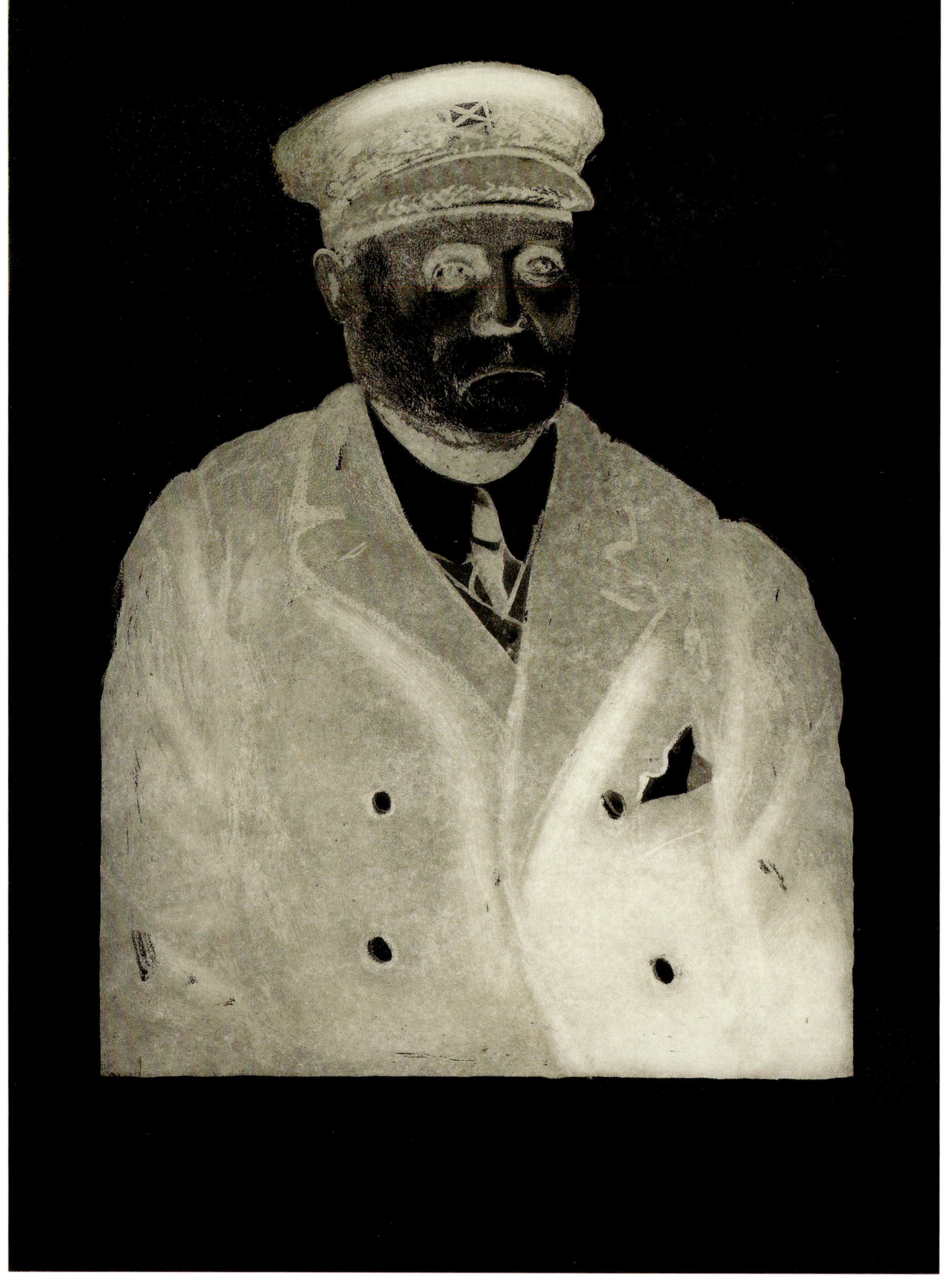

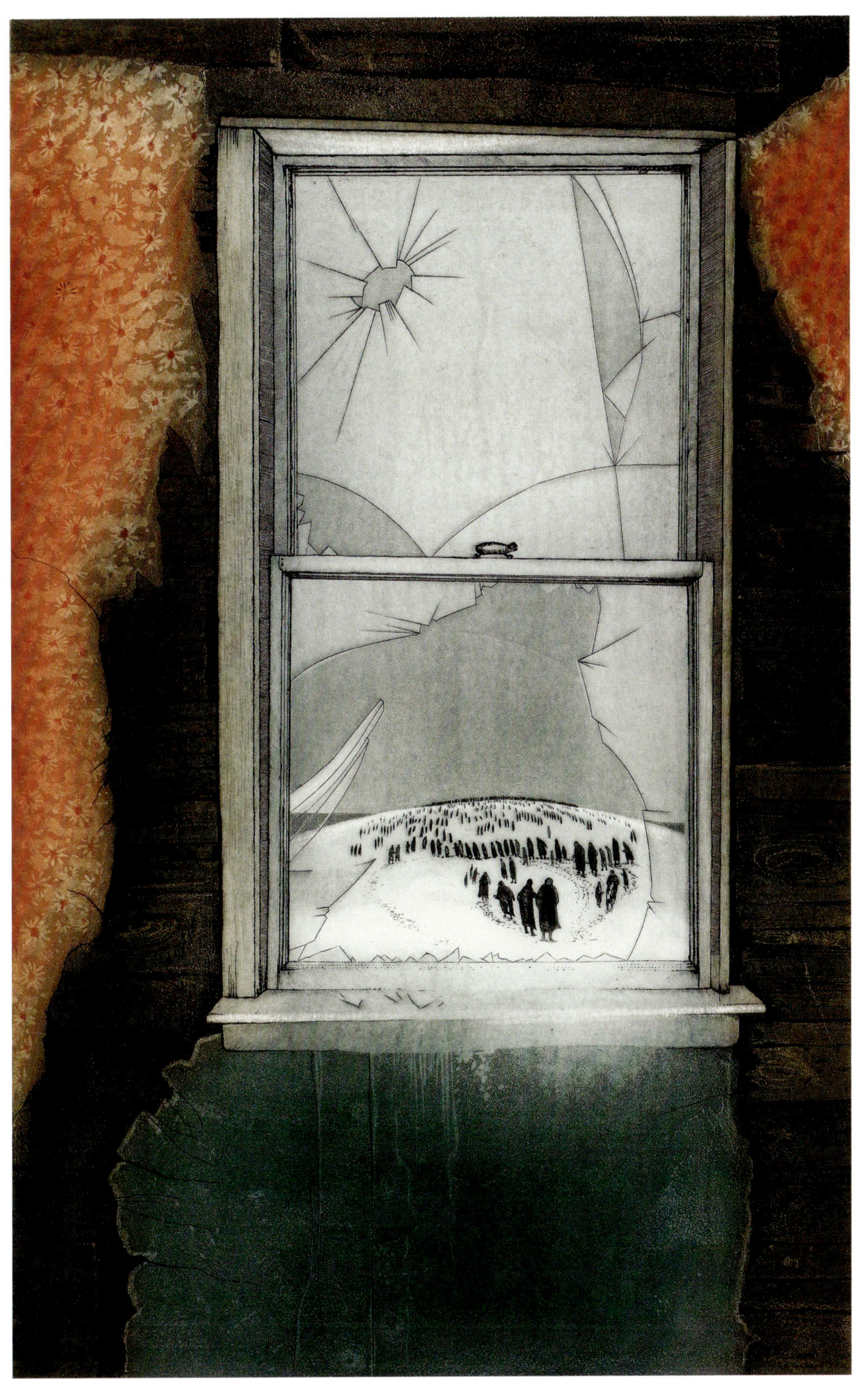

facing: 14. **Posthumous Portrait of Captain Abraham Kean**, 1968

left: 15. **Gram Glover's Dream**, 1968

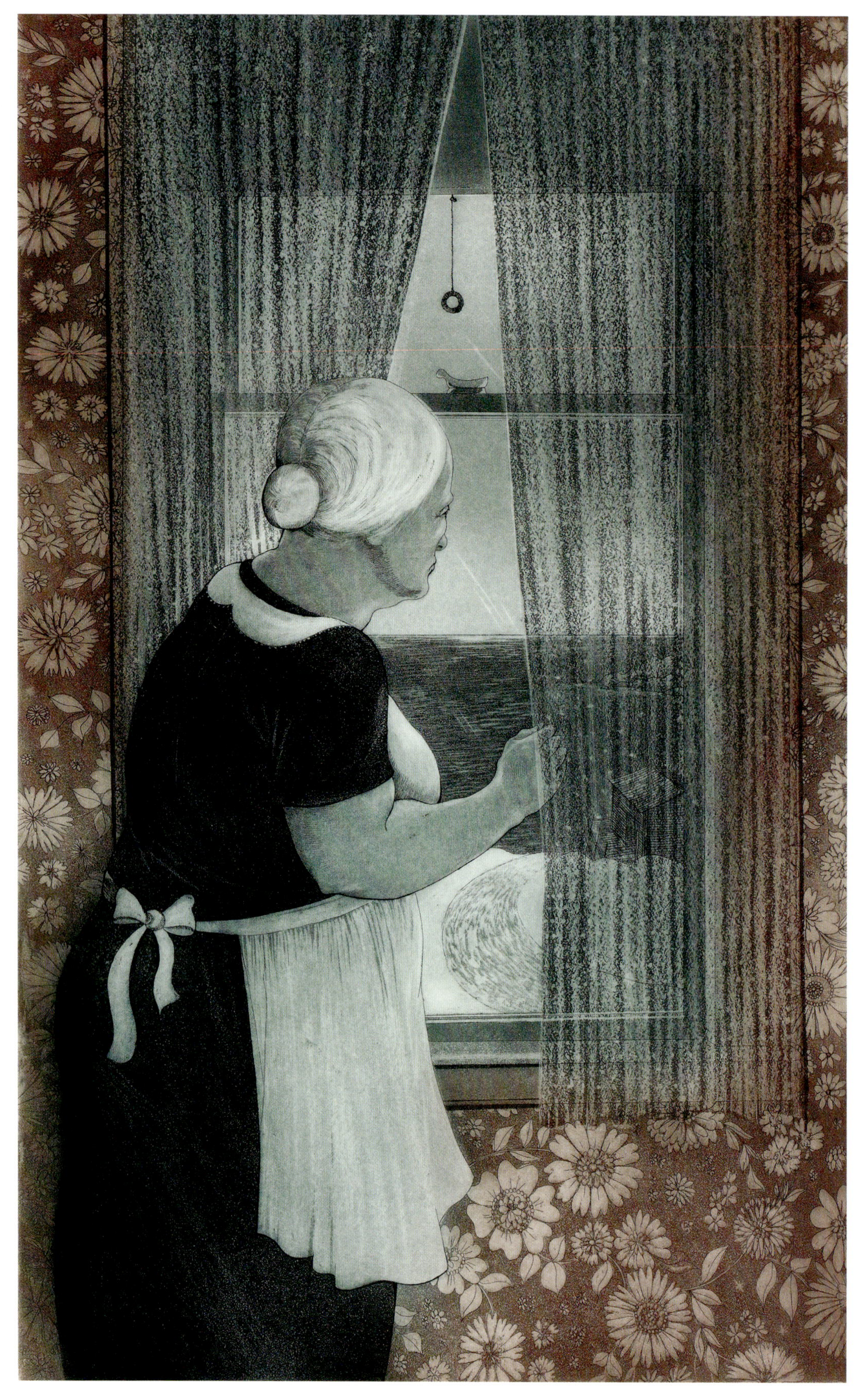

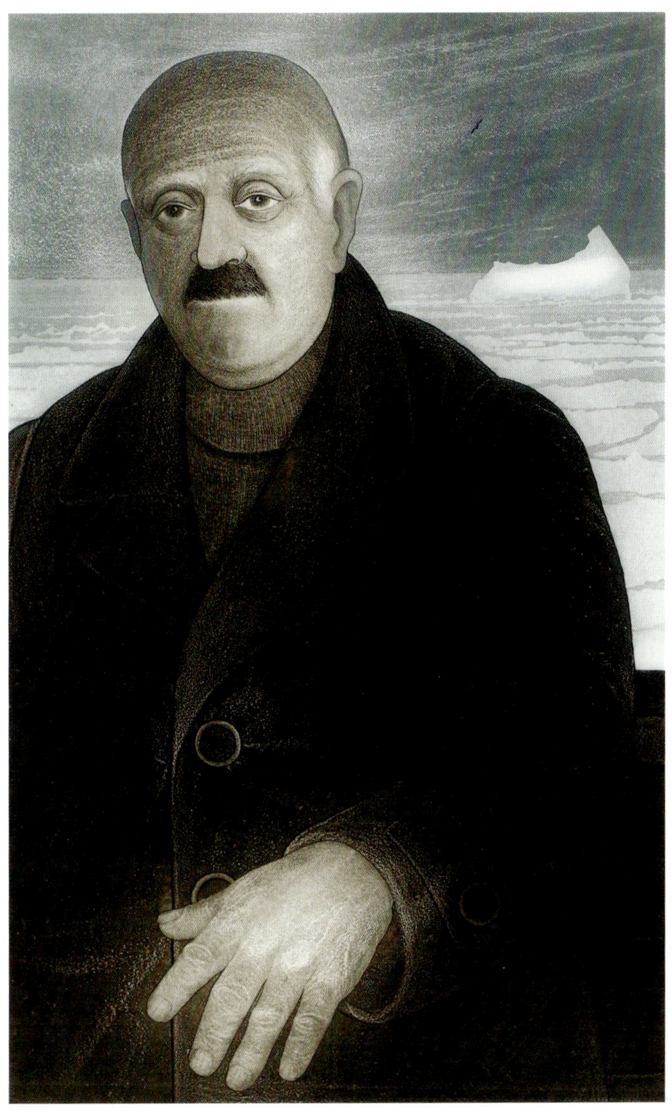

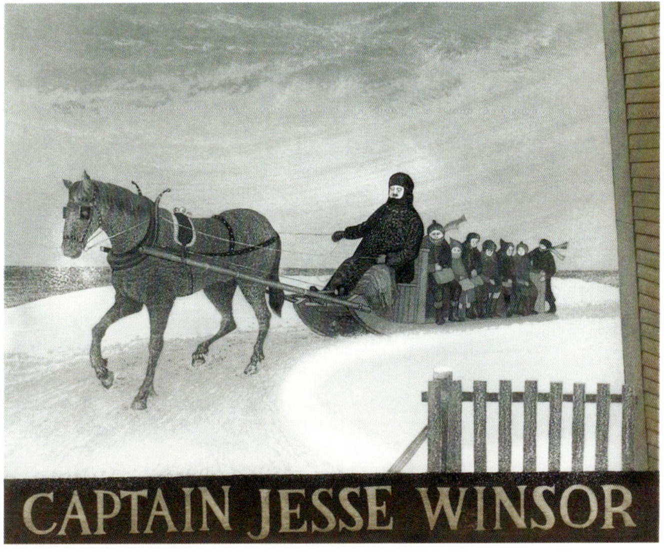

facing: 16. **Gram Glover Waiting**, 1972

left: 17. **Home in Wesleyville (Captain Jesse Winsor)**, 1975

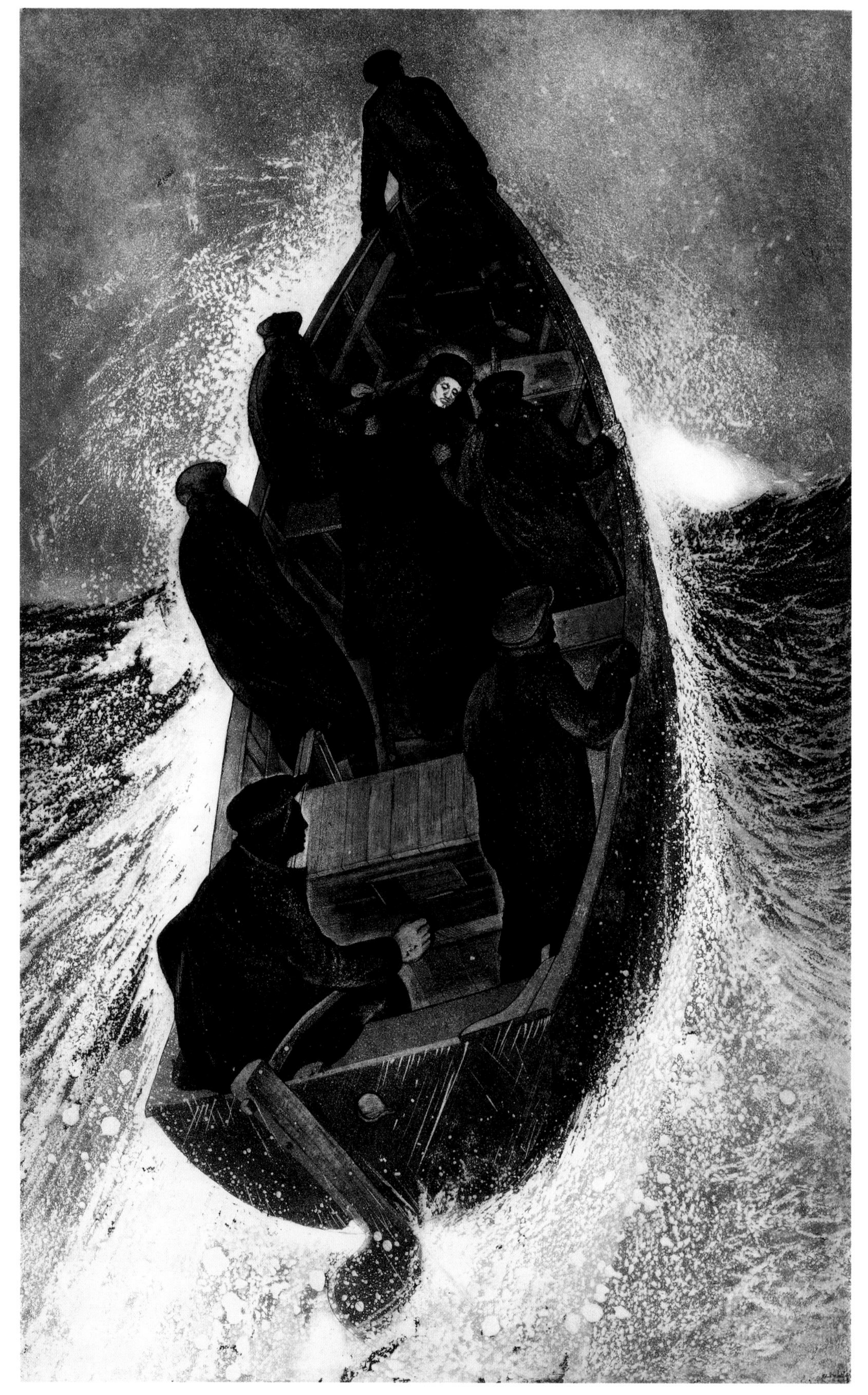

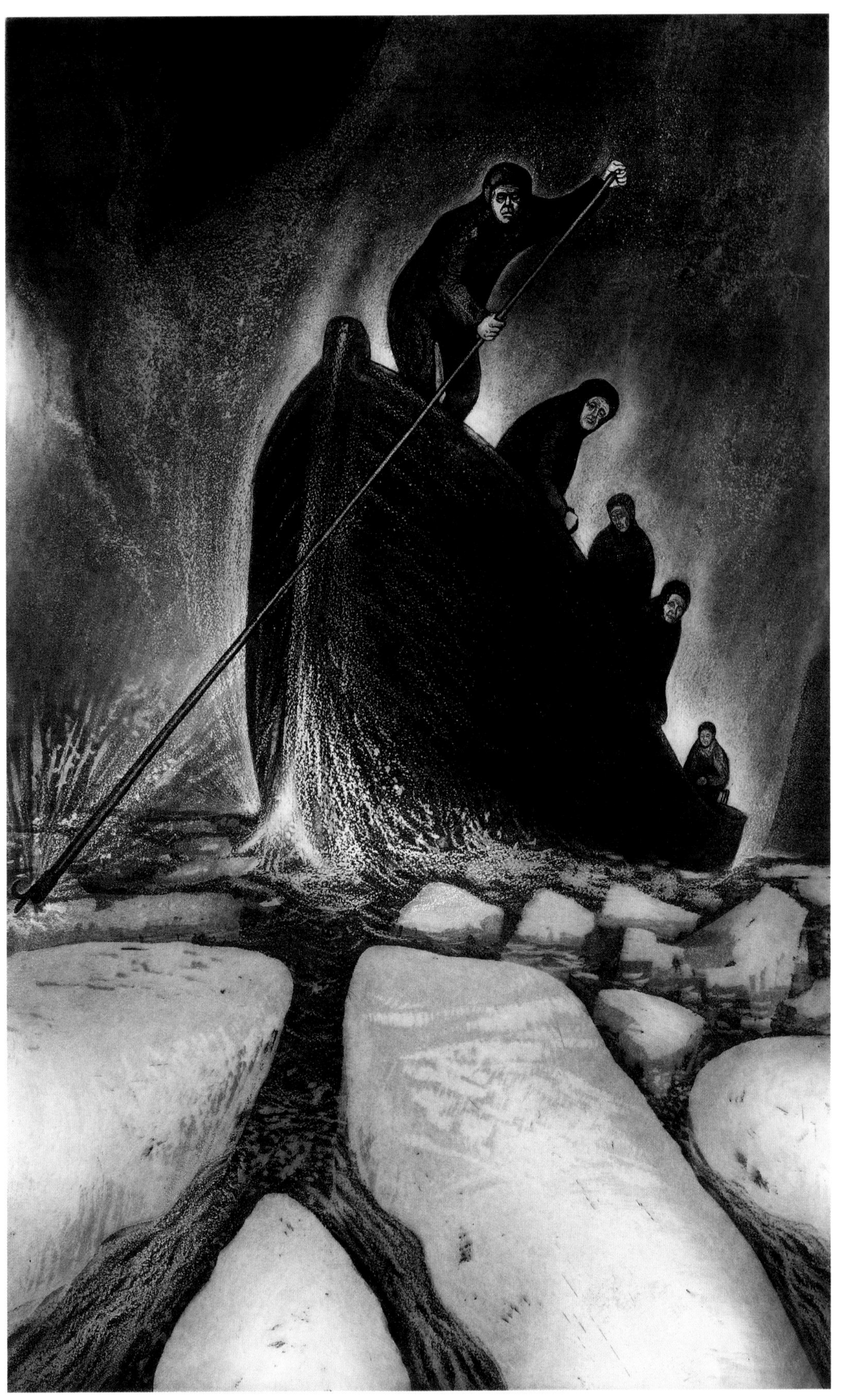

facing: 18. **Sick Captain Leaving**, 1971

left: 19. **Sick Captain Returning**, 1973

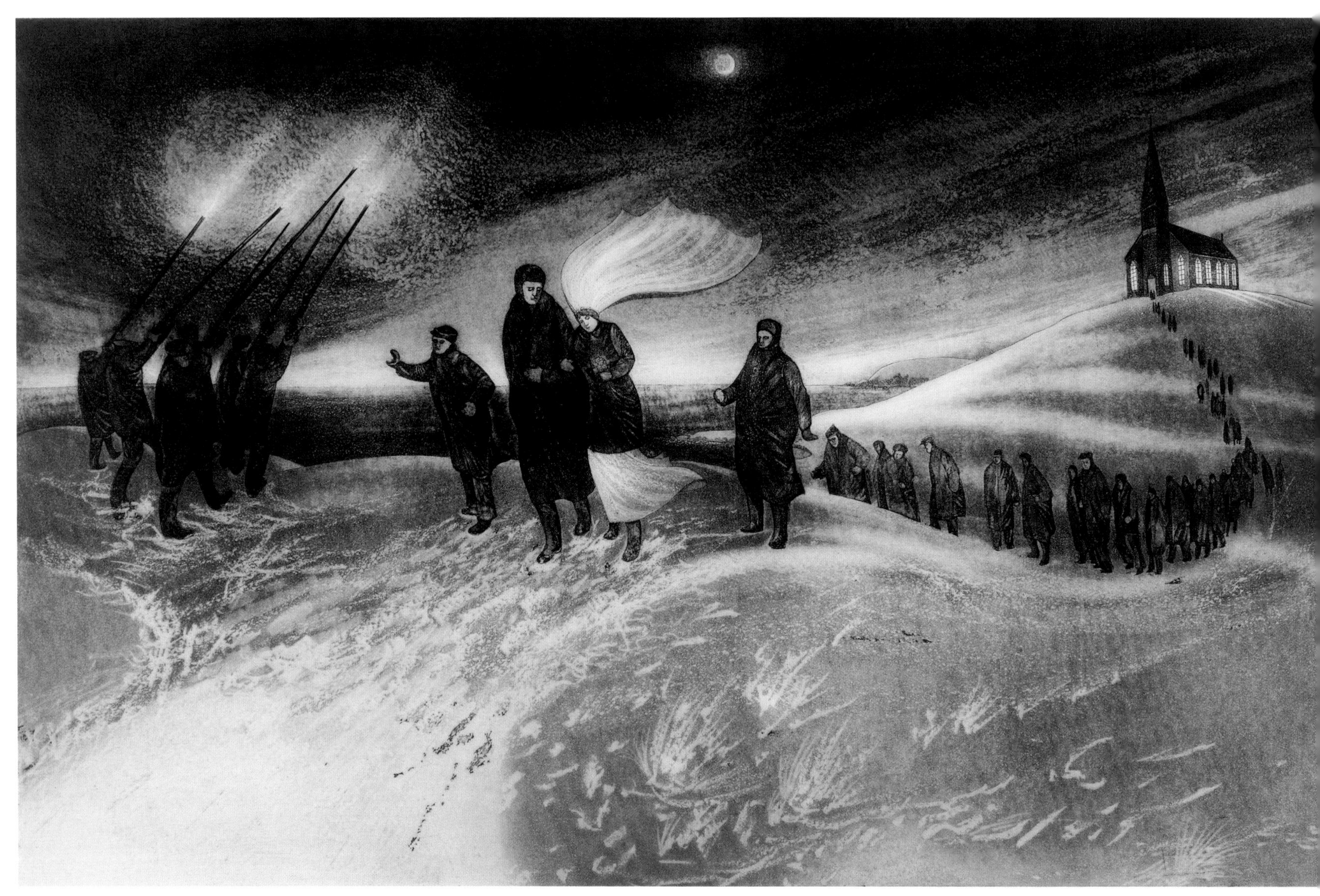

20. **Wedding on Bragg's Island**, 1973

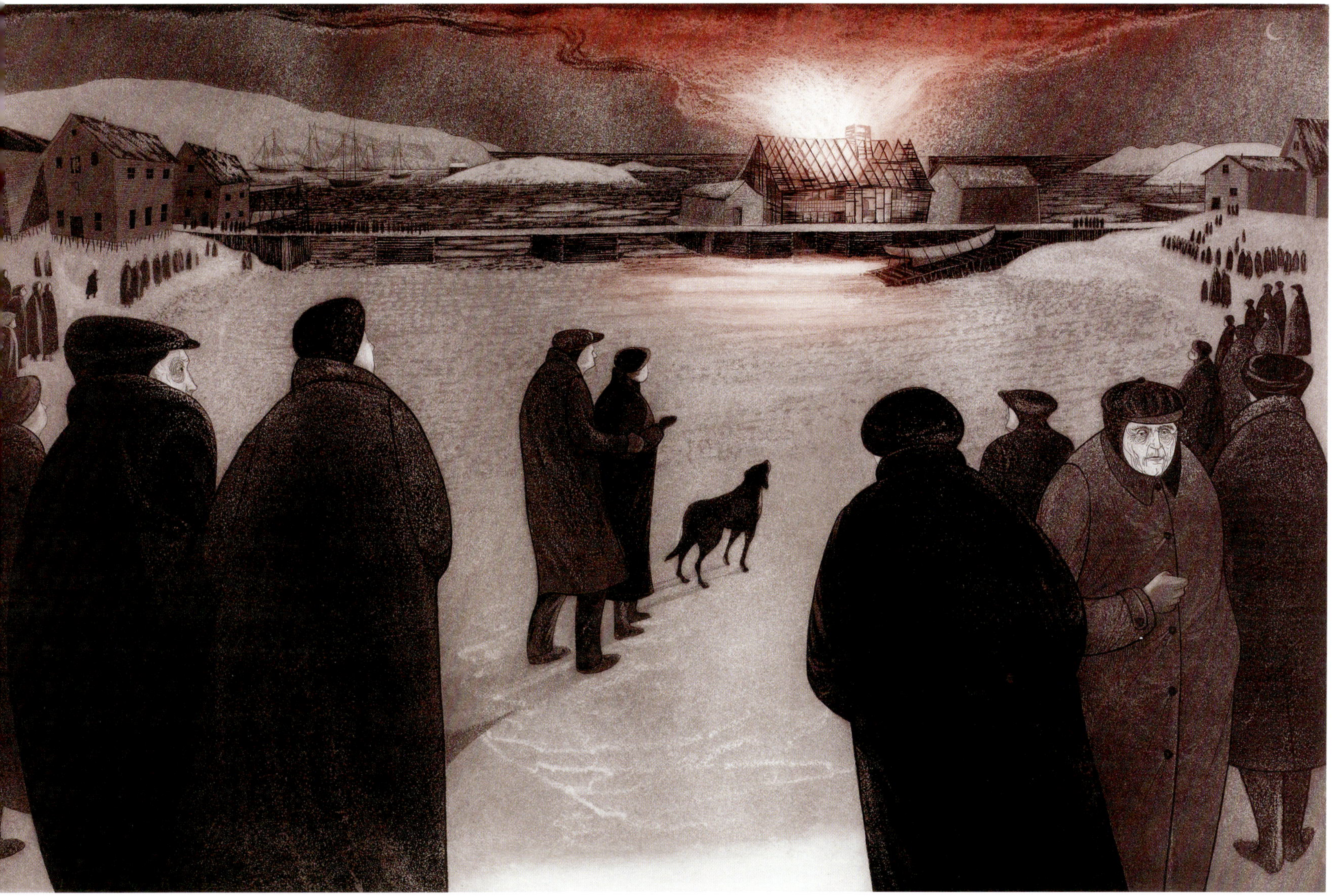

21. **The Burning of William Fifield's Forge,** 1975

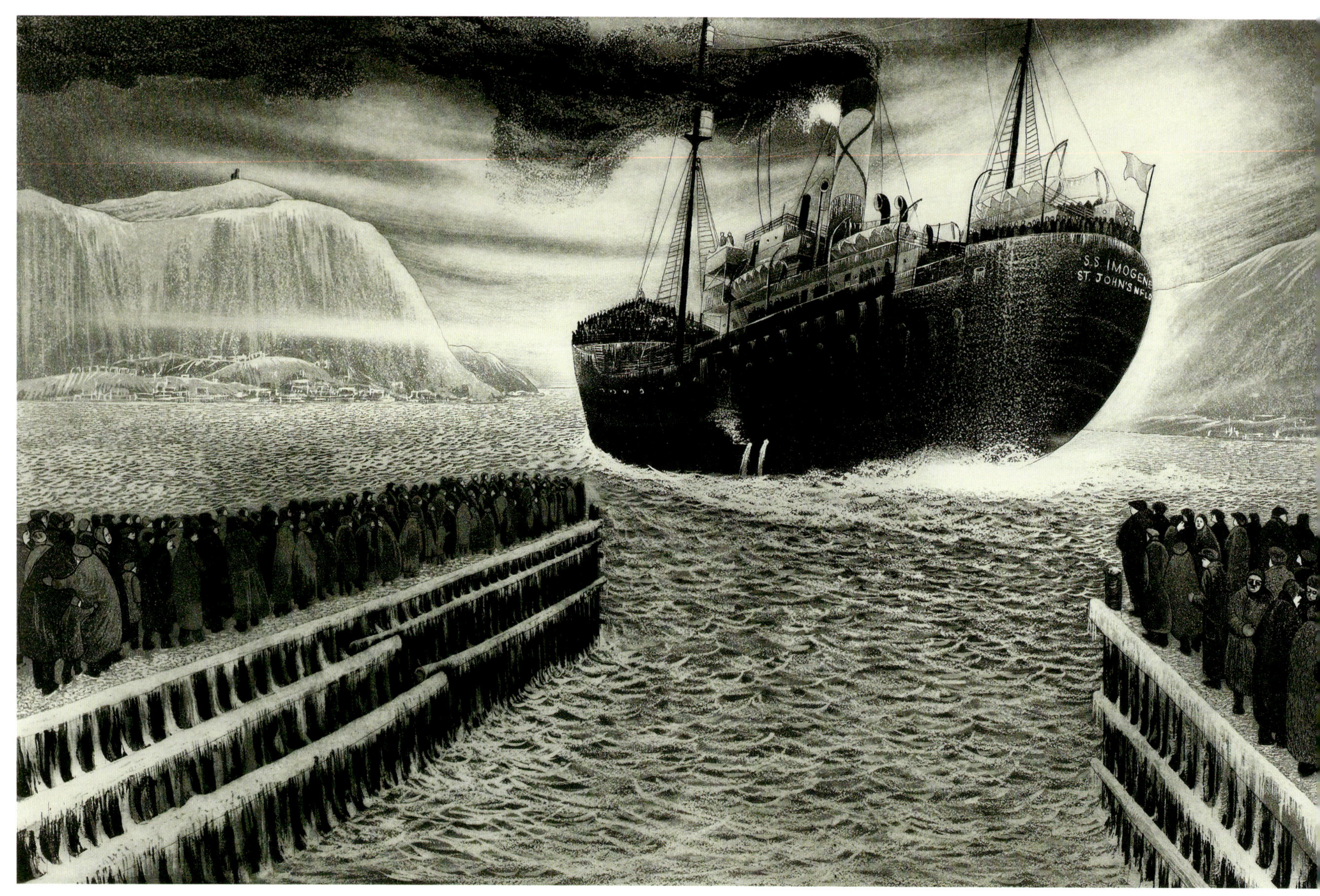

22. SS Imogene Leaving for the Icefields, 1973

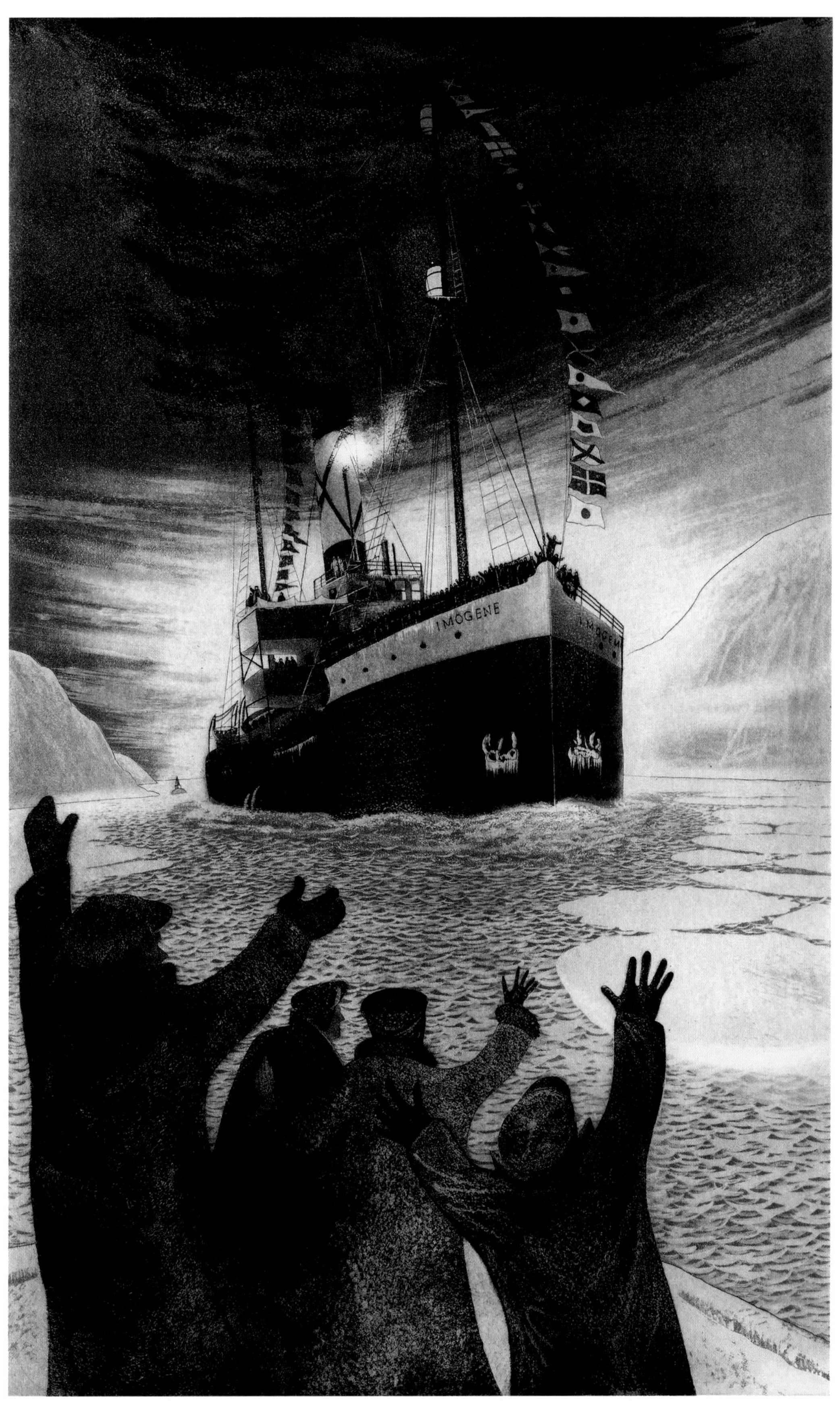

23. SS Imogene Home from the Icefields, 1972

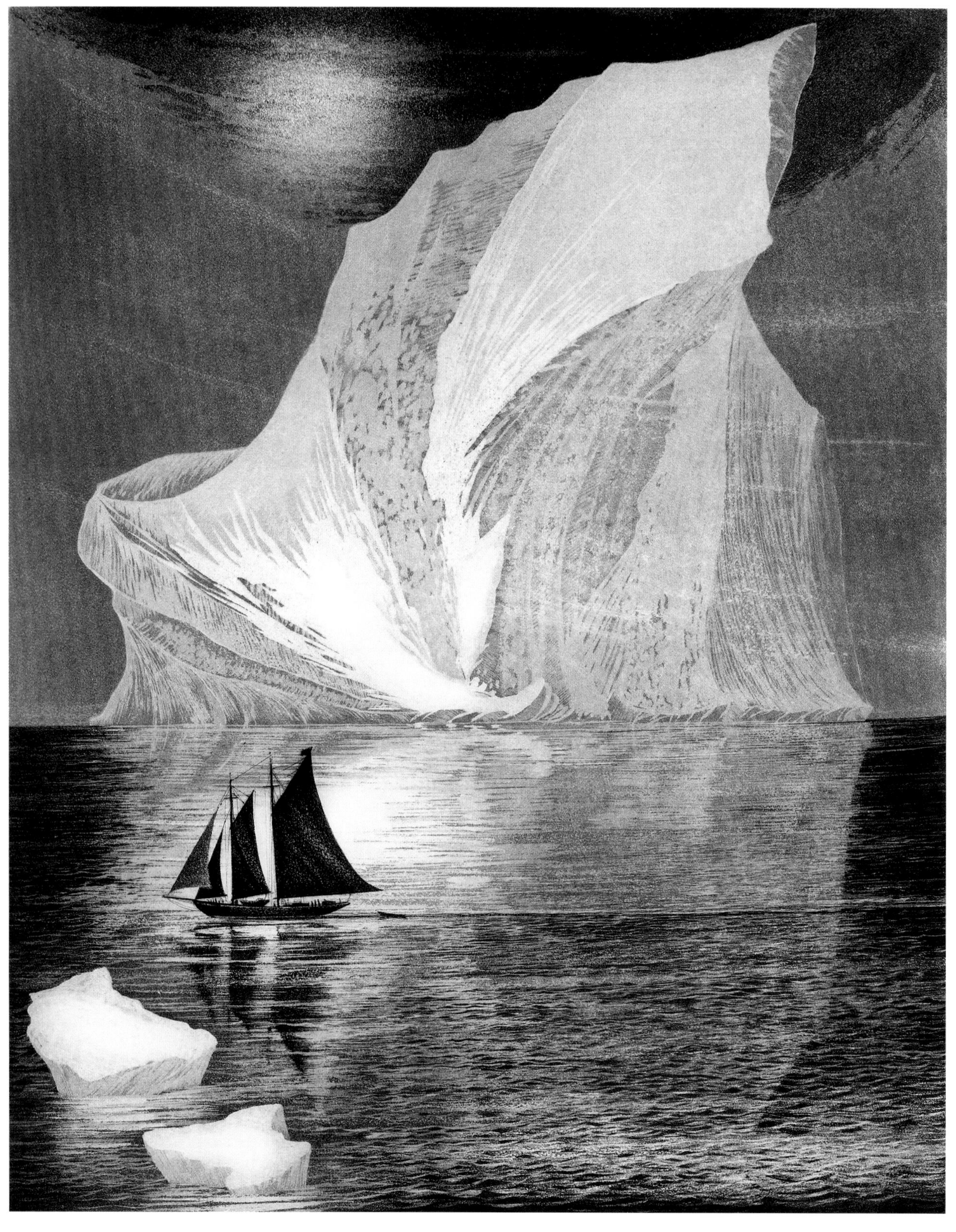

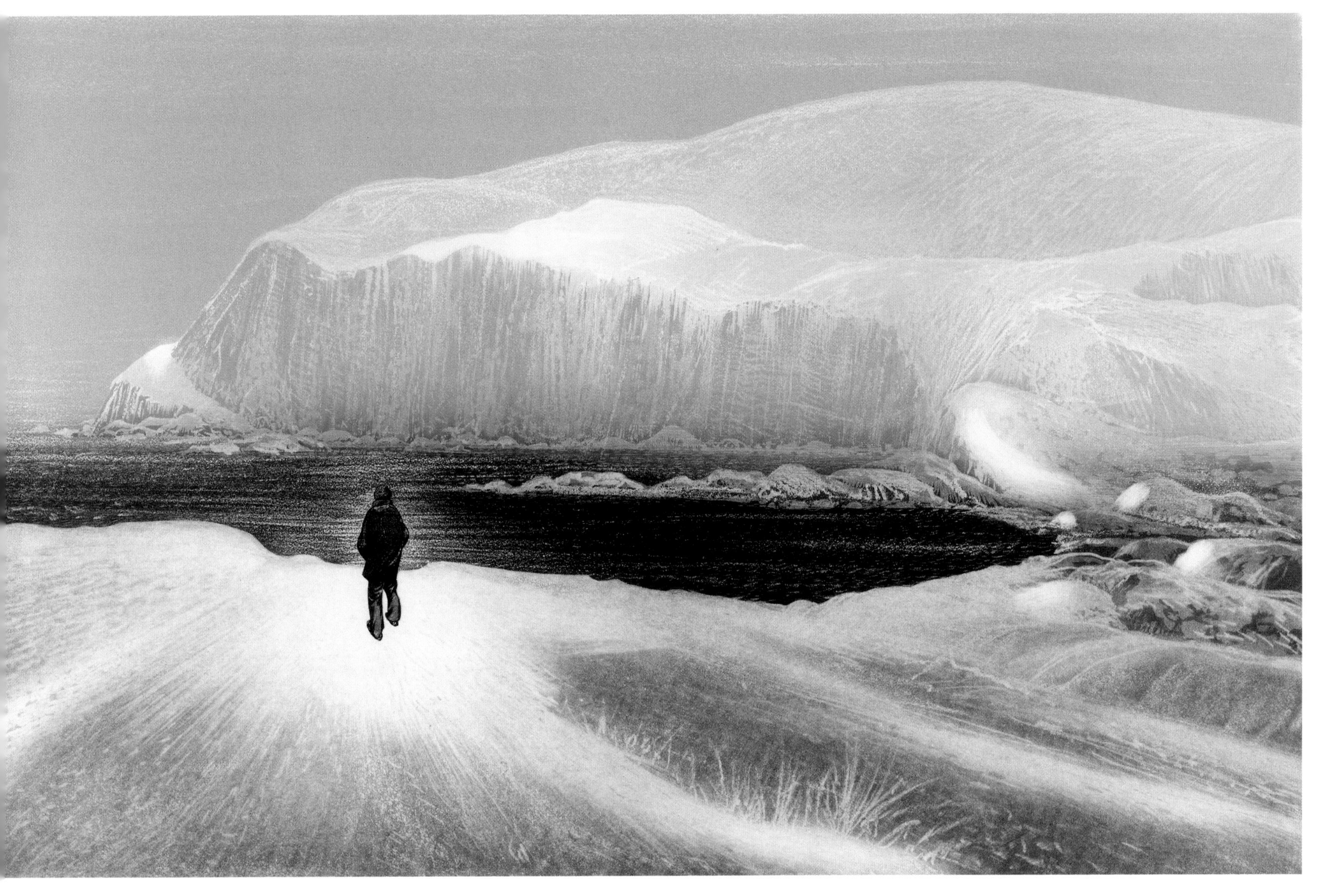

facing: 24. **Flora S. Nickerson Down on the Labrador,** 1978

above: 25. **January Visit Home,** 1975

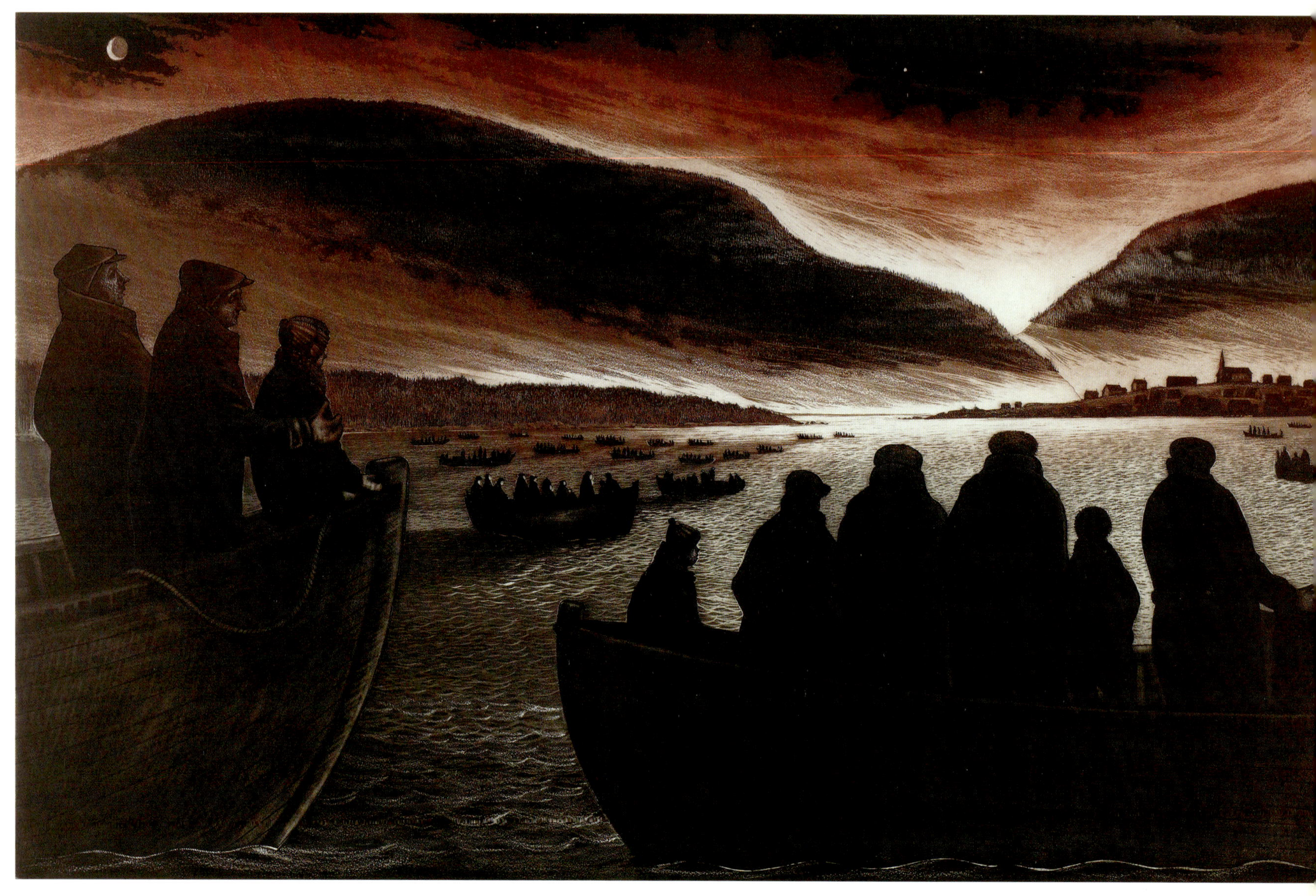

above: 26. **Fire in Indian Bay**, 1979

facing: 27. **Wesleyville: Burning of the Methodist Church**, 1976

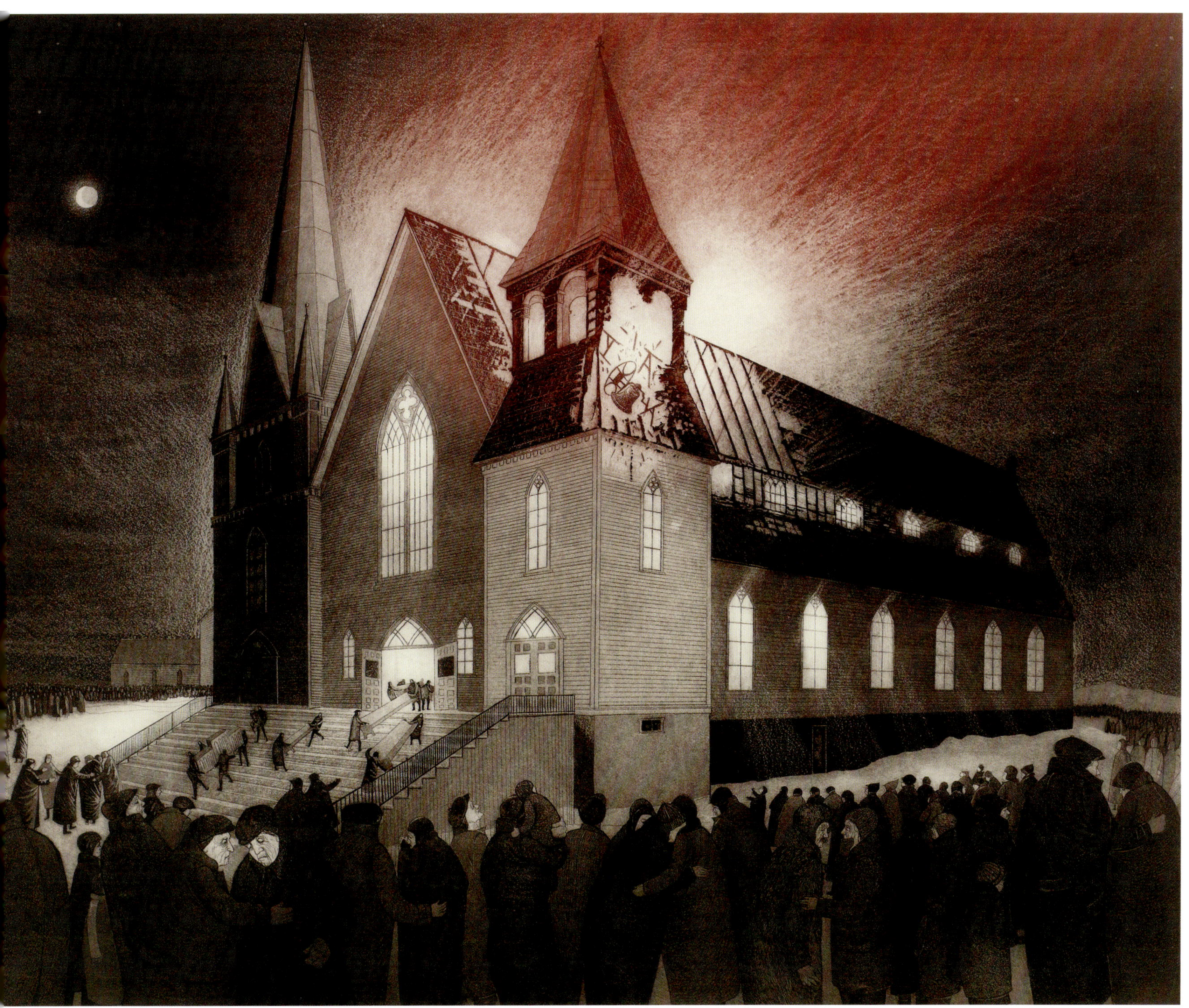

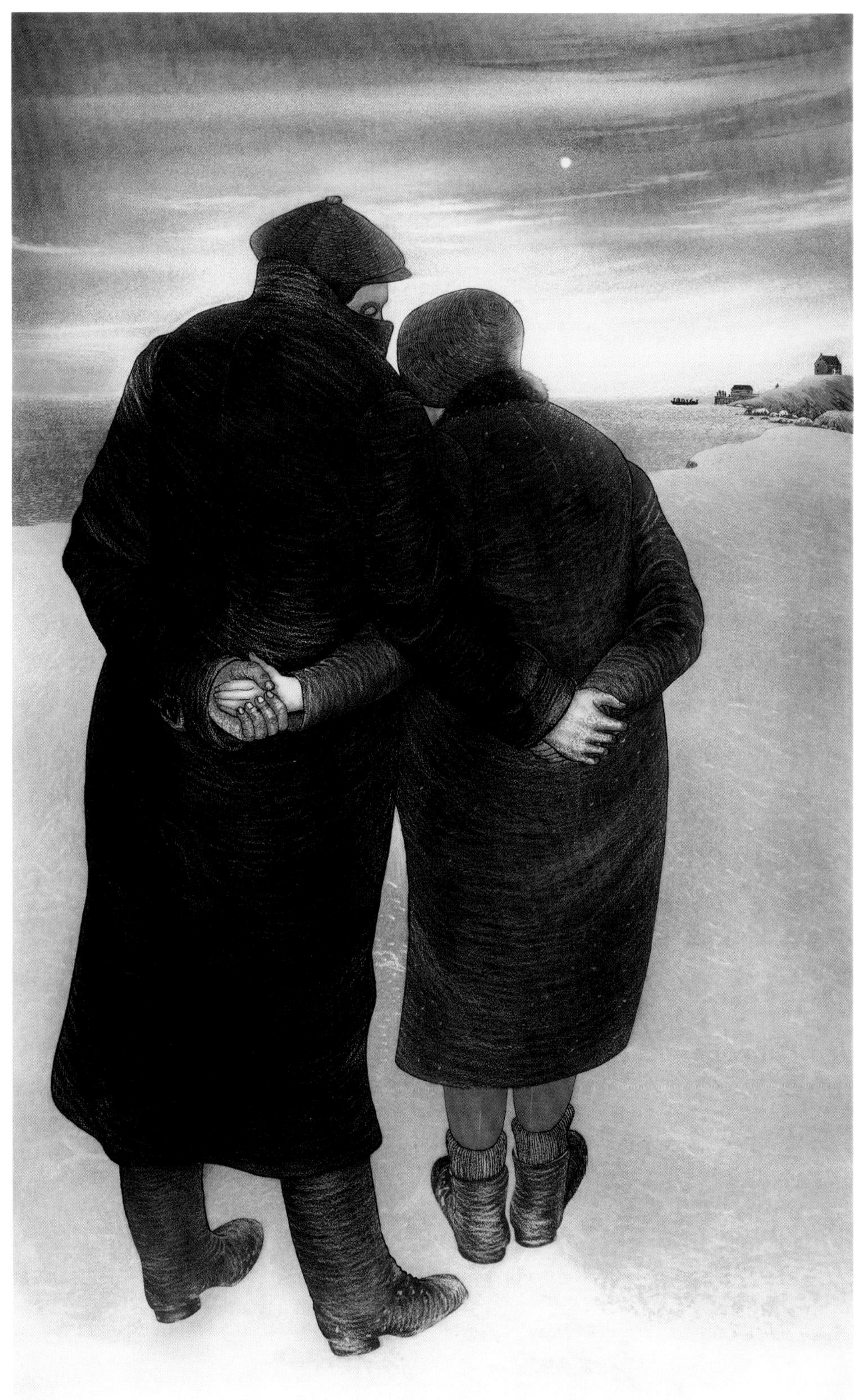

28. **Aunt Mag and Uncle Elias Feltham**, 1976

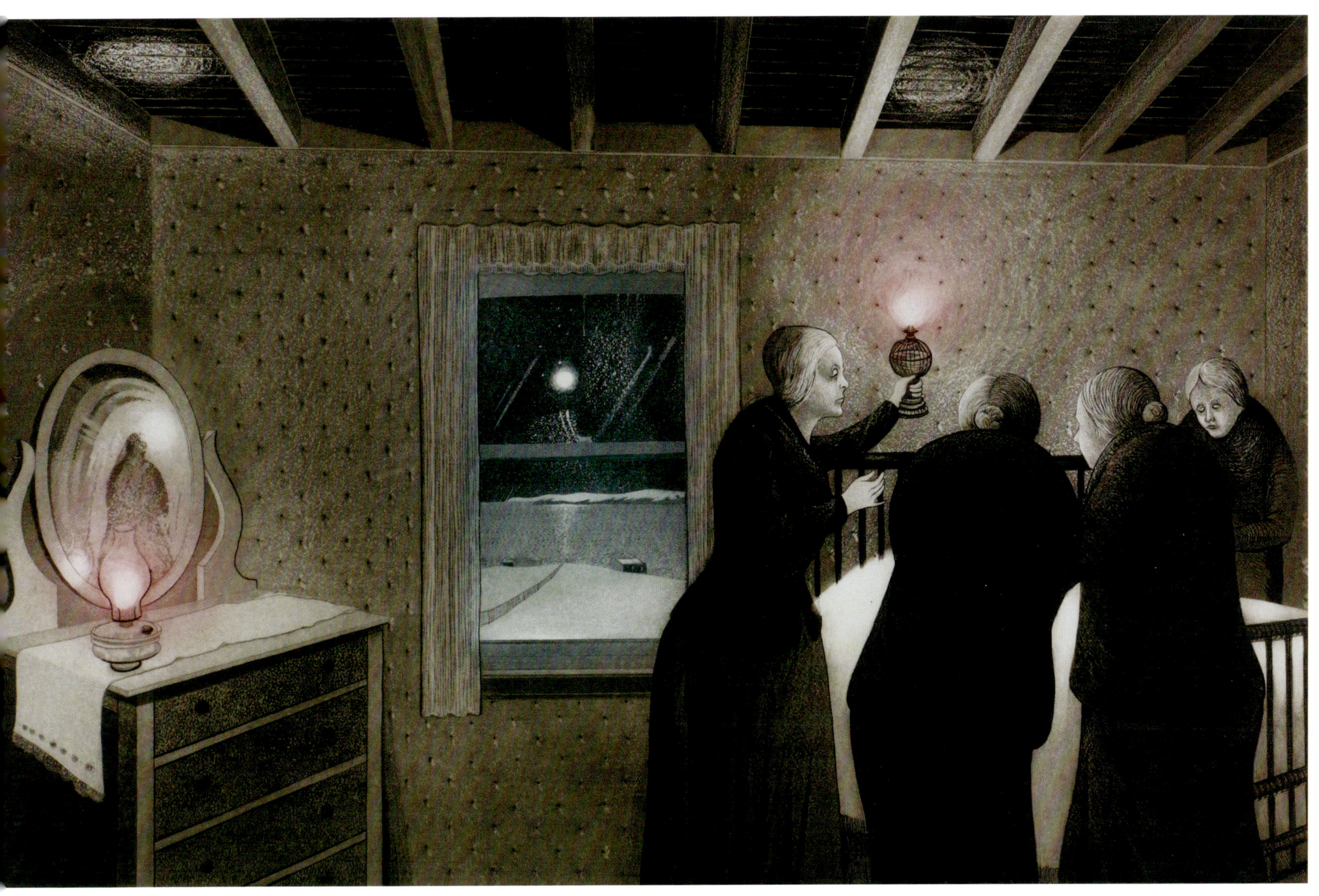

29. **Vigil on Bragg's Island**, 1973

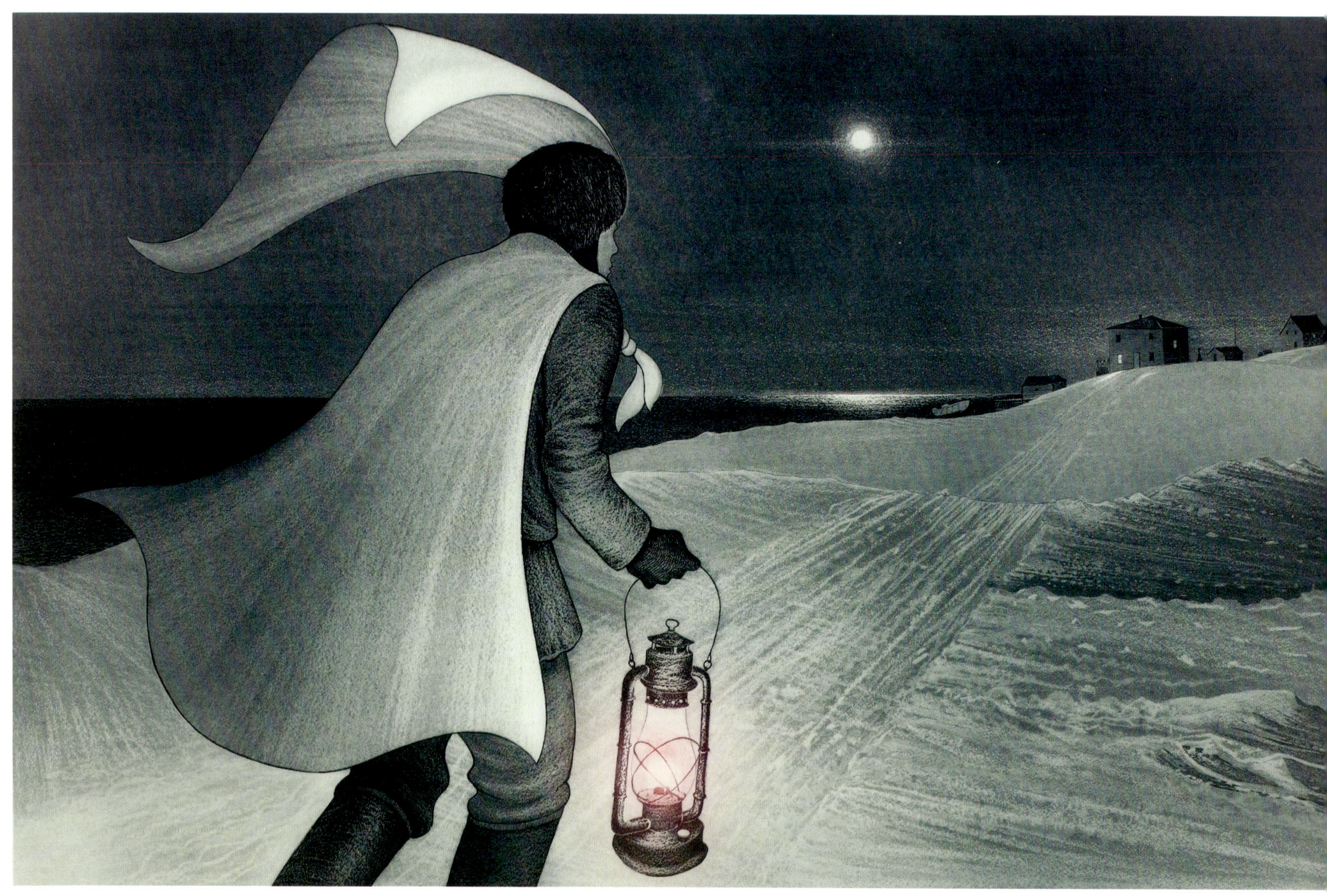

30. **Lone Mummer Approaching**, 1976

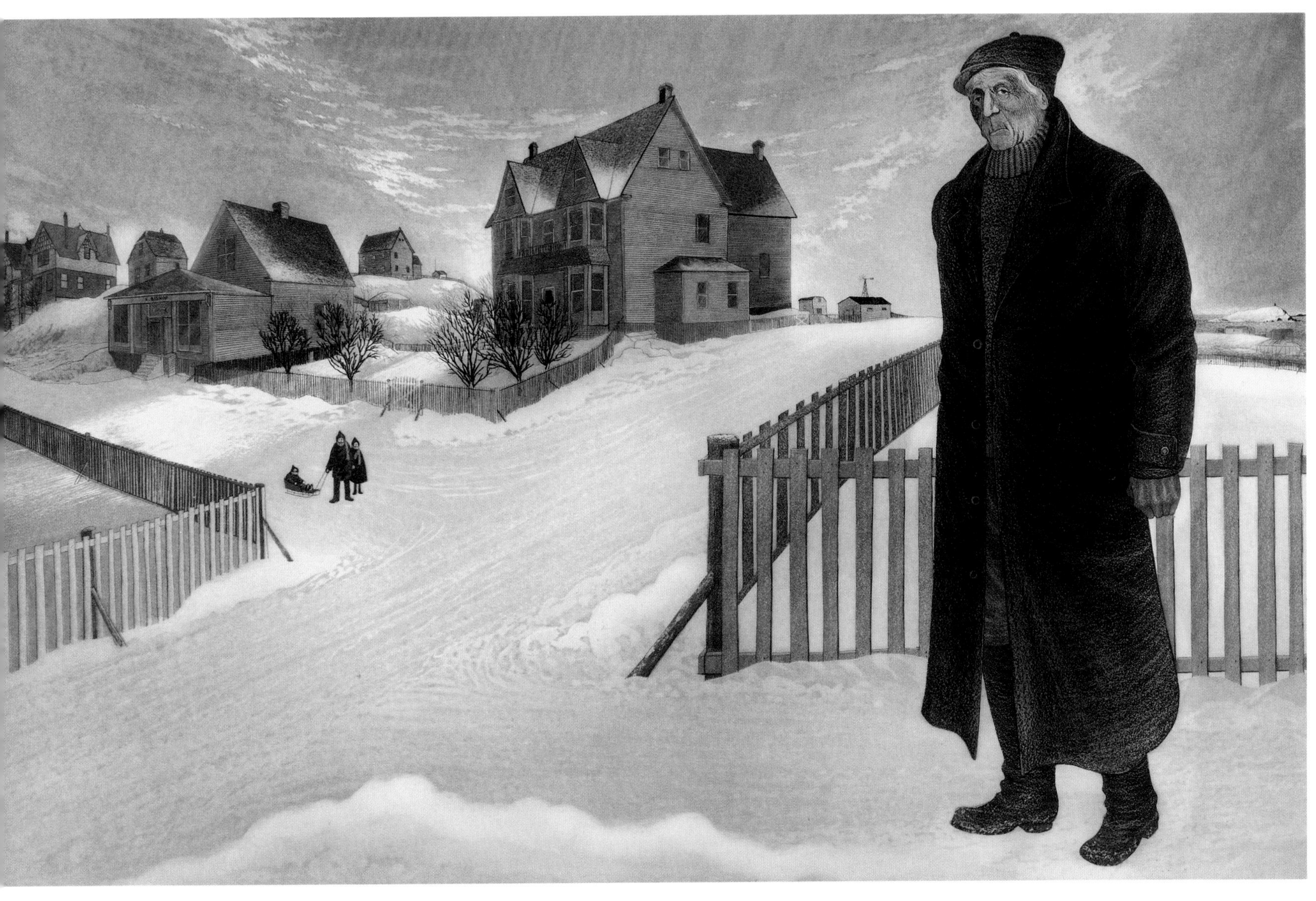

above: 31. **Captain Edward Bishop Home in Wesleyville,** 1976

overleaf: 32. **Hauling Job Sturge's House,** 1979

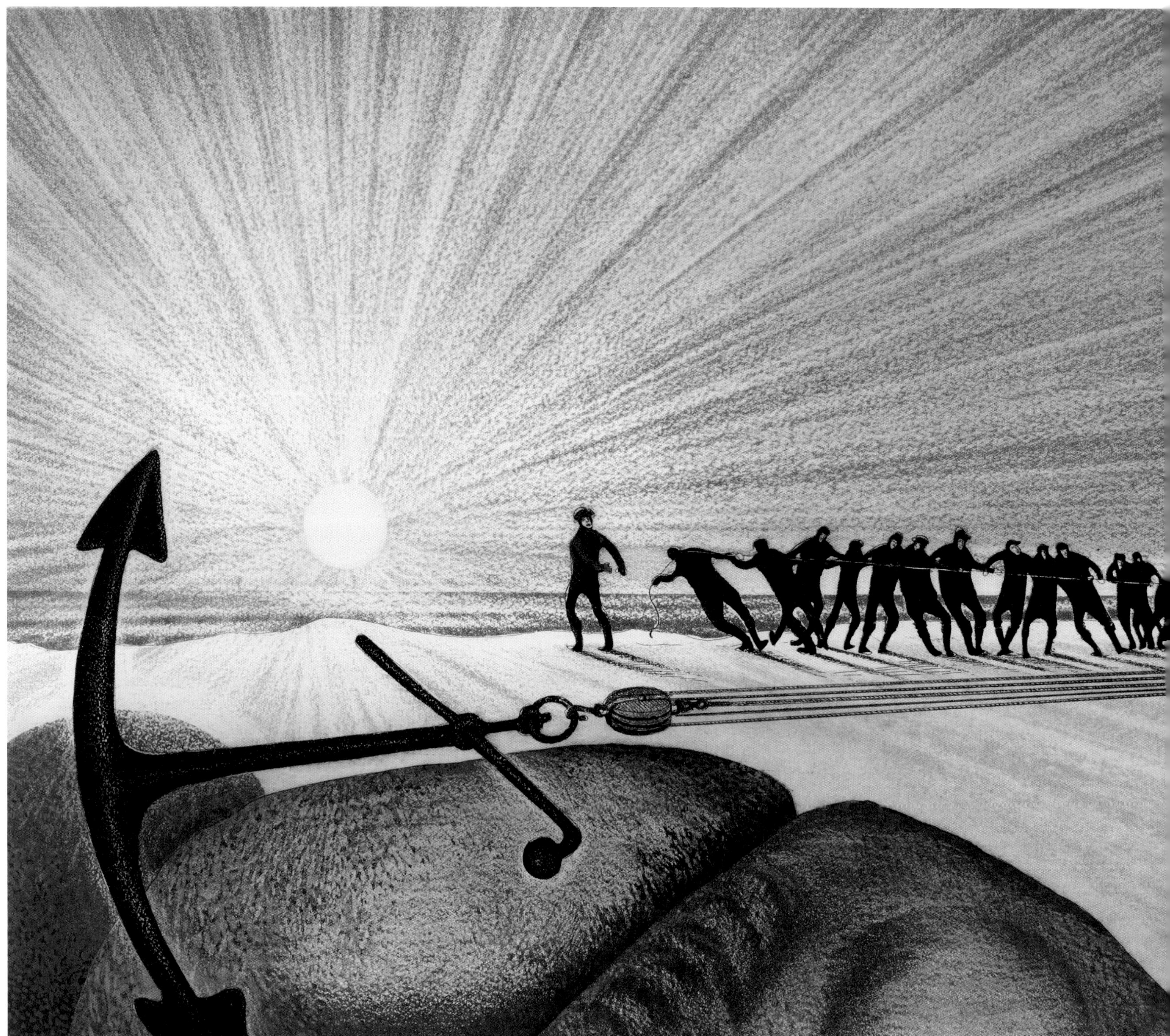

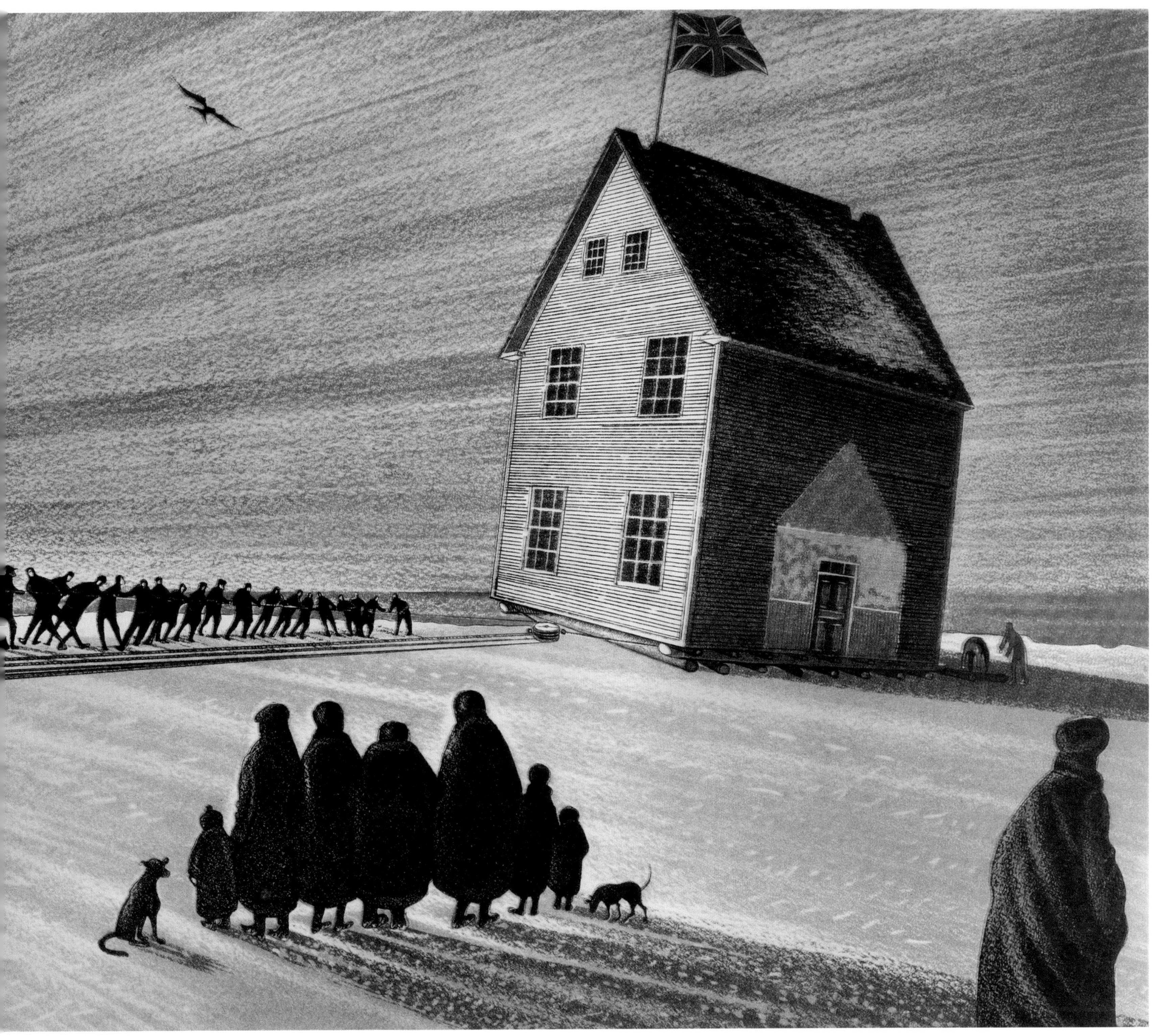

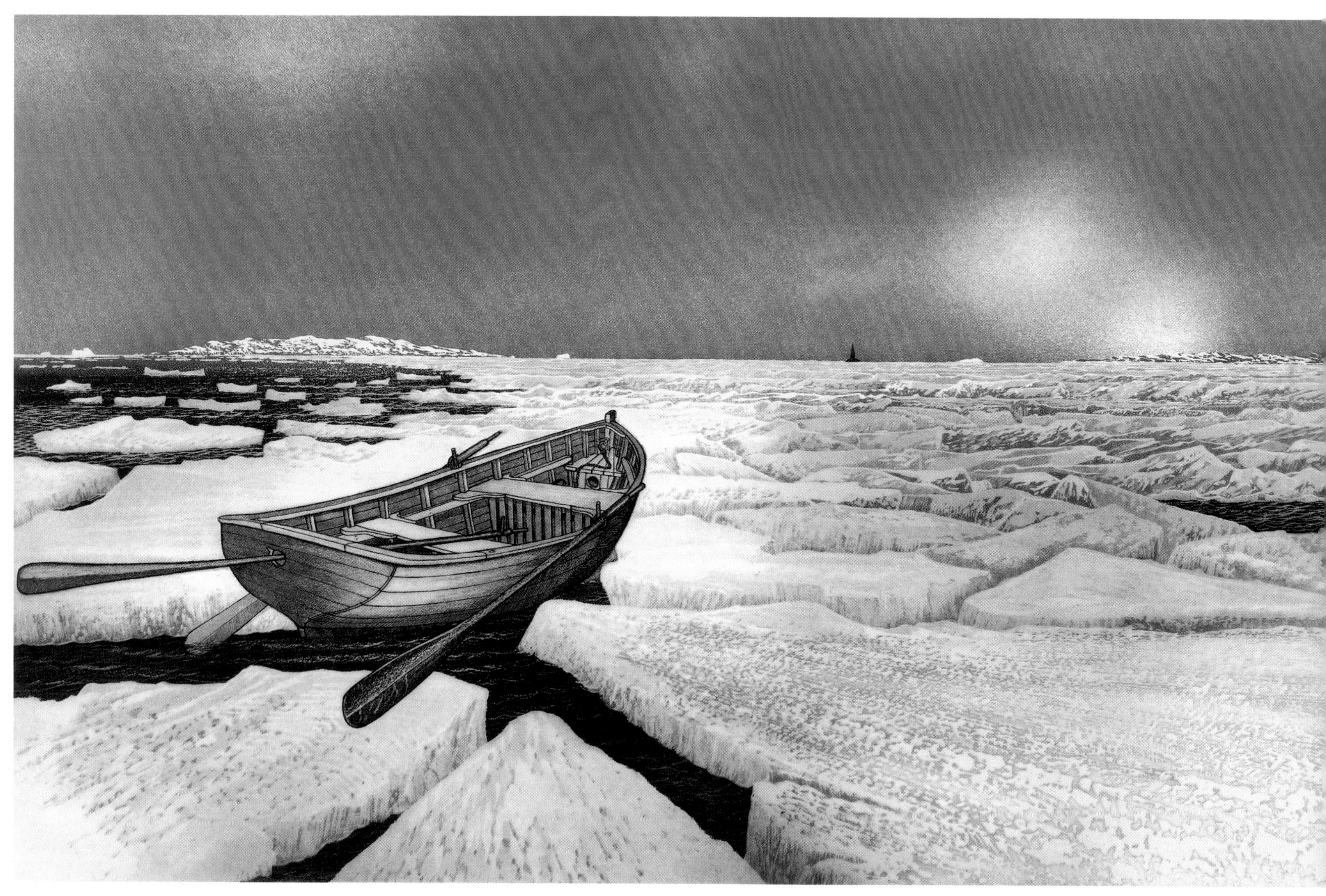

33. **Brian and Martin Winsor**, 1979

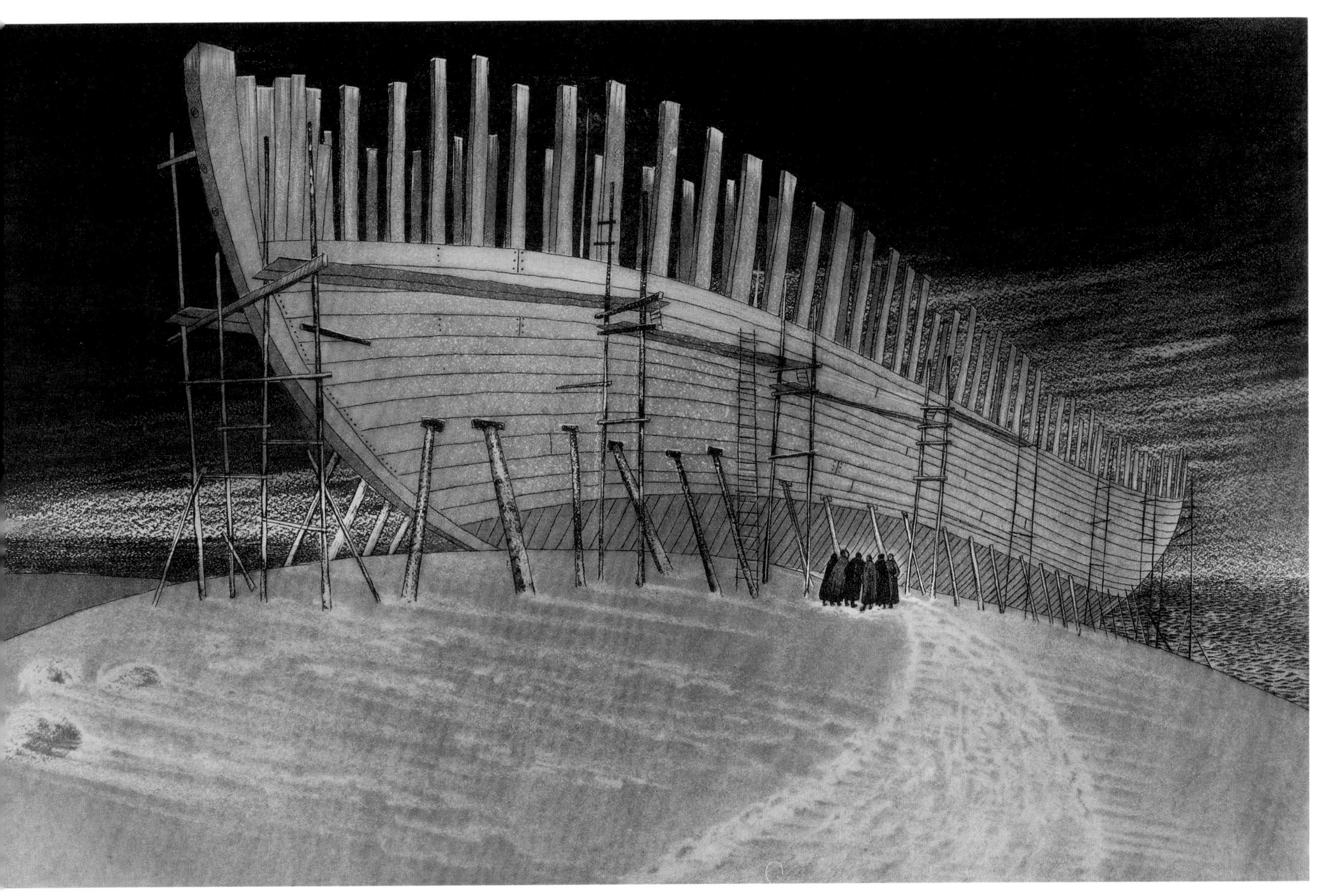

34. **Prince Andrew under Construction**, 1973

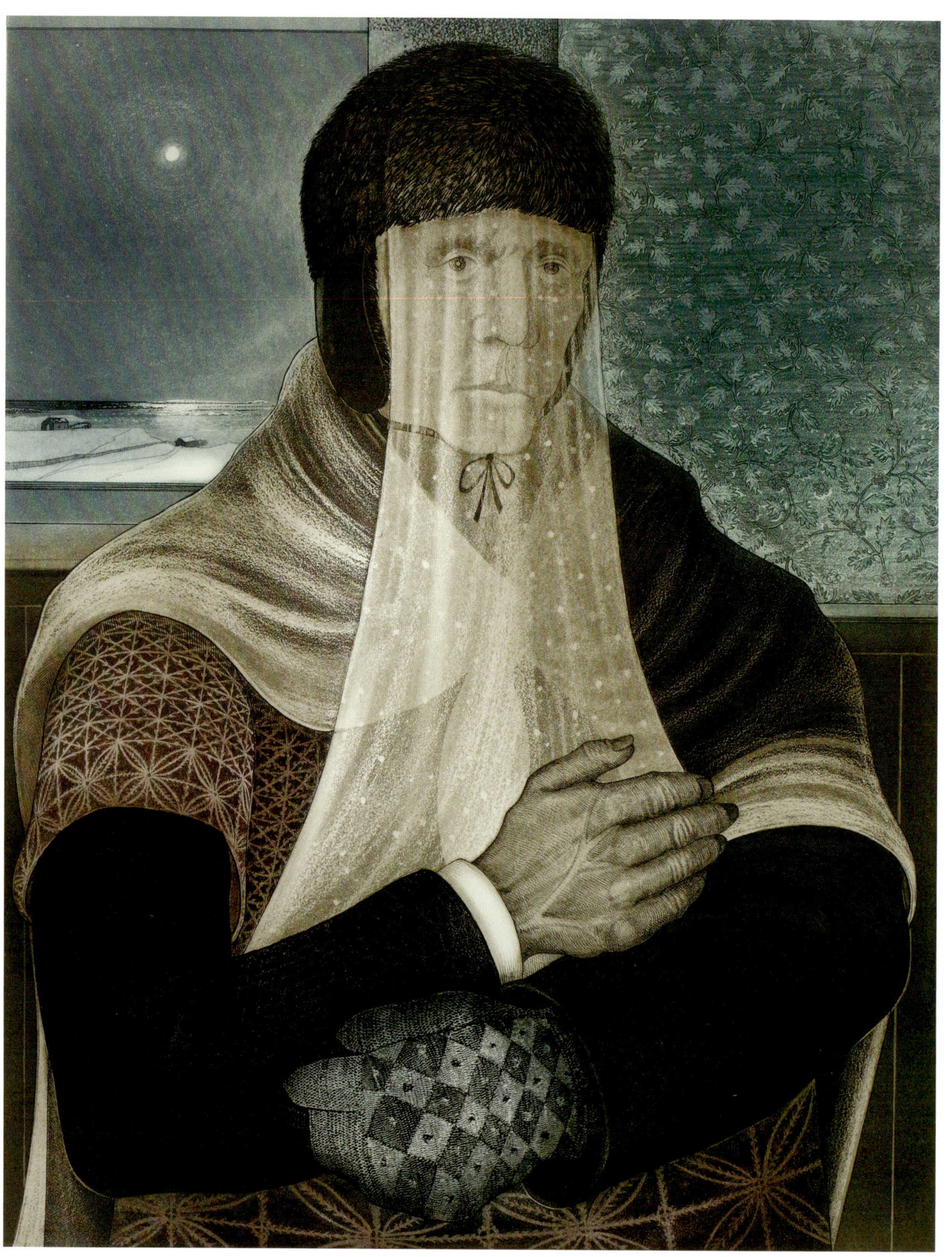

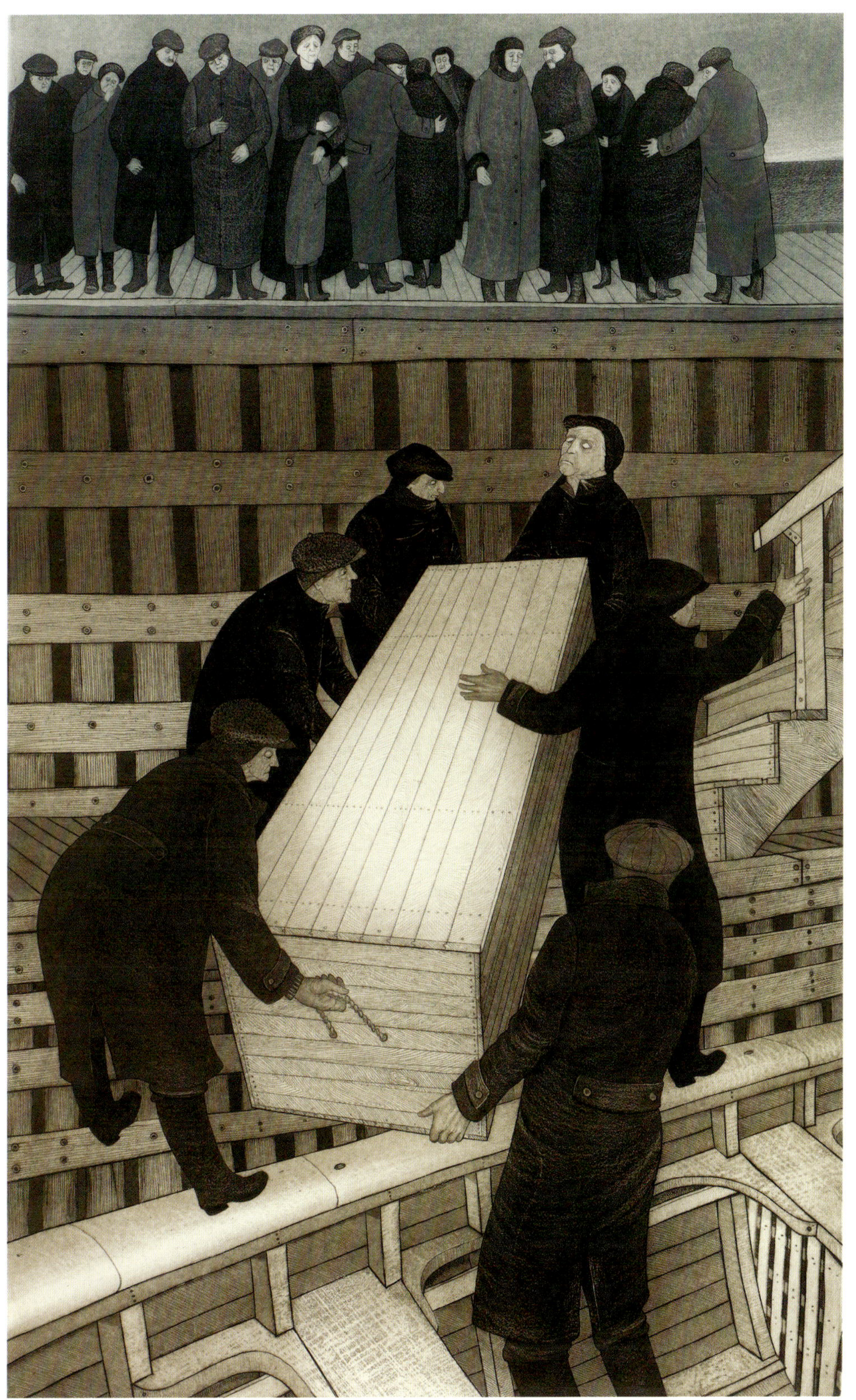

facing: 35. **Lone Mummer Inside,** 1979

left: 36. **Captain Jesse Winsor Home from the Labrador,** 1976

overleaf, left: 37. **Captain Lew Kean Passing,** 1979

overleaf, right: 38. **The Seabird Hunter,** 1978

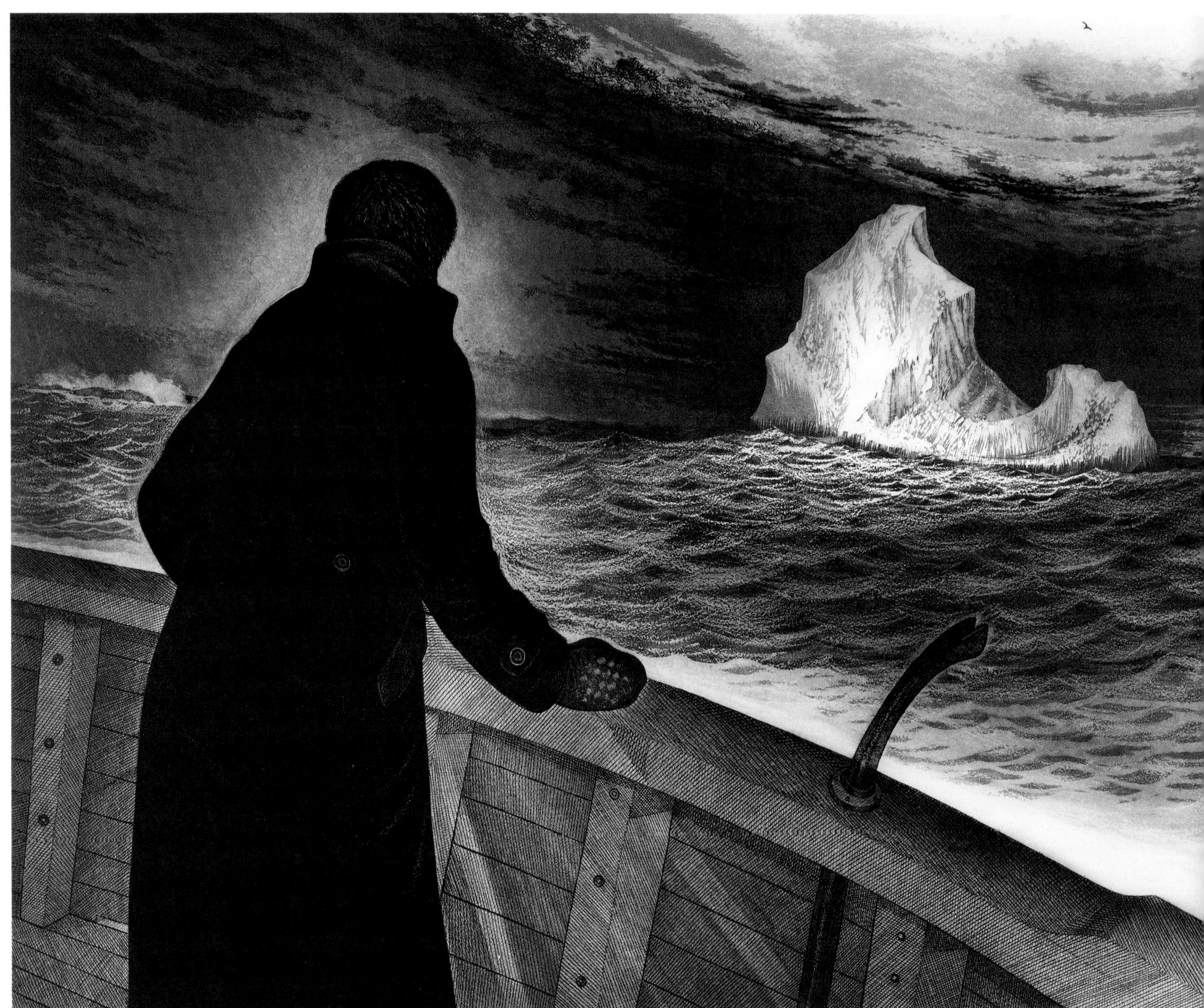

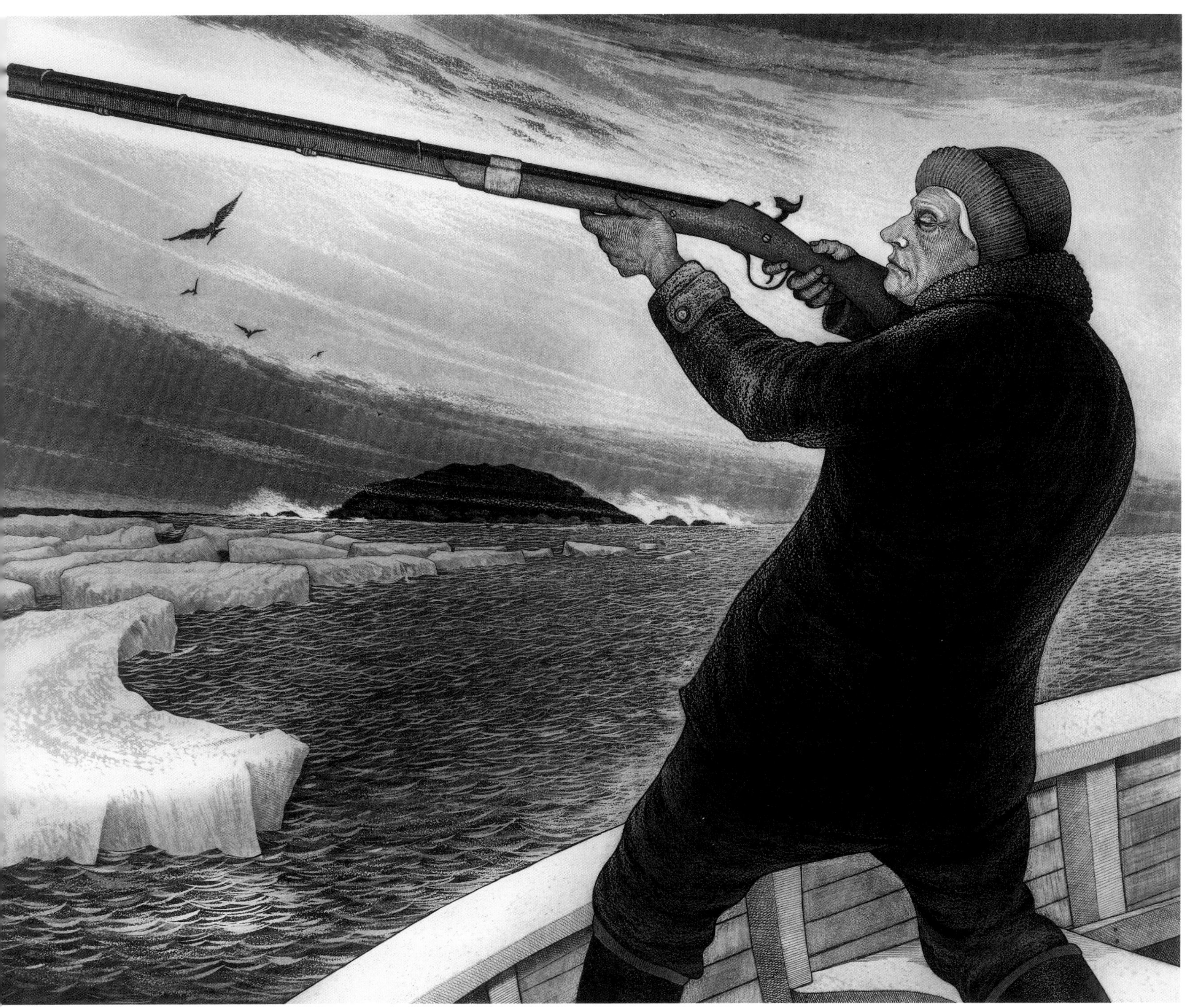

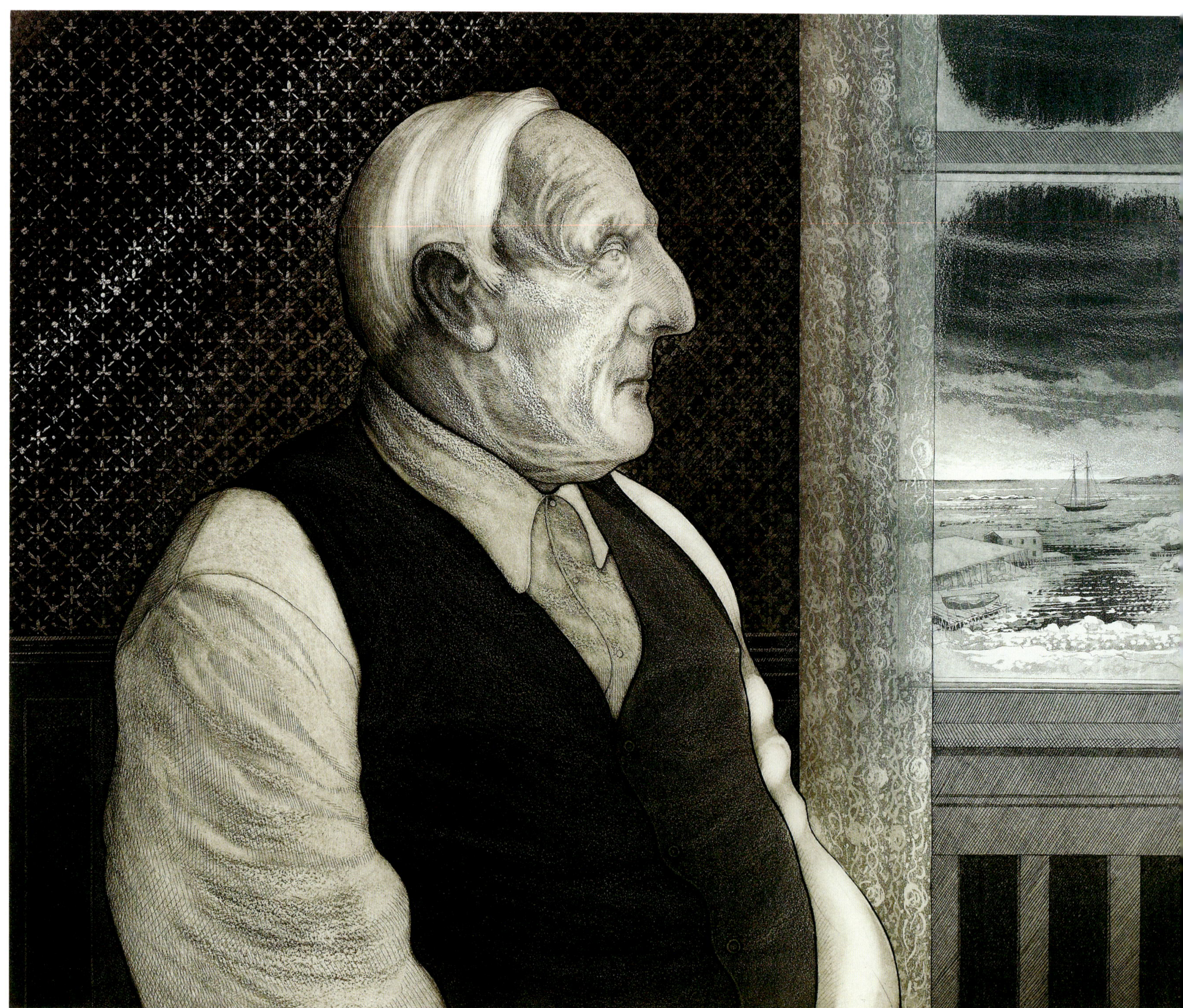

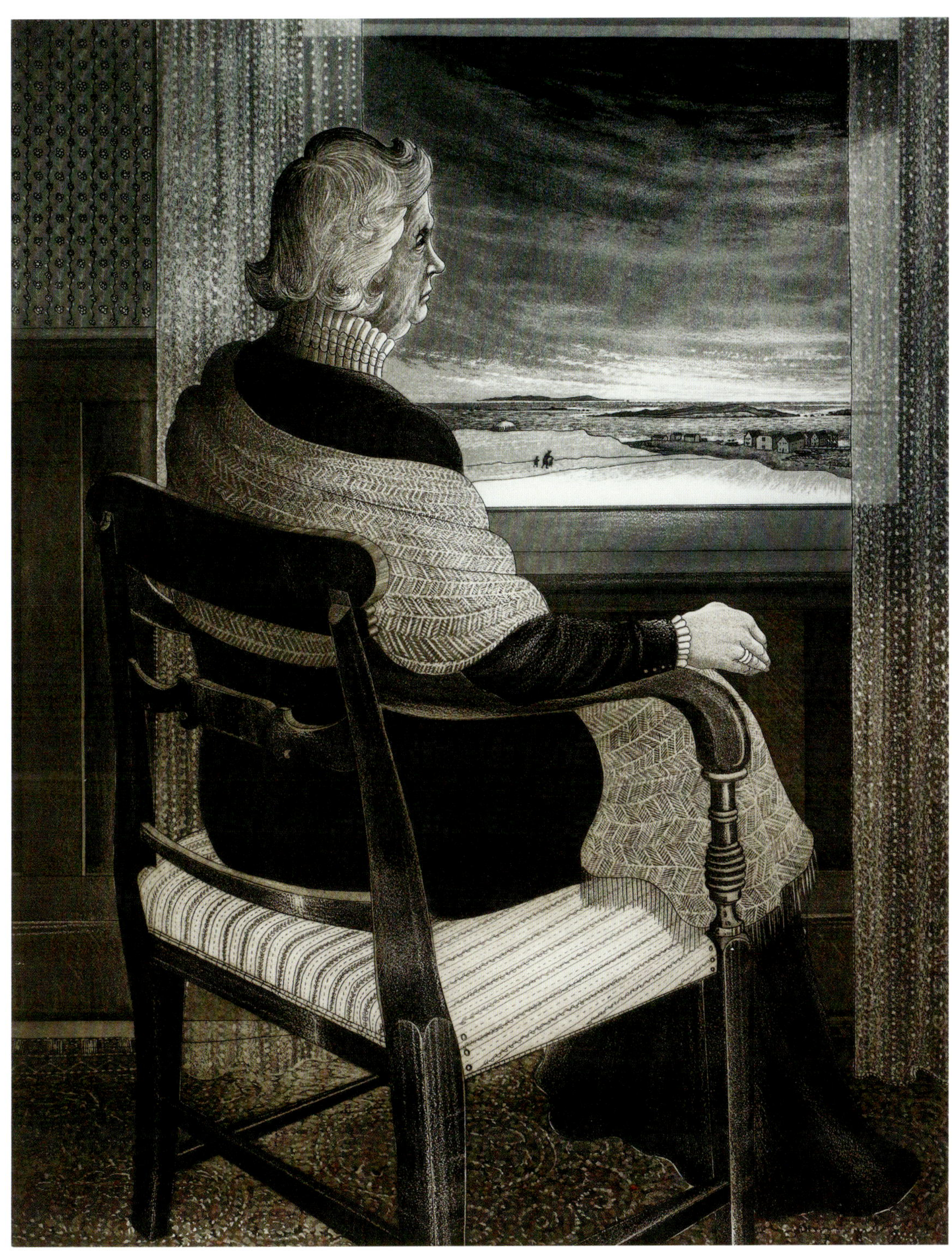

facing: 39. **Skipper Bax Ford Home in Wesleyville**, 1979

left: 40. **Mrs. Captain B. Home in Wesleyville**, 1979

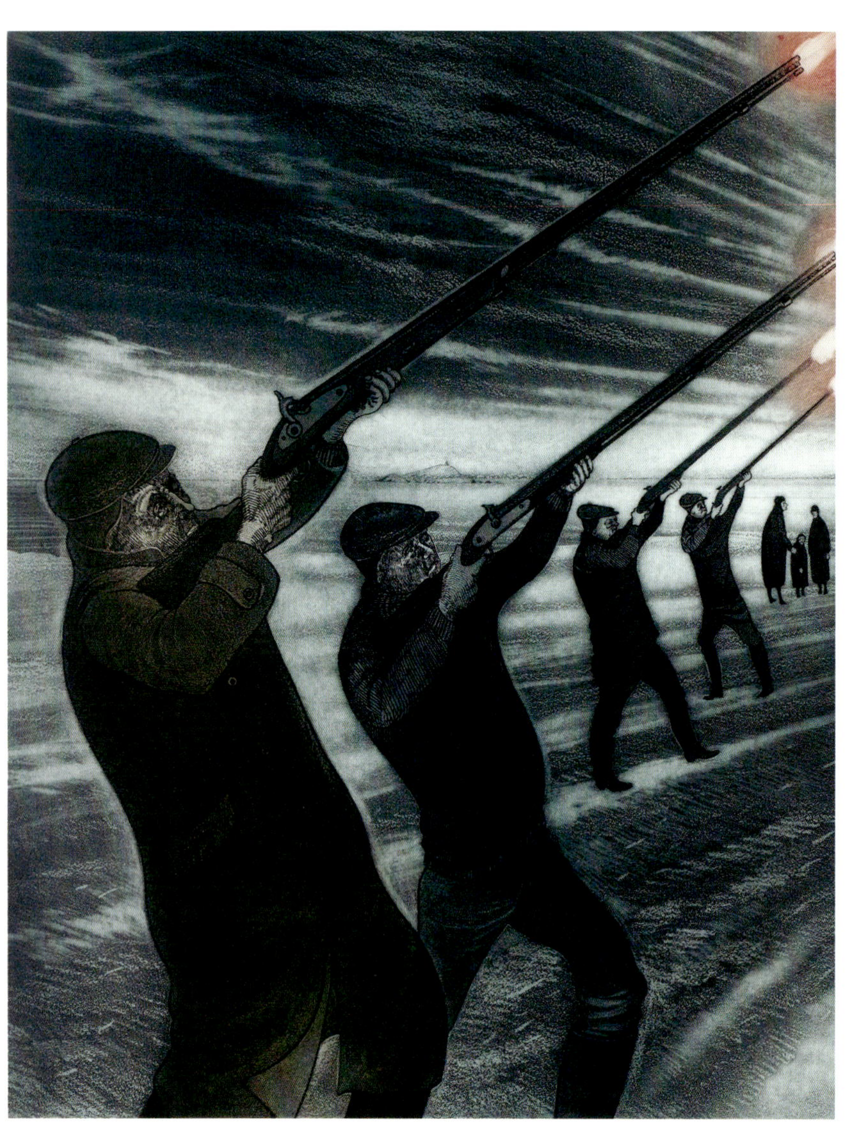

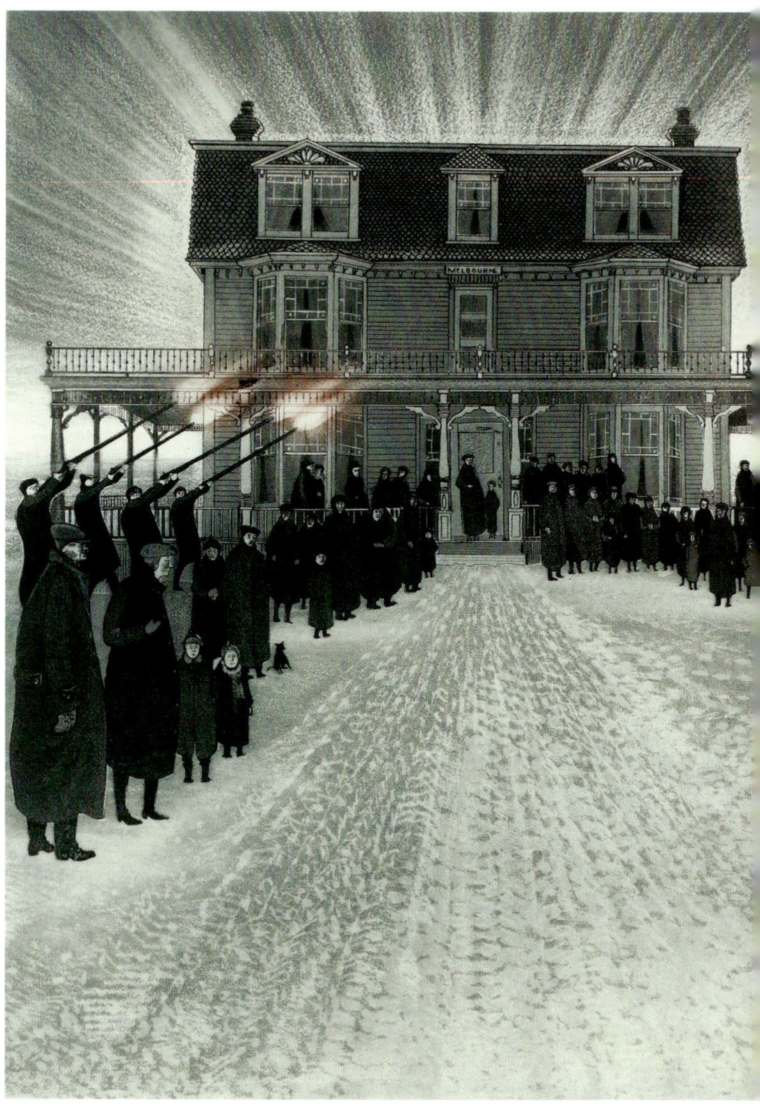
MELBOURNE

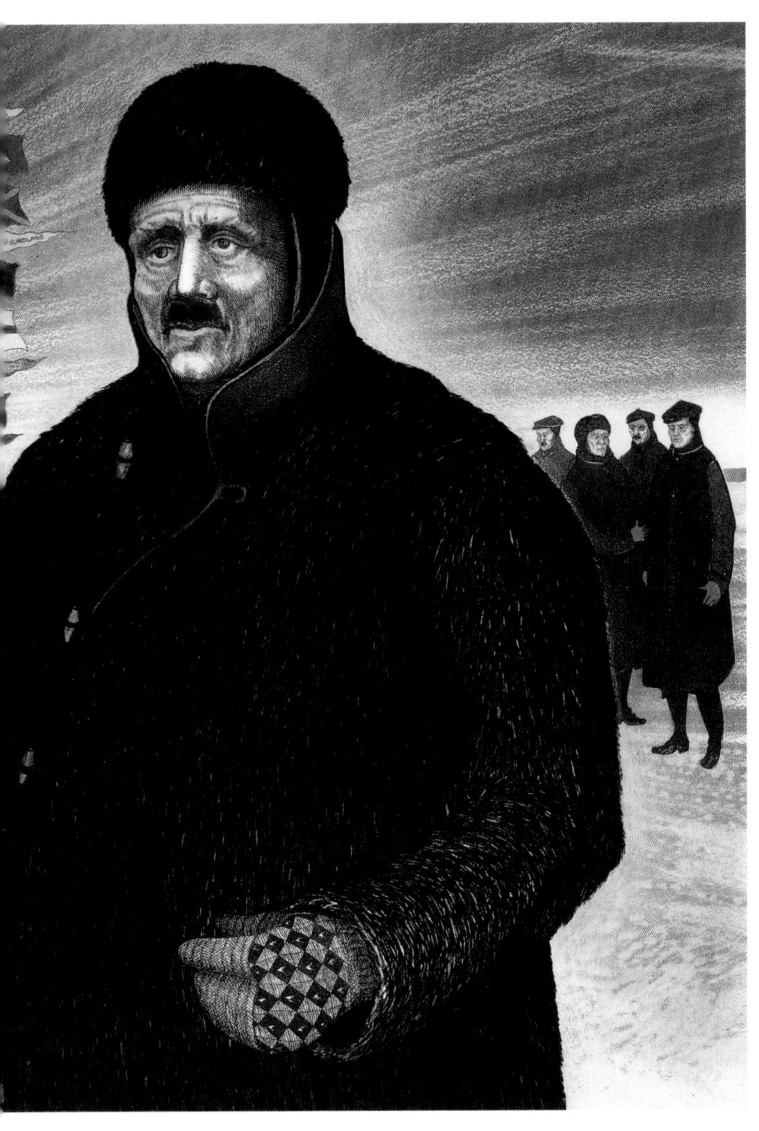
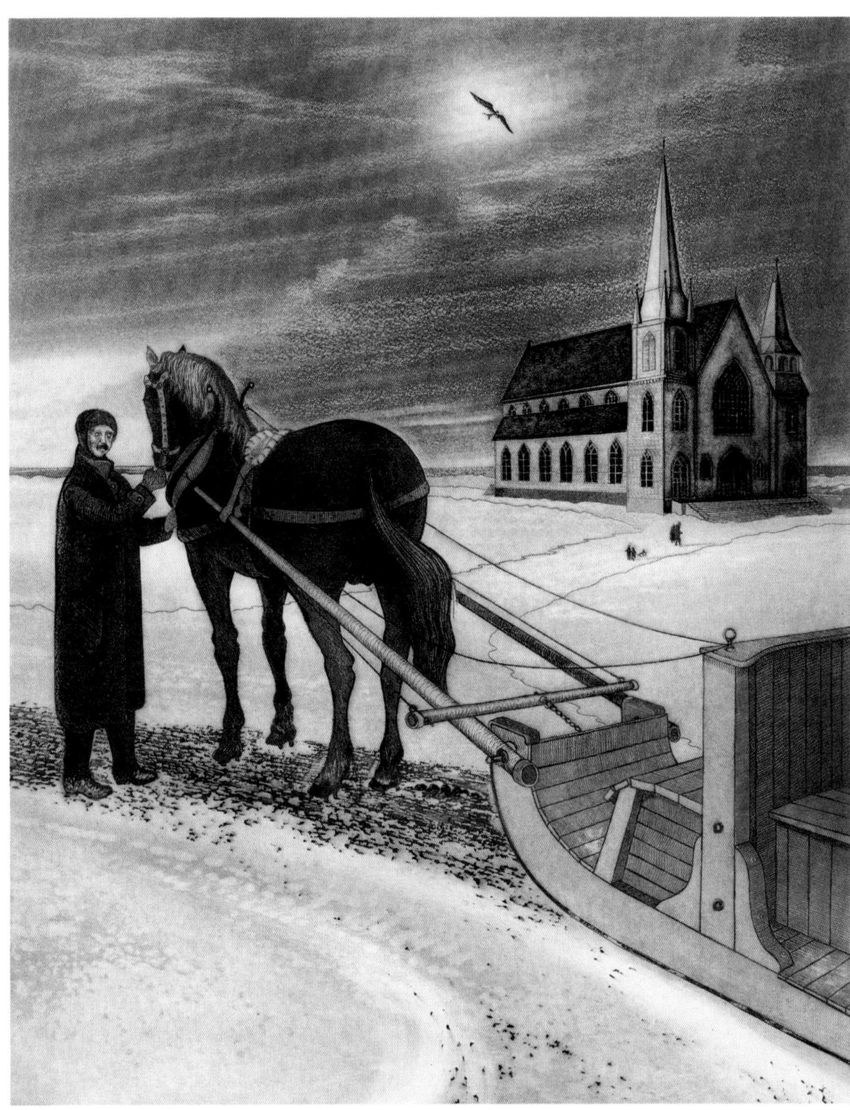

41. **Captain Jesse Winsor Home from the Icefields** (triptych), 1979

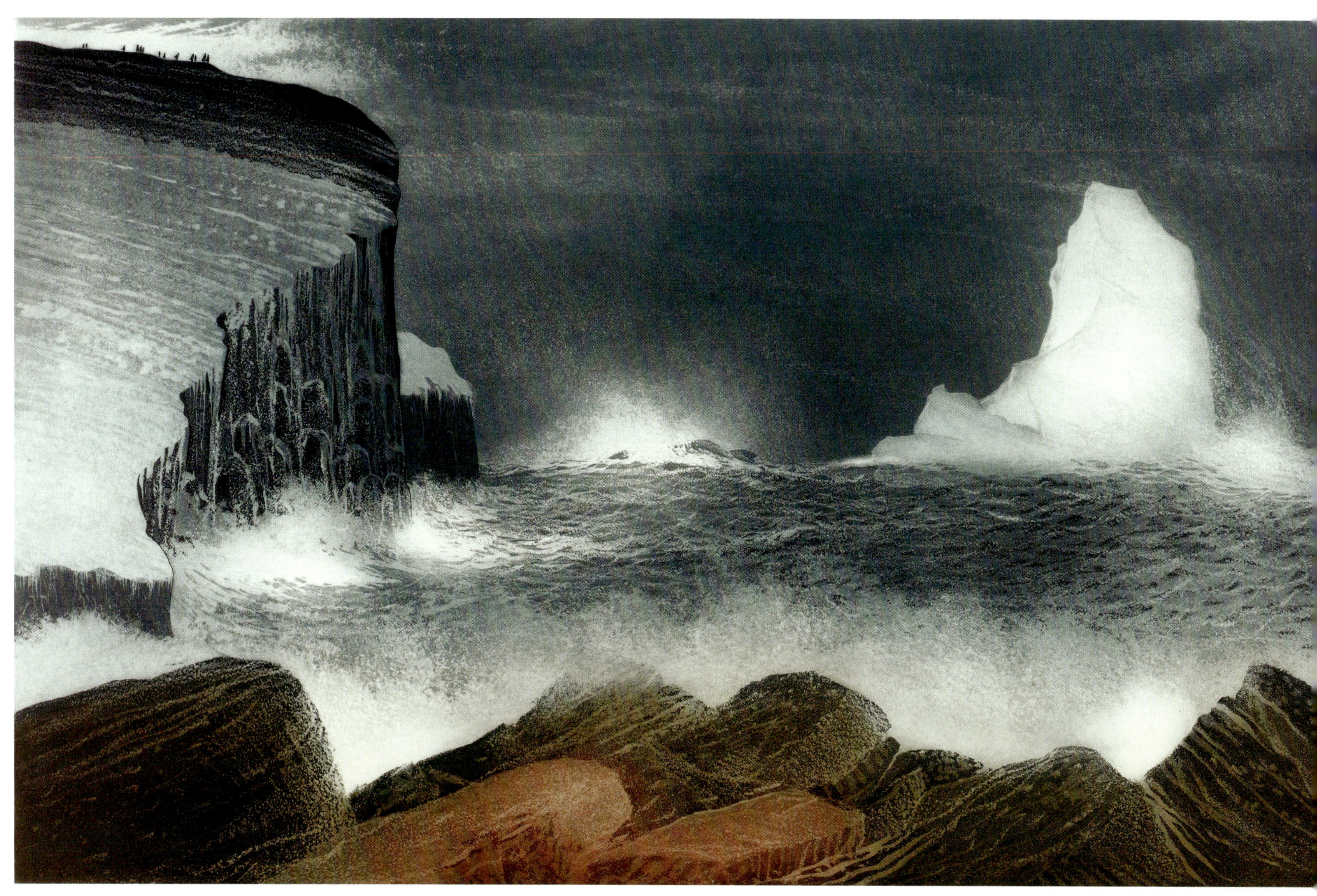

42. **April Iceberg off Bragg's Island**, 1976

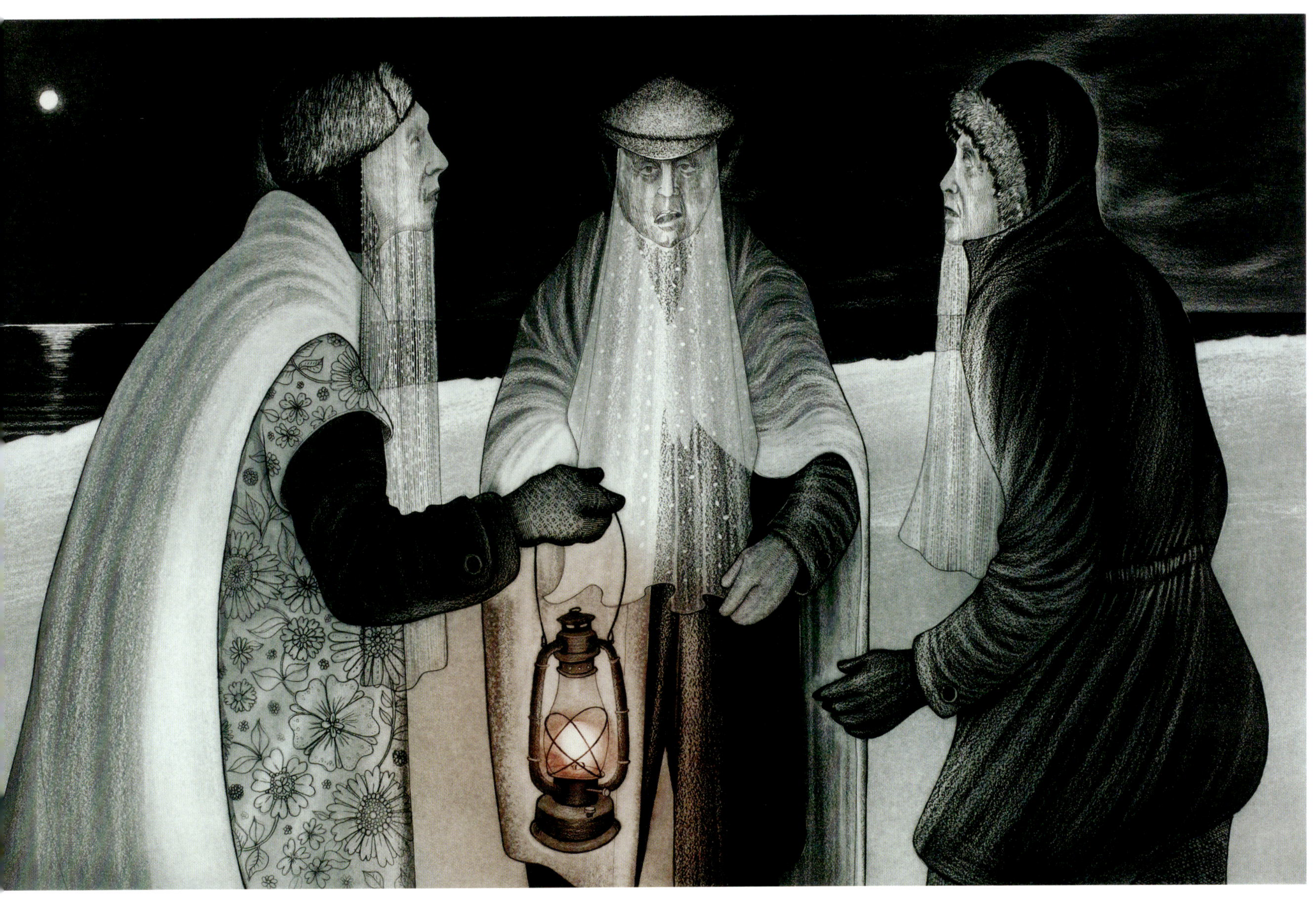

43. **Three Mummers on Winsor's Point**, 1979

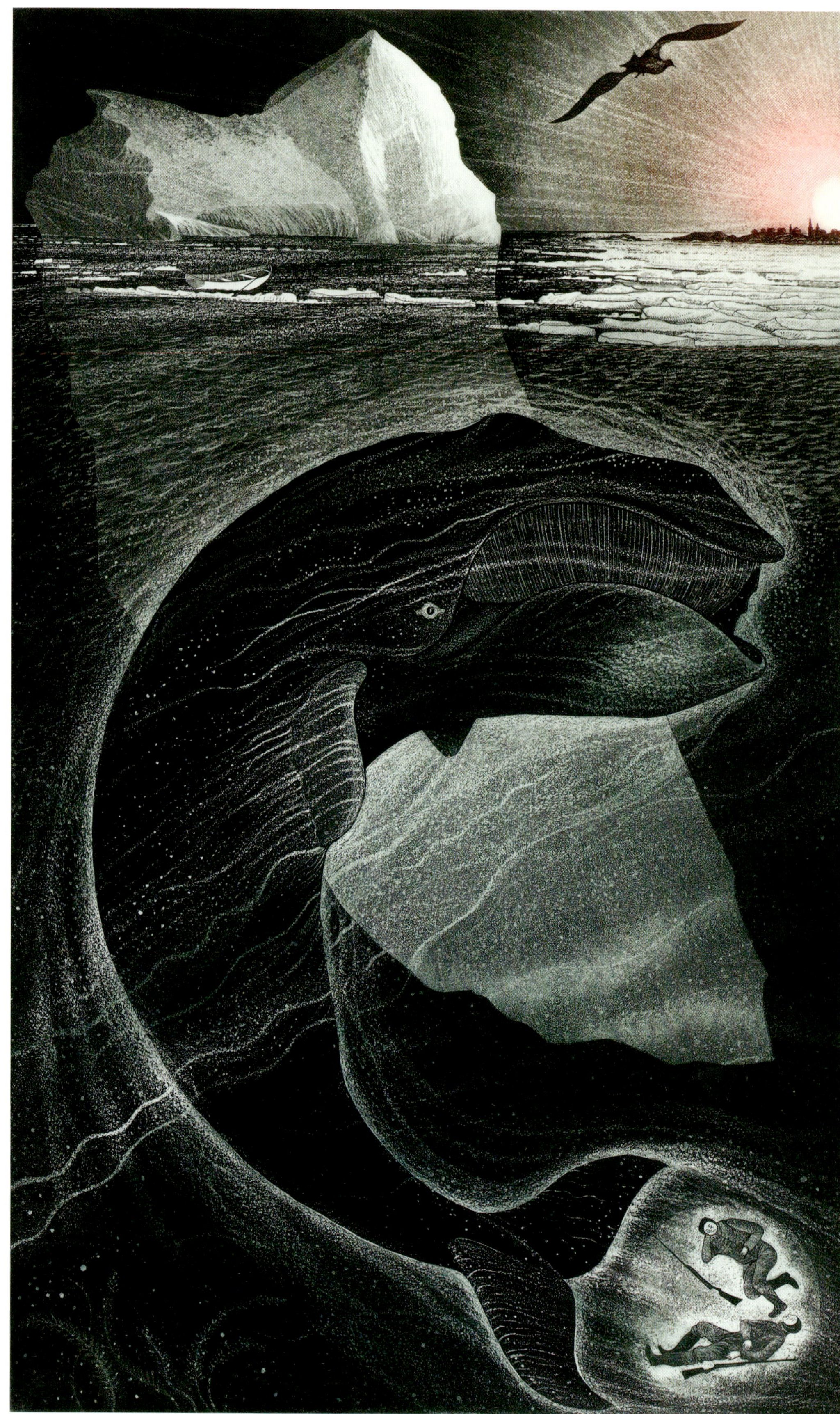

44. The Great Peace of Brian and Martin Winsor, 1982

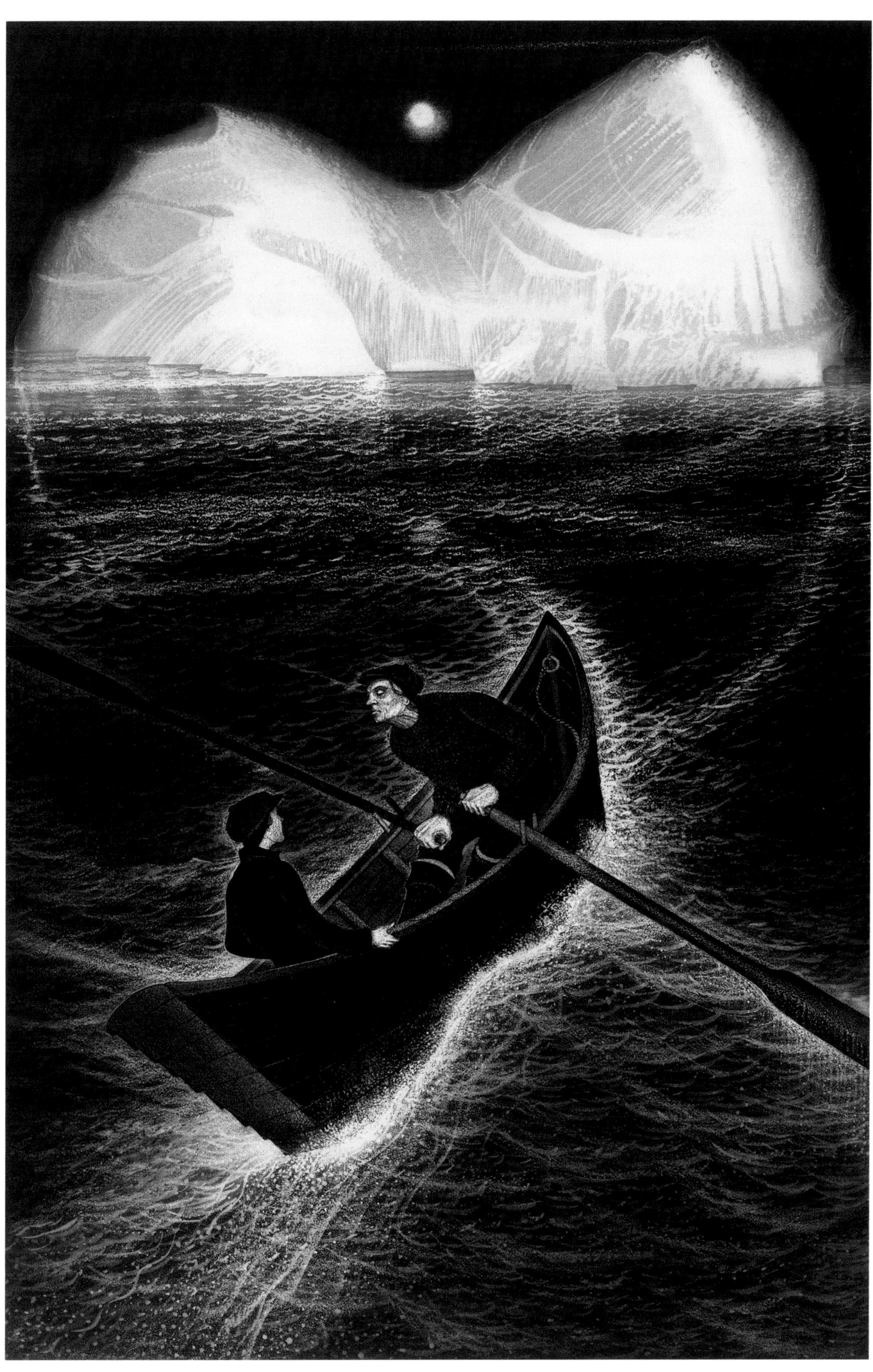

45. **His Father's Dreams**, 1985

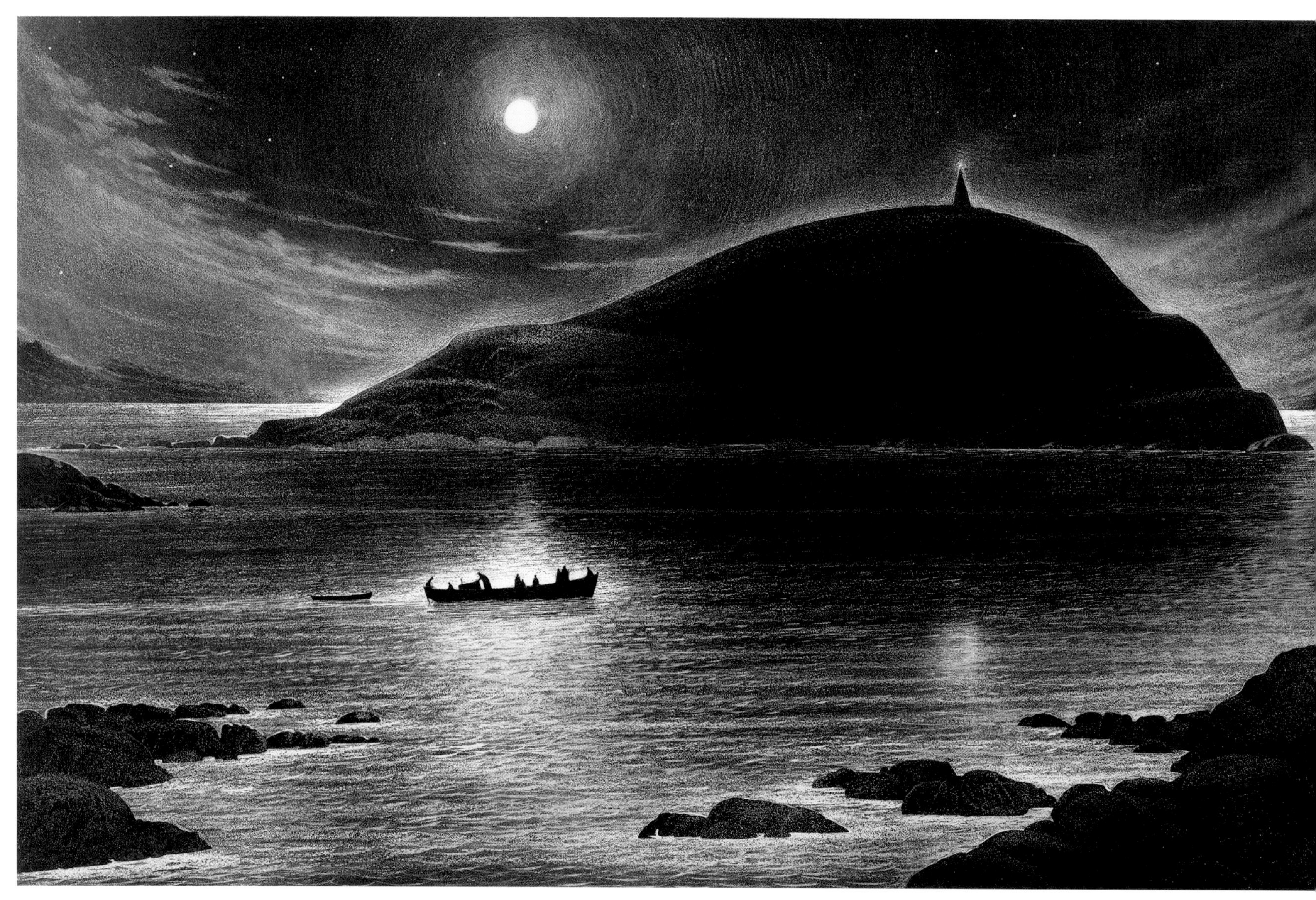

46. **Wesleyville: Night Passage Bennett's High Island** from **Bennett's Island Trilogy**, 1981

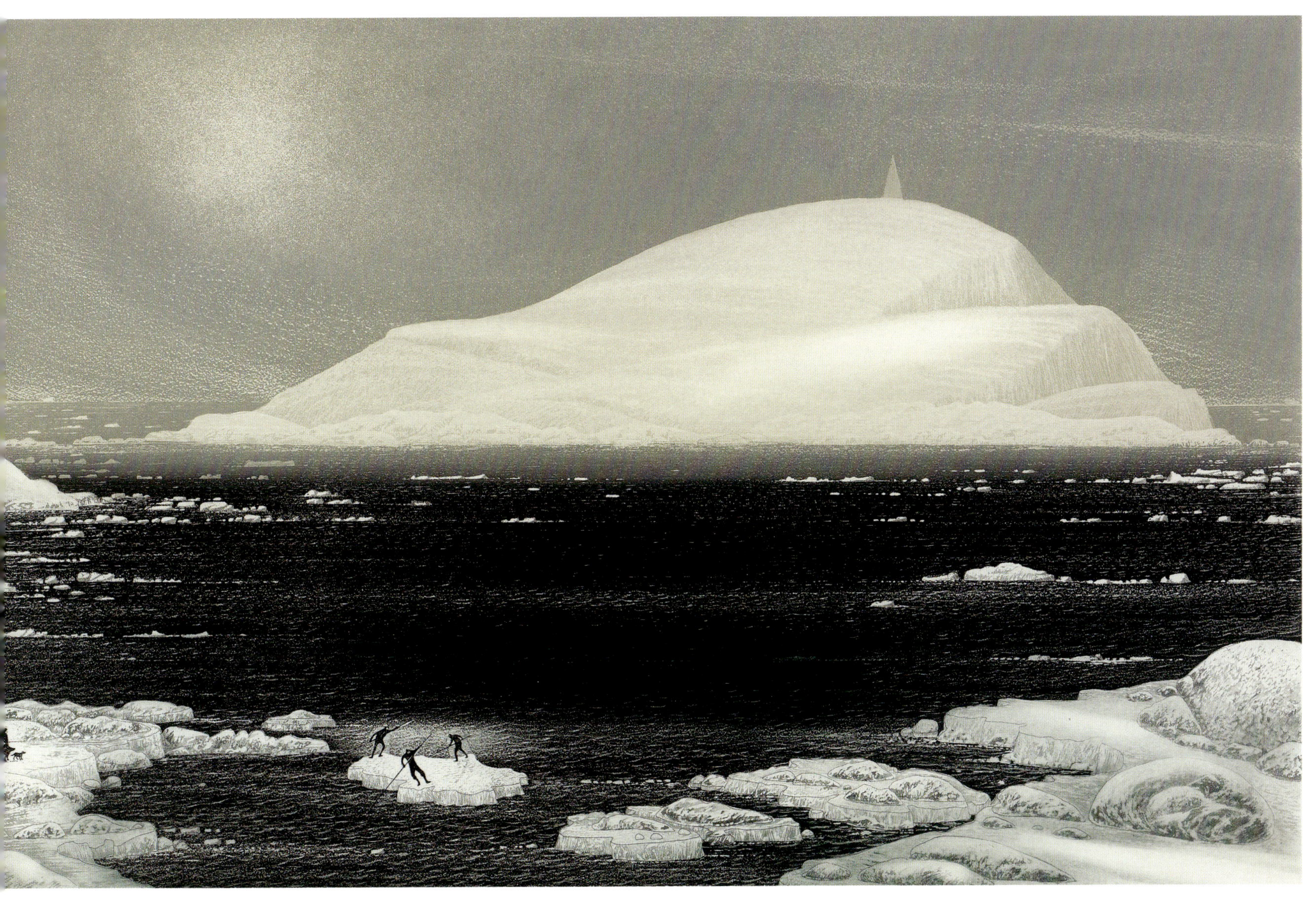

47. **Wesleyville: March Ice Raft** from **Bennett's Island Trilogy**, 1981

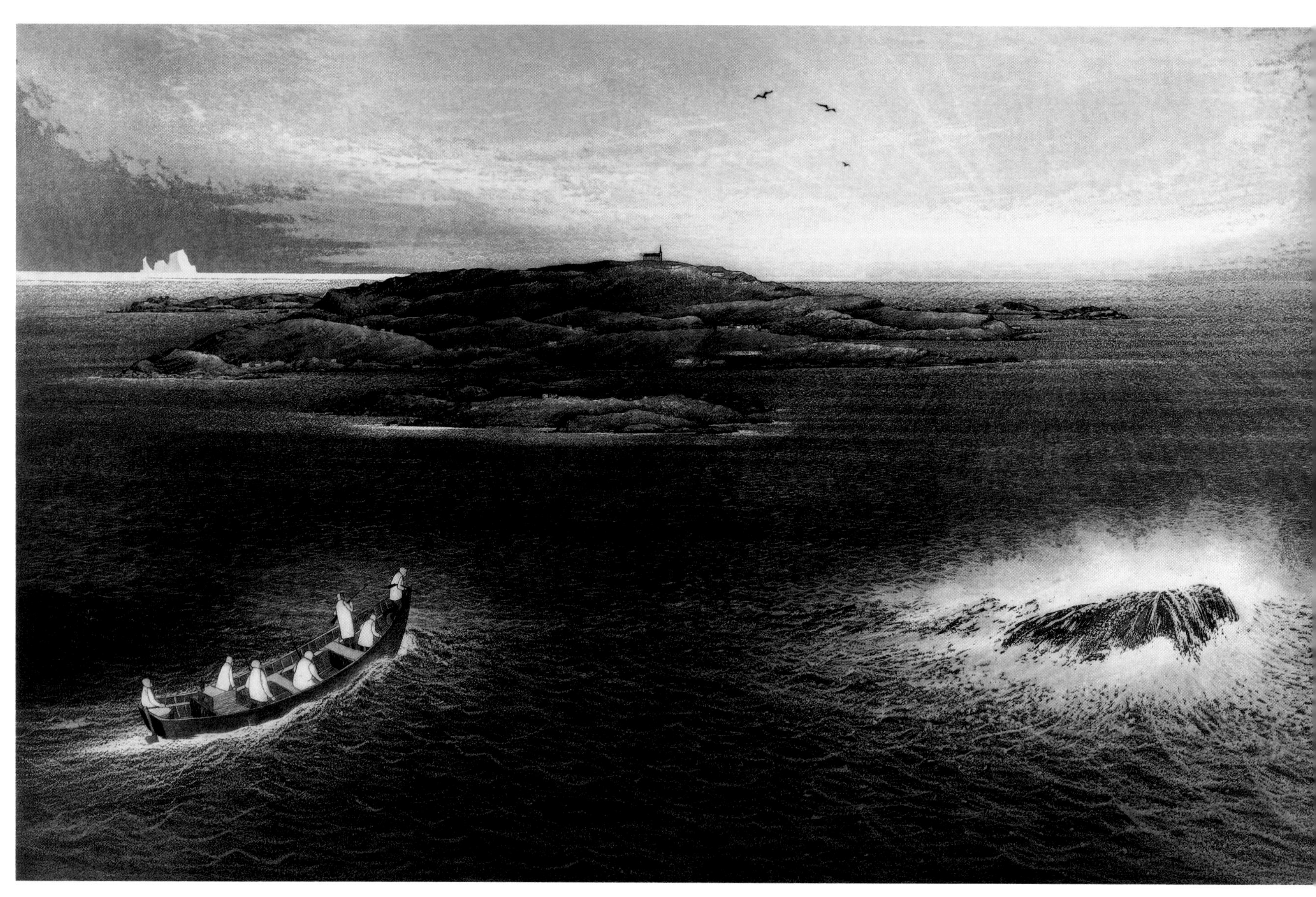

48. **Seabird Hunters Returning Home to Bragg's Island**, 1976

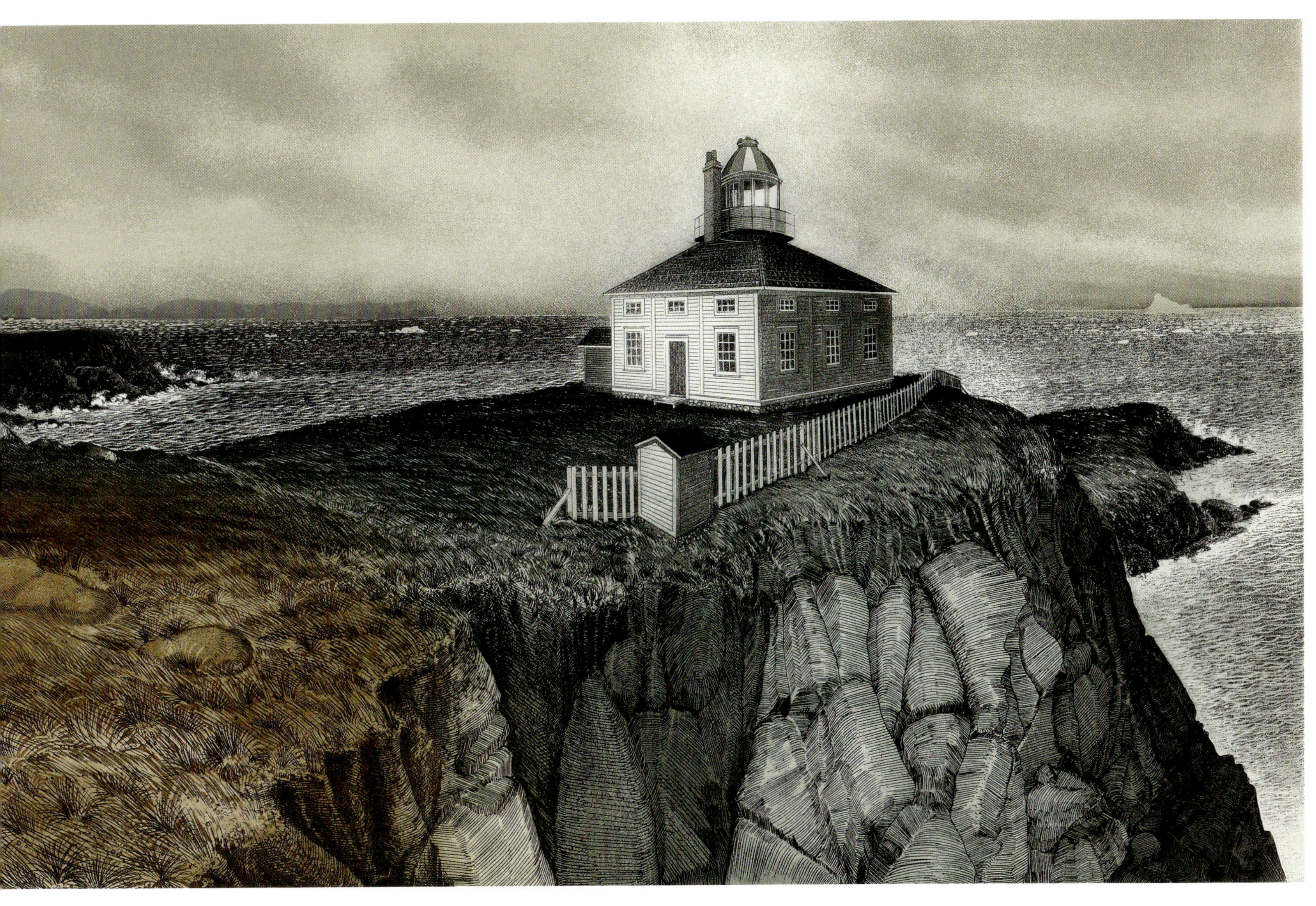

49. **Cape Spear, Newfoundland**, 1983

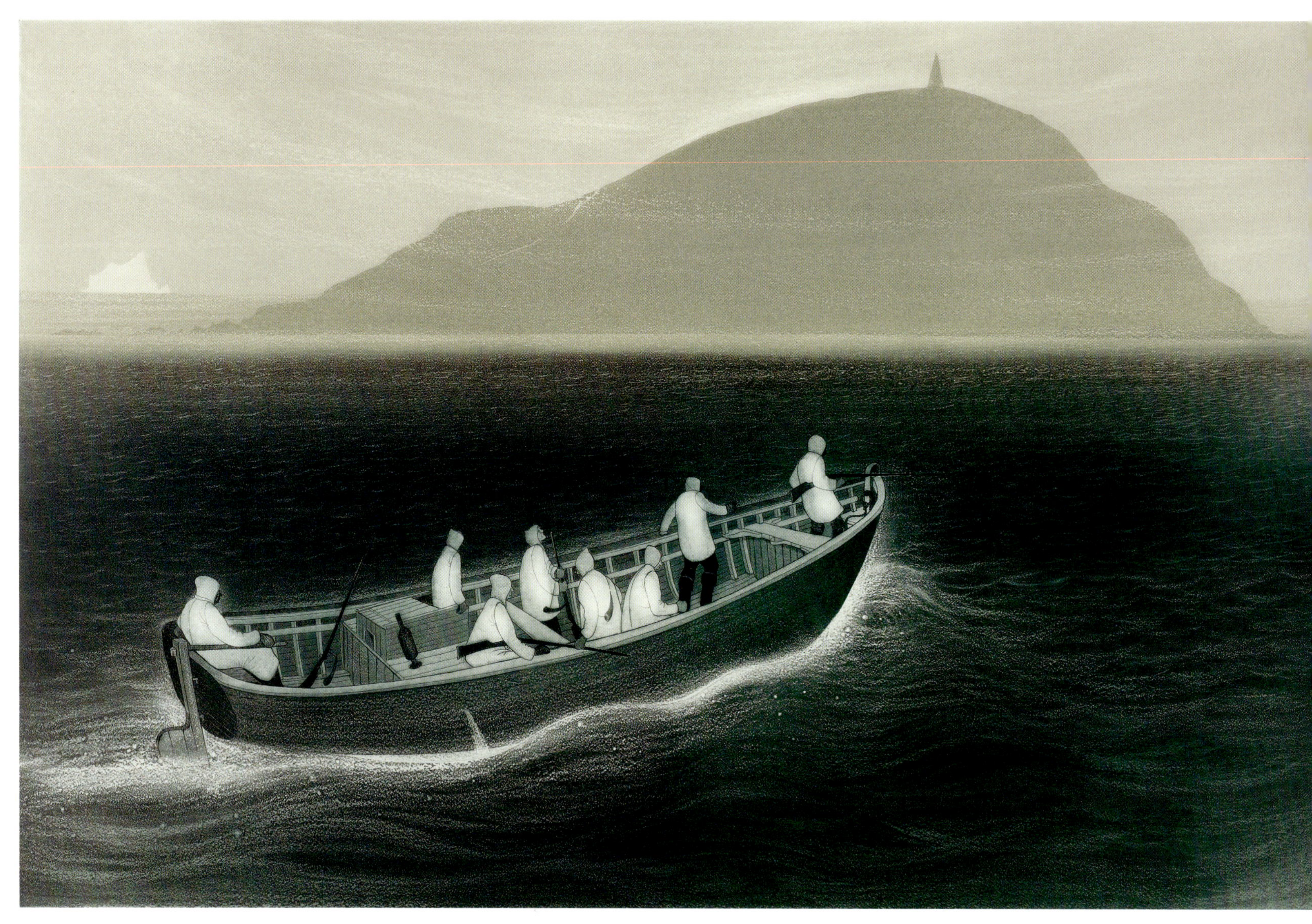

50. **Wesleyville: Seabird Hunters Crossing the Reach**, 1981

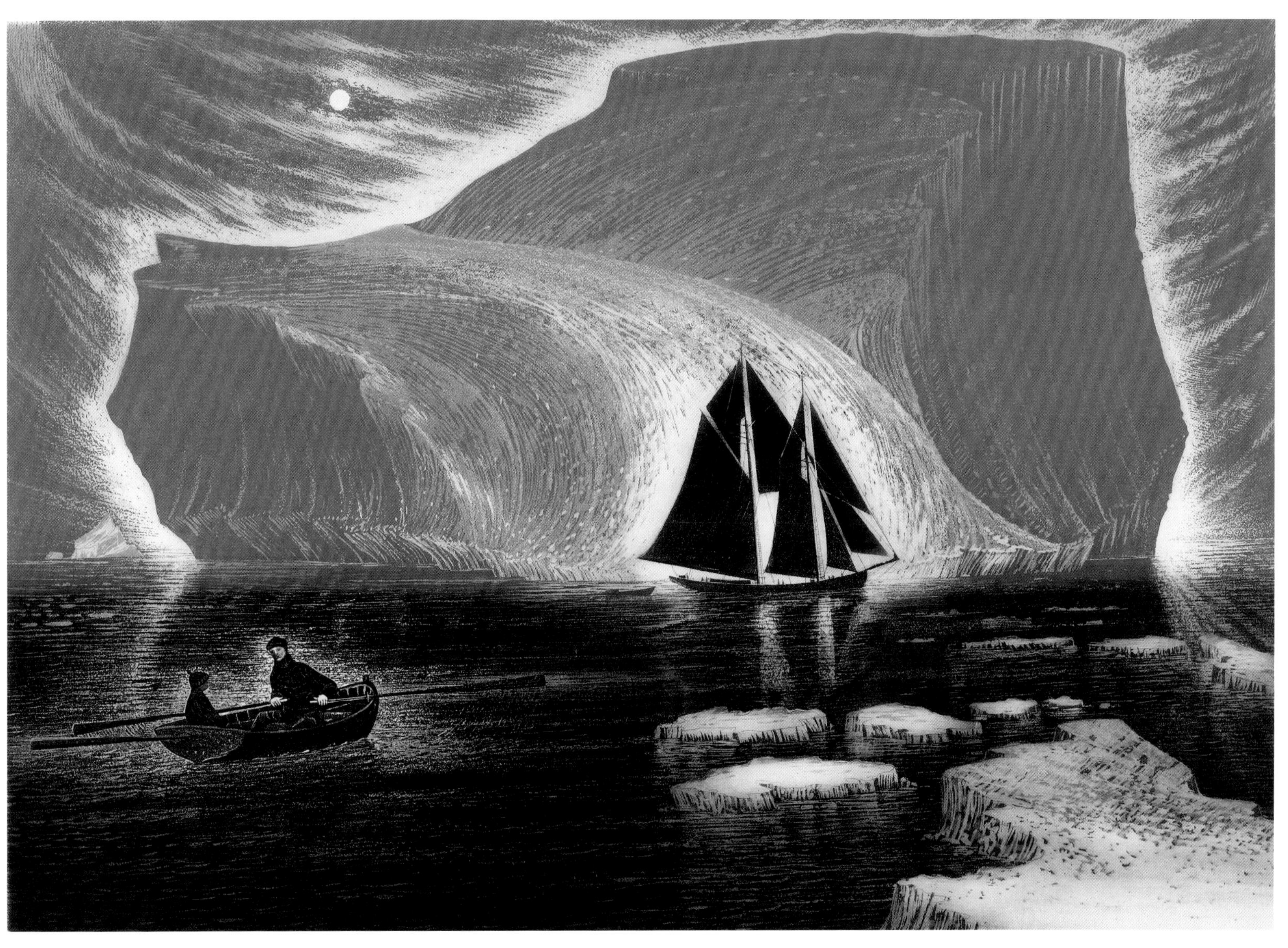

51. The Flora S. Nickerson
in the Labrador Sea, 1982

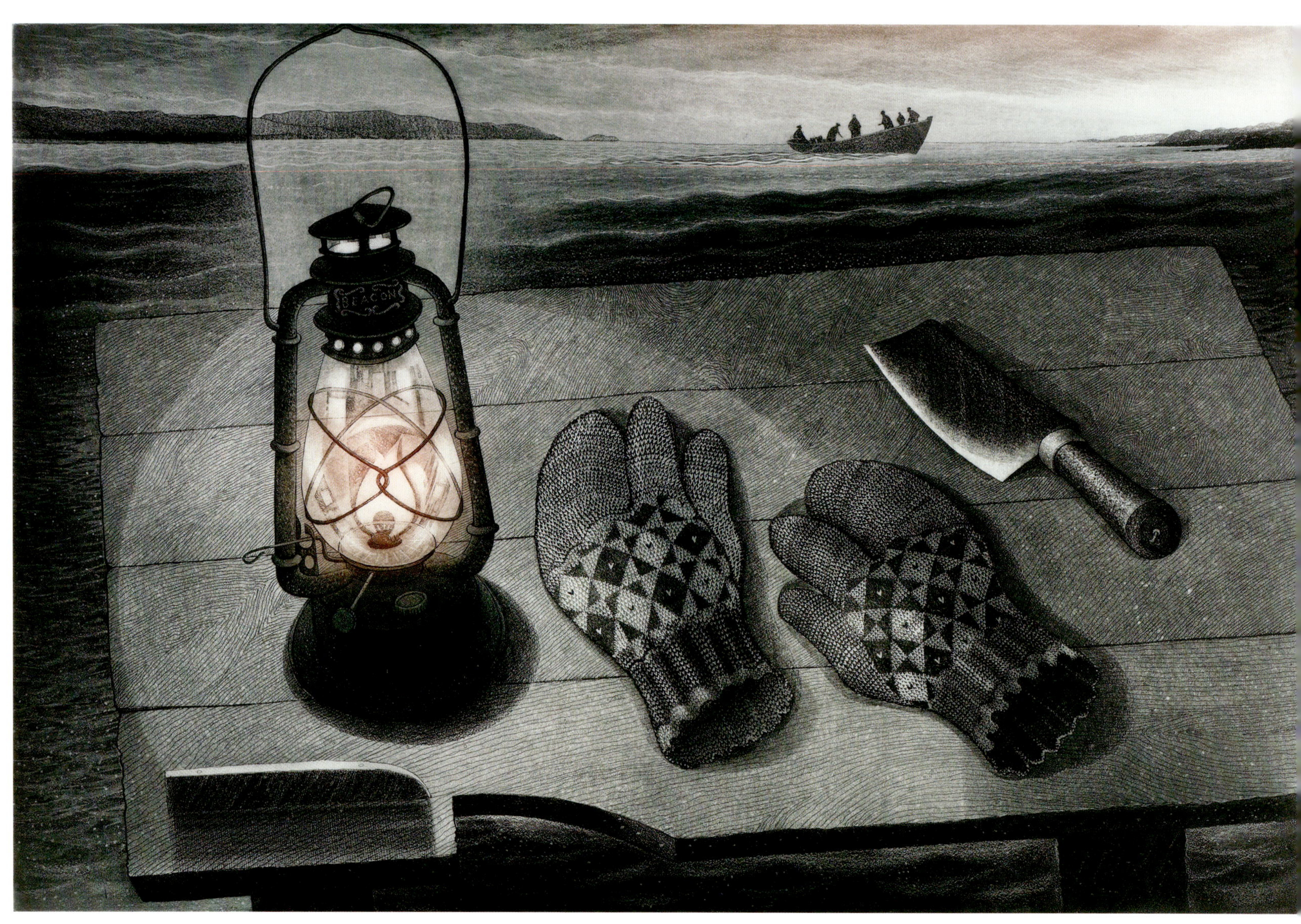

52. **For Edgar Glover: The Splitting Table**, 1999

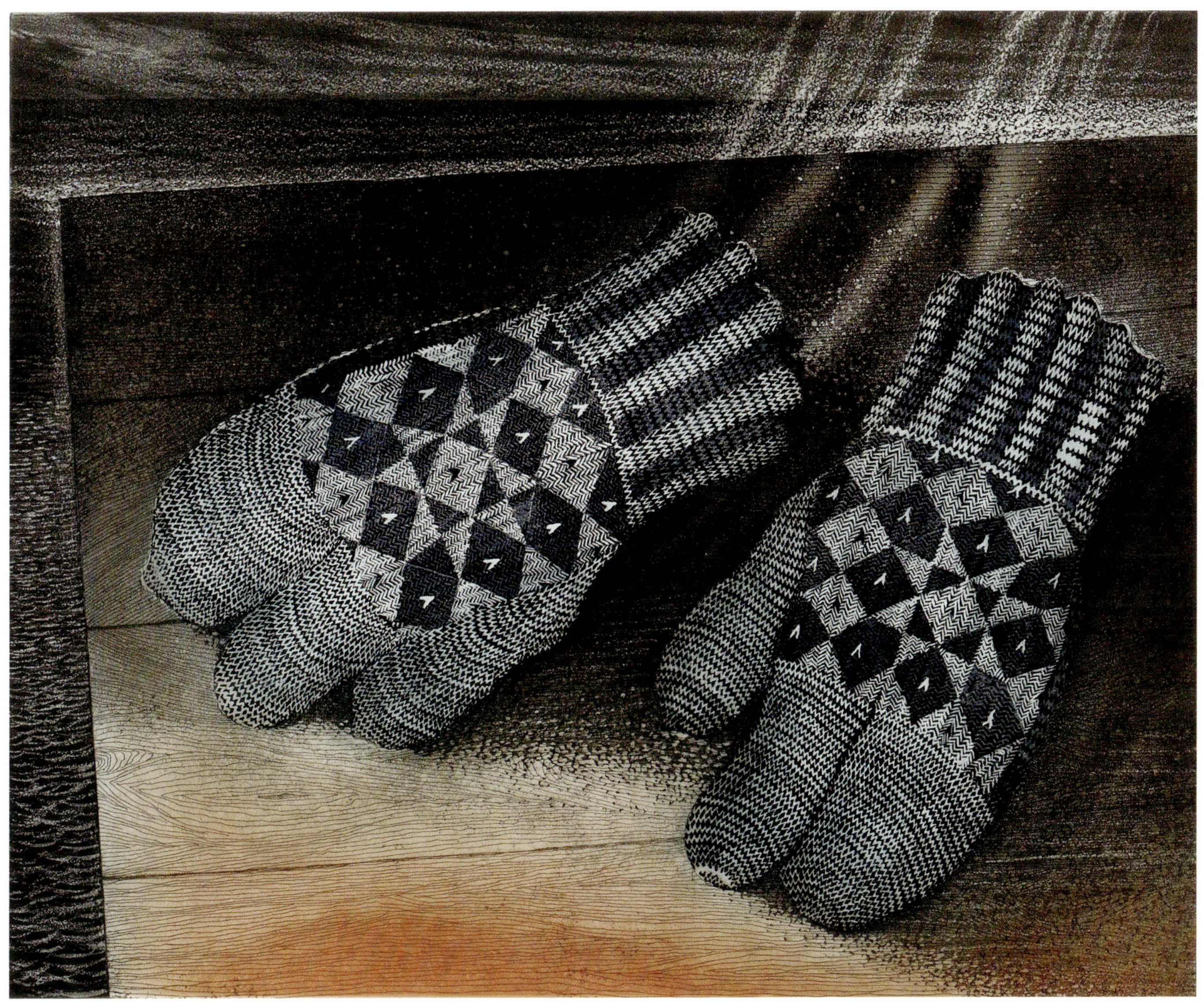

53. **Uncle Sam Kelloway**, 1983

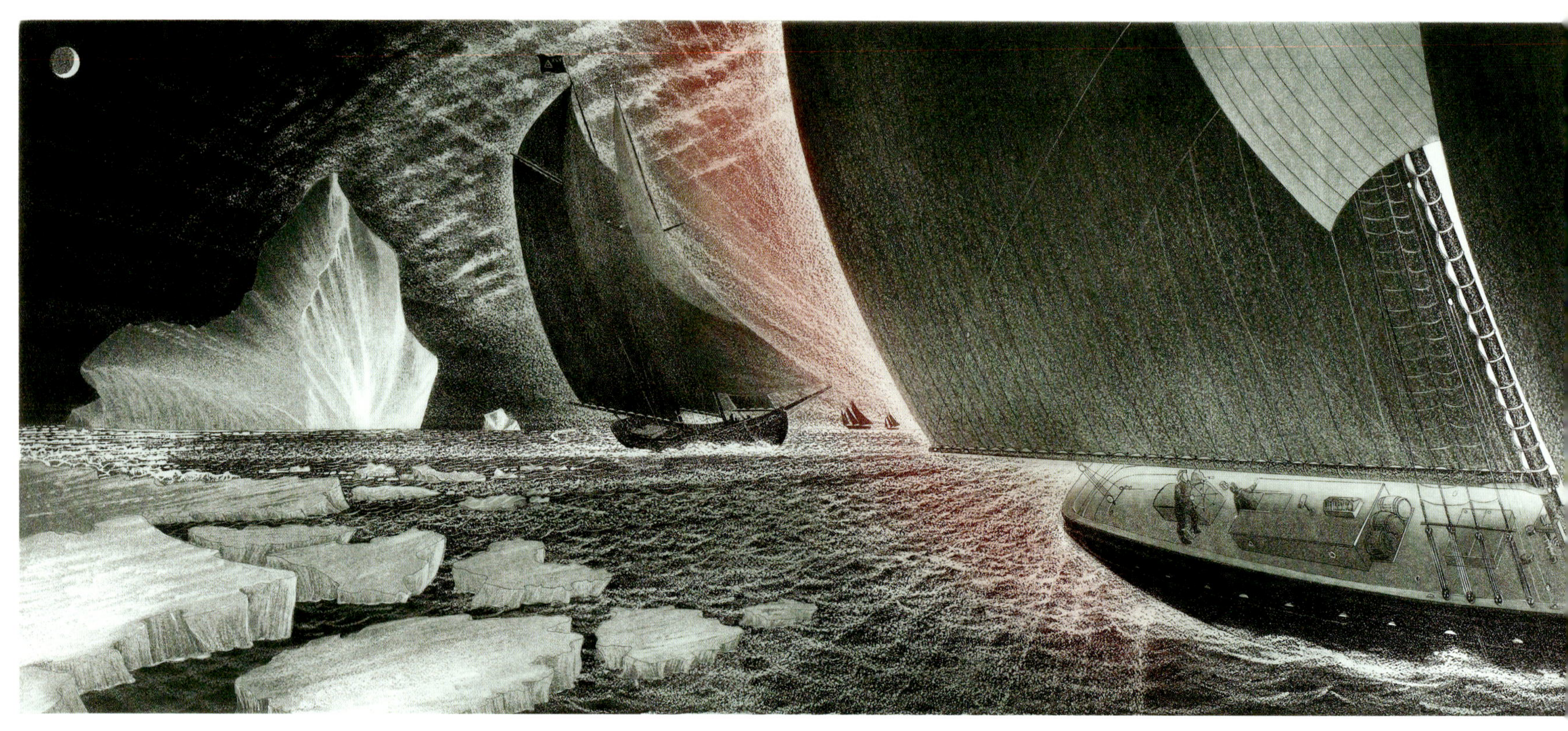

54. **Outward Bound for the Labrador**, 1987

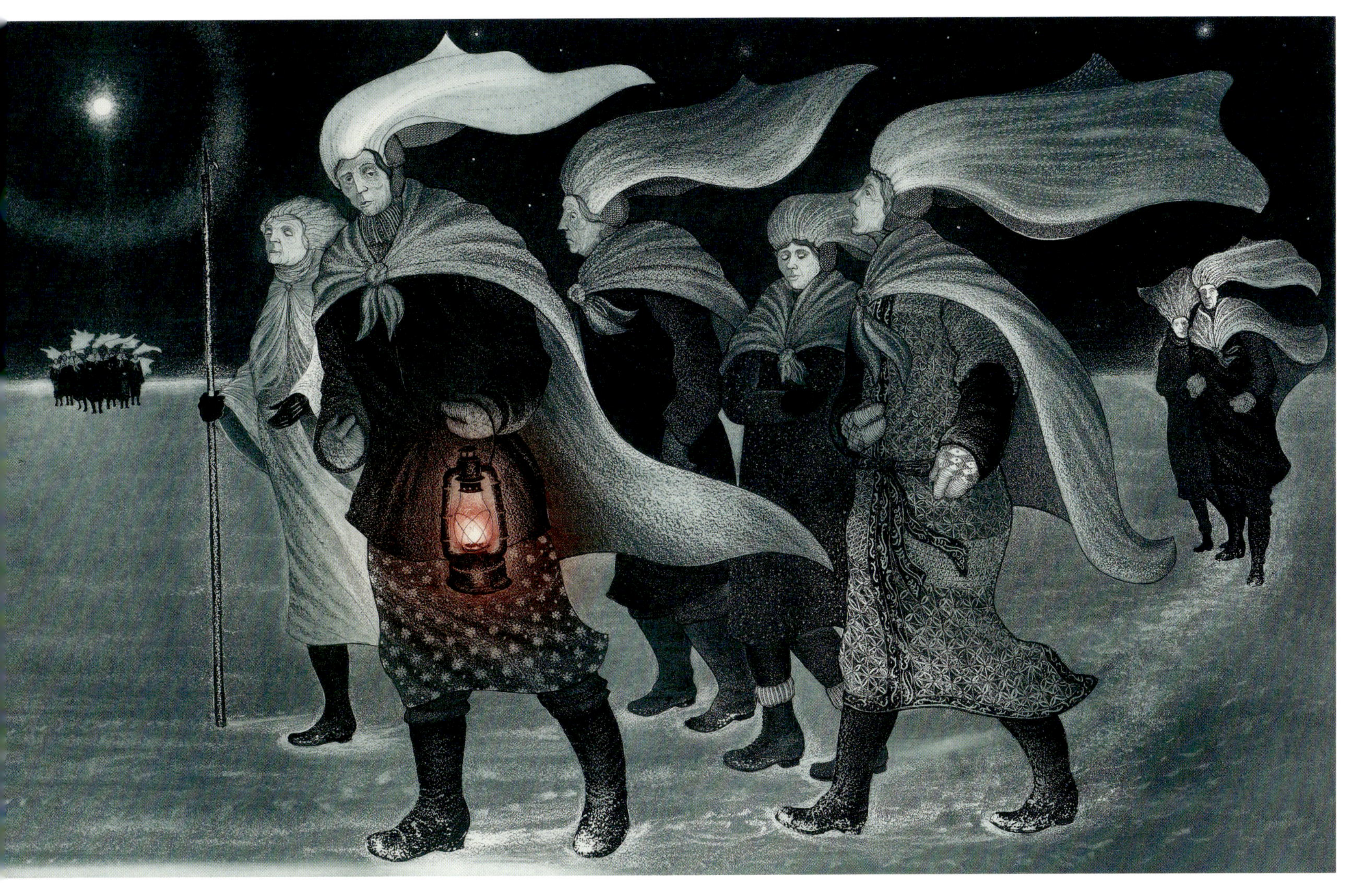

55. **Pound Cove Mummers Crossing Cold Harbour Pond**, 1985

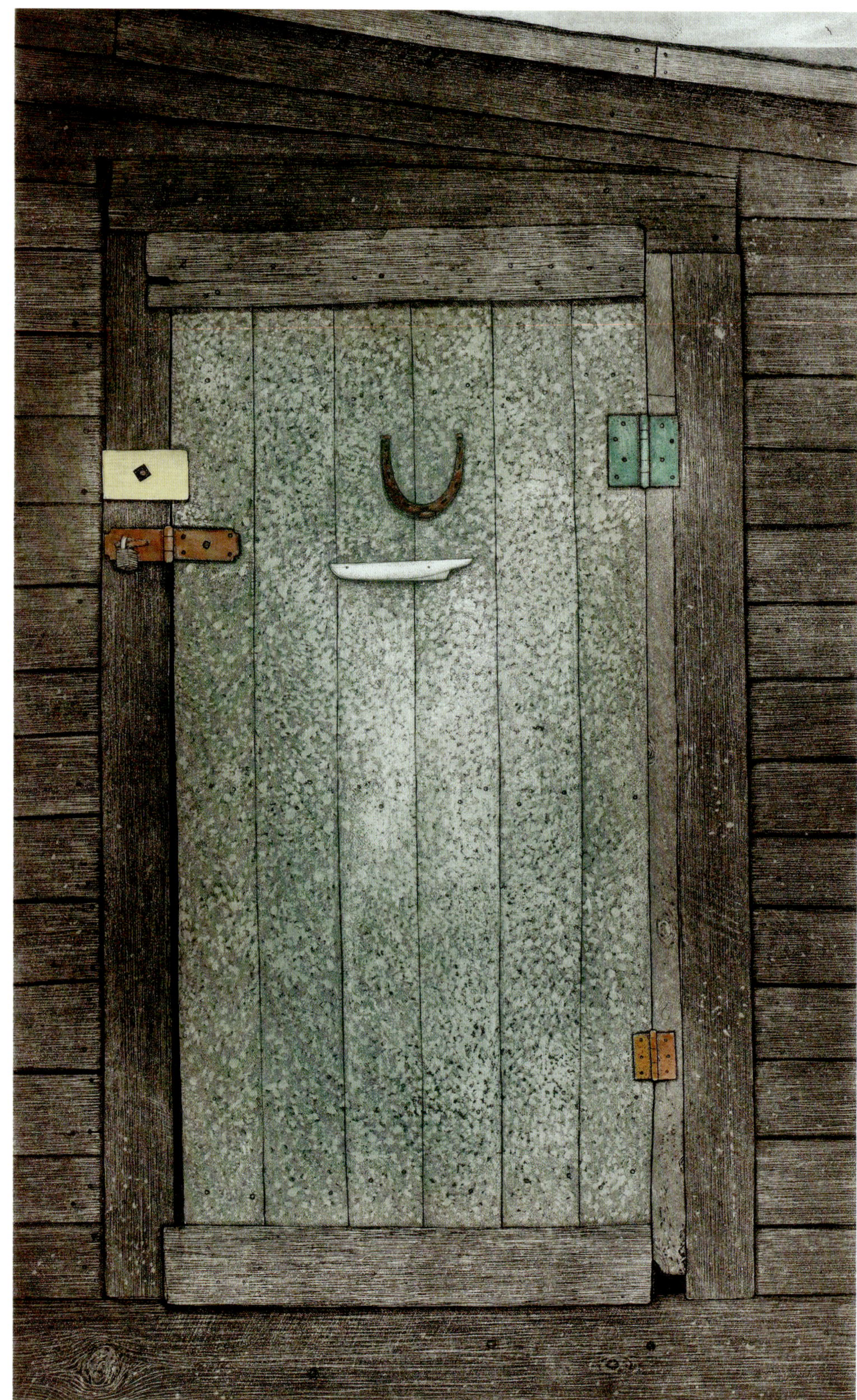

56. **Ephraim Kelloway's Door**, 1982

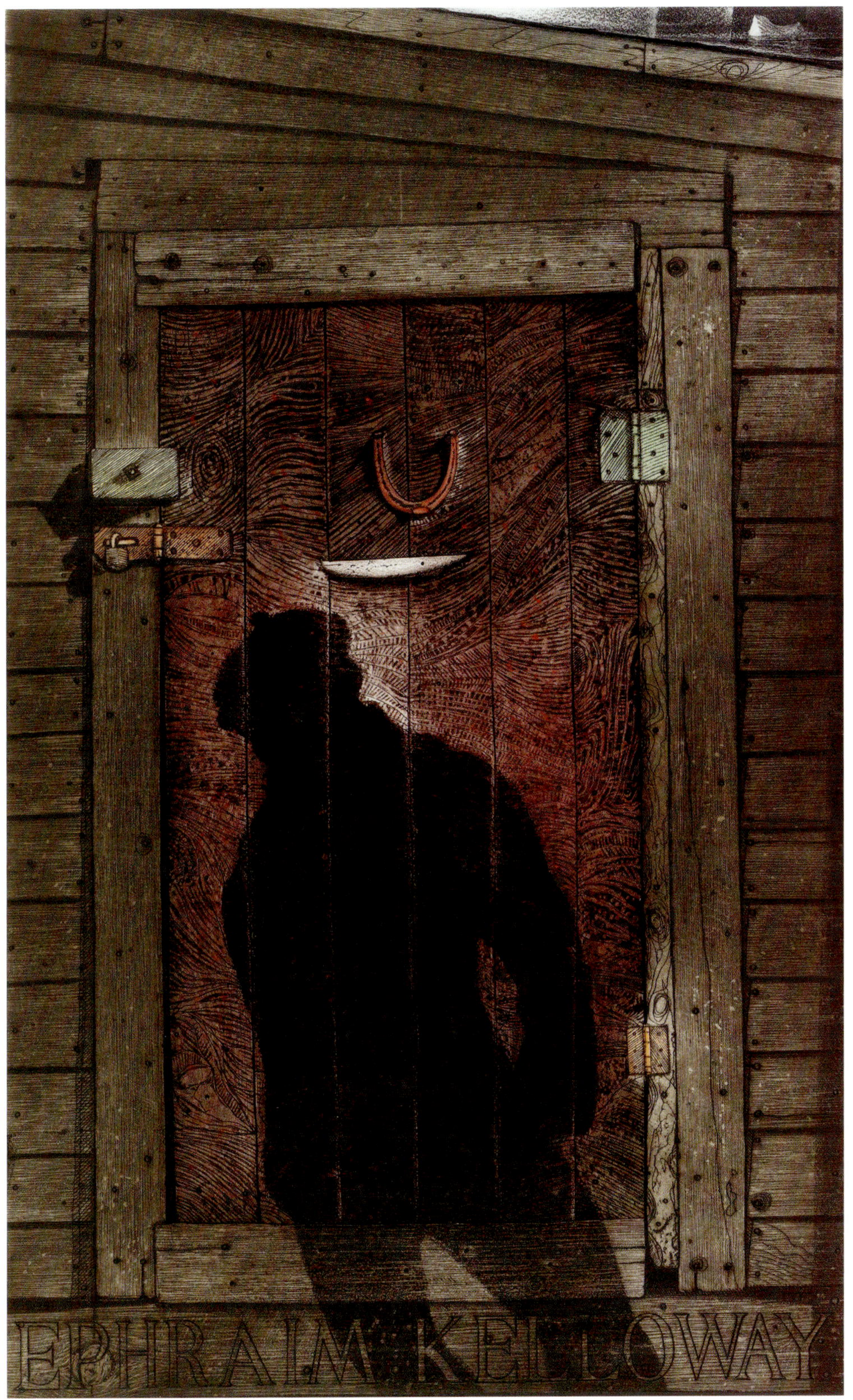

57. **Passing Shadow**, 1990

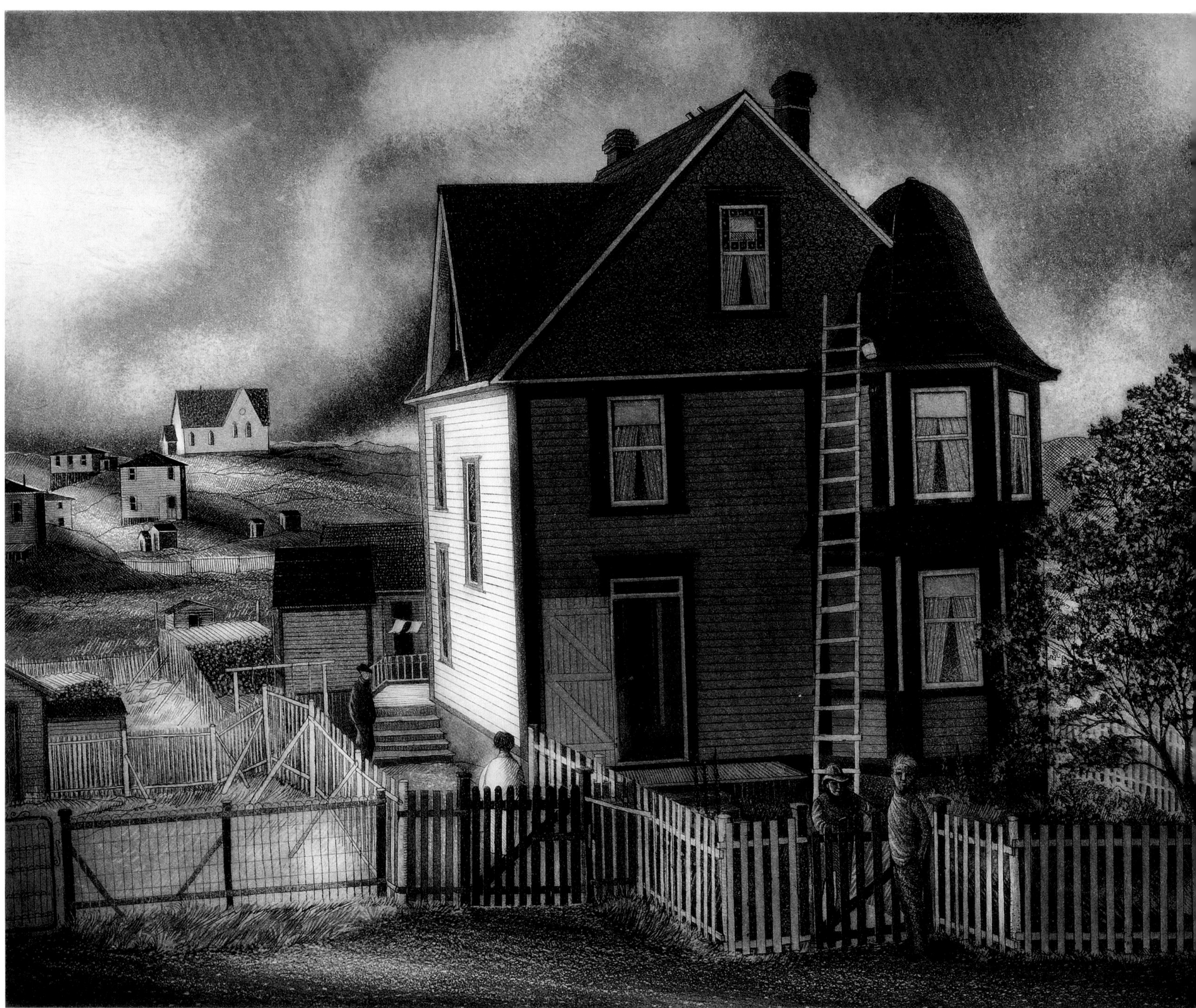

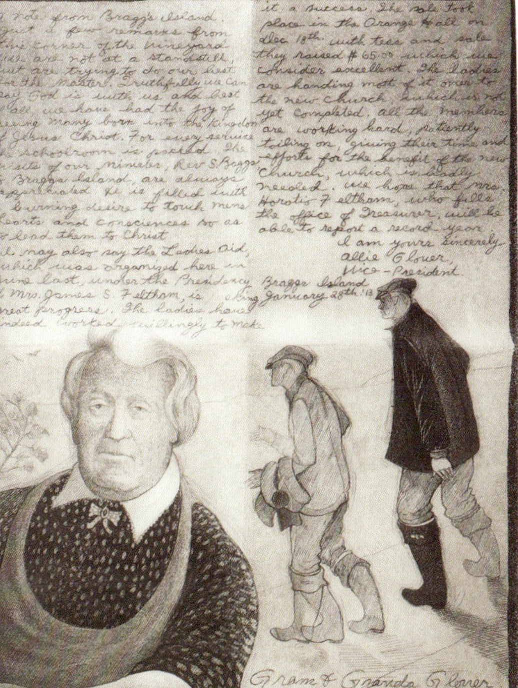

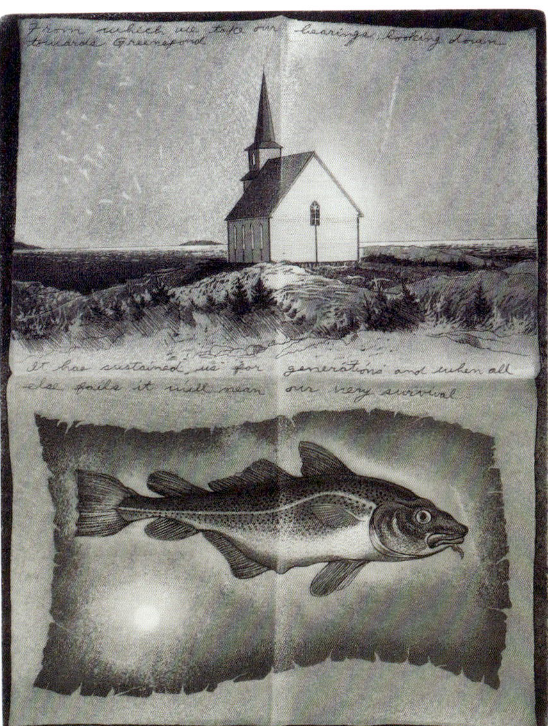

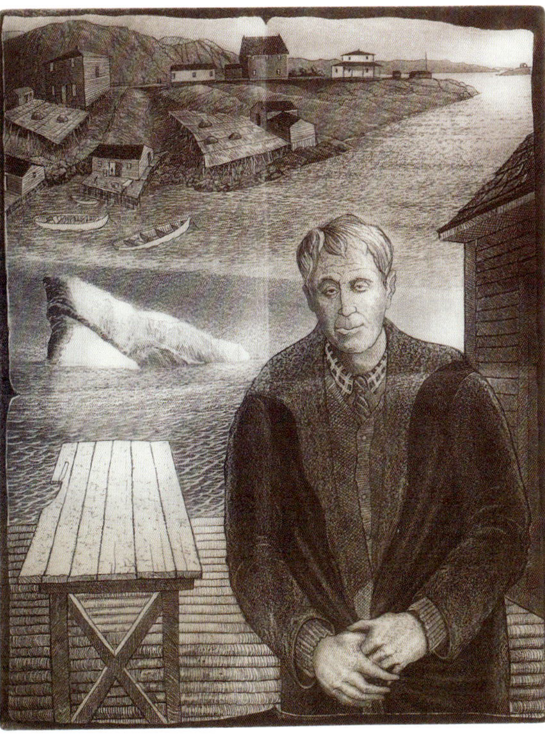

facing: 58. **Uncle Sam Kelloway's Place in Wesleyville**, 1999

above: 59. **Notes from Bragg's Island**, 1992

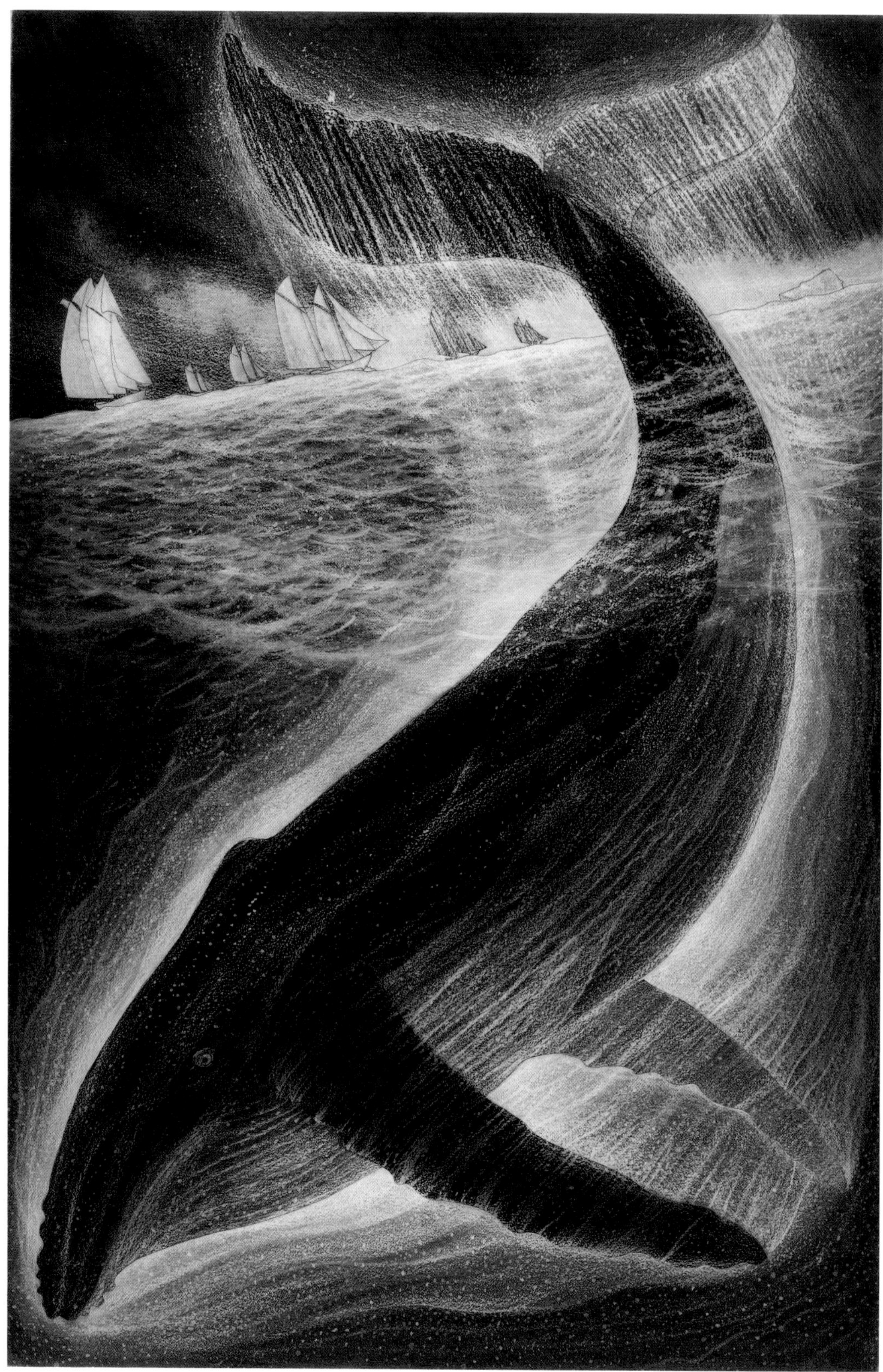

60. **Wesleyville Fleet in Labrador Sea**, 1995

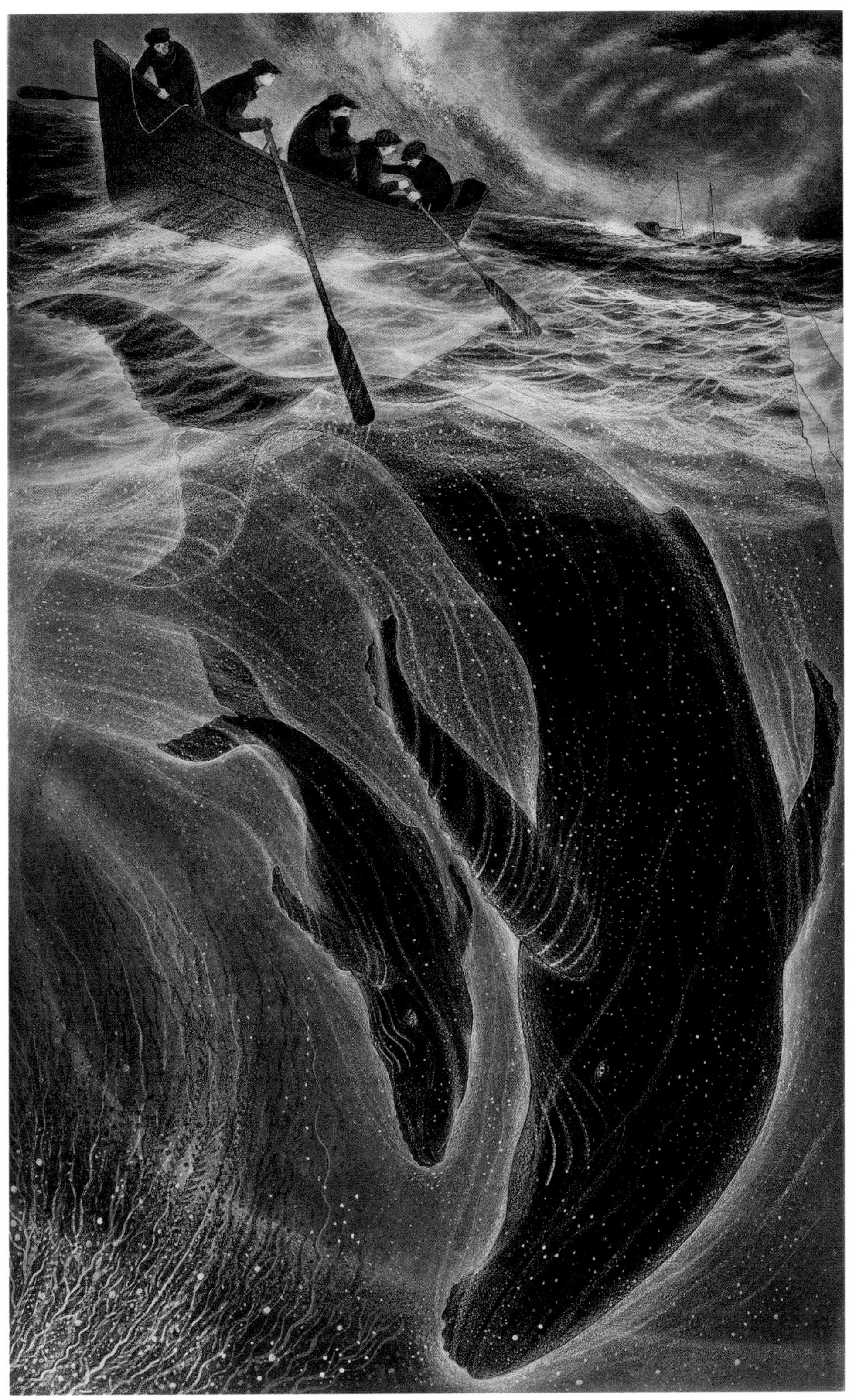

61. **Loss of Flora S. Nickerson**, 1993

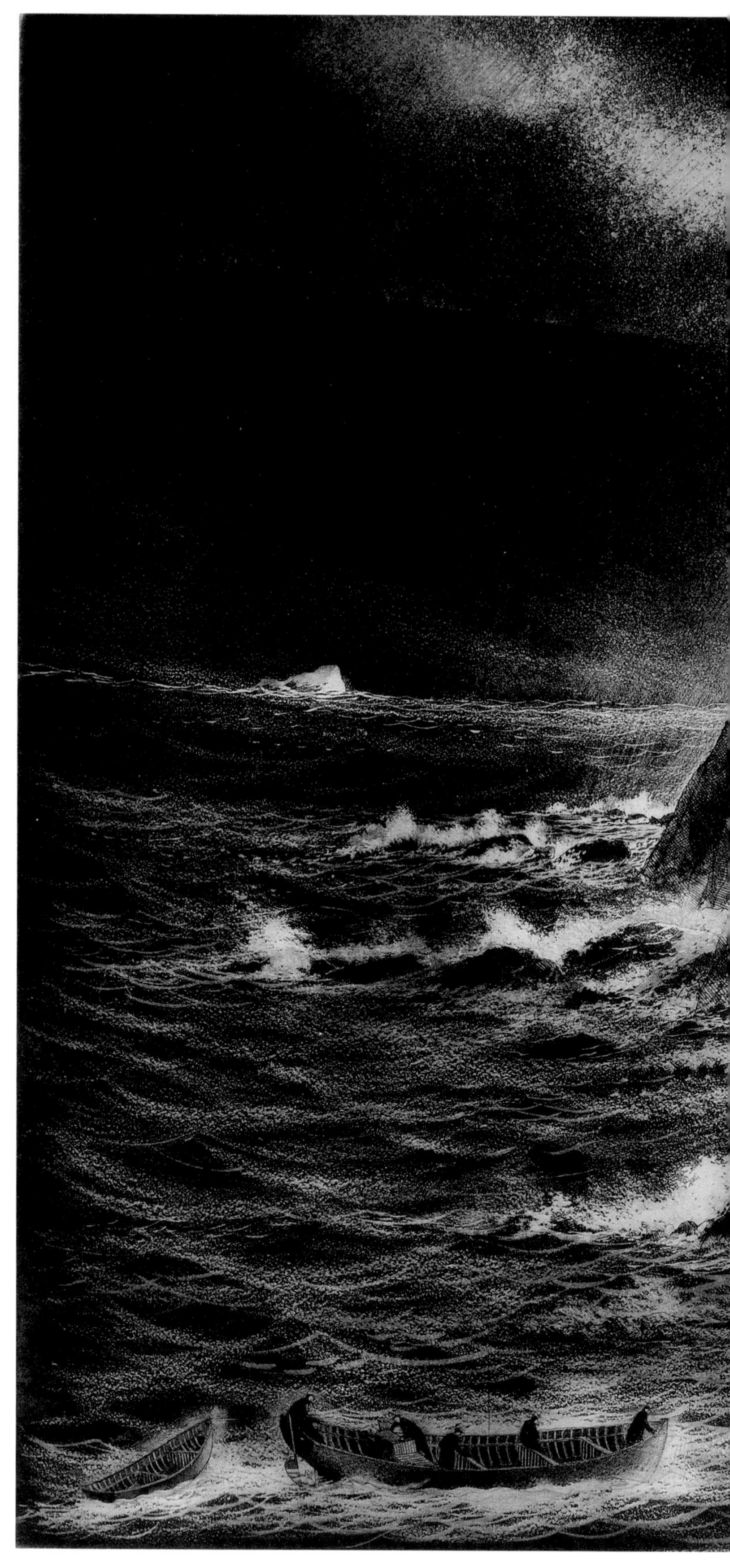

62. **Haven**, 1994

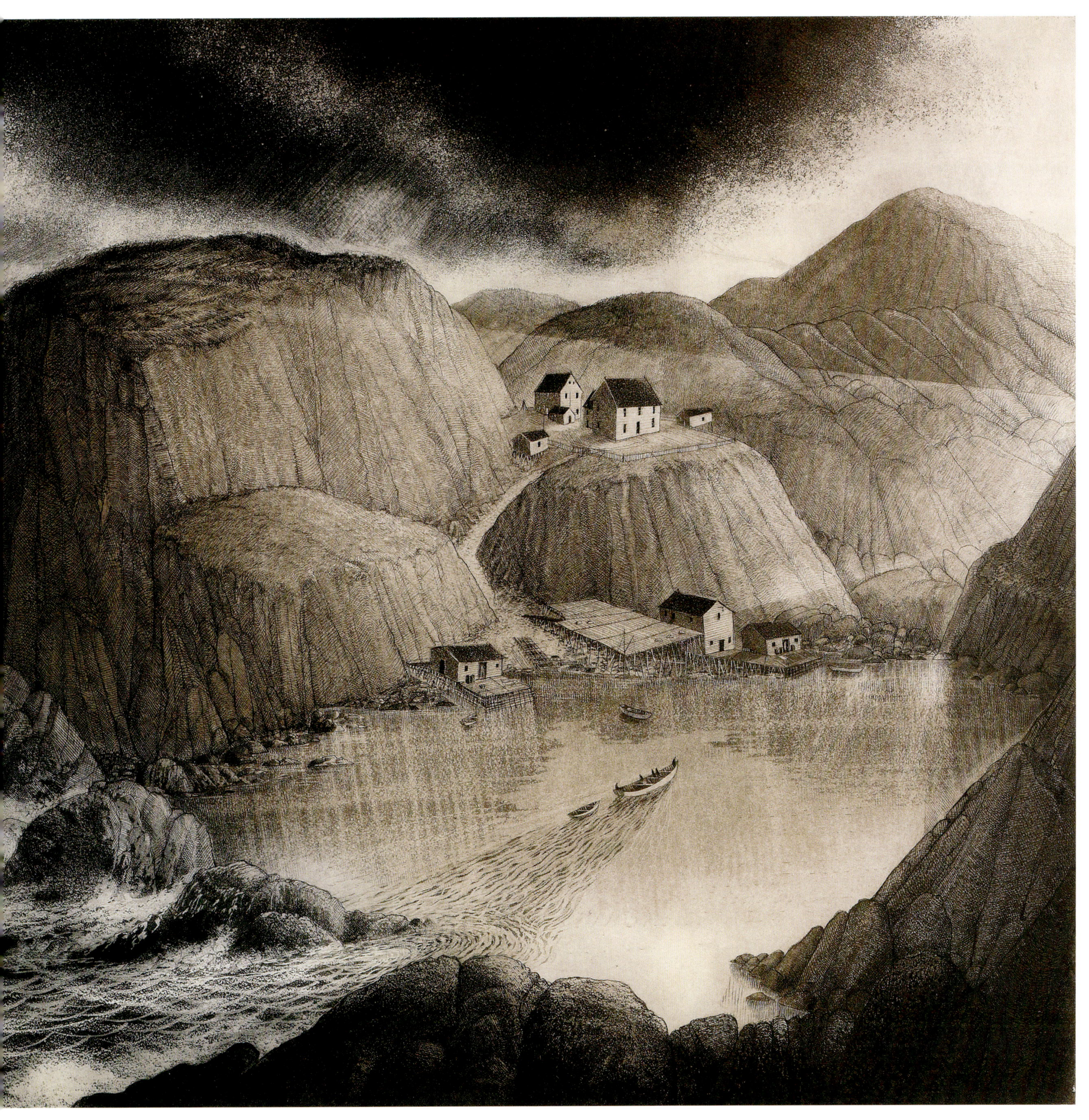

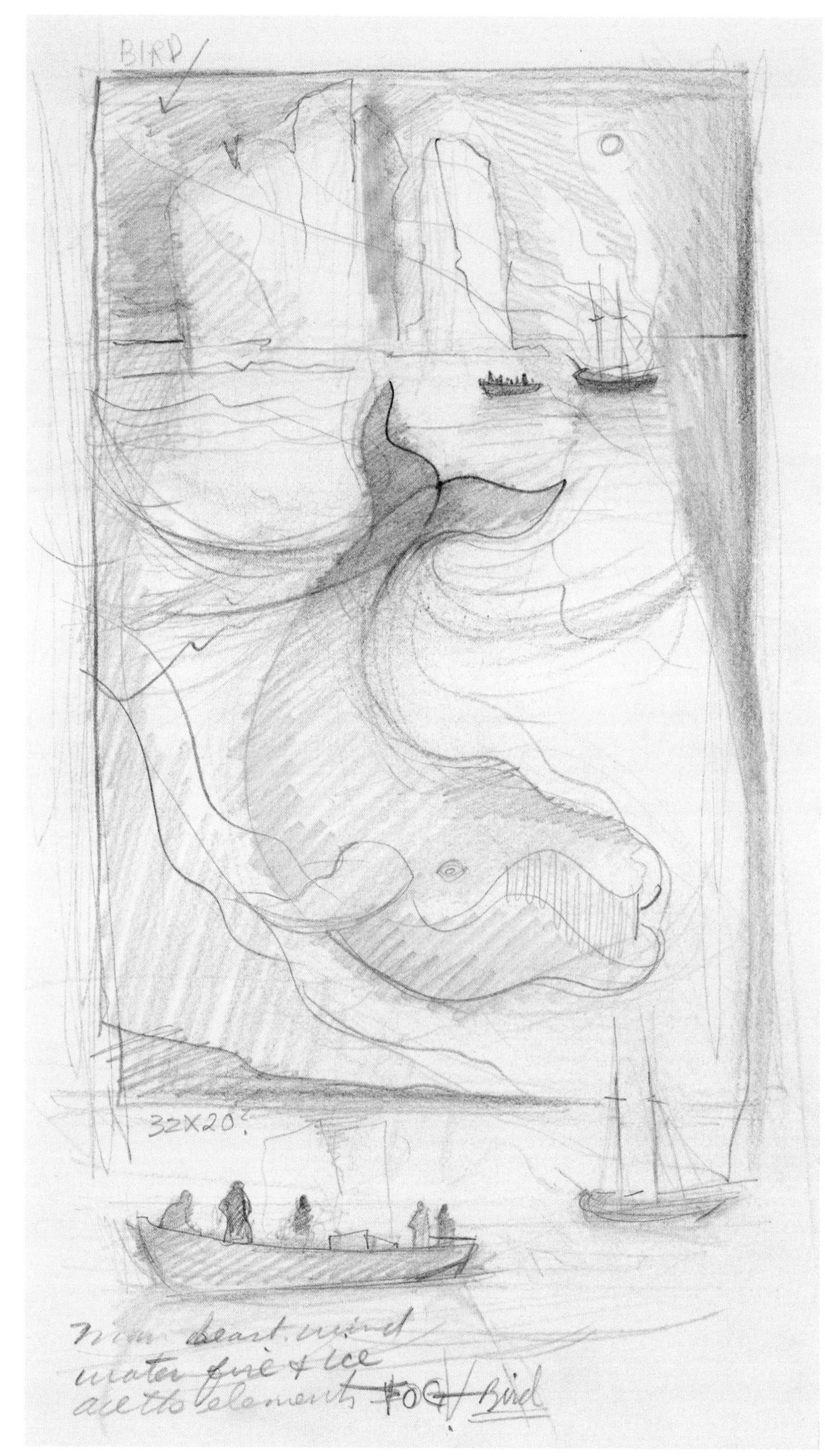

63. Sketch for **Fire Down on the Labrador**, 1979

FIRE DOWN ON THE LABRADOR

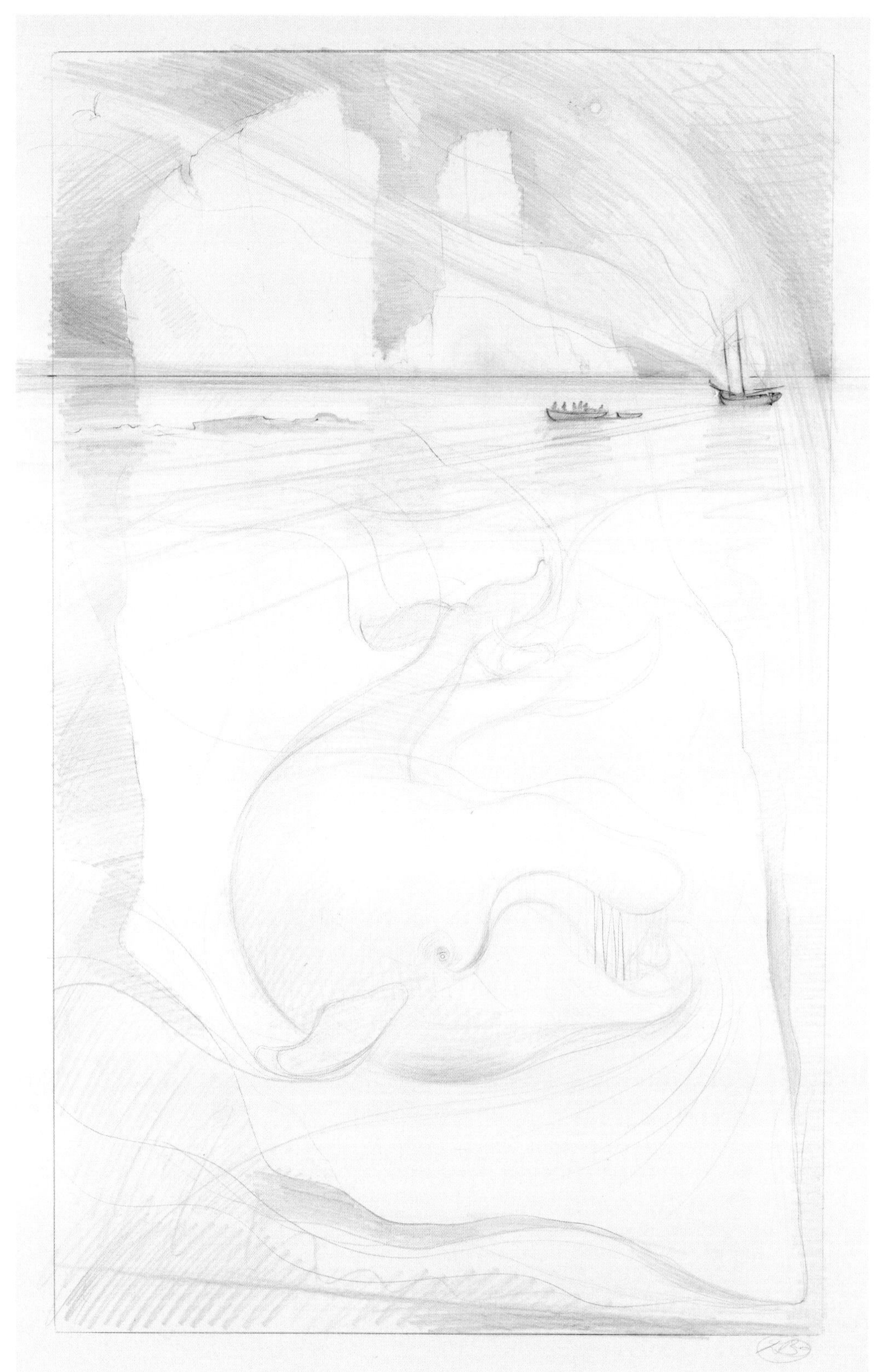

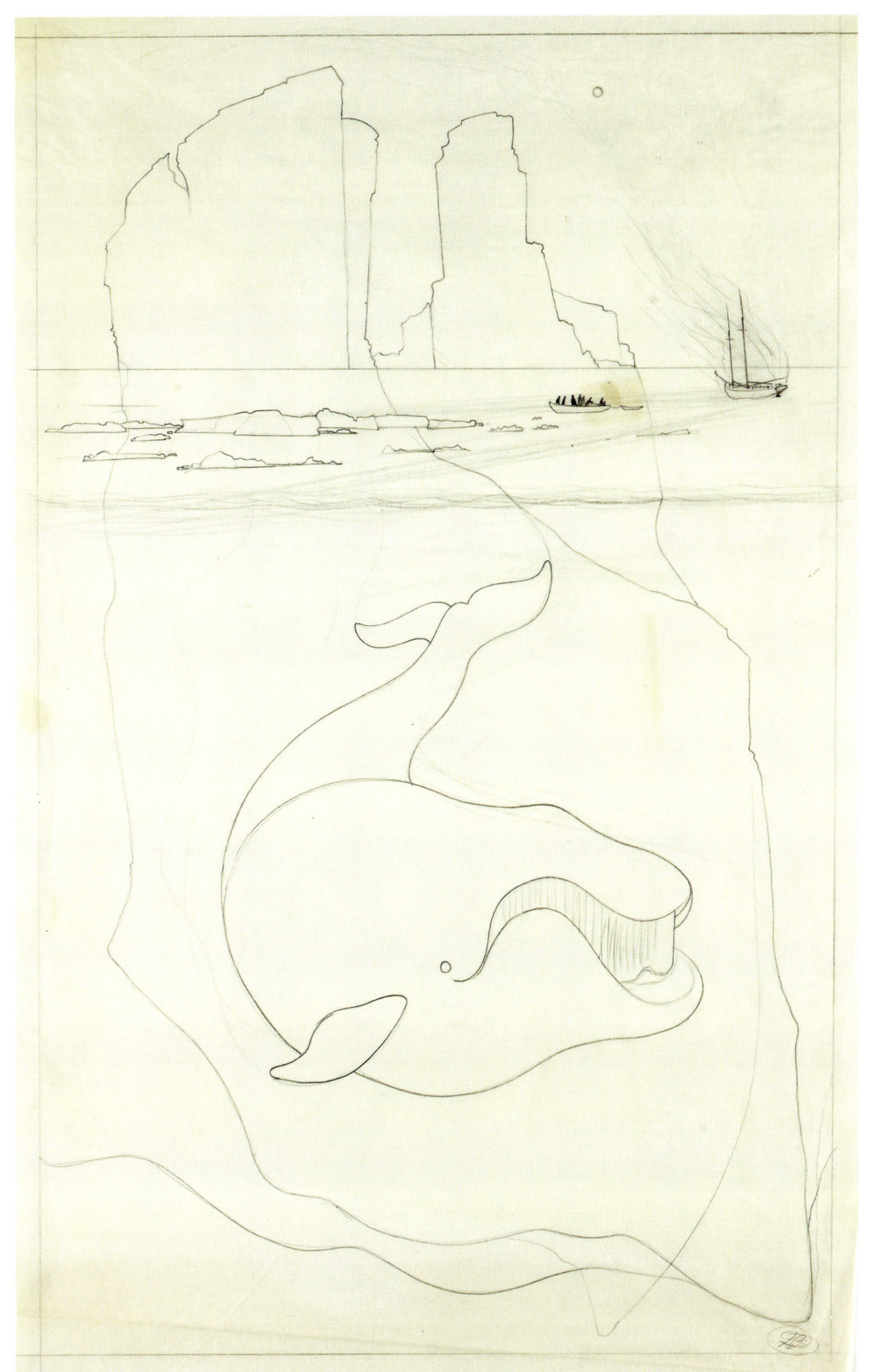

facing: 64. Graphite drawing for **Fire Down on the Labrador**, 1979

left: 65. Cartoon tracing for reverse transfer to the copper plate for **Fire Down on the Labrador**, 1980

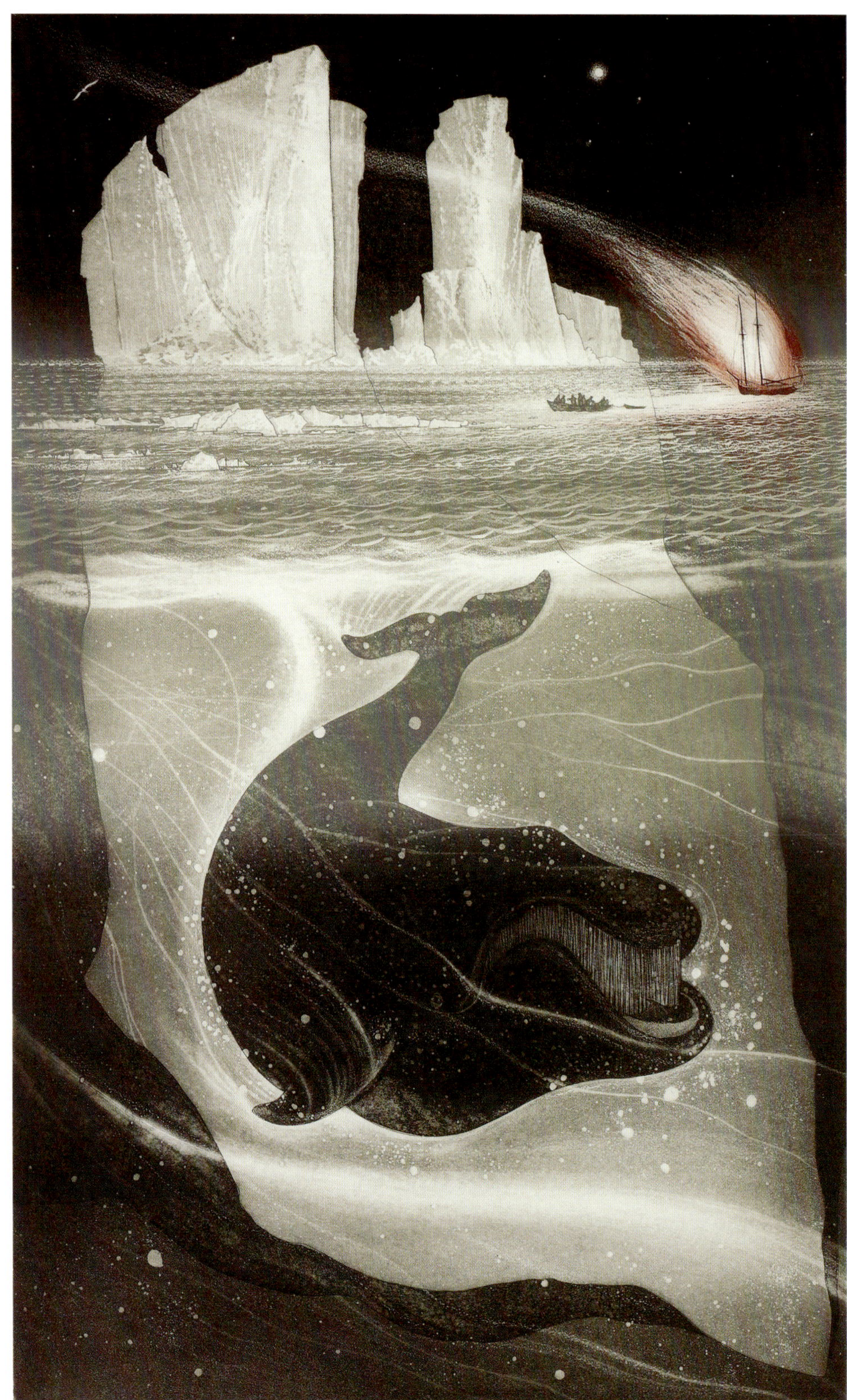

66. Experimental inking proof for **Fire Down on the Labrador**, 1980

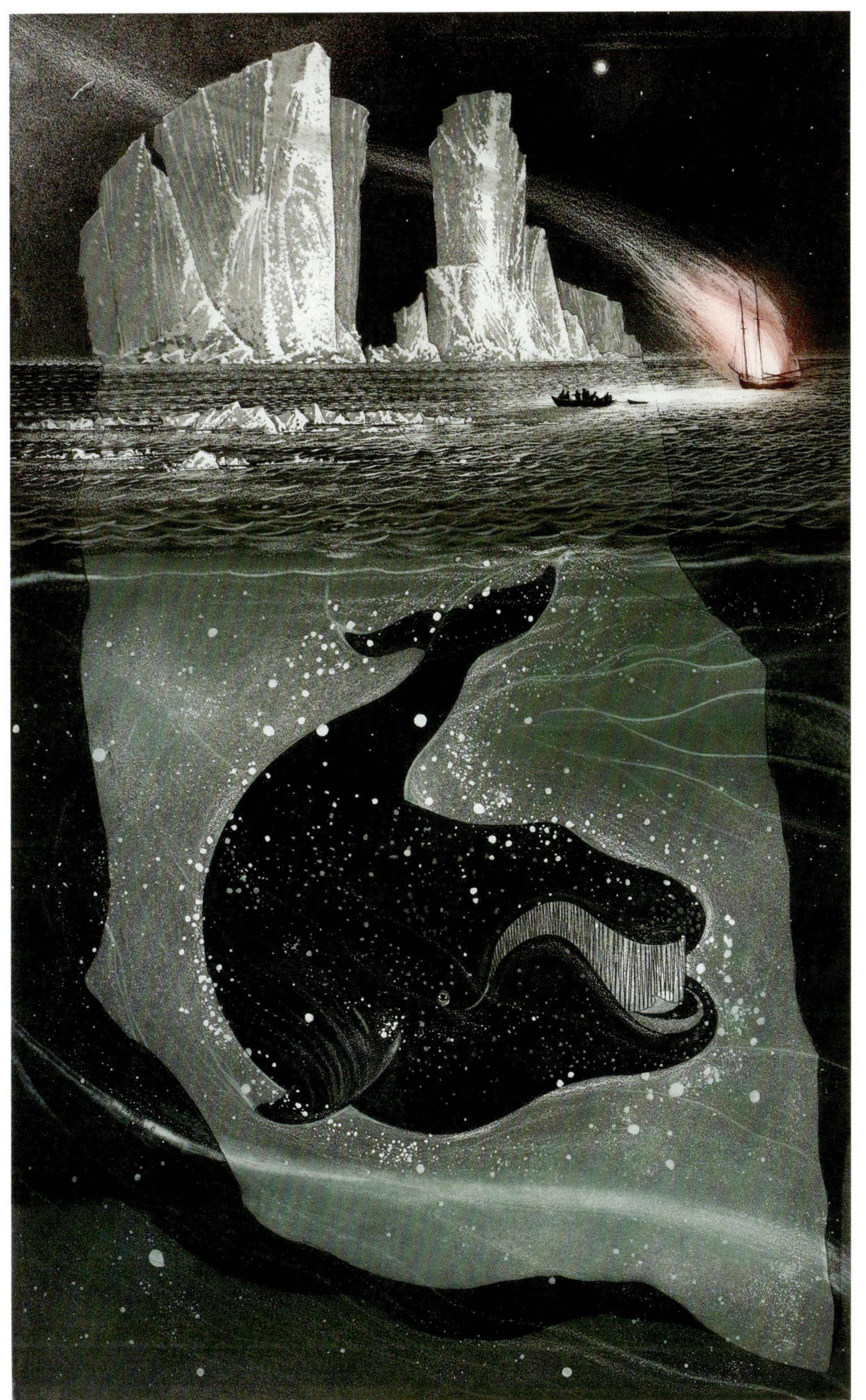

67. Working proof prior to scraper and burnisher use for **Fire Down on the Labrador**, 1980

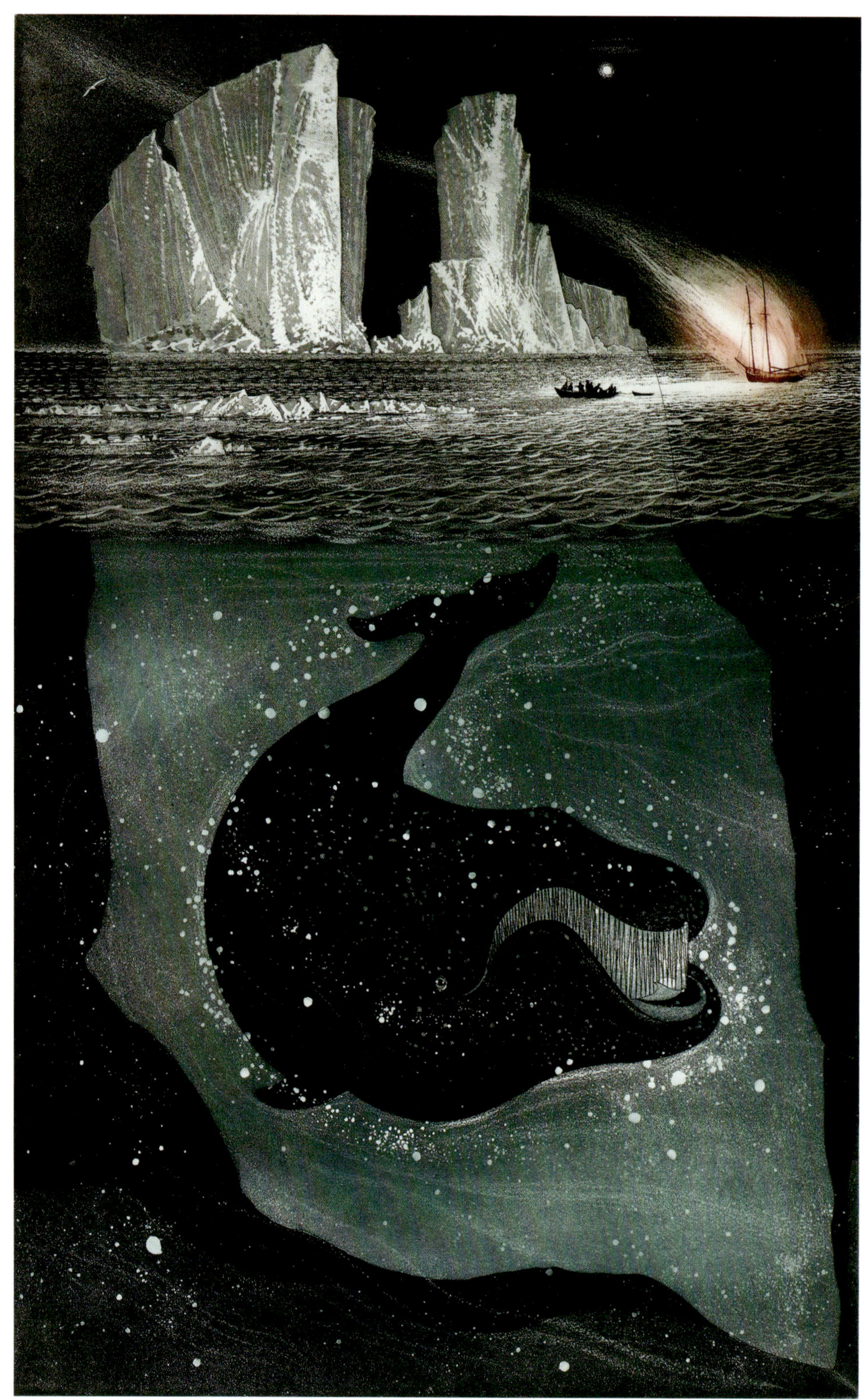

68. **Fire Down on the Labrador**, 1980
AP 3/6

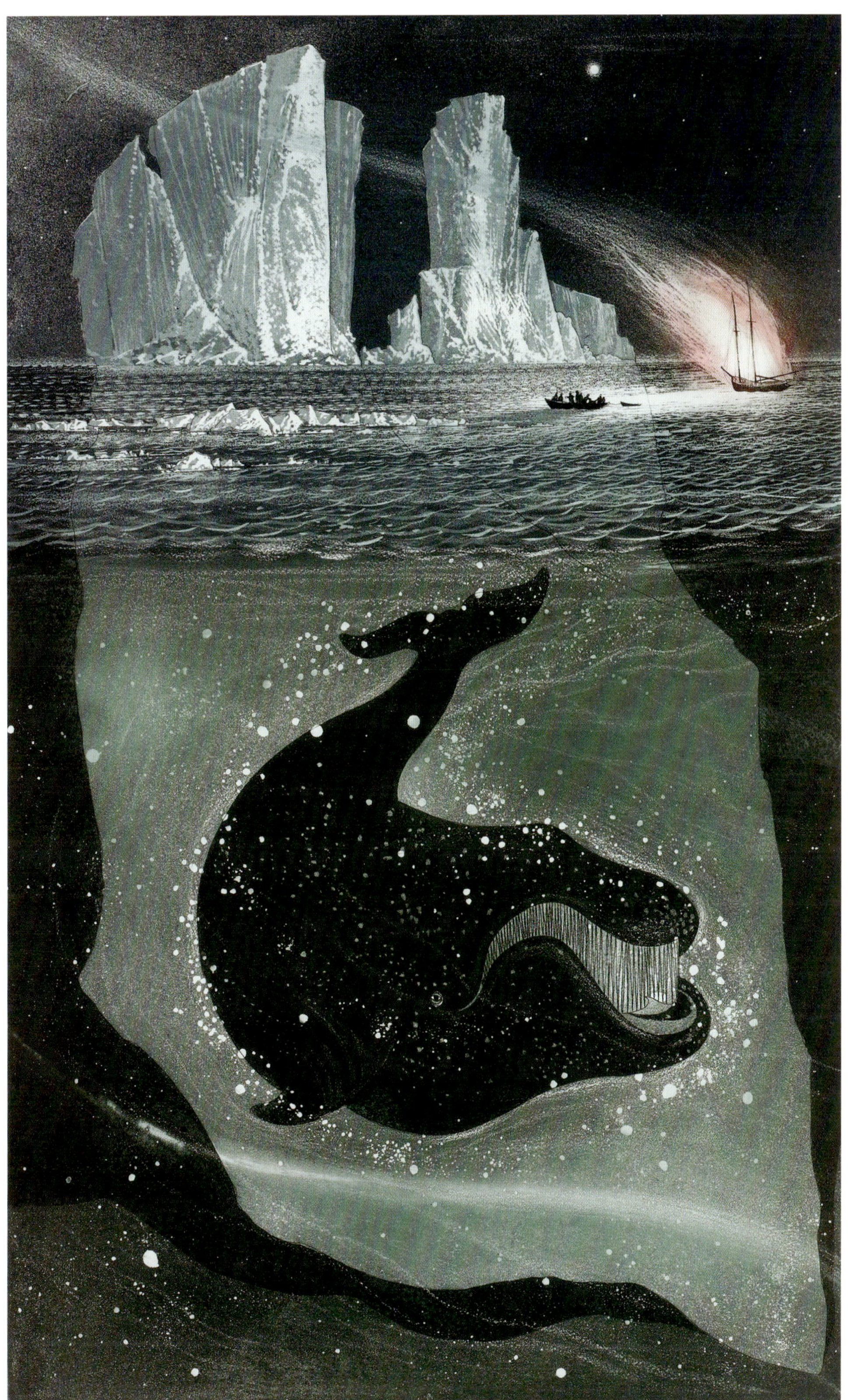

69. **Fire Down on the Labrador**, 1980
AP 4/6

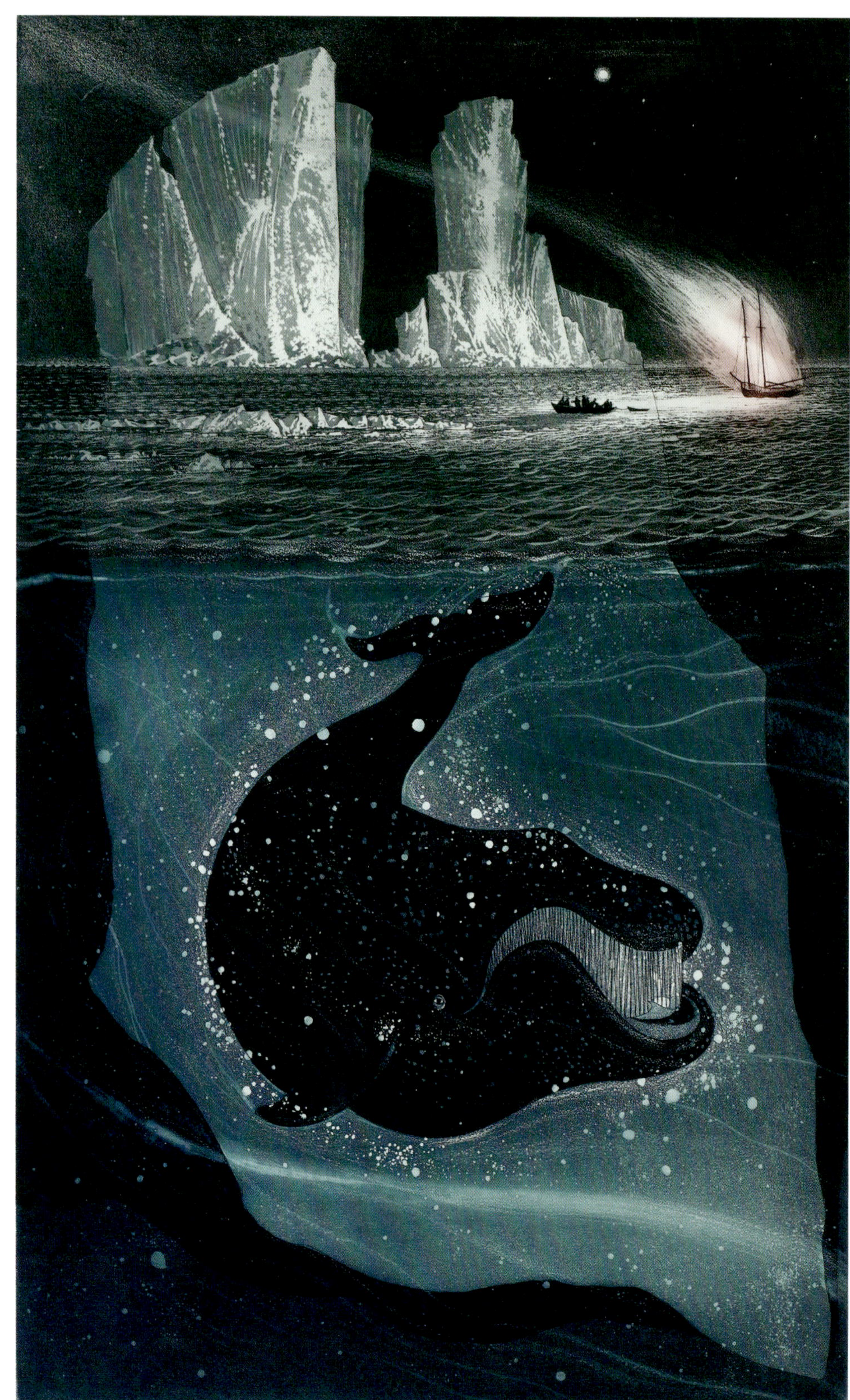

70. **Fire Down on the Labrador**, 1980
AP 5/6

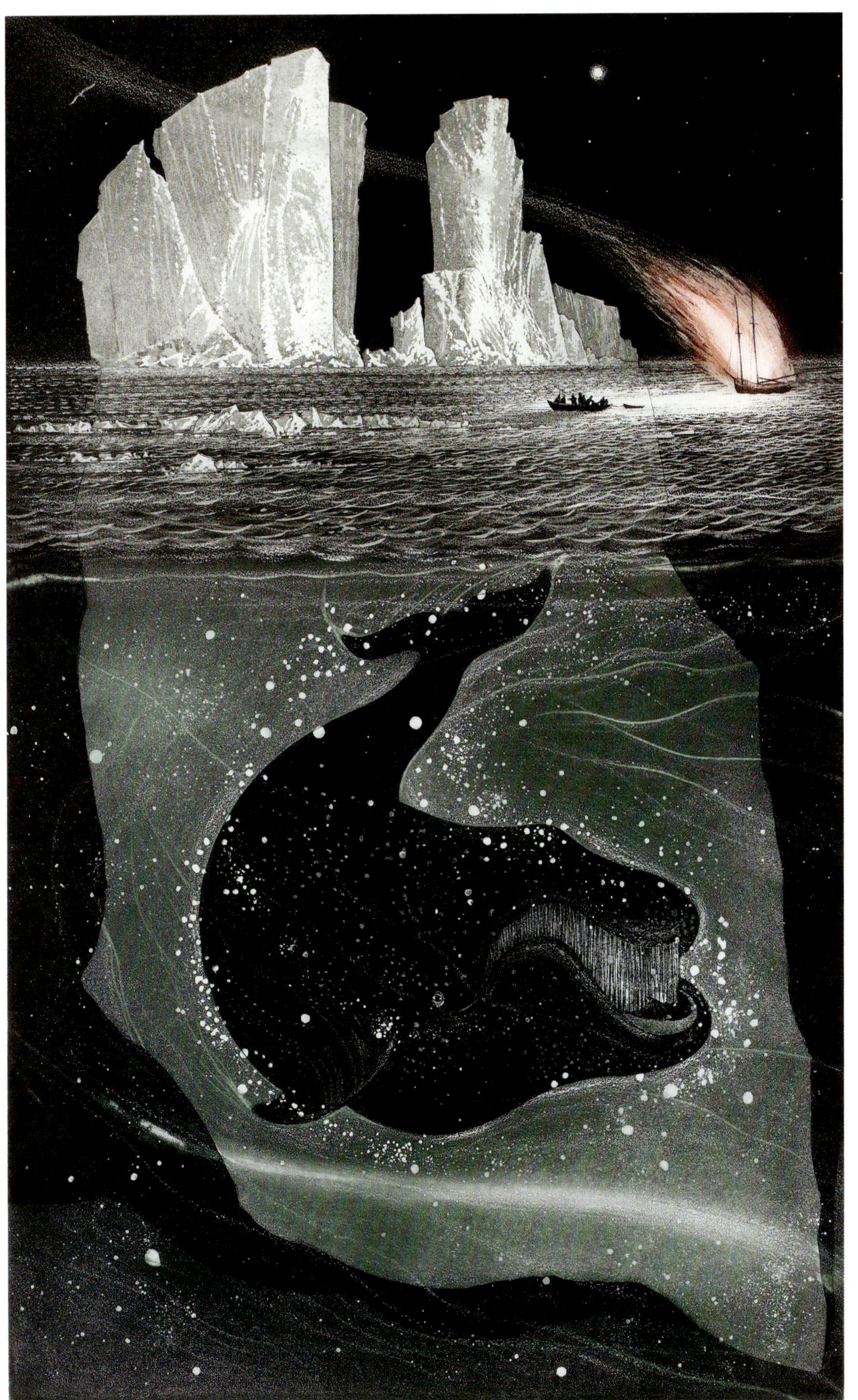

71. **Fire Down on the Labrador**, 1980
WP 6/6

Works in the Exhibition

All works are gifts or promised gifts of David and Anita Blackwood to the Art Gallery of Ontario, except for number 35. Height precedes width.
Abbreviations: AP: artist's proof; WP: working proof; imp.: plate impression

1. **The Search Party**
1963
etching, aquatint and drypoint on wove paper
74.7 × 50.0 cm (imp.)
Gift of David and Anita Blackwood, Port Hope, Ontario, 1999
Acc. No. 99/888

2. **Vision of the Lost Party**
1964
etching, aquatint and drypoint on wove paper
74.6 × 50.3 cm (imp.)
Gift of David and Anita Blackwood, Port Hope, Ontario, 1999
Acc. No. 99/897

3. **The Mirage**
1965
etching, engraving and aquatint on wove paper
50.5 × 22.6 cm (imp.)
Gift of David and Anita Blackwood, Port Hope, Ontario, 1999
Acc. No. 99/899

4. **Vision of the Lost Party: Outport Funeral**
1967
etching and aquatint on wove paper · I/10
75.7 × 50.5 cm (imp.)
Gift of David and Anita Blackwood, Port Hope, Ontario, 1999
Acc. No. 99/906

5. **Kean's Men Waiting for the SS Bellaventure**
1968
etching, aquatint and drypoint on wove paper · AP
50.4 × 80.5 cm (imp.)
Gift of David and Anita Blackwood, Port Hope, Ontario, 1999
Acc. No. 99/913

6. **Spirit Departing: Once Told Tale**
1968
etching and aquatint on wove paper · AP
80.7 × 50.5 cm (imp.)
Gift of David and Anita Blackwood, Port Hope, Ontario, 2008
Acc. No. 2008/276

7. **Great Lost Party Adrift**
1971
etching and aquatint on wove paper · AP
50.5 × 80.6 cm (imp.)
Gift of David and Anita Blackwood, Port Hope, Ontario, 2008
Acc. No. 2008/278

8. **Monday Morning, March 1**
1968
etching and aquatint on wove paper
50.5 × 80.9 cm (imp.)
Gift of David and Anita Blackwood, Port Hope, Ontario, 1999
Acc. No. 99/911

9. **Wreck off Bragg's Island**
1967
etching, aquatint and drypoint on wove paper · AP
50.5 × 75.7 cm (imp.)
Gift of David and Anita Blackwood, Port Hope, Ontario, 1999
Acc. No. 99/905

10. **Island Funeral**
1967
etching and aquatint on wove paper · AP
75.8 × 50.2 cm (imp.)
Gift of David and Anita Blackwood, Port Hope, Ontario, 1999
Acc. No. 99/907

11. **Cape Islanders Waiting**
1967
etching, aquatint and drypoint on wove paper · AP
75.8 × 50.3 cm (imp.)
Gift of David and Anita Blackwood, Port Hope, Ontario, 1999
Acc. No. 99/903

12. **Survivor Wandering**
1968
aquatint and embossing
on wove paper · AP
80.5 × 50.4 cm (imp.)
Gift of David and Anita
Blackwood, Port Hope,
Ontario, 1999
Acc. No. 99/912

13. **Sealer's Dream**
1968
aquatint · AP
50.6 × 40.5 cm (imp.)
Gift of David and Anita
Blackwood, Port Hope,
Ontario, 1999
Acc. No. 99/909

14. **Posthumous Portrait of Captain Abraham Kean**
1968
etching and aquatint
on wove paper · AP
50.4 × 37.8 cm (imp.)
Gift of David and Anita
Blackwood, Port Hope,
Ontario, 1999
Acc. No. 99/910

15. **Gram Glover's Dream**
1968
etching and aquatint
on wove paper · AP
81.0 × 50.5 cm (imp.)
Gift of David and Anita
Blackwood, Port Hope,
Ontario, 1999
Acc. No. 99/914

16. **Gram Glover Waiting**
1972
etching and aquatint
on wove paper · AP
81.0 × 50.4 cm (imp.)
Gift of David and Anita
Blackwood, Port Hope,
Ontario, 1999
Acc. No. 99/928

17. **Home in Wesleyville (Captain Jesse Winsor)**
1975
etching and aquatint
on wove paper · AP
81.0 × 50.4; 40.3 × 50.4 cm
(2 plates)
Gift of David and Anita
Blackwood, Port Hope,
Ontario, 1999
Acc. No. 99/937

18. **Sick Captain Leaving**
1971
etching and aquatint
on wove paper · 5/25
80.5 × 50.4 cm (imp.)
Gift of David and Anita
Blackwood, Port Hope,
Ontario, 1999
Acc. No. 99/923

19. **Sick Captain Returning**
1973
etching, aquatint and
drypoint on wove paper · AP
81.0 × 50.5 cm (imp.)
Gift of David and Anita
Blackwood, Port Hope,
Ontario, 1999
Acc. No. 99/933

20. **Wedding on Bragg's Island**
1973
etching and aquatint
on wove paper
50.5 × 81.0 cm (imp.)
Gift of David and Anita
Blackwood, Port Hope,
Ontario, 1999
Acc. No. 99/934

21. **The Burning of William Fifield's Forge**
1975
etching and aquatint
on wove paper · AP
50.4 × 80.4 cm (imp.)
Gift of David and Anita
Blackwood, Port Hope,
Ontario, 2008
Acc. No. 2008/290

22. **SS Imogene Leaving for the Icefields**
1973
etching and aquatint
on wove paper · final WP
50.5 × 80.7cm (imp.)
Gift of David and Anita
Blackwood, Port Hope,
Ontario, 1999
Acc. No. 99/930

23. **SS Imogene Home from the Icefields**
1972
etching and aquatint
on wove paper · AP (final imp.)
80.7 × 50.5 cm (imp.)
Gift of David and Anita
Blackwood, Port Hope,
Ontario, 1999
Acc. No. 99/929

24. **Flora S. Nickerson Down on the Labrador**
1978
etching and aquatint on wove paper · final WP
50.5 × 40.2 cm (imp.)
Gift of David and Anita Blackwood, Port Hope, Ontario, 1999
Acc. No. 99/943

25. **January Visit Home**
1975
etching and aquatint on wove paper · 13/50
50.5 × 80.7 cm (imp.)
Gift of David and Anita Blackwood, Port Hope, Ontario, 2008
Acc. No. 2008/277

26. **Fire in Indian Bay**
1979
etching, aquatint and drypoint on wove paper · WP
50.3 × 80.9 cm (imp.)
Gift of David and Anita Blackwood, Port Hope, Ontario, 2008
Acc. No. 2008/298

27. **Wesleyville: Burning of the Methodist Church**
1976
etching and aquatint on wove paper
55.4 × 70.9 cm (imp.)
Gift of David and Anita Blackwood, Port Hope, Ontario, 1999
Acc. No. 99/940

28. **Aunt Mag and Uncle Elias Feltham**
1976
etching, aquatint and drypoint on wove paper · AP
80.8 × 50.5 cm (imp.)
Gift of David and Anita Blackwood, Port Hope, Ontario, 2008
Acc. No. 2008/274

29. **Vigil on Bragg's Island**
1973
etching and aquatint on wove paper
50.4 × 80.7 cm (imp.)
Gift of David and Anita Blackwood, Port Hope, Ontario, 1999
Acc. No. 99/931

30. **Lone Mummer Approaching**
1976
etching and aquatint on wove paper
50.5 × 81.0 cm (imp.)
Gift of David and Anita Blackwood, Port Hope, Ontario, 1999
Acc. No. 99/939

31. **Captain Edward Bishop Home in Wesleyville**
1976
etching and aquatint on wove paper · AP
50.5 × 81.0 cm (imp.)
Gift of David and Anita Blackwood, Port Hope, Ontario, 2008
Acc. No. 2008/288

32. **Hauling Job Sturge's House**
1979
etching and aquatint on wove paper
32.9 × 80.6 cm (imp.)
Gift of David and Anita Blackwood, Port Hope, Ontario, 1999
Acc. No. 99/948

33. **Brian and Martin Winsor**
1979
etching, aquatint and drypoint on wove paper · AP
50.5 × 81.0 cm (imp.)
Gift of David and Anita Blackwood, Port Hope, Ontario, 2008
Acc. No. 2008/275

34. **Prince Andrew under Construction**
1973
etching and aquatint on wove paper
50.3 × 80.8 cm (imp.)
Gift of David and Anita Blackwood, Port Hope, Ontario, 1999
Acc. No. 99/932

35. **Lone Mummer Inside**
1979
etching and aquatint on wove paper · plate 10
70.9 × 55.5 cm (imp.)
Given by friends in memory of Norman Bruce Walford, Chief of Administration and Corporate Secretary, the Art Gallery of Ontario, 1981–1989, in appreciation of his devotion to the Arts, 1994
Acc. No. 93/415

36. **Captain Jesse Winsor Home from the Labrador**
1976
etching and aquatint on wove paper
80.3 × 50.5 cm (imp.)
Gift of David and Anita Blackwood, Port Hope, Ontario, 1999
Acc. No. 99/938

37. **Captain Lew Kean Passing**
1979
etching, aquatint and drypoint on wove paper · HC
55.5 × 70.5 cm (imp.)
Gift of David and Anita Blackwood, Port Hope, Ontario, 2008
Acc. No. 2008/280

38. **The Seabird Hunter**
1978
etching, aquatint and drypoint on wove paper
55.5 × 70.5 cm (imp.)
Gift of David and Anita Blackwood, Port Hope, Ontario, 1999
Acc. No. 99/944

39. **Skipper Bax Ford Home in Wesleyville**
1979
etching, aquatint and drypoint on wove paper · 50/50
40.3 × 50.5 cm (imp.)
Gift of David and Anita Blackwood, Port Hope, Ontario, 1999
Acc. No. 99/947

40. **Mrs. Captain B. Home in Wesleyville**
1979
etching and aquatint on wove paper
70.8 × 55.3 cm (imp.)
Gift of David and Anita Blackwood, Port Hope, Ontario, 1999
Acc. No. 99/946

41. **Captain Jesse Winsor Home from the Icefields** (tryptch)
1979
etching and aquatint on wove paper · AP
50.5 × 40.2 cm; 50.5 × 80.4 cm; 50.5 × 40.2 cm (3 plates)
Gift of David and Anita Blackwood, Port Hope, Ontario, 1999
Acc. No. 99/949.1–.3

42. **April Iceberg off Bragg's Island**
1976
etching and aquatint on wove paper · AP
50.3 × 80.6 cm (imp.)
Gift of David and Anita Blackwood, Port Hope, Ontario, 2008
Acc. No. 2008/273

43. **Three Mummers on Winsor's Point**
1979
etching and aquatint on wove paper · AP 1/10
50.4 × 80.7 cm (imp.)
Promised gift of David and Anita Blackwood, Port Hope, Ontario
Acc. No. n/a

44. **The Great Peace of Brian and Martin Winsor**
1982
etching, aquatint and drypoint on wove paper · final WP 9/9
81.0 × 50.2 cm (imp.)
Gift of David and Anita Blackwood, Port Hope, Ontario, 1999
Acc. No. 99/959

45. **His Father's Dreams**
1985
etching and aquatint on wove paper
90.9 × 60.7 cm (imp.)
Gift of David and Anita Blackwood, Port Hope, Ontario, 1999
Acc. No. 99/967

46. **Wesleyville: Night Passage Bennett's High Island** from **Bennett's Island Trilogy**
1981
etching and aquatint on wove paper · 43/50
50.5 × 80.4 cm (imp.)
Gift of David and Anita Blackwood, Port Hope, Ontario, 1999
Acc. No. 99/956

47. **Wesleyville: March Ice Raft** from **Bennett's Island Trilogy**
1981
etching and aquatint on wove paper · AP
50.4 × 80.9 cm (imp.)
Gift of David and Anita Blackwood, Port Hope, Ontario, 1999
Acc. No. 99/958

48. **Seabird Hunters Returning Home to Bragg's Island**
1976
etching and aquatint on wove paper · AP
50.4 × 81.0 cm (imp.)
Gift of David and Anita Blackwood, Port Hope, Ontario, 2008
Acc. No. 2008/272

49. **Cape Spear, Newfoundland**
1983
etching and aquatint on wove paper · AP 6 (2nd plate)
50.7 × 81.0 cm (imp.)
Gift of David and Anita Blackwood, Port Hope, Ontario, 1999
Acc. No. 99/964

50. **Wesleyville: Seabird Hunters Crossing the Reach**
1981
etching, aquatint and drypoint on wove paper · AP 3/10; Ed. 50
50.5 × 80.9 cm (imp.)
Gift of David and Anita Blackwood, Port Hope, Ontario, 1999
Acc. No. 99/957

51. **The Flora S. Nickerson in the Labrador Sea**
1982
etching, aquatint and drypoint on wove paper · AP
40.5 × 58.1 cm (imp.)
Gift of David and Anita Blackwood, Port Hope, Ontario, 2008
Acc. No. 2008/287

52. **For Edgar Glover: The Splitting Table**
1999
etching and aquatint on wove paper · AP 16
60.4 × 80.9 cm (imp.)
Gift of David and Anita Blackwood, Port Hope, Ontario, 2008
Acc. No. 2008/292

53. **Uncle Sam Kelloway**
1983
etching and aquatint on wove paper · AP 7/8
40.6 × 50.5 cm (imp.)
Gift of David and Anita Blackwood, Port Hope, Ontario, 2008
Acc. No. 2008/305

54. **Outward Bound for the Labrador**
1987
etching and aquatint on wove paper · AP
38.0 × 90.7 cm (imp.)
Gift of David and Anita Blackwood, Port Hope, Ontario, 2008
Acc. No. 2008/284

55. **Pound Cove Mummers Crossing Cold Harbour Pond**
1985
etching and aquatint on wove paper · AP
50.4 × 80.9 cm (imp.)
Gift of David and Anita Blackwood, Port Hope, Ontario, 1999
Acc. No. 99/968

56. **Ephraim Kelloway's Door**
1982
etching and aquatint, with hand-colouring on wove paper · final WP 8/8
80.9 × 50.4 cm (imp.)
Gift of David and Anita Blackwood, Port Hope, Ontario, 2008
Acc. No. 2008/289

57. **Passing Shadow**
1990
etching and aquatint with hand-colouring on wove paper · AP 3/5
81.0 × 50.5 cm (imp.)
Gift of David and Anita Blackwood, Port Hope, Ontario, 2008
Acc. No. 2008/291

58. **Uncle Sam Kelloway's Place in Wesleyville**
1999
etching and aquatint on wove paper · final WP 15/15
40.5 × 50.6 cm (imp.)
Gift of David and Anita Blackwood, Port Hope, Ontario, 2008
Acc. No. 2008/293

59. **Notes from Bragg's Island**
1992
etching and aquatint on wove paper · AP
35.2 × 27.6 cm; 35.2 × 27.8 cm; 35.2 × 27.6 cm (3 plates on one sheet)
Gift of David and Anita Blackwood, Port Hope, Ontario, 2008
Acc. No. 2008/283

60. **Wesleyville Fleet in Labrador Sea**
1995
etching and aquatint
on wove paper
WP 5/12
90.7 × 60.5 cm (imp.)
Gift of David and Anita
Blackwood, Port Hope,
Ontario, 2008
Acc. No. 2008/306

61. **Loss of Flora S. Nickerson**
1993
etching and aquatint
on wove paper · final WP
81.0 × 50.3 cm (imp.)
Gift of David and Anita
Blackwood, Port Hope,
Ontario, 2008
Acc. No. 2008/281

62. **Haven**
1994
etching and aquatint on
wove paper · final WP 9/9
50.4 × 80.9 cm (imp.)
Gift of David and Anita
Blackwood, Port Hope,
Ontario, 1999
Acc. No. 99/975

63. Sketch for **Fire Down on the Labrador**
1979
graphite on paper
30.2 × 17.8 cm (sheet)
Gift of David and Anita
Blackwood, Port Hope,
Ontario, 2008
Acc. No. 2008/310

64. Graphite drawing for
Fire Down on the Labrador
1979
graphite on paper
93.0 × 62.7 cm (sheet)
Gift of David and Anita
Blackwood, Port Hope,
Ontario, 2008
Acc. No. 2008/307

65. Cartoon tracing for reverse
transfer to the copper plate for
Fire Down on the Labrador
1980
92.1 × 57.5 cm (sheet)
Gift of David and Anita
Blackwood, Port Hope,
Ontario, 2008
Acc. No. 2008/308

66. Experimental inking proof for
Fire Down on the Labrador
1980
etching and aquatint
on wove paper
80.9 × 50.3 cm (imp.)
Gift of David and Anita
Blackwood, Port Hope,
Ontario, 2008
Acc. No. 2008/309

67. Working proof prior to
scraper and burnisher for
Fire down on the Labrador
1980
etching and aquatint
on wove paper
80.9 × 50.3 cm (imp.)
Gift of David and Anita
Blackwood, Port Hope,
Ontario, 2008
Acc. No. 2008/311

68. **Fire Down on the Labrador**
1980
etching and aquatint
on wove paper · AP 3/6
80.9 × 50.3 cm (imp.)
Gift of David and Anita
Blackwood, Port Hope,
Ontario, 1999
Acc. No. 99/954

69. **Fire Down on the Labrador**
1980
etching and aquatint
on wove paper · AP 4/6
80.9 × 50.3 cm (imp.)
Promised gift of David
and Anita Blackwood
Acc. No. n/a

70. **Fire Down on the Labrador**
1980
etching and aquatint
on wove paper · AP 5/6
80.9 × 50.3 cm (imp.)
Promised gift of David
and Anita Blackwood
Acc. No. n/a

71. **Fire Down on the Labrador**
1980
etching and aquatint
on wove paper · WP 6/6
80.9 × 50.3 cm (imp.)
Promised gift of David
and Anita Blackwood
Acc. No. n/a

Selected Bibliography

A Sense of Place: Explorations of the Landscape by David Blackwood, Thaddeus Holownia and Dan Steeves (Oakville, ON: Abbozzo Gallery, 2005).

Bell, Peter. *David Blackwood: The Lost Party Series.* Organized by the Extension Department of the Art Gallery of Ontario in Cooperation with David Blackwood, 1975.

Blackwood, David. Interview by Joan Murray, Port Hope, October 27, 1977. Tape recording. David Blackwood and Joan Murray Artist Files, Robert McLaughlin Gallery, Oshawa, Ontario.

David Blackwood (Vancouver: Heffel Gallery, 1998).

David Blackwood: A Survey of the Prints (Toronto: Gallery One, 1999).

David Blackwood: The Mummer's Veil (Oakville, ON: Abbozzo Gallery, 2003).

David Blackwood's Door Paintings (Toronto: Gallery One, 1990).

Gough, William. *The Art of David Blackwood.* Toronto: McGraw-Hill Ryerson, 1988.

Grattan, Patricia, and Michael Burtch. *David Blackwood Prints: 1962–1984.* St. John's: Art Gallery, Memorial University, 1985.

Horwood, Harold. Review of *Wake of the Great Sealers* by Farley Mowat, CBC.

Mowat, Farley. *Wake of the Great Sealers.* Prints and drawings by David Blackwood. Boston: Little, Brown, 1973.

Murray, Joan. "Blackwood's Newfoundland: An Interview with David Blackwood." *Canadian Forum,* May 1978, 6–10.

Murray, Neil. "Profile: Newfoundland Artist David Blackwood Portrays an Older Way of Life." *Newfoundland Herald TV Week,* March 1, 1978.

Porter, Edward. "David Blackwood: A Survey, 1965–1984." *Arts Atlantic,* January–February 1985, 16–17.

Purdie, James. "Blackwood's Prints a Loyal Record of Newfoundland in Better Days." *Globe and Mail,* March 1, 1975.

Scott, Michael. "Life in Isolation: A Talk with David Blackwood." *Vancouver Sun,* March 21, 1998.

Image Credits

All plates were photographed by Craig Boyko, Ian Lefebvre and Sean Weaver of the Art Gallery of Ontario. Other images are credited as follows:

Blackwood Collection, p. vi
Katharine Lochnan, p. viii
© Stephen Amini, p. x
Ian Lefebvre © 2010 Art Gallery of Ontario, p. xii
© 2010 Alexander Spraetz/ www.spraetz.net, pp. xiv–xv
Blackwood Collection, p. 3
Blackwood Collection, p. 4
Blackwood Collection, p. 5
Blackwood Collection, p. 7
John de Visser, Blackwood Collection; John de Visser, Blackwood Collection; Blackwood Collection; John de Visser, Blackwood Collection, p. 8 (clockwise from top left)
Library and Archives Canada/ National Film Board of Canada, Still Photography Division Collection/ PA-128080, p. 9
Blackwood Collection, p. 11
Blackwood Collection, Ian Lefebvre © 2010 Art Gallery of Ontario, p. 14
Ian Lefebvre © 2010 Art Gallery of Ontario, p. 16
Blackwood Collection, Ian Lefebvre © 2010 Art Gallery of Ontario, p. 17
© Estate of Käthe Kollwitz/ SODRAC (2010), Blackwood Collection, Ian Lefebvre © 2010 Art Gallery of Ontario, p. 18 (left)
© Estate of Marc Chagall/ SODRAC (2010), Blackwood Collection, Ian Lefebvre © 2010 Art Gallery of Ontario, p. 18 (right)
Blackwood Collection, Ian Lefebvre © 2010 Art Gallery of Ontario, p. 19
© Estate of Georges Rouault/ SODRAC (2010), Blackwood Collection, Ian Lefebvre © 2010 Art Gallery of Ontario, p. 20
Blackwood Collection, p. 21
Katharine Lochnan, p. 24
© Barrett & MacKay Photo, pp. 26–27
Ian Lefebvre © 2010 Art Gallery of Ontario, p. 30
Ian Lefebvre © 2010 Art Gallery of Ontario, p. 31
Blackwood Collection, p. 33
Eli Noseworthy, Blackwood Collection, p. 35
John E. Maunder, c. 1910 to c. 1935, Library and Archives Canada/ John E. Maunder Collection/ PA-057899, p. 36
Edgar Blackwood, Blackwood Collection, p. 39
Blackwood Collection, p. 40
Blackwood Collection, Ian Lefebvre © 2010 Art Gallery of Ontario, p. 44
Blackwood Collection, Ian Lefebvre © 2010 Art Gallery of Ontario, p. 45
Blackwood Collection, p. 46 (top)
Blackwood Collection, Ian Lefebvre © 2010 Art Gallery of Ontario, p. 46 (bottom)
Blackwood Collection, Ian Lefebvre © 2010 Art Gallery of Ontario, p. 47
© Barrett & MacKay Photo, Newfoundland and Labrador Tourism, pp. 48–49
After H. Williams, "Geologic Ancestors to the Atlantic: The Geology of Newfoundland," *Newfoundland Quarterly* 96, no. 3 (2003), p. 52
Captain James Cook, Blackwood Collection, p. 53
Eric Leinberger, after map by Tina Riche © 2002, Newfoundland and Labrador Heritage Web Site Project (www.heritage.nf.ca/environment/ecoregions_nfld.html), p. 54
Eric Leinberger, adapted from C. MacNiocaill and M.A. Smethurst, "Palaeozoic Palaeogeography of Laurentia and Its Margins: A Reassessment of Palaeomagnetic Data," *Geophysical Journal International* 116 (1994): 715–25, p. 55
Eric Leinberger, adapted from http://geology.com/pangea.htm, p. 56
From K.J.W. McCaffrey, M. Feely, R. Hennessy and J. Thompson, "Visualisation of Folding in Marble Outcrops, Connemara, Western Ireland: An Application of Virtual Outcrop Technology," *Geosphere* 4, no. 3 (2008): 588–99, p. 57
Martin Feely, p. 58 (top)
Derek Wilton, p. 58 (bottom)
Katharine Lochnan, p. 59
Katharine Lochnan, p. 60
S.J. O'Brien and A.F. King, "Ediacaran Fossils from the Bonavista Peninsula (Avalon Zone), Newfoundland: Preliminary Descriptions and Implications for Regional Correlation," Newfoundland Department of Mines and Energy, Geological Survey, Report 04-1 (2004): 203–12, p. 63

Blackwood Collection, p. 64
Ian Lefebvre © 2010 Art Gallery of Ontario, p. 66
© Barrett & MacKay Photo, Newfoundland and Labrador Tourism, pp. 68–69
Blackwood Collection, p. 72
John E. Maunder, Library and Archives Canada/ John E. Maunder Collection/ PA-057831, p. 74
Blackwood Collection, p. 75
John E. Maunder, Library and Archives Canada/ John E. Maunder Collection/ PA-077760, p. 76
Library and Archives Canada/ Elizabeth Rosetta Glover fonds/PA-165350, p. 78
Blackwood Collection, p. 81
Blackwood Collection, p. 82
B. Brooks, Library and Archives Canada/National Film Board of Canada. Photothèque Collection, PA-154122, © Government of Canada. Reproduced with the permission of the Minister of Public Works and Government Services Canada (2010), p. 83
John E. Maunder, Library and Archives Canada/ John E. Maunder Collection/ PA-077542, p. 86 (top)
John E. Maunder, Library and Archives Canada/ John E. Maunder Collection/ PA-057903, p. 86 (bottom)
Holloway Studio, Blackwood Collection, p. 87
Blackwood Collection, p. 88
The Rooms Provincial Archives Division, A 61-72/ Parsons family fonds, p. 89 (top)
Holloway Studio, Blackwood Collection, p. 89 (bottom)
Holloway Studio, Blackwood Collection, p. 90
The Rooms Provincial Archives Division, LS 51/Robert Palfry Holloway, Holloway family fonds, p. 91
The Rooms Provincial Archives Division, LS 50/Robert Palfry Holloway, Holloway family fonds, p. 92
The Rooms Provincial Archives Division, A 9-19, p. 93
© Barrett & MacKay Photo, Newfoundland and Labrador Tourism, pp. 94–95
Blackwood Collection, p. 98
John de Visser, Blackwood Collection, p. 101
John de Visser, Blackwood Collection, p. 102
Rupert Maas, London, p. 106
© Barrett & MacKay Photo, Newfoundland and Labrador Tourism, pp. 108–09
Photos by Michael Crummey, p. 113
Blackwood Collection, p. 114 (left)
Collection of Helen Crummey, p. 114 (right)
Collection of Helen Crummey, p. 117
Photo by Michael Crummey, p. 118
Eli Noseworthy, Blackwood Collection, p. 121
Ian Lefebvre © 2010 Art Gallery of Ontario, p. 122